Philosophers of Our Times

Philosophers of Our Times

EDITED BY
Ted Honderich

OXFORD
UNIVERSITY PRESS

OXFORD
UNIVERSITY PRESS

Great Clarendon Street, Oxford, OX2 6DP,
United Kingdom

Oxford University Press is a department of the University of Oxford.
It furthers the University's objective of excellence in research, scholarship,
and education by publishing worldwide. Oxford is a registered trade mark of
Oxford University Press in the UK and in certain other countries

First Edition published in 2015

Impression: 2

Published in the United States of America by Oxford University Press
198 Madison Avenue, New York, NY 10016, United States of America

British Library Cataloguing in Publication Data

Data available

Library of Congress Control Number: 2014941572

ISBN 978-0-19-871250-3

Printed and bound in Great Britain by
Clays Ltd, St Ives plc

Acknowledgements

Chapter 1: Thomas Nagel, 'Conceiving the Impossible and the Mind-Body Problem'. This was the first Royal Institute of Philosophy Annual Lecture. It was given in London on 18 February 1998.

Chapter 2: P. F. Strawson, 'Perception and its Objects'. A car accident prevented the author from giving an arranged Royal Institute of Philosophy Annual Lecture. The editor and the publisher of the present volume have decided to include the present paper.

Chapter 3: Tyler Burge, 'Perception: Where Mind Begins'. The Royal Institute of Philosophy Annual Lecture 2013.

Chapter 4: Jerry Fodor, 'The Revenge of the Given: Mental Representation Without Conceptualization'. The Royal Institute of Philosophy Annual Lecture 2006.

Chapter 5: Ned Block, 'Attention and Mental Paint'. Originally published in *Philosophical Issues* 20, 2010, pp. 23–63. The author is grateful to the following audiences for responses to earlier versions of this paper, starting in October 2008: the University of California at Berkeley, the University of California at Santa Barbara, the University of Warwick, the Australian National University, the NYU Consciousness Project discussion group, the Rutgers cognitive science group, the UCLA Philosophy Department, the University of Victoria Philosophy Department, the Searle conference at Santa Clara University, the NYU Mind & Language Seminar, Brown University, and the Royal Institute of Philosophy. He thanks Tyler Burge, Imogen Dickie, Geoffrey Lee, Farid Masrour, Chris Peacocke, Jesse Prinz, Frédérique de Vignemont, and Sebastian Watzl for comments on earlier drafts.

Chapter 6: John McDowell, 'Some Remarks on Intention in Action'. Originally published in *The Amherst Lecture in Philosophy* 6 (2011): 1–18. Earlier versions of some of this material were given as a Royal Institute of Philosophy Lecture in London; as a Howison Lecture at the University of California, Berkeley; and as part of the author's Hägerström Lectures at Uppsala University.

Chapter 7: Christine M. Korsgaard, 'On Having a Good'. This paper was delivered as the Royal Institute of Philosophy Annual Lecture in March 2012, Suarez Lecture at Fordham in April 2013, and as one of the Agnes Cumin Lectures at University College Dublin in March. The author is indebted to the audiences for helpful discussion on all of these occasions and at colloquia at Stanford, the CUNY Graduate Center, SUNY-Binghamton, Brandeis, and the Georg-August University in Göttengen.

Chapter 8: T. M. Scanlon, 'Reasons Fundamentalism'. This is a revised version of the author's 2008 Royal Institute of Philosophy Annual Lecture 'Reasons and Rationality'. A slightly different version appears as Lecture 1 of his *Being Realistic about Reasons* (Oxford: Oxford University Press, 2013).

Chapter 9: Simon Blackburn, 'The Majesty of Reason'. The Royal Institute of Philosophy Annual Lecture 2009.

Chapter 10: Mary Warnock, 'What Is Natural? And Should We Care?' The Royal Institute of Philosophy Annual Lecture 2002.

Chapter 11: John R. Searle, 'Free Will as a Problem in Neurobiology'. This article is an extension of some of the ideas presented in the author's lecture to the Royal Institute of Philosophy, in February 2001. That lecture was based on an earlier article in the *Journal of Consciousness Studies*, 'Consciousness, Free Action and the Brain', volume 10, number 10, October 2000. Some of the arguments in the early part of this article are developed in more detail in the author's book *Rationality in Action* (MIT Press, 2001).

Chapter 12: Derek Parfit, 'We Are Not Human Beings'. This lecture is taken from material written with the support of a Foundational Research Grant from the Ammonius Foundation, for whose generosity the author is very grateful. He has been much helped by comments from Eric Olson, Sydney Shoemaker, and Ingmar Persson.

Chapter 13: Anthony Kenny, 'Knowledge, Belief, and Faith'. The Royal Institute of Philosophy Annual Lecture 2007.

Chapter 14: Noam Chomsky, 'Simple Truths, Hard Problems: Some Thoughts on Terror, Justice, and Self-Defence'. The Royal Institute of Philosophy Annual Lecture 2004.

Chapter 15: Alasdair MacIntyre, 'Social Structures and their Threats to Moral Agency'. The Royal Institute of Philosophy Annual Lecture 1999.

Chapter 16: Jürgen Habermas, 'Religious Tolerance—The Pacemaker for Cultural Rights'. The Royal Institute of Philosophy Annual Lecture 2003.

Chapter 17: Bernard Williams, 'Philosophy as a Humanistic Discipline'. The Royal Institute of Philosophy Annual Lecture 2000.

Chapter 18: David J. Chalmers, 'Why Isn't There More Progress in Philosophy?' The Royal Institute of Philosophy Annual Lecture 2014.

Contents

Introduction

Ted Honderich

How is what it is like to be a bat related to the bat?
What are you really aware of in seeing?
Where did mind begin? With spiders?
Is there no thinking inside your seeing?
Is there mental paint?
What is the intending in your acting?

Are there goods that are not goods *for* anyone?
What *are* reasons?
Is a fundamentalism about reasons in morality almost entirely misdirected?
What is natural and does it matter? Much? At all?

Is the problem of free will a solved problem of consciousness but a remaining
    problem for neurobiology?
Are *you* a human being?
Is belief in God possibly false but nonetheless reasonable?

Are there simple, available, and refuting truths about terrorism, justice, antici-
    patory self-defence, and more?
What about tolerance, religious tolerance, cultural rights, church bells, and calls
    to prayer?
What are moral agents and what societies are against them?

What has philosophy in general been, and what should it be?
Is there less progress in philosophy than in science, and if so, why?

These questions and their answers, five groups of them, are the stuff of seventeen Royal
Institute of Philosophy Annual Lectures and one paper that could have been a lecture
that was not given. They are by Tom Nagel, Peter Strawson, Tyler Burge, Jerry Fodor,
Ned Block, John McDowell, Christine Korsgaard, Tim Scanlon, Simon Blackburn,
Mary Warnock, John Searle, Derek Parfit, Anthony Kenny, Noam Chomsky, Alasdair
MacIntyre, Jürgen Habermas, Bernard Williams, and David Chalmers.

Philosophy in my view is a greater concentration than that of science on the logic of ordinary intelligence—on clarity, consistency and validity, completeness, and generality. These lectures are instances of the reality of this philosophy as it is in the universities of the United Kingdom and the United States. They are, I say, about as good an introduction to and exemplification of the subject in these times as you are likely to lay hands on. They are not popular philosophy, not the stuff of books for the general reader, not surveys, not philosophy as journalism can convey it. They are the actual content of undergraduate and postgraduate degrees in philosophy.

They have the extent of clarity that is to be expected in the work of leaders of the subject. But each is preceded by the editor's introduction, that is, I hope, a decent guide through what is to come. If reading main-line philosophy is never like reading a novel, it is something you can be prepared for.

While waiting to go into prison for sponsoring an anti-war pamphlet in 1916, Bertrand Russell gave his *Lectures on Logical Atomism* in a lecture room in London's Bloomsbury, a lecture room to be much used thereafter. Stanley Balfour, then Home Secretary in the government of the day, instructed that he should have writing materials in his cell for the book *Introduction to Mathematical Philosophy*. Russell, Balfour, the liberal political theorist and sociologist L. T. Hobhouse, and the socialist political theorist and economist Harold Laski were the principal founders of the Royal Institute of Philosophy, in 1925.

The Royal Institute of Philosophy Annual Lectures, which began in 1998, are by leaders of the subject in the United Kingdom and the United States. They were chosen by a democracy comparable to the democracies in which we live, limited but real, maybe a little less limited. Nominations were invited from members of the Council of the Royal Institute and from other outside philosophers as well as some editors in prominent publishers of the subject.

This selection of lecturers, if still in and of the real world, not entirely above human nature, was not the known method of quickly remembering old pals, or of keeping in mind those to whom favours are to be repaid, or of high principles to do with mutuality and reciprocity in the future. Nor, although eminence by location in an ancient or other university will have played a role, was the selection a choosing by a minority—geographical, from a favoured part or parts of a subject, guided by feminist or other high principle, or influenced by email cabals however confident.

The first of the five groups of questions is concerned with the philosophy of mind, the second with moral or value philosophy, the next with the free-standing subjects of freedom and determinism, personal identity, and religion, the fourth with political and social philosophy, and the last with philosophy in general. That the first group of questions is a little larger is perhaps owed to the prominence of the philosophy of mind in our times. Metaphysics, however unavoidable, and however in the background of various questions, is not to the fore.

Having listened to all the lectures as chairman, most of them given in University College London, and spent time with them again for the writing of the little introductions,

I commend them to you with all the confidence allowed by the scepticism natural to the discipline of philosophy. They contain truths, distinctions, acuteness, judgements on other judgements, arresting propositions, ingenuities, maybe some shocks, and a lot else, including sharp disagreement between lecturers in the morals and values section, and the last two philosophers being in different philosophical worlds.

Reading all the lectures is reading mainstream philosophy, which is indeed unlike reading a novel or anything else. The lectures have strengths and shortcomings not had by their counterparts in science, a fact that the very last lecture in a way contemplates. They demonstrate the falsehood, perhaps the hopeful falsehood, of the utterance of a noted scientist that philosophy is dead, a scientist unaware of the truth among others that the subject has always buried its undertakers.

Most lectures in lecture rooms end with a question period. Certainly the Royal Institute of Philosophy Annual Lectures as given ended with half an hour's questions from the audience, usually out of different preoccupations. The strongest philosophers, like the strongest philosophy, can be a little confused. They can be wrong. Remember that who wins in philosophy will be decided over time by those final judges, Fact and Logic. So you who read this book should also ask questions. By way of encouragement to the bashful, and indulgence in my portion of the philosophical ego, I will mention one or two or some of my own at the ends of my introductions.

Introduction to Thomas Nagel's Lecture

Ted Honderich

Tom Nagel was born in Serbia into a Jewish family, studied at Cornell University, then Oxford, and then at Harvard under John Rawls. He taught at Berkeley and Princeton before settling at New York University. He was chosen as the first of the Royal Institute of Philosophy Annual Lecturers after he became widely known for a paper whose leading idea is that something's being conscious is *there being something it is like to be that thing*, say a bat, or you. The question of the title 'What Is It Like to Be a Bat?' has done more than any other to unsettle confidence among hard physicalists about the nature of consciousness. It gives content and salience to common talk of subjectivity.

This contribution to the contemporary philosophy of mind, perhaps more than any other contribution, raises or involves the question of how our consciousness is related to the brain, often called the mind-body problem. This question of relation, perhaps inadvisably, has been given more attention than the direct question of what it is to be conscious, the nature of that fact, what that fact is.

What Nagel persistently contemplates in the present lecture is the philosophical and scientific consensus, if a conflicted consensus, that a state or event of being conscious *is* an objective physical state. More particularly, is your having a thought or a feeling right now a physical state of your brain? Is it, more particularly, as in the theory of functionalism, and in all or most cognitive science, a physical state that 'functions' in a certain way, which is to say no more than that it is a state or event that stands in certain causal connections with earlier and later events, say something seen and arm movements?

Nagel allows that indeed there is causal connection between conscious states or events and such resulting physical events as arm movements, which is often taken as an irresistible argument for a physicalism about consciousness. Nagel contemplates, differently, that there is some or necessary connection between your conscious thinking and your brain. There could not be a zombie—something physically absolutely identical to you but unconscious.

But he denies that we understand such a relation, understand how there can be such a relation of necessity. We cannot make sense of *how* there can be necessary connection between consciousness and brain. That is on the way to being as incomprehensible for us as the thought or utterance that the number 379 has parents. For the thought of necessary connection between consciousness and brain, we need concepts we just have not got, including concepts dealing with our hesitation about consciousness even being in space at all.

He insists to real effect that we really must not suppose we can rightly believe or try to believe what we cannot understand. Our situation, therefore, is that we must admit we have no answer to how consciousness is related to the brain, no theory of how it is or is not physical. So the old and disdained dualism of body and mind, the first physical and the second not, may still be true in this age of a plethora of physicalist theories. Whatever may happen in the unforeseeable future, after we are all dead, we have to accept that the mind-body problem is for us a mystery. This has prompted some others into as much or greater pessimism, and given pause to more of us.

Nagel's four immediately relevant books are *Mortal Questions* (1979), which contains the paper 'What Is It Like to Be a Bat?' as well as papers on matters of life and death, *The View From Nowhere* (1986), *What Does It All Mean?* (1987), ideal as an introduction to philosophy, and *Mind and Cosmos: Why the Materialist Neo-Darwinian Conception of Nature is Almost Certainly False* (2012), whose audacity has given rise to some controversy about evolution. His moral and political writings, as individual, include *The Possibility of Altruism* (1970) and *Equality and Partiality* (1991).

They and the lecture raise questions of which he is aware but which may trouble you still more. What is an objective physical fact? If your being conscious is not an objective physical fact, maybe not taking up space, how indeed *can* it cause the objective physical fact of the movement of your arm? If there are different kinds of physicality, what are they? Could there be subjective physicality? Can it be that our present situation with respect to consciousness is not that we really know a requirement of which we also know that is not fulfilled? Is our situation rather that it is not really clear what the requirement of necessary connection is, a requirement of which Nagel speaks in various ways? And that it will not be clear until it *is* fulfilled, until an analysis is seen to show what was needed all along?

1

Conceiving the Impossible and the Mind-Body Problem

Thomas Nagel

I

Intuitions based on the first-person perspective can easily mislead us about what is and is not conceivable.[1] This point is usually made in support of familiar reductionist positions on the mind-body problem, but I believe it can be detached from that approach. It seems to me that the powerful appearance of contingency in the relation between the functioning of the physical organism and the conscious mind—an appearance that depends directly or indirectly on the first-person perspective—must be an illusion. But the denial of this contingency should not take the form of a reductionist account of consciousness of the usual type, whereby the logical gap between the mental and the physical is closed by conceptual analysis—in effect, by analysing the mental in terms of the physical (however elaborately this is done—and I count functionalism as such a theory, along with the topic-neutral causal role analyses of mental concepts from which it descends).

In other words, I believe that there is a necessary connection in both directions between the physical and the mental, but that it cannot be discovered *a priori*. Opinion is strongly divided on the credibility of some kind of functionalist reductionism, and I won't go through my reasons for being on the antireductionist side of that debate. Despite significant attempts by a number of philosophers to describe the functional manifestations of conscious mental states, I continue to believe that no purely functionalist characterization of a system entails—simply in virtue of our mental concepts—that the system is conscious.

[1] See Sydney Shoemaker, 'The First-Person Perspective,' in *The First-Person Perspective and Other Essays* (Cambridge University Press, 1996).

So I want to propose an alternative. In our present situation, when no one has a plausible answer to the mind-body problem, all we can really do is to try to develop various alternatives, one of which may prove in the long run to be an ancestor of a credible solution. This is a plea for the project of searching for a solution that takes conscious points of view as logically irreducible to, but nevertheless necessarily connected with, the physical properties of the organisms whose points of view they are. Consciousness should be recognized as a conceptually irreducible aspect of reality that is necessarily connected with other equally irreducible aspects—as electromagnetic fields are irreducible to but necessarily connected with the behavior of charged particles and gravitational fields with the behavior of masses, and vice versa. But the task of conceiving how a necessary connection might hold between the subjective and the physical cannot be accomplished by applying analogies from within physical science. This is a new ballgame. Yet I believe it is not irrational to hope that some day, long after we are all dead, people will be able to observe the operation of the brain and say, with true understanding, 'That's what the experience of tasting chocolate looks like from the outside.'

Of course we already know what it looks like from far enough outside: the subject taking the first reverent mouthful of a hot fudge sundae, closing his eyes in rapture, and saying 'Yum.' But I have in mind some view or representation of the squishy brain itself, which in light of our understanding we will be able to *see* as tasting chocolate. While that is at the moment inconceivable, I think that it is what we would need in order to grasp the truth about these matters. My reading of the situation is that our inability to come up with an intelligible conception of the relation between mind and body is a sign of the inadequacy of our present concepts, and that some development is needed. At this point, however, all one can hope to do is to state some of the conditions that more adequate concepts would have to satisfy. One can't expect actually to come up with them.[2] But I shall begin by describing the present impasse.

II

When we try to reason about the possible relations between things, we have to rely on our conceptual grasp of them. The more adequate the grasp, the more reliable our reasoning will be. Sometimes a familiar concept clearly allows for the possibility that what it designates should also have features not implied by the concept itself—often features very different in kind from those directly implied by the concept. Thus ordinary prescientific concepts of kinds of substances, such as water or gold or blood, are in themselves silent with regard to the microscopic composition of those substances

---

[2] My position is fairly close to that of Colin McGinn, but without his pessimism. See for example his essay 'Consciousness and the Natural Order,' in *The Problem of Consciousness* (Blackwell, 1991). What I have to say here is also a development of a suggestion in *The View From Nowhere* (Oxford University Press, 1986), pp. 51–3.

but nevertheless open to the scientific discovery, often by very indirect means, of such facts about their true nature. If a concept refers to something that takes up room in the spatio-temporal world, it provides a handle for all kinds of empirical discoveries about the inner constitution of that thing.

On the other hand, sometimes a familiar concept clearly excludes the possibility that what it designates has certain features: for example we do not need a scientific investigation to be certain that the number 379 does not have parents. There are various other things that we can come to know about the number 379 only by mathematical or empirical investigation, such as what its factors are, or whether it is greater than the population of Chugwater, Wyoming, but we know that it does not have parents just by knowing that it is a number. If someone rebuked us for being closed-minded, because we can't predict in advance what future scientific research might turn up about the biological origins of numbers, he would not be offering a serious ground for doubt.

The case of mental processes and the brain is intermediate between these two. Descartes thought it was closer to the second category, and that we could tell just by thinking about it that the human mind was not an extended material thing and that no extended material thing could be a thinking subject. But this is, to put it mildly, not nearly as self-evident as that a number cannot have parents. What does seem true is that the concept of a mind, or of a mental event or process, fails to plainly leave space for the possibility that what it designates should turn out also to be a physical thing or event or process, as the result of closer scientific investigation, in the way that the concept of blood leaves space for discoveries about its composition. The trouble is that mental concepts don't obviously pick out things or processes that take up room in the spatio-temporal world to begin with. If they did, we could just get hold of some of those things and take them apart or look at them under a microscope or subject them to chemical analysis. But there is a prior problem about how those concepts might refer to anything that could be subjected to such investigation: they don't give us the comfortable initial handle on the occupants of the familiar spatio-temporal world that prescientific physical substance concepts do.[3]

Nevertheless it is overconfident to conclude, from one's inability to imagine how mental phenomena might turn out to have physical properties, that the possibility can be ruled out in advance. We have to ask ourselves whether there is more behind the Cartesian intuition than mere lack of knowledge, resulting in lack of imagination.[4] Of course it is not enough just to say, 'You may be mistaking your own inability to imagine something for its inconceivability.' One should be open to the possibility of withdrawing a judgment of inconceivability if offered a reason to think it might be

---

[3] See Colin McGinn, 'Consciousness and Space,' *Journal of Consciousness Studies* 2 (1995), pp. 220–30.
[4] This is the objection that Arnauld made to Descartes, in the fourth set of objections to the *Meditations*.

mistaken, but there does have to *be* a reason or at least some kind of story about how this illusion of inconceivability might have arisen.

If mental events really have physical properties, an explanation is needed of why they seem to offer so little purchase for the attribution of those properties. Still, the kind of incomprehensibility here is completely different from that of numbers having parents. Mental events, unlike numbers, can be roughly located in space and time, and are causally related to physical events, in both directions. The causal facts are strong evidence that mental events have physical properties, if only we could make sense of the idea.[5]

Consider another case where the prescientific concept did not obviously allow for the possibility of physical composition or structure—the case of sound. Before the discovery that sounds are waves in air or another medium, the ordinary concept permitted sounds to be roughly located, and to have properties like loudness, pitch, and duration. The concept of a sound was that of an objective phenomenon that could be heard by different people, or that could exist unheard. But it would have been very obscure what could be meant by ascribing to a sound a precise spatial shape and size, or an internal, perhaps microscopic, physical structure. Someone who proposed that sounds have physical parts, without offering any theory to explain this, would not have said anything understandable. One might say that in advance of the development of a physical theory of sound, the hypothesis that sounds have a physical microstructure would not have a clear meaning.

Nevertheless, at one remove, the possibility of such a development is evidently not excluded by the concept of sound. Sounds were known to have certain physical causes, to be blocked by certain kinds of obstacles, and to be perceptible by hearing. This was already a substantial amount of causal information, and it opened the way to the discovery of a physically describable phenomenon that could be identified with sound because it had just those causes and effects—particularly once further features of sound, like variations of loudness and pitch, could also be accounted for in terms of its precise physical character. Yet it is important that *in advance*, the idea that a sound has a physical microstructure would have had no clear meaning. One would not have known how to go about imagining such a thing, any more than one could have imagined a sound having weight. It would have been easy to mistake this lack of clear allowance for the possibility in the concept for a positive exclusion of the possibility by the concept.

The analogy with the case of mental phenomena should be clear. They too occupy causal roles, and it has been one of the strongest arguments for some kind of physicalism that those roles may prove upon investigation to be occupied by organic processes. Yet the problem here is much more serious, for an obvious reason: identifying sounds with waves in the air does not require that we ascribe phenomenological

---

[5] Compare Donald Davidson, 'Mental Events,' in his *Essays on Actions and Events* (Oxford University Press, 1980).

qualities and subjectivity to anything physical, because those are features of the perception of sound, not of sound itself. By contrast, the identification of mental events with physical events requires the unification of these two types of properties in a single thing, and that remains resistant to understanding. The causal argument for identification may make us believe that it is true, but it doesn't help us to understand it, and in my view, we really shouldn't believe it unless we can understand it.

The problem lies in the distinctive first-person/third-person character of mental concepts, which is the grammatical manifestation of the subjectivity of mental phenomena. Though not all conscious beings possess language, our attribution of conscious states to languageless creatures implies that those states are of the kind that in the human case we pick out only through these distinctive concepts, concepts which the subject applies in his own case without observation of his body.

They are not pure first-person concepts: to try to detach their first-person application from the third person results in philosophical illusions: e.g. that the subject of my consciousness might have been replaced five minutes ago and all my memories, personality, etc. transferred to a new subject in this same body, without any outwardly or inwardly perceptible sign—without any other physical or psychological change. If the pure first-person idea of 'I' defined an individual, that would make sense, but it seems reasonably clear that the real idea of 'I' has lost its moorings in this philosophical thought experiment. The point goes back to Kant, who argued that the subjective identity of the consciousness of myself at different times is not sufficient to establish the objective identity of a subject or soul.[6]

That is not to say that I understand just how the first person and the third form two logically inseparable aspects of a single concept—only that they do. This applies to all conscious mental states and events, and their properties. They are subjective, not in the sense that they are the subjects of a purely first-person vocabulary, but in the sense that they can be accurately described only by concepts in which nonobservational first-person and observational third-person attributions are logically inseparable. Such states are modifications of the point of view of an individual subject.

The problem, then, is how something that is an aspect or element of an individual's subjective point of view could also be a physiologically describable event in the brain—the kind of thing which, considered under that description, involves no point of view and no distinctively immediate first-person attribution at all. I believe that as a matter of fact you can't have one without the other, and furthermore that the powerful intuition that it is conceivable that an intact and normally functioning physical human organism could be a completely unconscious zombie is an illusion—due to the limitations of our understanding. Nevertheless those limitations are real. We do not at present possess the conceptual equipment to understand how subjective and physical features could both be essential aspects of a single entity or process.

---

[6] See Kant, 'The Paralogisms of Pure Reason,' *Critique of Pure Reason*, A363–4.

III

Suppose, as seems likely, that I taste the smoke of my cigar when and only when my brain is in a certain physical state. What gets in the way of the thought that the experiential state of which I am introspectively aware is the physical state? The problem lies in the lack of any conceivable internal connection between a modification of my subjective point of view and a modification of the physico-chemical activity of my brain. The two may correspond extensionally as exactly as you like, but identity requires more than that. If they are the same state, it must be impossible for the one to exist without the other. And while we may have good empirical reasons to believe that that is true, the *understanding* of such an impossibility requires that the necessity of the connection between the two become intellectually transparent to us. In the case of conscious states and physiological states, it isn't just that we don't see such a necessary connection: it seems in advance that a necessary connection between two such different things is unimaginable. They seem logically unrelated.

It is very different from trying to imagine the possibility of a physico-chemical analysis of embryonic development, before one has the slightest inkling of what the analysis might be. In that case we can nevertheless understand the possibility in the abstract: there are no grounds for ruling it out *a priori*, since we know in general terms what it is to exhaustively analyse a large-scale process into its microscopic or submicroscopic components. But that model will not help us with the mind and the brain. We are entitled to identify a familiar physical phenomenon like fire with a theoretically described process at the atomic level because the macroscopic properties of fire, including its causes and effects, can be derived from the microscopic account— can be seen to be necessitated by it. The chemical analysis of fire and air reveals, for example, that it is a necessary truth that a fire confined to a small, airtight space will quickly go out. But we cannot see how a detailed account of what is going on in the brain could exhaustively explain the taste of a cigar—not even if we could see how it explained all the physical effects of such an experience. So long as this explanatory gap remains, the identification of the states remains problematic.[7]

This does seem to call for some revision in our way of conceiving of mind, or matter, or both. The difficulty is to do this without denying what is in front of your nose. What we need is not a reductionist or eliminative revision but an expansionist one. By this I mean a conception that will permit subjective points of view to have an objective physical character *in themselves*. The reason such an expansion does not seem to me out of the question is that it doesn't involve a contradiction with the essential nature of subjective experience. Our problem is that there is no room for a necessary connection with physiology in the space of possible development defined by the

---

[7] Joseph Levine has stressed this point, though I believe he is too ready to describe the problem as epistemological rather than metaphysical. See 'Materialism and Qualia: The Explanatory Gap,' *Pacific Philosophical Quarterly* 64 (1983), pp. 354–61.

concept of mind. But that does not rule out the possibility of a successor concept of mind which will both preserve the essential features of the original and be open to the discovery of such connections. This kind of thing happens all the time in the course of scientific history, as with the concepts of sound, or element, or species, or space, or number. A new concept is developed to talk about the same things as the old, one that includes most of the features of the old concept but puts them in a relation to one another and to other features that is new, and that makes it possible to see or explore further connections.

Without such an expanded conception of the mental, there is no prospect of overcoming the explanatory gap. But it seems to me entirely possible that a more adequate conception of subjective experience should see it as the phenomenological 'inside' of certain physical processes, and that what we need is to dismantle the barriers to such a conception. If it became possible for us to think of experiences as essentially what it is like subjectively for a physical organism to be in some physiological state, the way would be open for the discovery of *a posteriori* necessary truths about what physiological state a particular kind of experience is. But the big step is the first one, of expanding the concept of experience by the recognition that what it contains explicitly—including its behavioral or functional implications—gives an incomplete account of the nature of experience.

The ordinary concept of water is unsaturated, so to speak, since it contains a blank space to be filled in by the discovery of the real, and essential, chemical composition of water. Just as we make room for the possibility of such discovery by denying that the manifest properties of water exhaust its nature, so we can open the possibility of an *a posteriori* answer to the mind-body problem by denying that the manifest properties of experience exhaust its nature. This means thinking of experiences, contrary to intuition, as events whose full nature is not revealed to experience—and more generally, thinking of the mind, contrary to Cartesian intuition, as only partially available, even in principle, to introspection. If we can do this without denying the phenomenology or reducing it to something else, we will be on the first step toward an expansionist but still non-dualist response to the mind-body problem. This is so far pure fantasy, but it is the fantasy of a theoretical identification of mental events with an inner constitution that includes but is not exhausted by their introspectible or manifest character.

The search for the possible form of a theory of the relation between mind and brain has to continue, and if there can be no such theory, that too requires explanation. I believe that the explanatory gap in its present form cannot be closed—that so long as we work with our present mental and physical concepts no transparently necessary connection will ever be revealed, between physically described brain processes and sensory experience, of the logical type familiar from the explanation of other natural processes by analysis of their physico-chemical constituents. We have good grounds for believing that the mental supervenes on the physical—i.e. that there is no mental difference without a physical difference. But pure, unexplained supervenience is not a solution but a sign that there is something fundamental we don't know. We cannot regard pure supervenience as the end of the story because that would require the physical to necessitate the mental without there being any answer to the question *how* it does so. But there *must* be a 'how,' and our task is to understand it. An obviously systematic connection that remains unintelligible to us calls out for a theory.

IV

The subjectivity of consciousness seems to block all reductionist proposals because, given any physicalist or functionalist description, however sophisticated, it *seems* logically possible that there should be an organism or system satisfying those conditions but nevertheless lacking any subjective point of view—a *zombie*, in current jargon. That is, there seems nothing to bar us from conceiving positively the existence of any kind of physical or functionally organized system, and then conceiving negatively that there is no subjective experience connected with it.[8] The two types of conception are so completely unrelated that the first seems incapable of ruling out the second: all we have to do is imagine the physical system from the outside, and then imagine it from the inside—as not having any inside in the experiential sense.

I said at the outset that we should be very cautious in the use of intuitions that depend on the first-person point of view, and that includes intuitions about persons or beings other than ourselves that depend on taking up their point of view in imagination. In this case the very disparity between the two forms of conception that gives rise to the strong intuition of conceivability should make us suspicious. The absence of any conceptual connection when phenomena are grasped by such disparate concepts may conceal a deeper necessary connection that is not yet conceptual because not accessible to us by means of our present forms of thought.

I still think we can rely on such thought experiments to refute the most common types of *conceptual* reductionism, however. Even if there is some kind of entailment of the mental by the physical-functional, it is not analytic or definitional. There is no hidden verbal contradiction in the description of a zombie—even if in reality a zombie is logically impossible. There remains the question of a possible weaker conceptual link in the other direction—from the mental to the physical—through the necessity of public criteria for the application of mental concepts, which go with their distinctive first-person/third-person character. But while such public criteria may be necessary for the operation of mental concepts, they are not sufficient, and their logical relation to the reference of those concepts is not obvious. In any case, the public criteria are functional rather than physiological, on the usual interpretation, and what I am talking about here is the relation between mental states and the brain, not

---

[8] This argument has recently been given much prominence by David Chalmers; see *The Conscious Mind* (Oxford University Press, 1996).

between mental states and behavior. Let me try to say what is wrong with conceptual arguments against the necessity of the former relation. I shall return to the private language issue later.

The following things seem *prima facie* conceivable which are pretty certainly impossible in a very strong sense, namely:

1) a living, behaving, physiologically and functionally perfect human organism that is nevertheless completely lacking in consciousness, i.e. a zombie,

2) a conscious subject with an inner life just like ours that behaves and looks just like a human being but has electronic circuitry instead of brains.

To repeat, I believe the apparent conceivability of these things reveals something about our present concepts but not about what is really possible. Analytic psychophysical reductionism is false, but there is independent reason to believe that these are not true logical possibilities, and if so, our concepts are missing something. Our current concepts don't lead to contradiction—it's not as bad as that—but they fail to reveal a logical impossibility.

Contrast these thought experiments with the *a priori* inconceivability of a number having parents. The latter involves a straightforward clash between concepts, not merely a disparity. No number could enter into the kind of biological relation with a predecessor that is a necessary condition of being a child or offspring. In that case we see a contradiction between the conditions of numberhood and the conditions of being the child of anything or anyone. In the relation of consciousness to the physical world, by contrast, our concepts fail to reveal a necessary connection, and we are tempted to conclude to the absence of any such connection. Our intuition is of a logical compatibility, not a logical incompatibility. We conceive the body from outside and the mind from inside, and see no internal connection, only an external one of correlation or perhaps causation. But in spite of the vividness of the intuition, I believe that it reflects our conceptual limitations rather than the truth: the difference between the modes of conception is so great that there is every reason to suspect that we would be unable to see an internal necessary connection even if there were one.

Conceivability and inconceivability are the main evidence we have for possibility and necessity, but they can be misleading, and conceivability that depends on the relation between first and third-person reference is particularly treacherous terrain. It may be that the physical description of the brain states associated with consciousness is an incomplete account of their essence—that it is merely the outside view of what we recognize from within as conscious experience. If anything like that is true, then our present conceptions of mind and body are radically inadequate to the reality, and do not provide us with adequate tools for *a priori* reasoning about them. That poses the general question of how we can attempt to develop conceptions that reflect the actual necessary connections and are therefore reliable tools for reasoning, and what determines whether there is hope of developing such concepts for a domain where we do not yet have them. After all, humans did not always have logical, geometrical, and arithmetical concepts, but had to develop them.

V

Obviously we cannot will a new conceptual framework into existence. It has to result from trying to think, in light of the evidence, about the subject we want to understand, and devising concepts that do better justice to it than the ones we have. Considered as a form of revisionism rather than analysis, the physicalist-functionalist movement in philosophy of mind might be thought to have had a similar aim, but I believe it has failed because it is too conservative: it has tried to reinterpret mental concepts so as to make them tractable parts of the framework of physical science. What is needed instead is a search for something more unfamiliar, something which starts from the conceptual unintelligibility, in its present form, of the subjective-objective link. The enterprise is one of imagining possibilities: identity theorists like Smart, Armstrong, and Lewis tried to explain how the identity of mental with physical states could be a contingent truth; I am interested in how some sort of mind-brain identity might be a necessary truth. That would require not only the imagination of concepts that might capture the connection, but also some account of how our existing concepts would have to be related to these and to one another. Specifically, we must think about the first-person and third-person conditions of application of mental concepts, and the physical concepts used to describe the brain. What would something be like to which *all* of these applied noncontingently?

If we think of a standard case of reference-fixing (in Kripke's sense) like 'water,' we observe that, prescientifically, the reference is fixed not only by contingent features of the substance, such as its being what falls from the sky as rain and fills the lakes and oceans, what comes out of the tap, and what we bathe in—but also by noncontingent manifest features, such as its density, its liquidity at room temperature, and its propensity to freeze or boil under certain conditions. We can adopt a reference-fixing model (rather than the reductionist model) for the relation between functional states and mental states provided we do not think of the functional states as *contingent* reference-fixers. I think the right view is not that functional role characterizations contingently pick out inner states whose intrinsic nature must be physically or phenomenologically specified, but rather that *all* the types of features by which we standardly identify mental states, from within and from without, are noncontingent features of those states, and that their physiological nature is also noncontingent.

That could be true only if they were identified with neurophysiological states whose connection, at least dispositionally, with characteristic functional roles in the organism was noncontingent. This does not seem out of the question: integrated visual and motor systems in the brain might be part of the specification of the neurophysiological nature of colour phenomenology, for example. What I am saying is not incompatible with Kripke's claim that the reference of a term like 'pain' is fixed by an essential property of the referent, namely its immediate phenomenological quality—but it goes beyond this. My suggestion is that the immediate phenomenological quality, the functional role, and the physiological basis of pain are all essential properties of it, and that the apparent conceivability of their separation is an illusion.

To be precise, I conjecture that being a pain entails (nonanalytically) all three features—functional, phenomenological, and physiological—but that only the latter two entail pain. This is because the phenomenological and the physical entail the functional (and one another) whereas the functional does not entail them. It is parallel to the case of water. There could be a watery liquid that wasn't the compound H_2O and therefore wasn't water, but being H_2O entails having the essential gross properties of water. Similarly, it is possible that there could be a state functionally equivalent to pain in a mechanism with a completely different internal constitution, but if it were both physically and phenomenologically different, it would not be the same mental state and would not be pain. Phenomenological and physiological features of mental states entail their functional features, but not vice versa.

So the proposal is that mental states may have a tripartite essence—phenomenological, functional, and physiological—but we still don't understand how this could be, since our modal intuitions go against it. In particular, we still have to deal with the apparent conceivability of an exact physical-functional replica of a conscious human being that nevertheless has no phenomenological 'interior' at all—a zombie. It is clear that first-person imagination is doing the work in this thought experiment. The task of defending a necessary connection between the physical and the phenomenological would require some account of how a connection that is in fact internal remains stubbornly external from the point of view of our understanding. But I believe that can be done.

VI

Suppose I think about the taste of the cigar I am now smoking. What I must do first is to regard the experience as a state of myself of whose subjective qualities I am immediately aware, and which has certain publicly observable functional relations to stimuli and discriminatory capacities. There is already a natural illusion of contingency with respect to these latter relations, because they are concealed in my introspective identification of the experience. But this introspective identification is itself one of those mental acts that—because of the first-person/third-person link—cannot be logically separated from its functional connections (for example the capacity to distinguish this taste from that of a cigarette). Recognizing this, I can see that the Cartesian thought experiment of imagining myself having this experience without having a body at all is an unreliable guide to what is really possible. It depends on the concealment of the necessary conditions of reference of the phenomenological concept that I am employing to think about the experience. (This is the anti-private-language point.)

But now what of the relation between the experience and its physiological basis? Here I seem to be able to imagine either myself or someone else tasting exactly this flavor of cigar—and its having all the usual functional connections as well—although my brain or the other person's brain is in a completely different state. Indeed it seems imaginable, though unlikely, that when I offer a friendly cigar to an exotic visitor from outer space who has a completely different physiology, it should taste the same to him. But here too the imagination is a poor guide to possibility, because it relies on an assumption of the completeness of the manifest conditions of reference of the concept (now taken to include functional conditions).

The first thing to acknowledge is that if there were a necessary connection between the phenomenology and the physiology of tasting a cigar, it would not be evident *a priori* on the basis of the ordinary concept of that experience, since the possession of that concept involves no awareness of anything about the brain. It isn't just that, like the behavioral connections, the relation to the brain is *hidden from view* in my first-person use of the concept: the relation is completely absent from the concept, and cannot be retrieved by philosophical analysis. Nevertheless, if there is such a relation, having the full concept (including the first-person aspect) would require having a brain, indeed a brain with exactly the right physiological characteristics, the brain would be directly involved in the act of imagination—though its involvement would be completely outside the range of my awareness in employing the concept. To imagine a mental state from the inside would be what I have called an act of *sympathetic* imagination—putting myself in a conscious state *resembling* the thing imagined—and it would be impossible to do this without putting my brain in a corresponding physical state.[9]

This shows that I cannot rely on the apparent imaginability of the separation of phenomenology and physiology to establish the contingency of the relation, since I can know in advance that this act of imagination would seem subjectively the same whether the relation were contingent or necessary. If the relation is necessary, then I have not really succeeded in imagining the phenomenology without the physiology. The imagination here is essentially ostensive, and I cannot point to one without pointing to the other. But now, how am I to form the conception that the relation might actually be necessary—as opposed to merely acknowledging that I can't discover *a priori* that it isn't? I have to think that these two ways of referring—by the phenomenological concept and the physiological concept—pick out a single referent, in each case rigidly, but that the logical link cannot be discovered by inspecting the concepts directly: rather it goes only through their common link to the referent itself.

---

[9] See 'What Is It Like to Be a Bat?' (*Philosophical Review*, 1974), fn 11. This was an earlier response to the modal argument against materialism. See also Christopher Hill, 'Imaginability, Conceivability, Possibility and the Mind-Body Problem,' *Philosophical Studies*, 1995.

The idea would have to be, then, that there is a single event to which I can refer in two ways, both of them via concepts that apply to it noncontingently. One is the mental concept that I am able to acquire in both first- and third-person applications because I am a subject of this state, which has the special character of consciousness and introspective accessibility—the state of tasting a cigar. The other is a (so far unspecified) physiological concept that describes the relevant physical state of the brain. To admit the possibility of a necessary connection here, we have to recognize that the mental concept as it now operates has nothing to say about the physiological conditions for its own operation, and then consider the hypothesis of a successor concept that leaves a place for such a condition—a place that can be filled only *a posteriori*, by a theory of the third type of event that admits these two types of access, internal and external.

VII

What will be the point of view, so to speak, of such a theory? If we could arrive at it, it would render transparent the relation between mental and physical, not directly, but through the transparency of their common relation to something that is not merely either of them. Neither the mental nor the physical point of view will do for this purpose. The mental will not do because it simply leaves out the physiology, and has no room for it. The physical will not do because while it includes the behavioral and functional manifestations of the mental, this doesn't, in view of the falsity of conceptual reductionism, enable it to reach to the mental concepts themselves. The right point of view would be one which, contrary to present conceptual possibilities, included both subjectivity and spatio-temporal structure from the outset, all its descriptions implying both these things at once, so that it would describe inner states and their functional relations to behavior and one another from the phenomenological inside and the physiological outside simultaneously—not in parallel. The mental and physiological concepts and their reference to this same inner phenomenon would then be seen as secondary and each partial in its grasp of the phenomenon: each would be seen as referring to something that extends beyond its grounds of application.

The difficulty is that such a viewpoint cannot be constructed by the mere conjunction of the mental and the physical. It has to be something genuinely new, otherwise it will not possess the necessary unity. Truly necessary connection could be revealed only by a new theoretical construction, realist in intention, contextually defined as part of a theory that explained both the familiarly observable phenomenological and the physiological characteristics of these inner events. Its character would have to be inferred from what it was introduced to explain—like the electromagnetic field, gravity, the atomic nucleus, or any other theoretical postulate. This could only be done in the context of a theory containing real laws and not just dispositional definitions, otherwise the theoretical entity would not have independent reality.

To summarize. The conjecture is essentially this: that even though no transparent *and direct* explanatory connection is possible between the physiological and the phenomenological, but only an empirically established extensional correlation, we may hope and ought to try as part of a scientific theory of mind to form a third conception that does directly entail both the mental and the physical, and through which their actual necessary connection with one another can therefore become transparent to us. Such a conception will have to be created; we won't just find it lying around. All the great reductive successes in the history of science have depended on theoretical concepts, not natural ones—concepts whose whole justification is that they permit us to replace brute correlations with reductive explanations. At present such a solution to the mind-body problem is literally unimaginable, but it may not be impossible.

Introduction to P. F. Strawson's Lecture

Ted Honderich

Sir Peter Strawson, born of teachers in north London, read philosophy, politics, and economics in Oxford, and, after returning from the war, became a Fellow at University College, Oxford, and subsequently Oxford's Waynflete Professor of Metaphysics. At 31 he became known for his contending against Bertrand Russell's theory of descriptions, and subsequently he was distinguished by his metaphysics in the English descriptive or analytic way, not speculative in the German way, and by his books *Introduction to Logical Theory* (1952), *Individuals* (1959), *The Bounds of Sense* (1966), and many articles.

A car accident resulted in his being unable to give an arranged and anticipated Royal Institute of Philosophy Annual Lecture. The editor and the publisher of the present volume have decided to include the present paper. It, like most of the lectures, is not in much need of an introduction for clarification but more to lead readers into a confident anticipation that even if the thinking is not easy, concentration on it will be rewarded.

The paper is an adjudication of two views of our ordinary sense perception of things and a defence of a third view. The first is that of the Logical Positivist A. J. Ayer in the tradition of what is called phenomenalism, having to do with internal and somehow subjective entities in perception, what historically were called ideas and subsequently have been spoken of as sense data, qualia, representations, and the like. The second view, John Mackie's, is in a tradition of what is called scientific realism, having to do with the science of perception and the nature of what is perceived. As against these two views, the third view or attitude, to which Strawson is at least inclined, is what he speaks of as a kind of common-sense realism about the world.

Ayer, we are reminded, takes it in a late book that our ordinary perceptual experience of a thing, seeing it, is such that what we judge or think about what we see *goes beyond* what we actually experience. What we have in mind, maybe a room, is more than what, strictly speaking, we do experience in the subjective episode. That is accepted in a certain careful way by Strawson. But it is also maintained that we do not need to embrace sense data, which need is a myth. We have to remember instead that our perceptual experience in a way immediately includes or involves a concept of the object itself. It is only the theory of phenomenalist philosophers that in a way leads us away from this fact. We can and must stick to common-sense realism.

Mackie's scientific realism is approached first by way of a comparison with a fourth view, which, for Strawson, has still less claim to attention. This is what has laboured under the name of naïve realism—but has recently had at least the sympathy of strong philosophers. It is in fact a confused realism in Strawson's judgement, since it fails to draw a distinction that it itself must presuppose, say the distinction between our visual experience of dappled deer and the deer themselves. Mackie's scientific realism, also very different indeed from common-sense realism, is to the effect that objects have only the physical properties allowed to them in scientific theory, say a psychology of vision, and that we cannot perceive them as they really are, that our representations of them do not deliver their reality.

Strawson's common-sense realism is taken by him to be a real realism, something of which scientific realism is a distortion. It credits things with visual and tactile properties that are immediately or directly perceived by us. They are not a matter of any inference or construction on our part, either in the phenomenalist way or a scientific way. A causal story about them can be told, despite impediments. Much more is explained about the bases and defence of this realism. More is explained too of the weakness of the two alternatives, including some nonsense, and an attempt to blend the two together.

It is possible to question and to disagree with common-sense realism, as I myself do. Are the dappled deer yet more, and more literally, the story of your seeing them than Strawson supposes? Is it possible to go still further in Strawson's realist direction and to suppose that our actual consciousness in perception can be very explicitly analysed? But one cannot but be affected by his line of thought in its informal astuteness. What is conveyed and evoked has the excellence of making you think. It is easy, too, to be enlightened by much along the way, say the incidental observation near the end that science is not the only offspring of common sense, and remains its dependant.

2

Perception and its Objects

P. F. Strawson

I

Ayer has always given the problem of perception a central place in his thinking. Reasonably so; for a philosopher's views on this question are a key both to his theory of knowledge in general and to his metaphysics. The movement of Ayer's own thought has been from phenomenalism to what he describes in his latest treatment of the topic as 'a sophisticated form of realism'.[1] The epithet is doubly apt. No adequate account of the matter can be simple; and Ayer's account, while distinguished by his accustomed lucidity and economy of style, is notably and subtly responsive to all the complexities inherent in the subject itself and to all the pressures of more or less persuasive argument which have marked the course of its treatment by philosophers. Yet the form of realism he defends has another kind of sophistication about which it is possible to have reservations and doubts; and, though I am conscious of being far from clear on the matter myself, I shall try to make some of my own doubts and reservations as clear as I can. I shall take as my text Chapters 4 and 5 of *The Central Questions of Philosophy*; and I shall also consider a different kind of realism—that advocated by J. L. Mackie in his book on Locke.[2] There are points of contact as well as of contrast between Ayer's and Mackie's views. A comparison between them will help to bring out the nature of my reservations about both.

According to Ayer, the starting point of serious thought on the matter of perception consists in the fact that our normal perceptual judgements always 'go beyond' the sensible experience which gives rise to them; for those judgements carry implications which would not be carried by any 'strict account' of that

[1] A. J. Ayer, *The Central Questions of Philosophy* (London: Weidenfeld and Nicolson, 1973), Chapters 4 and 5, pp. 68–111.

[2] J. L. Mackie, *Problems from Locke* (Oxford: Clarendon Press, 1976), Chapters 1 and 2, pp. 7–71.

experience.[3] Ayer sees ordinary perceptual judgements as reflecting or embodying what he calls the common-sense view of the physical world, which is, among other things, a realist view; and he sees that view itself as having the character of 'a theory with respect to the immediate data of perception'.[4] He devotes some space to an account of how the theory might be seen as capable of being developed by an individual observer on the basis of the data available to him; though he disavows any intention of giving an actual history of the theory's development. The purpose of the account is, rather, to bring out those features of sensible experience which make it possible to employ the theory successfully and which, indeed, justify acceptance of it. For it is, he holds, by and large an acceptable theory, even though the discoveries of physical science may require us to modify it in certain respects.

Evidently no infant is delivered into the world already equipped with what Ayer calls the common-sense view of it. That view has to be acquired; and it is open to the psychologist of infant learning to produce at least a speculative account of the stages of its acquisition. Ayer insists, as I have remarked, that his own account of a possible line of development or construction of the common-sense view is not intended as a speculative contribution to the theory of infant learning. It is intended, rather, as an analysis of the nature of mature or adult perceptual experience, an analysis designed to show just how certain features of mature sensible experience vindicate or sustain the common-sense view which is embodied or reflected in mature perceptual judgements. Clearly the two aims here distinguished—the genetic—psychological and the analytic—philosophical—are very different indeed, and it will be of great importance not to confuse them. In particular it will be important to run no risk of characterizing mature sensible experience in terms adequate at best only for the characterization of some stage of infantile experience. It is not clear that Ayer entirely avoids this danger.

What is clear is that if we accept Ayer's starting point, if we agree that our ordinary perceptual judgements carry implications not carried by a 'strict account' of the sensible experience which gives rise to them, then we must make absolutely sure that our account of that experience, in the form it takes in our mature life, is indeed strict—in the sense of strictly correct. Only so can we have any prospect of making a correct estimate of the further doctrines that the common-sense view of the world has the status of a *theory* with respect to a type of sensible experience which provides *data* for the theory; that this experience supplies the *evidence* on which the theory is based;[5] that the common-sense view can be regarded as *inferred* or at least inferrable from this evidence; and that our ordinary perceptual judgements have the character of *interpretations*,[6] in the light of theory, of what sensible experience actually presents us with.

[3] Ayer, *Central Questions*, pp. 81, 89.   [4] Ayer, *Central Questions*, p. 88.
[5] Ayer, *Central Questions*, p. 89.   [6] Ayer, *Central Questions*, p. 81.

But can we—and should we—accept Ayer's starting point? I think that, suitably interpreted, we both can, and should, accept it. Two things will be required of a strict account of our sensible experience or of any particular episode or slice of sensible experience: first, as I have just remarked, that it should in no way distort or misrepresent the character of that experience as we actually enjoy it, i.e. that it should be a true or faithful account; secondly, that its truth, in any particular case, should be independent of the truth of the associated perceptual judgement, i.e. that it should remain true even if the associated perceptual judgement is false. It is the second requirement on which Ayer lays stress when he remarks that those judgements carry implications which would not be carried by any strict account of sensible experience; or, less happily in my opinion, that in making such judgements we take a step beyond what our sensible experience actually presents us with. But it is the first requirement to which I now wish to give some attention.

Suppose a non-philosophical observer gazing idly through a window. To him we address the request, 'Give us a description of your current visual experience', or 'How is it with you, visually, at the moment?' Uncautioned as to exactly what we want, he might reply in some such terms as these: 'I see the red light of the setting sun filtering through the black and thickly clustered branches of the elms; I see the dappled deer grazing in groups on the vivid green grass…'; and so on. So we explain to him. We explain that we want him to amend his account so that, without any sacrifice of fidelity to the experience as actually enjoyed, it nevertheless sheds all that heavy load of commitment to propositions about the world which was carried by the description he gave. We want an account which confines itself strictly within the limits of the subjective episode, an account which would remain true even if he had seen nothing of what he claimed to see, even if he had been subject to total illusion.

Our observer is quick in the uptake. He does not start talking about lights and colours, patches and patterns. For he sees that to do so would be to falsify the character of the experience he actually enjoyed. He says, instead, 'I understand. I've got to cut out of my report all commitment to propositions about independently existing objects. Well, the simplest way to do this, while remaining faithful to the character of the experience as actually enjoyed, is to put my previous report in inverted commas or *oratio obliqua* and describe my visual experience such as it would have been natural to describe in these terms, had I not received this additional instruction. Thus: "I had a visual experience such as it would have been natural to describe by saying that I saw, etc.… [or, to describe in these words, 'I saw… etc.'] were it not for the obligation to exclude commitment to propositions about independently existing objects." In this way [continues the observer] I *use* the perceptual claim—the claim it was natural to make in the circumstances—in order to characterize my experience, without actually making the claim. I render the perceptual judgement internal to the characterization of the experience without actually asserting the content of the judgement. And this is really the best possible way of characterizing the experience. There are perhaps alternative locutions which might serve the purpose, so long as they are understood as being to the same effect—on the whole, the more artificial the better, since their artificiality will help to make it clearer just to what effect they are intended to be. Thus we might have: "It sensibly seemed to me just as if I were seeing such-and-such a scene" or "My visual experience can be characterized by saying that I saw what I saw, supposing I saw anything, *as* a scene of the following character...".'

If my observer is right in this—and I think he is—then certain general conclusions follow. Our perceptual judgements, as Ayer remarks, embody or reflect a certain view of the world, as containing objects, variously propertied, located in a common space, and continuing in their existence independently of our interrupted and relatively fleeting perceptions of them. Our making of such judgements implies our possession and application of concepts of such objects. But now it appears that we cannot give a veridical characterization even of the sensible experience which these judgements, as Ayer expresses it, 'go beyond', without reference to those judgements themselves; that our sensible experience itself is thoroughly permeated with those concepts of objects which figure in such judgements. This does not mean, i.e. it does not follow directly from this feature of sensible experience, that the general view of the world which those judgements reflect must be true. That would be too short a way with scepticism. But it does follow, I think, that our sensible experience could not have the character it does have unless—at least before philosophical reflection sets in—we unquestioningly *took* that general view of the world to be true. The concepts of the objective which we see to be indispensable to the veridical characterization of sensible experience simply would not be in this way indispensable unless those whose experience it was initially and unreflectively took such concepts to have application in the world.

This has a further consequence: the consequence that it is quite inappropriate to represent the general, realist view of the world which is reflected in our ordinary perceptual judgements as having the status of a *theory* with respect to sensible experience; that it is inappropriate to represent that experience as supplying the *data* for such a theory or the *evidence* on which it is based or from which it is *inferred* or *inferrable*; that it is inappropriate to speak of our ordinary perceptual judgements as having the character of an *interpretation*, in the light of theory, of the content of our sensible experience. The reason for this is simple. In order for some belief or set of beliefs to be correctly described as a theory in respect of certain data, it must be possible to describe the data on the basis of which the theory is held in terms which do not presuppose the acceptance of the theory on the part of those for whom the data *are* data. But this is just the condition we have seen not to be satisfied in the case where the so-called data are the contents of sensible experience and the so-called theory is a general realist view of the world. The 'data' are laden with the 'theory'. Sensible experience is permeated by concepts unreflective acceptance of the general applicability of which is a condition of its being so permeated, a condition of that experience being what it is; and these concepts are of realistically conceived objects.

I must make it quite clear what I am saying and what I am not saying here. I am talking of the ordinary non-philosophical man. I am talking of us all before we felt, if ever we did feel, any inclination to respond to the solicitations of a general scepticism, to regard it as raising a problem. I am saying that it follows from the character of sensible experience as we all actually enjoy it that a common-sense realist view of the world does not in general have the status of a theory in respect of that experience; while Ayer, as I understand him, holds that it does. But I am not denying that to one who has seen, or thinks he has seen, that sensible experience might have the character it does have and yet a realist view of the world be false; to him the idea may well present itself that the best way of accounting for sensible experience as having that character is to accept the common realist view of the world or some variant of it. He might be said to adopt, as a theory, the doctrine that the common realist view of the world is, at least in some basic essentials, true. But this will be a philosopher's theory, designed to deal with a philosopher's problem. (I shall not here discuss its merits as such.) What I am concerned to dispute is the doctrine that a realist view of the world has, for any man, the status of a theory in relation to his sensible experience, a theory in the light of which he interprets that experience in making his perceptual judgements.

To put the point summarily, whereas Ayer says we take a step beyond our sensible experience in making our perceptual judgements, I say rather that we take a step back (in general) from our perceptual judgements in framing accounts of our sensible experience; for we have (in general) to include a reference to the former in framing a veridical description of the latter.

It may seem, on a superficial reading, that Ayer had anticipated and answered this objection. He introduces, as necessary for the characterization of our sensible experience, certain concepts of types of pattern, the names for which are borrowed from the names of ordinary physical objects. Thus he speaks of visual leaf patterns, chair patterns, cat patterns, and so on.[7] At the same time, he is careful, if I read him rightly, to guard against the impression that the use of this terminology commits him to the view that the employment of the corresponding physical-object concepts themselves is necessary to the characterization of our sensible experience.[8] The terminology is appropriate (he holds) simply because those features of sensible experience to which the terminology is applied are the features which govern our identifications of the physical objects we think we see. They are the features, 'implicitly noticed',[9] which provide the main clues on which our everyday judgements of perception are based.

This is ingenious, but I do not think it will do. This we can see more clearly if we use an invented, rather than a derived, terminology for these supposed features and then draw up a table of explicit correlations between the invented names and the physical-object names. Each artificial feature name is set against the name of a type of physical object: our perceptual identifications of seen objects as of that type are held

---

[7] Ayer, *Central Questions*, p. 91.   [8] Ayer, *Central Questions*, p. 96.
[9] Ayer, *Central Questions*, p. 91.

to be governed by implicit noticings of that feature. The nature and significance of the feature names is now quite clearly explained and we have to ask ourselves whether it is these rather than the associated physical-object terms that we ought to use if we are to give a quite strict and faithful account of our sensible experience. I think it is clear that this is not so; that the idea of our ordinary perceptual judgements as being invariably based upon, or invariably issuing from, awareness of such features is a myth. The situation is rather, as I have already argued, that the employment of our ordinary, full-blooded concepts of physical objects is indispensable to a strict, and strictly veridical, account of our sensible experience.

Once again, I must make it clear what I am, and what I am not, saying. I have been speaking of the typical or standard case of mature sensible and perceptual experience. I have no interest at all in denying the thesis that there also occur cases of sensible experience such that the employment of full-blooded concepts of physical objects would not be indispensable, and may be inappropriate, to giving a strict account of the experience. Such cases are of different types, and there is one in particular which is of interest in the present connection. An observer, gazing through his window, may perhaps, by an effort of will, bring himself to see, or even will-lessly find himself seeing, what he knows to be the branches of the trees no longer *as* branches at all, but as an intricate pattern of dark lines of complex directions and shapes and various sizes against a background of varying shades of grey. The frame of mind in which we enjoy, if we ever do enjoy, this kind of experience is a rare and sophisticated, not a standard or normal, frame of mind. Perhaps the fact, if it is a fact, that we can bring ourselves into this frame of mind when we choose may be held to give a sense to the idea of our 'implicitly noticing' such patterns even when we are not in this frame of mind. If so, it is a sense very far removed from that which Ayer's thesis requires. For that thesis requires not simply the possibility, but the actual occurrence, in all cases of perception, of sensible experience of this kind. One line of retreat may seem to lie open at this point: a retreat to the position of saying that the occurrence of such experiences may be *inferred*, even though we do not, in the hurry of life, generally notice or recall their occurrence. But such a retreat would be the final irony. The items in question would have changed their status radically: instead of data for a common-sense theory of the world, they would appear as consequences of a sophisticated theory of the mind.

This concludes the first stage of my argument. I have argued that mature sensible experience (in general) presents itself as, in Kantian phrase, an *immediate* consciousness of the existence of things outside us. (*Immediate*, of course, does not mean *infallible*.) Hence, the common realist conception of the world does not have the character of a 'theory' in relation to the 'data of sense'. I have not claimed that this fact is of itself sufficient to 'refute' scepticism or to provide a philosophical 'demonstration' of the truth of some form of realism; though I think it does provide the right starting point for reflection upon these enterprises. But that is another story and I shall not try to tell it here. My point so far is that the ordinary human commitment to a conceptual scheme of a realist character is not properly described, even in a stretched sense of the words, as a theoretical commitment. It is, rather, something given with the given.

II

But we are philosophers as well as men; and so must examine more closely the nature of the realist scheme to which we are pre-theoretically committed and then consider whether we are not rationally constrained, as Locke and Mackie would maintain we are, to modify it quite radically in the light of our knowledge of physics and physiology. Should we not also, as philosophers, consider the question of whether we can rationally maintain any form of realism at all? Perhaps we should; but, as already remarked, that is a question I shall not consider here. My main object, in the present section, is to get a clear view of the main features of our pre-theoretical scheme before considering whether it is defensible, as it stands, or not. I go in a somewhat roundabout way to work.

I have spoken of our pre-theoretical scheme as realist in character. Philosophers who treat these questions commonly distinguish different forms of realism. So do both Ayer and Mackie. They both mention, at one extreme, a form of realism which Mackie calls 'naive' and even 'very naive', but which might more appropriately be called 'confused realism'. A sufferer from confused realism fails to draw any distinction between sensible experiences (or 'perceptions') and independently existing things (or 'objects perceived') but is said (by Mackie expounding Hume) to credit the former with persistent unobserved existence.[10] It should be remarked that, if this is an accurate way of describing the naive realist's conception of the matter, he must be very confused indeed, since the expression 'unobserved' already implies the distinction which he is said to fail to make. Speaking in his own person, Mackie gives no positive account of the naive realist's view of things, but simply says that there is, historically, in the thought of each of us, a phase in which we fail to make the distinction in question.[11] It may indeed be so. The point is one to be referred to the experts on infantile development. But in any case the matter is not here of any consequence. For we are concerned with mature perceptual experience and with the character of the scheme to which those who enjoy such experience are pre-theoretically committed. And it seems to me as certain as anything can be that, as an integral part of that scheme, we distinguish, naturally and unreflectively, between our seeings and hearings and feelings—our perceivings—of objects and the objects we see and hear and feel; and hence quite consistently accept both the interruptedness of the former and the continuance in existence, unobserved, of the latter.

At the opposite extreme from naive realism stands what may be called scientific or Lockian realism. This form of realism credits physical objects only with those of

---

[10] Mackie, *Problems*, p. 67.   [11] Mackie, *Problems*, p. 68.

their properties which are mentioned in physical theory and physical explanation, including the causal explanation of our enjoyment of the kind of perceptual experience we in fact enjoy. It has the consequence that we do not, and indeed cannot, perceive objects as they really are. It might be said that this consequence does not hold in an unqualified form. For we perceive (or seem to perceive) objects as having shape, size, and position; and they really do have shape, size, and position and more or less such shape, size, and position as we seem to perceive them as having. But this reply misconstrues the intended force of the alleged consequence. We cannot in sense perception—the point is an old one— become aware of the shape, size, and position of physical objects except by way of awareness of boundaries defined in some sensory mode—for example, by visual and tactile qualities such as scientific realism denies to the objects themselves; and no change in, or addition to, our sensory equipment could alter this fact. To perceive physical objects as, according to scientific realism, they really are would be to perceive them as lacking any such qualities. But this notion is self-contradictory. So it is a necessary consequence of this form of realism that we do not perceive objects as they really are. Indeed, in the sense of the pre-theoretical notion of perceiving—that is, of immediate awareness of things outside us—we do not, on the scientific realist view, perceive physical objects at all. We are, rather, the victims of a systematic illusion which obstinately clings to us even if we embrace scientific realism. For we continue to enjoy experience *as of* physical objects in space, objects of which the spatial characteristics and relations are defined by the sensible qualities we perceive them as having; but there are no such physical objects as these. The only true physical objects are items systematically correlated with and causally responsible for that experience; and the only sense in which we *can* be said to perceive them is just that they cause us to enjoy that experience.

These remarks are intended only as a *description* of scientific realism. I do not claim that they show it to be untenable. I shall return to the topic later.

In between the 'naive' and the 'scientific' varieties, Ayer and Mackie each recognize another form of realism, which they each ascribe to 'common sense'. But there is a difference between Ayer's version of common-sense realism and Mackie's. For Mackie's version, unlike Ayer's, shares one crucial feature with scientific realism.

The theory of perception associated with scientific or Lockian realism is commonly and reasonably described as a representative theory. Each of us seems to himself to be perceptually aware of objects of a certain kind: objects in space outside us with visual and tactile qualities. There are in fact, on this view, no such objects; but these object appearances can in a broad sense be said to be representative of those actual objects in space outside us which are systematically correlated with the appearances and causally responsible for them. The interesting feature of Mackie's version of common-sense realism is that the theory of perception associated with it is no less a representative theory than that associated with Lockian realism. The difference is simply that common sense, according to Mackie, views object appearances as more faithful representatives of actual physical objects than the Lockian allows: in that common sense, gratuitously by scientific standards, credits actual objects in space outside us with visual and tactile as well as primary qualities. As Mackie puts it, common sense allows 'colours-as-we-see-them to be *resemblances* of qualities actually in the things'.[12] On both views, sensible experience has its own, sensible objects; but the common-sense view, according to Mackie, allows a kind of resemblance between sensible and physical objects which the scientific view does not.

I hope it is already clear that this version of common-sense realism is quite different from what I have called our pre-theoretical scheme. What we ordinarily take ourselves to be aware of in perception are not resemblances of physical things but the physical things themselves. This does not mean, as already remarked, that we have any difficulty in distinguishing between our experiences of seeing, hearing, and feeling objects and the objects themselves. That distinction is as firmly a part of our pre-theoretical scheme as is our taking ourselves, in general, to be immediately aware of those objects. Nor does it mean that we take ourselves to be immune from illusion, hallucination, or mistake. We can, and do, perfectly adequately describe such cases without what is, from the point of view of the pre-theoretical scheme, the quite gratuitous introduction of sensible objects interposed between us and the actual physical objects they are supposed to represent.

The odd thing about Mackie's presentation is that at one point he shows himself to be perfectly well aware of this feature of the real realism of common sense; for he writes, 'What we seem to see, feel, hear and so on... *are seen as real things without us*—that is, outside us. We just see things as being simply there, of such-and-such sorts, in such-and-such relations...'[13] He goes on, of course, to say that 'our seeing them so is logically distinct from their being so', that we might be, and indeed are, wrong. But he would scarcely dispute that what is thus *seen as* real and outside us is also *seen as* coloured, as possessing visual qualities; that what *is felt as* a real thing outside us is also felt as hard or soft, smooth or rough-surfaced—as possessing tactile qualities. The real realism of common sense, then, does indeed credit physical things with visual and tactile properties; but it does so not in the spirit of a notion of representative perception, but in the spirit of a notion of direct or immediate perception.

Mackie's version of common-sense realism is, then, I maintain, a distortion of the actual pre-theoretical realism of common sense, a distortion which wrongly assimilates it, in a fundamental respect, to the Lockian realism he espouses. I do not find any comparable distortion in Ayer's version. He aptly describes the physical objects we seem to ourselves, and take ourselves, to perceive as 'visuo-tactual continuants'. The scheme as he presents it allows for the distinction between these items and the experiences of perceiving them and for the causal dependence of the latter on the former; and does so, as far as I can see, without introducing the alien features I have

---

[12] Mackie, *Problems*, p. 64.   [13] Mackie, *Problems*, p. 61.

discerned in Mackie's account. It is perhaps debatable whether Ayer can consistently maintain the scheme's freedom from such alien elements while continuing to represent it as having the status of a 'theory' in relation to the 'data' of sensible experience. But, having already set out my objections to that doctrine, I shall not pursue the point.

Something more must be said, however, about the position, in the common-sense scheme, of the causal relation between physical object and the experience of perceiving it. Although Ayer admits the relation to a place in the scheme, he seems to regard it as a somewhat sophisticated addition to the latter, a latecomer, as it were, for which room has to be made in an already settled arrangement.[14] This seems to me wrong. The idea of the presence of the thing as accounting for, or being responsible for, our perceptual awareness of it is implicit in the pre-theoretical scheme from the very start. For we think of perception as a way, indeed the basic way, of informing ourselves about the world of independently existing things: we assume, that is to say, the general reliability of our perceptual experiences; and that assumption is the same as the assumption of a general causal dependence of our perceptual experiences on the independently existing things we take them to be of. The thought of my fleeting perception as a *perception* of a continuously and independently existing thing implicitly contains the thought that if the thing had not been there, I should not even have *seemed* to perceive it. It really should be obvious that with the distinction between independently existing objects and perceptual awareness of objects we already have the general notion of causal dependence of the latter on the former, even if this is not a matter to which we give much reflective attention in our pre-theoretical days.

Two things seem to have impeded recognition of this point. One is the fact that the correctness of the description of a perceptual experience as the perception of a certain physical thing *logically* requires the existence of that thing; and the *logical* is thought to exclude the *causal* connection, since only logically distinct existences can be causally related. This is not a serious difficulty. The situation has many parallels. Gibbon would not be the historian of the decline and fall of the Roman Empire unless there had occurred some actual sequence of events more or less corresponding to his narrative. But it is not enough, for him to merit that description, that such a sequence of events should have occurred and he should have written the sentences he did write. For him to qualify as the *historian* of these events, there must be a causal chain connecting them with the writing of the sentences. Similarly, the memory of an event's occurrence does not count as such unless it has its causal origin in that event. And the recently much-canvassed 'causal theory of reference' merely calls attention to another instance of the causal link which obtains between thought and an independently (and anteriorly) existing thing when the former is rightly said to have the latter as its object.

¹⁴ Ayer, *Central Questions*, pp. 87–8.

The second impediment is slightly more subtle. We are philosophically accustomed—it is a Humean legacy—to thinking of the simplest and most obvious kind of causal relation as holding between types of item such that items of both types are observable or experienceable and such that observation or experience of either term of the relation is distinct from observation or experience of the other: i.e. the causally related items are not only distinct existences, but also the objects of distinct observations or experiences. We may then come to think of these conditions as constituting a requirement on all primitive belief in causal relations, a requirement which could be modified or abandoned only in the interests of theory. Since we obviously cannot distinguish the observation of a physical object from the experience of observing it—for they are the same thing—we shall then be led to conclude that the idea of the causal dependence of perceptual experience on the perceived object cannot be even an implicit part of our pre-theoretical scheme, but must be at best an essentially theoretical addition to it.

But the difficulty is spurious. By directing our attention to causal relations between *objects* of perception, we have simply been led to overlook the special character of perception itself. Of course, the requirement holds for causal relations between distinct objects of perception; but not for the relation between perception and its object. When x is a physical object and y is a perception of x, then x is *observed* and y is *enjoyed*. And in taking the enjoyment of y to be a perception of x, we *are* implicitly taking it to be caused by x.

This concludes the second phase of my argument. I have tried to bring out some main features of the real realism of common sense and of the associated notion of perception. From the standpoint of common-sense realism we take ourselves to be immediately aware of real, enduring physical things in space, things endowed with visual and tactile properties; and we take it for granted that these enduring things are causally responsible for our interrupted perceptions of them. The immediacy which common sense attributes to perceptual awareness is in no way inconsistent either with the distinction between perceptual experience and thing perceived or with the causal dependence of the former on the latter or the existence of other causally necessary conditions of its occurrence. Neither is it inconsistent with the occurrence of perceptual mistake or illusion—a point, like so many others of importance, which is explicitly made by Kant.[15] Both Ayer and Mackie, explicitly or implicitly, acknowledge that the common-sense scheme includes this assumption of immediacy—Mackie in a passage I have quoted, Ayer in his description of the common-sense scheme. Unfortunately, Mackie's acknowledgement of the fact is belied by his describing common-sense realism as representative in character and Ayer's acknowledgement of it is put in doubt by his describing the common-sense scheme as having the status of a theory in relation to sensible experience.

[15] Kant, 'The Refutation of Idealism', in *Critique of Pure Reason*, B274–9.

III

It is one thing to describe the scheme of common sense; it is another to subject it to critical examination. This is the third and most difficult part of my task. The main question to be considered, as already indicated, is whether we are rationally bound to abandon, or radically to modify, the scheme in the light of scientific knowledge.

Before addressing ourselves directly to this question, it is worth stressing—indeed, it is essential to stress—the grip that common-sense non-representative realism has on our ordinary thinking. It is a view of the world which so thoroughly permeates our consciousness that even those who are intellectually convinced of its falsity remain subject to its power. Mackie admits as much, saying that, even when we are trying to entertain a Lockian or scientific realism, 'our language and our natural ways of think-ing keep pulling us back' to a more primitive view.[16] Consider the character of those ordinary concepts of objects on the employment of which our lives, our transactions with each other and the world, depend: our concepts of cabbages, roads, tweed coats, horses, the lips and hair of the beloved. In using these terms we certainly intend to be talking of independent existences and we certainly intend to be talking of immedi-ately perceptible things, bearers of phenomenal (visuo-tactile) properties. If scientific or Lockian realism is correct, we cannot be doing both at once; it is confusion or illu-sion to suppose we can. If the things we talk of really have phenomenal properties, then they cannot, on this view, be physical things continuously existing in physical space. Nothing perceptible—I here drop the qualification 'immediately', for my use of it should now be clear—is a physically real, independent existence. No two persons can ever, in this sense, perceive the same item: nothing at all is publicly perceptible.

But how deep the confusion or the illusion must go! How radically it infects our concepts! Surely we mean by a cabbage a kind of thing of which most of the specimens we have encountered have a characteristic range of colours and visual shapes and felt textures; and not something unobservable, mentally represented by a complex of sensible experiences which it causes. The common consciousness is not to be fobbed off with the concession that, after all, the physical thing has—in a way—a shape. The way in which scientific realism concedes a shape is altogether the wrong way for the common consciousness. The lover who admires the curve of his mistress' lips or the lover of architecture who admires the lines of a building takes himself to be admiring features of those very objects themselves; but it is the visual shape, the visually defined shape, that he admires. Mackie suggests that there is a genuine *resemblance* between subjective representation and objective reality as far as shape is concerned;[17] but this suggestion is quite unacceptable. It makes no sense to speak of a phenomenal property as *resembling* a non-phenomenal, abstract prop-erty such as physical shape is conceived to be by scientific realism. The property of looking square or round can no more resemble the property, so conceived, of being

---

[16] Mackie, *Problems*, p. 68.   [17] Mackie, *Problems*, Chapters 1 and 2, passim.

physically square or round than the property of looking intelligent or looking ill can resemble the property of being intelligent or being ill. If it seems to make sense to speak of a resemblance between phenomenal properties and physical properties, so conceived, it is only because we give ourselves pictures—phenomenal pictures— of the latter. The resemblance is with the picture, not the pictured.

So, then, the common consciousness lives, or has the illusion of living, in a phe- nomenally propertied world of perceptible things in space. We might call it the lived world. It is also the public world, accessible to observation by all: the world in which one man, following another's pointing finger, can see the very thing that the other sees. (Even in our philosophical moments we habitually contrast the colours and visual shapes of things, as being publicly observable, with the subjective contents of consciousness, private to each of us, though not thereby unknowable to others.)

Such a reminder of the depth and reality of our habitual commitment to the common-sense scheme does not, by itself, amount to a demonstration of that scheme's immunity from philosophical criticism. The scientific realist, though no Kantian, may be ready, by way of making his maximum concession, with a reply modelled on Kant's combination of empirical realism with transcendental idealism. He may distinguish between the uncritical standpoint of ordinary living and the crit- ical standpoint of philosophy informed by science. We are humanly, or naturally—he may say—constrained to 'see the world' in one way (i.e. to think of it as we seem to perceive it) and rationally, or critically, constrained to think of it in quite another. The first way (being itself a causal product of physical reality) has a kind of validity at its own level; but it is, critically and rationally speaking, an inferior level. The second way really is a correction of the first.

The authentically Kantian combination is open to objection in many ways; but, by reason of its very extravagance, it escapes one specific form of difficulty to which the scientific realist's soberer variant remains exposed. Kant uncompromisingly declares that space is in us; that it is 'solely from the human standpoint that we can speak of space, of extended things etc.';[18] that things as they are in themselves are not spatial at all. This will not do for the scientific realist. The phenomenally propertied items which we take ourselves to perceive and the apparent relations between which yield (or contribute vitally to yielding) our notion of space are indeed declared to have no independent reality; but, when they are banished from the realm of the real, they are supposed to leave behind them—as occupants, so to speak, of the evacuated terri- tory—those spatially related items which, though necessarily unobservable, never- theless constitute the whole of physical reality. Ayer refers in several places to this consequence; and questions its coherence.[19] He writes, for example, 'I doubt whether the notion of a spatial system of which none of the elements can be observed is even intelligible.'

---

[18] Kant, 'The Refutation of Idealism', in *Critique*, B42.
[19] Ayer, *Central Questions*, pp. 84, 86–7, 110.

It is not clear that this difficulty is insuperable. The scientific realist will claim to be able to abstract the notion of a position in physical space from the phenomenal integuments with which it is originally and deceptively associated; and it is hard to think of a conclusive reason for denying him this power. He will say that the places where the phenomenally propertied things we seem to perceive seem to be are, often enough, places at which the correlated physically real items really are. Such a claim may make us uneasy; but it is not obvious nonsense.

Still, to say that a difficulty is not clearly insuperable is not to say that it is clearly not insuperable. It would be better to avoid it if we can. We cannot avoid it if we embrace unadulterated scientific realism and incidentally announce ourselves thereby as the sufferers from persistent illusion, however natural. We can avoid it, perhaps, if we can succeed in combining elements of the scientific story with our common-sense scheme without downgrading the latter. This is the course that Ayer recommends[20] and, I suspect, the course that most of us semi-reflectively follow. The question is whether it is a consistent or coherent course. And at bottom this question is one of identity. Can we coherently identify the phenomenally propertied, immediately perceptible things which common sense supposes to occupy physical space with the configurations of unobservable ultimate particulars by which an unqualified scientific realism purports to replace them?

I approach the question indirectly, by considering once again Mackie's version of common-sense realism. According to this version, it will be remembered, physical things, though not directly perceived, really possess visual and tactile qualities which resemble those we seem to perceive them as possessing; so that if, *per impossibile*, the veil of perception were drawn aside and we saw things in their true colours, these would turn out to be colours indeed and, on the whole, just the colours with which we were naively inclined to credit them. Mackie does not represent this view as absurd or incoherent. He just thinks that it is, as a matter of fact, false. Things *could* really be coloured; but, since there is no scientific reason for supposing they are, it is gratuitous to make any such supposition.

Mackie is surely too lenient to his version of common-sense realism. That version effects a complete logical divorce between a thing's being red and its being red-looking. Although it is a part of the theory that a thing which is, in itself, red has the power to cause us to seem to see a red thing, the logical divorce between these two properties is absolute. And, as far as I can see, that divorce really produces nonsense. The ascription of colours to things becomes not merely gratuitous, but senseless. Whatever may be the case with shape and position, colours are visibilia or they are nothing. I have already pointed out that this version of common-sense realism is not the real realism of common sense: *that* realism effects no logical divorce between being red and being red-looking, for it is a perceptually direct and not a perceptually representative

[20] Mackie, *Problems*, pp. 110–11.

realism. The things seen as coloured are the things themselves. There is no 'veil past which we cannot see'; for there is no veil.

But this does not mean that a thing which is red, i.e. red-looking, has to look red all the time and in all circumstances and to all observers. There is an irreducible relativity, a relativity to what in the broadest sense may be called the perceptual point of view, built into our ascriptions of particular visual properties to things. The mountains are red-looking at this distance in this light; blue-looking at that distance at that light; and, when we are clambering up them, perhaps neither. Such-and-such a surface looks pink and smooth from a distance; mottled and grainy when closely examined; different again, perhaps, under the microscope.

We absorb this relativity easily enough for ordinary purposes in our ordinary talk, tacitly taking some range of perceptual conditions, some perceptual point of view (in the broad sense) as standard or normal, and introducing an explicit acknowledgement of relativity only in cases which deviate from the standard. 'It looks purple in this light', we say, 'but take it to the door and you will see that it's really green.' But sometimes we do something else. We shift the standard. Magnified, the fabric appears as printed with tiny blue and yellow dots. So those are the colours it really is. Does this ascription contradict 'it's really green'? No; for the standard has shifted. Looking at photographs, in journals of popular science, of patches of human skin, vastly magnified, we say, 'How fantastically uneven and ridgy it really is.' We study a sample of blood through a microscope and say, 'It's mostly colourless.' But skin can still be smooth and blood be red; for in another context we shift our standard back. Such shifts do not convict us of volatility or condemn us to internal conflict. The appearance of both volatility and conflict vanishes when we acknowledge the relativity of our 'reallys'.

My examples are banal. But perhaps they suggest a way of resolving the apparent conflict between scientific and common-sense realism. We can shift our point of view within the general framework of perception, whether aided or unaided by artificial means; and the different sensible-quality ascriptions we then make to the same object are not seen as conflicting once their relativity is recognized. Can we not see the adoption of the viewpoint of scientific realism as simply a more radical shift—a shift to a viewpoint from which no characteristics are to be ascribed to things except those which figure in the physical theories of science and in 'the explanation of what goes on in the physical world in the processes which lead to our having the sensations and perceptions that we have'?[21] We can say that this is how things really are so long as the relativity of this 'really' is recognized as well; and, when it is recognized, the scientific account will no more conflict with the ascription to things of visual and tactile qualities than the assertion that blood is really a mainly colourless fluid conflicts with the assertion that it is bright red in colour. Of course, the scientific point of view is not, in

---

[21] Mackie, *Problems*, p. 18.

one sense, a point of *view at all*. It is an intellectual, not a perceptual, standpoint. We could not occupy it at all, did we not first occupy the other. But we can perfectly well occupy both at once, so long as we realize what we are doing.

This method of reconciling scientific and common-sense realism requires us to recognize a certain relativity in our conception of the real properties of physical objects. Relative to the human perceptual standpoint the grosser physical objects are visuo-tactile continuants (and within that standpoint the phenomenal properties they possess are relative to particular perceptual viewpoints, taken as standard). Relative to the scientific standpoint, they have no properties but those which figure in the physical theories of science. Such a relativistic conception will not please the absolute-minded. Ayer recommends a different procedure. He suggests that we should conceive of perceptible objects (i.e. objects perceptible in the sense of the common-sense scheme) as being literally composed of the ultimate particles of physical theory, the latter being imperceptible, not in principle, but only empirically, as a consequence of their being so minute.[22] I doubt, however, whether this proposal, which Ayer rightly describes as an attempt to *blend* the two schemes, can be regarded as satisfactory. If the impossibility of perceiving the ultimate components is to be viewed as merely empirical, we can sensibly ask what the conceptual consequences would be of supposing that impossibility not to exist. The answer is clear. Even if there were something which we counted as perceiving the ultimate particles, this would still not, from the point of view of scientific realism, count as perceiving them as they really are. And nothing could so count; for no phenomenal properties we seemed to perceive them as having would figure in the physical explanation of the causal mechanisms of our success. But, so long as we stay at this point of view, what goes for the parts goes for any wholes they compose. However gross those wholes, they remain, from this point of view, imperceptible in the sense of common sense.

Ayer attempts to form one viewpoint out of two discrepant viewpoints; to form a single, unified description of physical reality by blending features of two discrepant descriptions, each valid from its own viewpoint. He can seem to succeed only by doing violence to one of the two viewpoints: the scientific. I acknowledge the discrepancy of the two descriptions, but claim that, once we recognize the relativity in our conception of the real, they need not be seen as in contradiction with each other. Those very things which from one standpoint we conceive as phenomenally propertied we conceive from another as constituted in a way which can only be described in what are, from the phenomenal point of view, abstract terms. 'This smooth, green, leather table-top', we say, 'is, considered scientifically, nothing but a congeries of electric charges widely separated and in rapid motion.' Thus we combine the two standpoints in a single sentence. The standpoint of common-sense realism, not explicitly

---

[22] Ayer, *Central Questions*, p. 110.

signalled as such, is reflected in the sentence's grammatical subject phrase, of which the words are employed in no esoteric sense. The standpoint of physical science, explicitly signalled as such, is reflected in the predicate. Once relativity of description to standpoint is recognized, the sentence is seen to contain no contradiction; and, if it contains no contradiction, the problem of identification is solved.

I recognize that this position is unlikely to satisfy the determined scientific realist. If he is only moderately determined, he may be partially satisfied, and may content himself with saying that the scientific viewpoint is superior to that of common sense. He will then simply be expressing a preference, which he will not expect the artist, for example, to share. But, if he is a hardliner, he will insist that the common-sense view is wholly undermined by science; that it is shown to be false; that the visual and tactile properties we ascribe to things are nowhere but in our minds; that we do not live in a world of perceptible objects, as understood by common sense, at all. He must then accept the consequence that each of us is a sufferer from a persistent and inescapable illusion and that it is fortunate that this is so, since, if it were not, we should be unable to pursue the scientific enterprise itself. Without the illusion of perceiving objects as bearers of sensible qualities, we should not have the illusion of perceiving them as space-occupiers at all; and without that we should have no concept of space and no power to pursue our researches into the nature of its occupants. Science is not only the offspring of common sense; it remains its dependant. For this reason, and for others touched on earlier, the scientific realist must, however ruefully, admit that the ascription to objects of sensible qualities, the standard of correctness of such ascription being (what we take to be) intersubjective agreement, is something quite securely rooted in our conceptual scheme. If this means, as he must maintain it does, that our thought is condemned to incoherence, then we can only conclude that incoherence is something we can perfectly well live with and could not perfectly well live without.

Introduction to Tyler Burge's Lecture

Ted Honderich

Tyler Burge began studying philosophy at Wesleyan University in Connecticut, got his doctorate from Princeton, and went on to teach at the University of California at Los Angeles, from which he has not strayed. He is the originator of a theory that what individuates or distinguishes a thought or belief of yours is not within you, but out there in the world. This particular externalism or anti-individualism, which stands apart from Hilary Putnam's earlier declaration and argument that 'meanings ain't in the head', and stands apart from other externalisms and of course cranialisms, is not Burge's only claim to attention. He also does some of the history of philosophy, notably the work of the German logician Gottlob Frege.

The lecture here begins with the scale of things upwards from rocks through plants, trees, bacteria, worms, spiders, bees, snakes, and dogs, up to us humans. In that sequence, related to evolutionary process, where does *mind* first come in? To answer that question, it is Burge's conviction that we don't need what he calls a *definition* of mind in order to go ahead. But he takes it that mind includes, non-controversially, a fact of consciousness and a fact of representation. Here he considers the second subject, and in particular representation in the case of perception.

Representation in general consists in something's having as a part of its nature that it is capable of being *veridical* with respect to something else. That is to say the first thing is related to the second; say, in the way something's being true of something else is related to that thing, or a desire for a glass of wine is related to getting one. Something's having veridicality conditions or accuracy or suchlike conditions is therefore at least akin to the sort of fact that has elsewhere been spoken of as something's being *satisfied* by something else.

The fact of representation, therefore, as Burge goes on to contemplate, is not to be understood, as it is simplest to report, merely in terms of something's being an effect of certain other things and a cause of certain other things—as the mercury level in a thermometer is the effect of temperature. Functionalism in its several forms, say the form of information registration or in terms of cognitive science, is a mistake about representation. Its idea of representation is not representation as in the mature science of psychology.

The lecture, like others in this volume, challenges the summarizer. Still, it can certainly be said to include other arresting propositions, of which the first is that the fact of perception, the most primitive type of representation, is a natural kind in psychology—a natural kind being a class of things familiar in science, such as a chemical element, a class that does not depend on *our* somehow bringing the things in it together. A second proposition has to do with the fact that in perception we have single *objects* that we get from a rich variation in sensory inputs, say retinal items. This fact of our objectifying in perception has to do with perceptual constancies—for example, giving a constant shape to something despite our different perceptions of it.

We come finally to the answer to an initial question. In the scale of things from rocks to us, representation or representational mind begins with bees, spiders, locusts, and other arthropods. They are the simplest things to exhibit perceptual representation, including constancies.

Implicit in all this is the conviction that there can be perception without consciousness, and that we don't know where on the scale consciousness as distinct from representation begins. The lecture is an instance of the lecturer's resistance to over-intellectualizing in philosophy. If it is to me philosophy understood as concentration on ordinary logic, it is also an instance of what can non-pejoratively be called a scientizing of philosophy. Psychology figures large in it, and its initial question is indeed a question that is at home in the theory of evolution, wherever else it may turn up.

In my case the lecture is a stiff reminder of the fact that philosophy that has in it a good deal with which you do not agree can be nothing less than exemplary philosophy, can properly reduce self-confidence. The questions it raises are several. If we do not need a definition of mind or consciousness to get going, do we anyway need an adequate initial clarification—in order to make sure that if we disagree or seem to disagree we are giving answers to one and the same question? Is the limited externalism having to do with individuation, off-stage in this lecture but certainly relevant, the full reply to cranialism? Does the truth about the nature of perceptual representation settle that it begins with the arthropods?

3

Perception: Where Mind Begins

Tyler Burge

Where does mind begin? This seems like a natural question. Rocks and fires, floating in empty space, are overwhelmingly the dominant large citizens of the universe.
Most of us are confident that rocks and fires do not have minds. *We humans* have
minds. Do any other terrestrial beings have minds? If so, which ones?

There is a philosophical question about how each of us knows that others have
minds. That is not my question. I refuse to worry about whether other people have
minds, at least not in this talk. I will not try to answer sceptics about mind in general or about how knowledge of minds is possible. I am more interested here in what
we know than in sceptical questions about whether we know, or how we know.

I do have some sympathy with scepticism about whether some *particular*
humans—certain politicians for example—have minds. But I will not be dealing even
with these sceptical questions. I will assume that we do have some knowledge that
will help answer our question. My task is to explain that knowledge.

So our question is: Do other types of terrestrial animals have minds? If so,
which ones?

Most of us think that apes and dolphins have minds. And cats and dogs. The cats
seem willful. The dogs seem to want to be with us. Both have eyes that seem to express
mindfulness. And we hear all the time about how smart apes and dolphins are.
Willfulness, wanting, expressiveness, smarts all seem to be signs of mind.

What about birds, with their bird brains? What of fish with their lifeless eyes? What
of snakes with their robotic, mindless-seeming reflexes?

What of spiders, ants, bees? They lack the endearing eyes that cats and dogs have.
Like snakes, the bees and the spiders seem to act in "pre-programmed" ways. Their
repertoire of behavior is limited. What they do is relatively easy to predict. So maybe
insects lack minds.

But the ants and bees do seem to cooperate in making and doing stuff. They seem
to act in each other's interests. Aren't interests things that minds have? Spiders
know how to spin webs, and know how to get away when we threaten them. Surely

knowledge is something that occurs in minds. Bees communicate with one another. Doesn't communication involve some mental state? So maybe bees and ants do have minds.

What of worms? What of jellyfish? What of amoebae, paramecia, bacteria? They move around purposively and seem to find places where they thrive and avoid places where they do not thrive. They seem to know how to navigate. Purpose and knowing seem to be states of mind.

Well, what of plants?

Aren't we going overboard? But wait. Plants grow in ways that are purposive and beneficial to them. Recently a biologist claimed in *Scientific American* that trees see. Surely seeing requires a mind. Are we being parochial to exclude plants from having minds? Maybe excluding plants is just a prejudice that one day we will look down on. Why shouldn't purposeful growth count as a kind of planning and realization of self-interest? Why shouldn't knowledge and perception be ascribed to plants?

But then, there is a regularity and order in all of nature. Maybe that order is mindful or mindlike. Maybe rocks *like* to move in the ways they do. Maybe fires *enjoy* their dancing. Do rocks and fires have minds after all?

Somewhere in this line of questioning, it is easy to feel that things have gotten out of hand. Some of the questions seem silly. But it is also easy to feel that many of the questions aren't easy. People disagree about how to answer some of them.

Even where there is agreement, it is not easy to say why we agree.

Are the "right" answers just a matter of cultural habit or choice? Are they relative to what one feels for, or cares about? Are they just a matter of what stance one decides to take up toward other beings in the universe?

I think not. I think that there are definite answers, based on scientific knowledge.

In asking the questions, one is likely, if one is honest, to feel uneasy. What is one asking exactly? What *is* mind? Is one so sure of what one means? Is it so evident *what mind is*? If the meaning of the question is unclear, how can we even begin to answer it? For all that, there remains a sense that the initial question is a real question, and that it should have a real answer.

Philosophy takes up large, interesting-sounding questions that on reflection need to be clarified before they can be well answered. The larger the question, the more need for clarification. Commonly, philosophy must worry about the meaning of its questions at the same time that it tries to develop answers to those very questions.

That seems like a paradox to some. How can one answer a question that one doesn't understand?

In fact, a lot of our thinking involves terms or concepts that we do not understand very well. We talk about semi-conductors, electric fields, radio waves, lymphomas. We understand these terms well enough to use them. But many of us cannot explain them in any depth. So the first thing to remember here is that it is not so uncommon to ask questions that we don't understand very well. Part of finding the answer is improving our understanding of terms in our questions. Questions about mind are like that.

But don't we need *definitions* to ask a serious question about what individuals have minds? People often ask philosophers "what is your definition?" for this or that. Here, the question might be, "what is your definition of 'mind'?"

Philosophers rarely give definitions. They are not shirking their duty. Definitions are not what they are commonly cracked up to be. In fact, we know from some very good work in philosophy by Quine and Putnam that useful definitions are not secure starting places. They can incorporate mistaken theories. Even when they are invoked in science, they are open to questioning and improvement.

We can have security if we *stipulate* meanings. But stipulation yields no new understanding. To be useful, definitions must capture something that we already understand. To be accurate, they must accord with facts. They do not come for free. In fact, they belong, if anywhere, more toward the end of inquiry than at the beginning.

How are we to attack our problem? I will start with some very general remarks about mind. "Mind" is not a well-entrenched scientific term. Ordinary speech allows quite a range of applications. My initial discussion brings out how unsteady ordinary talk is when it comes to deciding whether certain animals have minds. We say that worms know things (that safety is downward into the earth) and want things (to be left alone). But we also see worms as mindless organisms driven by their biological programs.

The tradition of reflecting on mind in philosophy can help. The tradition has focused on two large features, each of which has been taken to be a mark of mind. Some philosophers have taken all minds to involve both features. Others have favored one over the other.

The two large features are *consciousness* and *representation*.

Consciousness needs little introduction. It is what it is like to be awake. If you *are* awake, you probably get it. Notice: no definition.

There are unconscious aspects of mind. In fact, most of what goes on in our minds is unconscious. But the unconscious parts serve the conscious parts. And an individual that is not *capable* of being conscious counts, for some philosophers, as lacking a mind. So for many philosophers being *capable* of consciousness is a mark of having a mind.

I will not be saying much about consciousness, though I will return to it at the end. I won't say much because, although a lot of philosophy and some science have gone into studying consciousness, consciousness is not very well understood. We do not know where, in the evolutionary process, consciousness begins. We can be confident that we are conscious, that apes, monkeys, dolphins, whales, dogs, and cats are conscious. We can be confident because we know that consciousness depends in some way on the brain—for example sensory centers like pain centers. And we know that these animals have brains that are similar enough to ours to infer that they are conscious. They feel pain. We do not know whether insects or worms are conscious. In fact, we do not yet know how to determine scientifically whether they are conscious.

The other large feature of mind is *representation*. I will focus on representation.[1] The term "representation" is used in several ways. I want to clarify a use that centers on a distinctively psychological or mental kind.[2] *Representational* psychological states are those that have veridicality conditions *as an aspect of their natures—as an aspect of fundamental explanation-grounding kinds that they instantiate.*

Let me provide some commentary on the ideas in this point.[3]

First, veridicality conditions. Veridicality is being right about a subject matter. *Veridicality* has two main species: *accuracy* and *truth*. I use the term "truth" for the veridicality of propositions. Propositions, or propositional representational contents, are simply things that can be true or false and that have the same structure as complete sentences or complete thoughts.[4] I use the term "accurate" for veridicality that is not propositional. Symbols that are accurate or inaccurate are drawings and maps. Perceptions are examples of psychological states that do not have propositional structure and that are accurate or inaccurate, but not true or false.

A veridicality condition is a condition for being right about a subject matter. A representational content is such a condition. If the condition is fulfilled, the representational content (whether it be propositional or non-propositional) is veridical. If the condition is not fulfilled, the content is not veridical. A propositional representational content is true or false. For example, a belief that dolphins are friendly to humans has a truth condition, a propositional representational content, that is fulfilled if dolphins are in fact friendly to humans, and not fulfilled otherwise. Since representational contents are kinds of psychological states, the associated kind of psychological state—in this case, the belief—is true or false, as well.

Similarly, a non-propositional representational content sets a condition for being accurate about a subject matter. If the condition is met, the content and the associated perception are accurate. If the condition is not met, they are not. Representational

---

[1] Philosophers used to call representation "intentionality". This term was closely associated with some bad philosophical theories, and it is easily confused with being intentional in the sense of being on purpose. So I prefer the term "representation".

[2] Although some philosophers distinguish the kinds *psychology* and *mind*, I begin by taking them to be the same kind. The notion <u>mind</u> is more often associated with consciousness. The notion <u>psychology</u> (as in having a psychology) is more often associated with representation. Descartes is an early source of this distinction. I shall return to it at the end of the talk. Through most of the talk, however, I will not be drawing any such distinction.

[3] Much of what follows in this talk is elaborated in much greater detail in my *Origins of Objectivity* (Oxford: Clarendon Press, 2010), chapters 8 and 9; and in my 'Origins of Perception', *Disputatio* 4:29 (2011), 1–38.

[4] The reference here to sentences is just illustrative. Sentences have and exhibit propositional structure. I do not think that propositions are sentences, or that all propositional contents are expressed by sentences. I take the notion of propositional structure to be more basic than the notion of structure of complete sentences.

contents of perceptions are kinds of perceptions. A perception of something as spherical is accurate if that something is spherical. Otherwise, the perception is not accurate.

So much for exposition of the notion of veridicality condition. The rest of my explication of the term "representational" holds that to be representational a state must have veridicality conditions *as an aspect of its nature—as an aspect of fundamental explanation-grounding kind(s) that it instantiates.*

Nearly any state can be treated instrumentally, as if it had veridicality conditions. Doing so enables us to treat states as psychological or mental when we do not think that they really are. We can say that a planet wants to get around the sun in the usual way; and its want is fulfilled, made true, if it does so. Bacteria can be treated as more or less accurately representing light or oxygen, and as knowing light or oxygen to be harmful and wanting to get away from them.

Treating bacterial states as if they had veridicality conditions can be useful, but treating them that way does not make it so. In the psychologies of some individuals, having veridicality conditions is an aspect of the *natures* of the states—the kinds of states they are. A scientific understanding of the states themselves invokes veridicality conditions. The veridicality conditions are aspects of the kinds of states that are involved. The laws that the states figure in are specifiable partly in terms of veridicality conditions. Science does not explain bacterial movement in terms of veridicality conditions. Bacteria do not think or perceive. Science does explain the formation of certain psychological states—most impressively perceptual states—in terms of veridicality conditions. Certain animals, including human beings, have veridicality conditions—kinds of representational states—as real aspects of their psychologies.

As noted, it is often convenient, though metaphorical, to invoke veridicality conditions in a description of a phenomenon. Some have taken having veridicality conditions as simply a status accorded those states for the purposes of someone who describes the states. Such a view is sceptical that veridicality conditions, or representation, in the strong sense that I have laid out, are real psychological kinds. Such a view holds that representationality is, in general, a matter of our stance toward a state, not a real feature of the state.[5] The instrumentalist position just sketched has, I think, few adherents now. It is incompatible with the usual realist view of science. Science invokes representation as a kind embedded in law-like patterns. The most developed science of this sort is perceptual psychology. There is empirical reason to take representation, in our strong sense, as a real kind in the world.

Another, more common, way of avoiding appeal to the notion of representation that I have outlined is to substitute for it certain other notions, commonly expressed with the word "representation", that are also present in scientific explanations. I shall call this family of notions *"information registration"*.

---

[5] For the instrumentalist view, see Daniel C. Dennett, 'Intentional Systems', *The Journal of Philosophy* 68 (1971), 87–106; reprinted in *The Intentional Stance* (Cambridge, Massachusetts: MIT Press, 1989).

The core of this family is the technical notion of Shannon *information*. In this sense of "information", one state X "gives information about" another state Y, if X is statistically correlated with Y to some relevant degree. Thus if workers getting off from work in China is correlated with a cock's crowing in Nova Scotia, then each gives information about the other. And it can be said, on the relevant usage, that one type of event "represents" the other. Clearly, this notion of information, as statistical correlation, is not the same notion as the notion of representation that I am explicating. The latter notion is distinctively associated with a psychology. The former is an all-purpose notion of regular correlation.

Sometimes, this information-theoretic notion is adjoined to further notions to yield an explication of the term "representation". For example, for state X to represent state Y, state X must not only be statistically correlated with state Y; instances of state X must also be causally dependent on instances of state Y. Since neither the workers getting off from work in China nor a cock's crowing in Nova Scotia is causally dependent on the other, this more restrictive notion of representation would not apply.

Perception and many beliefs are causally dependent on what they represent. It is clear, however, that this causal information-theoretic notion is not the same as the notion of representation that I began with. A light bulb's being on can be causally dependent on, and informationally correlated with, the flipping of a switch. But the light's being on does not represent the flipping of the switch. Similarly, the direction of a shadow cast by a rock correlates with and is causally dependent on the direction of the sun. But the shadow does not represent the sun in any psychologically distinctive sense. No scientific account of the state of the light bulb takes representing the switch as part of its nature. No scientific account of the direction of the shadow makes any reference to veridicality conditions. Nothing about veridicality conditions and nothing of psychological interest resides in the electric circuitry of the lighting system, or in the interaction between the sun's rays and the rock. One can call the relevant relation "representation" if one wants. But one is using causal and correlational notions, not a psychologically distinctive notion of representation.

Sometimes, the information-theoretic notion, together with a causal notion, is adjoined to a notion of function, usually biological function. The result is often termed "representation". Thus for state X to "represent" state Y in this sense, X must not only correlate with Y and be causally dependent on Y; X must also have the biological function of correlating with Y. This conjunction of notions would exclude the light bulb's state from representing the switch's being flipped and the rock's shadow from representing the sun's direction. But this conjunction of notions is still vastly more inclusive than the notion of representation that is relevant to characterizing mind. A plant's growing in a certain direction correlates with, is caused by, and functions to correlate with the direction of the sun. But the plant's states do not represent the direction of the sun in any psychologically distinctive sense. No appeal to veridicality conditions figures systematically in accounts of processes in the plant.

Again, one can call the correlation-causal-functional complex "representation" if one wants. But one is not using a psychologically distinctive notion of representation. No science explains the plant's growth in terms of its having states with veridicality conditions as aspects of their natures. They are purely biological processes. There is a very broad, highly generic relation between this type of information registration and the psychological notion of representation that is used in perceptual psychology. But the differences are palpable.

Many of the sensitivities of plants and other organisms have been illuminatingly explained in terms of information registration. Many biologists and philosophers use the term "representation" very broadly to comprise all information registration. Doing so curries interest. It is sexier and gets more headlines and grant money to say that the bacterium represents oxygen and knows how to get away from it, or that the tree sees the sun. But nothing about veridicality conditions—no representation in a psychologically distinctive sense—enters into the scientific account. Explanations in science that use some notion of information registration do not use the notion in explaining the *formation* and *processing* of states. The notion enters only into background functional explanation—an account of what the biological structures are *for* in the survival of the organism. The basic states and processes of the plant are explained purely in bio-chemical terms or structural or statistical-informational terms that are not in any ordinary sense psychological.

There is, for example, a functional explanation of why a plant's bio-chemistry takes the form that it does, how the plant's growth is to be understood in evolutionary terms, and what function such growth has—how it was selected for. But no science takes the plant's internal states to have accuracy or truth conditions, with distinctive structures and semantics. Accuracy does not feature in the biology of plant processes. One should not confuse the information-registration sense of "representation" with the psychological sense of the same word. The extreme breadth of application of the information-registration notions indicates that they differ in significant ways from the notion of representation that has traditionally been thought to be involved in perception, belief, language, and reasoning.

There is nothing in itself wrong with using the term "representation" in the information-registration way. But such usage adds nothing to explanations in statistical, causal, or functional terms. And it obscures the distinctively psychological kind, *representation*. As I will explain, the more narrowly applicable, distinctively psychological notion of representation is central to a mature scientific enterprise. So substituting information-registration notions for the stricter, psychologically distinctive notion of representation encourages failure to recognize scientifically important distinctions. It also encourages either a romanticism to the effect that the whole living world is psychological or an unearned reductionist view that psychology is "just" biology.

There is a scientific difference between information registration and psychologically distinctive representation. In the latter, veridicality conditions play a role in *actual scientific explanation.* They play such a role most impressively in perceptual psychology. The point of perceptual psychology is to explain causally how individuals perceive particulars and attributes in the physical environment, and under what conditions individuals fall into perceptual illusions. This form of explanation has been present in psychology since Helmholtz's work in the late 19th century. But it has become the centerpiece of mathematically rigorous, systematic work that has become a mature science since the early 1970s. The science of *visual* perception has become a more impressive science than many parts of biology, including many parts of neuro-science. Since science is an unsurpassed basis for judging what sorts of things there are in the world, there is powerful reason to believe that representation, involving veridicality conditions as a key and apparently ineliminable feature, is a basic psychological kind.

Representationally successful perception is perception that is accurate about an environmental subject matter. Perceptual illusion is a mistake about a subject matter. States that are capable of being accurate or inaccurate about a subject matter are postulated in perceptual psychology both as things to be explained and as factors in causal explanations of other perceptual states. Representation, in the sense that I have outlined, lies at the center of a mature rigorous science.

The practice of perceptual psychology contrasts quite markedly with the science of plant biology and the sciences of very simple organisms like bacteria, paramecia, amoebae, and so on. Information registration, in various forms, enters into explanation in these sciences. States with veridicality conditions play no central role. In explanations that appeal to information registration, talk of veridicality conditions is an after-thought. Reference to veridicality conditions is no more central to scientific explanations of the states of plants and paramecia than to scientific explanation of planetary orbits. The key feature of representation—that it can be accurate/inaccurate or true/false—plays no role in the so-called representation involved in information registration.

There are reductionists who believe that the information-registration use of "representation" can do all the scientific work that the psychologically distinctive notion of representation does. They hold that the only scientifically acceptable notion of representation does apply just as literally to the sensitivity of plants to light and the sensitivity of paramecia to chemical compounds as it does to perceptual states and processes. They may simply regard the "real" explanation of psychological processing to be entirely at the neuro-biological level. Or they may simply hold that psychology can get by with correlation, causation, and biological function. What appear to be psychological explanations of processing are simply glosses on the biological function of the relevant processes, just as the functional glosses on plant growth are.

Of course, it is an empirical question whether one kind of scientific explanation can be reduced to another. But reductions must be earned. Explanation in perceptual psychology features veridicality conditions very centrally. It is not acceptable simply to assume such a reduction. Current scientific practice simply does not support such an assumption.

I believe that there are systematic reasons why reduction of representation to any of the types of information registration that figure in science is unlikely. I will not go into detail here. I will just sketch the main idea. The nearest thing to the notions of accuracy and error in the suite of ideas that comprise various types of information registration are notions of fulfillment or failure to fulfill biological function. Success in realizing a biological function is a practical matter—fitness for survival. But truth, accuracy, falsity, and inaccuracy are not practical matters. In principle, biological success could be correlated with inaccuracy, all the way down; biological failure could be correlated with accuracy, all the way down.

Error can contribute to fitness. A rabbit's repeated misperceptions of danger combined with quick-trigger reactions might not only insure against capture. Its expenditure of energy in acting on those misperceptions could make it more adept at fleeing. Conversely, accurate representation can contribute to failure of fitness. Accepting truths about how things really are can lead to disfunctional depression. The practical value of contribution to fitness is simply not the same as the representational value of veridicality.

Of course, contribution to biological fitness and accuracy *do* track one another by and large, especially at the most primitive levels of representation. The close connection between accuracy and fitness, however, does not affect my primary point. The difference between the practical notion of biological function and the notion of veridicality is so fundamental that an explanation that centers on biological (or artifactual) functionality inevitably explains something different from an explanation that centers on representation that involves veridicality conditions. So a purported reduction changes the subject.

In summary, I think it overwhelmingly unlikely that representation can be scientifically reduced to any type of information registration. There is no question that representation that sets veridicality conditions and information registration are different theoretical notions. I believe that they have irreducibly different explanatory potentials. Explanations of accuracy and of formation of perceptual states capable of accuracy or inaccuracy explain different matters than explanations of contribution to fitness. Perceptual psychology postulates representation as its central kind in its primary scientific explanations. In philosophizing about a science, the most reasonable starting point is to accept the commitments of the science itself.

I have been making some references to the science of perceptual psychology. Its postulation of representational states indicates that states with veridicality conditions are explanation-grounding kinds or natures. There appears to be no more primitive representational psychological state than perception. Perception is where representational mind begins. I will try to explicate commitments of perceptual psychology as a starting point for understanding this beginning.

The first basic point about perception is that it is a psychological state with veridicality conditions as part of its nature.

A second basic point depends on knowing something more about perceptual psychology. I will say a little about the shape of the science. The central problem of perceptual psychology, paradigmatically *visual* psychology, is to explain causally how veridical perception and perceptual illusions are formed from sensory input. The science presupposes explanations in physics that connect environmental events with impacts on the sensory receptors. For example, visual psychology assumes the account in optics of how light is propagated from a surface of a certain size, shape, reflectance, and in a certain position, to impacts on the sensory receptors. The optical laws of light, as it projects from a surface to a certain array of frequencies as they strike the retinal receptors, are well understood.

The psychological account has two main forms. One explains a causal chain of states that begins with the registration of the inputs into the visual system—for example, the first effects of the light array on the retinal sensors—and ends with perceptual states that represent the environment as being certain ways. The second form explains how environmental entities reflect light into the retina so as to yield perceptual states. This second form combines the first form with the background assumption of the optics. This second form enables the psychological science to explain accurate perception and illusion. Explanation of this sort can both anticipate general environmental conditions under which perception will be accurate or inaccurate, and explain successful perception and illusion in particular cases.

What makes both forms of explanation difficult and interesting is what is known in the science as the *under-determination problem*.

Visual perception represents particulars and attributes in the environment. But the initial states of the perceptual system are sensory registrations of proximal stimulation. Proximal stimulation is the stimulation closest to the sensory receptors. Such registrations of light arrays impacting the retina are not perceptions. But these and other registrations are all that the visual system has to go on.[6] Different environmental conditions can produce the same registrations of proximal stimulations. So in this sense proximal stimulations do not determine their environmental causal antecedents—the entities that are perceptually represented. Correspondingly, the registrations of proximal stimulation underdetermine perceptual states that are accurate or inaccurate with respect to the environmental, causal antecedents.[7] That is, a given registration of proximal stimulation is in itself compatible with many possible perceptual states.

---

[6] The visual system utilizes a wider range of input, not just stimuli of the retina. For example, it uses proprioceptive information about the direction and movement of the eyes. The underdetermination problem applies to the wider range as well.

[7] Underdetermination is a mathematical matter: it is logically and mathematically possible for the environmental causes of the registration of proximal stimulation (the causes that are potential objects of perception) to vary while the registration of proximal stimulation remains fixed. It is logically and mathematically possible for perceptual states to vary while a given registration of proximal stimulation remains fixed. In fact, these sorts of underdetermination are always not only logically and mathematically possible. They are also psycho-physically possible.

So there are two types of underdetermination that confront the central explanations of perceptual psychology. One is underdetermination of the environmental objects of perception by registration of proximal stimulation. The other is underdetermination of perceptual states by the registration of proximal stimulation.

The *underdetermination problem* is that of answering the following question. How are perceptual states that represent specific particulars and attributes in the environment produced, given that the proximal stimulations to which the system has immediate causal access do not determine either the environmental entities that the perceptual states represent as being there or the perceptual states that do the representing?

The initial registration, or encoding, of proximal stimulation—mainly registration of light—goes through a series of transformations in the visual system that eventuate in perceptual representations that represent entities in three-dimensional space. There is a determinate optical and geometrical solution to the problem of determining how a three-dimensional array projects onto a two-dimensional coding of that array. But there is no determinate mathematical solution to how a two-dimensional coding is transformed into a representation of, and as of, a three-dimensional scene. The retinal encodings, together with all other input from proximal stimulation, underdetermine even the *physically possible* environmental causes. Perceptual states sometimes accurately specify environmental attributes and refer to environmental particulars that have such attributes. So perceptual psychology must discover laws that govern how registrations of proximal stimulations cause visual perceptions, through a series of transformations. These formation laws are distinctively psychological. They systematically cite representational states in terms of the accuracy conditions of the states—for example, a perceptual state that specifies surface or body X as farther away, by such and such distance, from surface or body Y.

The formation laws, and law-like patterns of processing, in effect *privilege* certain possible environmental causes over others. The effect of the privileging is that the under determining registration of the proximal stimulation triggers, through a series of transformations, a perceptual state that represents exactly one of the many possible environmental causes that are optically compatible with the incoming light and its registration.

The underdetermination of environmental causes by proximal registrations renders the formation of perceptual states subject to error. Illusions occur when abnormal, "unprivileged" environmental causes produce the same types of registrations of proximal stimulations that are produced by normal, "privileged" distal causes. These conditions are a topic of the science.[8]

---

[8] Most points made here occur in any mainstream textbook on visual psychology. See Stephen E. Palmer, *Vision Science* (Boston, Massachusetts: MIT Press, 2002), 9–11, 18–24, 55–59; and Vicki Bruce and Patrick Green, *Visual Perception: Physiology, Psychology, and Ecology* (Hillsdale, New Jersey: Lawrence Erlbaum, 1985, 2004, fourth edition). The real science resides in journal articles.

The foregoing discussion of the underdetermination problem grounds my second point about perception. The point is this: formation of perceptual states constitutes a certain type of *objectification*.

Given that a process yields a perceptual state that specifies (has accuracy conditions regarding) environmental entities, formation of perceptual states involves a type of objectification. This objectification is formation of a state that functions to represent a subject matter beyond idiosyncratic features of the individual. The subject matter is the physical environment. The objectification involves a certain removal from the local or idiosyncratic.

Objectification resides in the ways perceptual systems overcome the two forms of underdetermination. The perceptual system distinguishes patterns coded in sensory registration that are likely to be adventitious, or idiosyncratic to the perceiver, from patterns that tend to correlate with specific aspects of the environment. When perceptual processing yields representation of the physical environment, it constitutes the relevant *objectification*. The sensory registration is local and idiosyncratic. The perceptual states represent a reality beyond proximal stimulation.

What marks a system or state as *perceptual* is a processing that contrasts registrations of proximal stimulation (and higher-order features of such stimulation), on one hand, with states that specify elements of the environment beyond the sensory receptors. Explanation of the formation of the relevant states benefits from taking the states as representing the environment rather than merely filtering and weighting proximal stimulation so as to make behavioral responses efficient in functioning to respond to environmental pressures.

Objectification in perception is implemented by *perceptual constancies*. Perceptual constancies are perceptual capacities systematically to represent some given particular or attribute as that very particular or attribute under significant variations in registration of proximal stimulation. In a perceptual constancy, a perceptual system can represent some given aspect of the physical environment as that aspect from different *perceptual perspectives*, produced by different proximal stimulation.

For example, *shape constancy* is a capacity to perceive a given shape under various stimulus and perspectival conditions. A square pattern can be seen as square whether viewed head on or at an angle. *Location constancy* is a capacity to represent a perceived particular as at a given distance and direction, under various types of stimulation deriving from various types of particulars perceived. The sonar systems of bats, whales, and dolphins and the visual systems of numerous animals can localize objects, even if the objects in a given location change many of their properties so as to produce very different proximal stimulation. *Luminance constancy* is the capacity to represent a given lightness—on the scale from black to white—as the same under various stimulus conditions, including different illuminations. There are numerous other types of perceptual constancies.

Perceptual constancies are marks of objectification. I conjecture that a sensory system is perceptual if and only if the system includes perceptual constancies. This conjecture is not based on conceptual analysis or definition. It is based on a judgment of conditions under which sciences are led to explain perception formation in terms of kinds of states that are accurate or inaccurate with respect to specific elements in the environment. The idea of the conjecture is that the central aspect of perceptual systems that makes it necessary to explain formation of their states in terms of representational contents with veridicality conditions is the presence of perspectival capacities inherent in perceptual constancies.

My conjecture is that, in the actual world, in the absence of perceptual constancies, a system's ability to connect sensorily with environmental entities can be adequately explained in terms that do not invoke representational contents with veridicality conditions. As a matter of scientific fact, explanations of many sensory capacities do not need to—and do not—invoke representational contents that set accuracy conditions. Such explanations do not ascribe perceptual constancies.

I believe that this difference in explanatory strategy corresponds to a difference in sensory capacities between those that involve perceptual constancies and those that do not. Representational accuracy and perceptual constancy are natural psychological kinds acknowledged in science.

As I have intimated, many species exhibit perceptual constancies. Some arthropods—bees, locusts, and some spiders; most reptiles, amphibians, and fish; and probably all birds and nearly all mammals have visual perception. Most of the *spatial* constancies occur in these visual systems. Color constancy is scattered through the animal kingdom, apparently depending on how central color is to the life of the species. Birds and bees tend to have it. Many mammals lack it. We are fortunate. Object constancy has been demonstrated in many birds and mammals. Various aspects of touch, proprioception, and hearing are perceptual, again in a wide variety of animals.[9]

Since certain arthropods have perception and since perception involves the most primitive type of representation, these animals have the most primitive type of representational mind. Representational mind begins with bees, spiders, locusts, and preying mantises.

Let me summarize my overall argument. Perception is a natural psychological kind, recognized in rigorous, mature science. Perception is marked by having accuracy conditions as part of the nature of the kind. The formation of perception involves a type of objectification. This objectification is a process that systematically contrasts phenomena that encode proximal stimulation, at various levels of abstraction, and phenomena that represent specific environmental entities. Objectification is marked by processes embedded in exercises of perceptual constancies. These are perceptual capacities to represent some environmental particular or attribute *as* that particular or attribute under a large variety of proximal stimulations, and from a large variety of corresponding perspectives. The simplest animals that are known to exhibit perceptual constancies are bees, certain spiders, and other arthropods, such as locusts

---

[9] See *Origins of Objectivity*, 419–421.

and preying mantises. So they have perceptual capacities. Perceptual capacities constitute the most primitive sort of representational mind. So representational mind begins in the arthropods.

I return to the other mark of mind—consciousness. In our current state of knowledge, I see no point in wrangling over priority between consciousness and representation. I think it better to follow out each of these marks of mind, to see where it leads. We may come to think that our concept of mind straddles importantly different kinds—representation and consciousness. Or we may come to understand some sort of unity between the two primary marks. If someone wants to reserve the term "mind" purely for systems capable of consciousness, I will not object. I prefer to talk about *representational mind*, or *representational aspects of mind*, and *conscious mind*, or if you insist, *representational psychology*. I think that understanding the main marks of mind or psychology is, at this stage, the main matter.

In any case, it is not a scientific requirement on perception that it be conscious. We know that bees and spiders have perception. We do not know whether they are conscious. Moreover, there is empirical reason to believe that some perception in bees, and in us, is unconscious.[10]

Moreover, not all consciousness involves perception, or even representation. Awareness of the felt quality of pain (as distinguished from proprioceptive locating of pain) does not require representational content or perceptual constancies.

There may be organisms that feel pain—and hence are conscious—but lack any representational capacities. There may be organisms that have representational capacities, but are never conscious.

---

[10] I cite three bodies of empirical evidence, among many others, with a sampling of relevant psychological literature.

(1) There is evidence that some color constancies—hence perceptions—in bumblebees occur at the retinal level, with nearly no processing. Such constancies almost surely occur before consciousness could occur, even if the bees *are* conscious. Adrian G. Dyer, 'Bumblebees Directly Perceive Variations in the Spectral Quality of Illumination', *Journal of Comparative Physiology A* 192 (2006), 333–338. There is reason to believe that similar, very primitive, color constancies occur at the retinal level in humans—again, well before consciousness is likely to arise. See M. T. Vanleeuwen, C. Joselevitch, and I. Fahrenfort, 'The Contribution of the Outer Retina to Color Constancy', *Visual Neuroscience* 24 (2007), 277–290.

(2) There are, in humans and other animals, certain states formed post-retinally, but in the first micro-seconds of visual processing, that seem to involve perceptual constancies, but seem not to be conscious. Again, it is likely that these constancies are formed before any kind of consciousness can occur. Such states are, at the very least, not consciously *accessible*. The individuals are oblivious to what they perceive. Steven J. Luck, Edward K. Vogel, and Kimron L. Shapiro, 'Word Meanings Can Be Accessed But Not Reported During the Attentional Blink', *Nature* 393 (1996), 616–618; Stanislas Dehaene, Lionel Naccache, Guryan Le Clec'H, Etienne Koechlin, Michael Mueller, Ghislaine Behaene-Lambertz, Pierre-Francois van de Moortele, and Denis Le Bihan, 'Imaging Unconscious Semantic Priming', *Nature* 395 (1998), 597–600; Rene Marois, Do-Joon Yi, and Marvin M. Chun, 'The Neural Fate of Consciously Perceived and Missed Events in the Attentional Blink', *Neuron* 41 (2004), 465–472.

We do not know where consciousness begins. We do not know where awareness of pain begins in the animal world. We do not know enough about consciousness even to know how to directly investigate the matter.

But we do know where representational mind begins. It begins with the arthropods. This result may not make us feel any special kinship with insects. They do not make good pets. They do not love or appreciate us. They lack endearing eyes. But we do have this in common. We are both capable of representing aspects of the physical environment, in a distinctively psychological sense of "represent". We both have representational mind. In this respect we are part of a small minority in this universe dominated by rock and fire. And we differ importantly from another minority with which we share life—the plants and other pre-psychological organisms.

(3) We know that blindsight patients perceive entities, again showing an array of perceptual constancies. It is likely that the relevant perceptions by blindsight patients are not phenomenally conscious. Blindsight is just one of many types of dissociation in which unconscious perception occurs. Prosopagnosia and extinction-neglect syndromes are others. I discuss these matters in greater depth in *Origins of Objectivity*, especially 374–376. For a sampling of relevant psychological literature, see L. Weiskrantz, *Blindsight* (New York: Oxford University Press, 1986); R. W. Kentridge, C. A. Heywood, and L. Weiskrantz, 'Spatial Attention Speeds Discrimination Without Awareness in Blindsight', *Neuropsychologia* 42 (2004), 831–835; James Danckert and Yves Rossetti, 'Blindsight in Action: What Can the Different Sub-types of Blindsight Tell Us about the Control of Visually Guided Actions?', *Neuroscience & Biobehavioral Reviews* 29 (2005), 1035–1046; Daniel L. Schacter, Mary Pat McAndrews, and Morris Moscovitch, 'Access to Consciousness: Dissociations between Implicit and Explicit Knowledge in Neuropsychological Syndromes', in L. Weiskrantz (ed.), *Thought Without Language* (Oxford: Clarendon Press, 1989); Martha J. Farah, 'Visual Perception and Visual Analysis After Brain Damage: A Tutorial Overview', in C. Umilta and M. Moscovitch (eds), *Attention and Performance XV: Conscious and Nonconscious Information Processing* (Cambridge, Mass.: MIT Press, 1995), 37–75, also in N. Block, O. Flanagan, and G. Güzeldere (eds), *The Nature of Consciousness* (Cambridge, Mass.: MIT Press, 1998). See also Bruce T. Volpe, Joseph E. Ledoux, and Michael S. Gazzaniga, 'Visual Processing of Visual Stimuli in an "Extinguished" Field', *Nature* 282 (1979), 722–724; M. Verfaellie, W. P. Milberg, R. McGlinchey-Berroth, L. Grande, and M. D'Esposito, 'Comparison of Cross-field Matching and Forced Choice Identification in Hemispatial Neglect', *Neuropsychology* 9 (1995), 427–434; James P. Morris, Kevin A. Pelphrey, and Gregory McCarthy, 'Face Processing Without Awareness in the Right Fusiform Gyrus', *Neuropsychologia* 45 (2007), 3087–3091.

Introduction to Jerry Fodor's Lecture

Ted Honderich

Jerry Fodor is among the strongest of philosophers and cognitive scientists, some say burliest, in a notable department of philosophy, that of Rutgers, the university of the state of New Jersey. He was born a New Yorker, went to Columbia and Princeton, and spent a year in Oxford. He is known for the theory that there is one language of thought, right there in all our human brains, not English or any other natural language. He is also known for understanding the mind in terms of modules, specialized entities responding to specific kinds of input. The philosophy of language has not escaped his attention and judgement, and he has taken on not merely much of cognitive science but also Darwin himself on evolution.

The sequence of the first half of his lecture, as he reports himself, begins with (i) the question about the mental—about the conscious and the unconscious mind—of whether there are things in it called *unconceptualized representations*, whether there is a *perceptual given* in that sense, as well as the conceptualized representations elaborated in some or all of the representative theories of the mind. That opening question, in the first of a number of metamorphoses or improvements of it, becomes the question of (ii) whether there are *just-representing* representations as well as *representing-as* ones, a distinction like the more familiar one between seeing something and seeing it *as* something.

That second question in turn becomes the question of (iii) whether there are what are called *iconic* mental representations as well as *discursive* ones. Are there iconic mental representations somehow akin, for example, to pictorial ones, maybe of a giraffe on paper? Not word-like and sentence-like representations in the particular and much-studied ways that those are composed of parts. And finally there is the last metamorphosis, the question (iv) of whether there are mental representations where representing something and *individuating* something comes apart—on which final understanding of the issue of givenness there *is* empirical evidence.

There is suggestive evidence in the psychological literature, that is, of representation without what is called an *item effect*. There is data to which your own experience, maybe of the chiming of a clock, and counting the chimes, is relevant. It takes and deserves slow reading. So we are invited to the conclusion that a certain perceptual *given* is quite likely—we are invited by the evidence of psychologists to an answer to what has hitherto been taken as a philosopher's question. Which is not to say that there isn't a given in some other sense or other senses.

Is all this about the given as hitherto heard of in philosophy? C. I. Lewis has much of his place in the history of American philosophy and logic for asserting the existence of some given, and his compatriot Wilfrid Sellars has some of his place for denying it. In this particular philosophical sense the given is qualia or qualities presented in our sense experience and also in rather more than that. They are qualia that are immediate, certain, and *true*—true despite their not involving conceptualization, which is a pretty good trick—and also what we construct reality out of.

Fodor sure isn't Lewis, for reasons starting with his inclusion of the unconscious mind, and also his nod to Freud, rarer these days than a decade ago. That isn't to say he hasn't got a subject for which he can use an old name. He isn't either, by the way, into what I call *actualism*, an enthusiasm of my own, about a very much plainer givenness, a fact of just all consciousness rather than also the rest of mentality. He has, as he hoped, limned one philosophical landscape, very discursively, and with what you could call New Yorker finesse. One question here is what distinguishes conscious from unconscious representation. We need to know, don't we? Despite similarity, conscious representation is a different sort of thing from a picture of a giraffe on paper or the printed word, isn't it?

4

The Revenge of the Given: Mental Representation Without Conceptualization

Jerry Fodor

1 Introduction

Could there be unconceptualized mental representations? What would they be like? Where might one look for some? How would you know if you had found one? I think these questions are, in the long run, largely empirical. But limning the landscape that they occupy is a philosophical enterprise within the meaning of the act, and that I shall presently try to do. I also propose to push at them and prod at them until they are in a form where psychological data can be brought to bear, and to say something about how the relevant data have come out so far.

For present purposes, I assume without argument that there are *conceptualized* mental representations. This assumption is the backbone of the "representational theory of mind" (RTM) which is, of course, itself famously tendentious. But I'm too old to worry about what to do if RTM isn't true.

I shall also assume what is maybe less familiar: that *conceptualized representation* is *representation as* and vice versa. So, to represent (e.g., mentally) Mr James as a cat is to represent him as falling under the concept CAT; and to represent Mr James as falling under the concept CAT is to represent him as a cat; and thinking of Mr James as a cat requires applying the concept CAT to Mr James. This is, to be sure, just the sort of "intellectualist" kind of thinking about thinking that mid-century logical behaviorists (notably Ryle and Wittgenstein) said that psychology and the philosophy of mind could profitably do without. Well, they were wrong.

If that is all granted, it suggests a first move: we have the option of exchanging "Can there be unconceptualized mental representation?" for "Can there be mental representing without mental representing as?" This serves to locate the present concerns in relation to a family of others that are philosophically familiar: For example, "represents X" is transparent to substitution of coextensive terms at the X position; but "represents as X as F" is opaque to substitution of coextensive predicates at the "F" position. If (a token of) "that cat" represents that cat, and if that cat is Granny's favorite cat, then that token of "that cat" represents Granny's favorite cat. But though a token of "that cat" represents that cat *as* that cat, it doesn't follow that "that cat" represents that cat as Granny's favorite, not even if that is the cat that Granny prefers to any other. In this respect the semantic distinction between *representing* and *representing as* works like the psychologist's distinction between *seeing* and *seeing as*. (You can see that cat without seeing it as that cat, but you can't see that cat *as* that cat without seeing it as a cat.) That's all implicit in RTM, according to which seeing X only requires mentally representing X somehow or other, but seeing X as F requires applying to X the mental representation that expresses the concept F. Seeing requires representation; seeing as requires representation as.

So, then: it is part of RTM that, if there is seeing without seeing as, then there is unconceptualized seeing. Piety recommends a more traditional formulation: if there is seeing without seeing as, then there is a "perceptual given." In what follows I will often put the matter the second way, but with a caveat: I assume, contrary to a main epistemological tradition, that the given may be both subpersonal and encapsulated; which is to say that it may be neither conscious nor (in Steven Stich's term) "inferentially promiscuous." This is, to be sure, the thin edge of a complicated tangle of issues. It is arguable, for example, that the content of a representation cannot be alienated from its accessibility to consciousness. That might be because (in the case of perceptual judgments or quite generally) the connection between content and first-person justifications of beliefs is itself inalienable. And it is likewise arguable that the connection between content and inferential role is inalienable because content is, in fact, a construct out of inferential role. On that sort of view, the notion of a kind of mental representation that is given rather than inferred, and that is unconscious to boot, is doubly a contradiction in terms.

Discussions of unconceptualized content in the philosophical literature (like, come to think of it, discussions of practically everything else) routinely beg both the question whether the identity of a mental representation is dissociable from its role in inference and the question whether the intentionality of a mental state is dissociable from its accessibility to consciousness. Speaking just for myself, I see no reason why the very same mental content that is de facto proprietary to unconscious processes of (as it might be) visual-form recognition in one mind might not be available to (as it might be) mechanisms of conscious problem-solving in another mind (or in the same mind at a different time). In effect, the received philosophical view has it that conceptual atomists have failed to recognize that the content of a representation supervenes on its inferential role, and computational psychologists have failed to recognize that mental states are *ipso facto* epistemologically transparent. Well, maybe; but I wouldn't bet much on either, and I wouldn't be flustered if the given flouts both.

2 Kinds of Representations

For reasons I'll presently set out, I think that there probably are non-conceptual perceptual representations. The line of argument I'll have on offer goes like this: on one hand, it is (empirically) plausible that some perceptual representation is iconic and, on the other hand, it is in the nature of iconic representation to be non-conceptual. That being the proposed polemical strategy, I had better now say something about what I mean by "iconic" representation.

First, then, my usage is idiosyncratic. In the semantics/semiotics literature, "iconic" frequently comports with notions like, for example, "pictorial" and "continuous." But it isn't always clear just what any of these come to, or just what the connections between them are supposed to be. As often as not, they are made to take in one another's wash. For the moment, I propose to pretend the slate is blank and stipulate the following.

First, "iconic" and "discursive" are mutually exclusive modes of representation: that a representation is either entails that it is not the other. I leave it open that some kinds of representation are neither iconic nor discursive. Offhand, I cannot think of a good candidate but it doesn't matter for the present purposes.

Second, I assume, for familiar reasons, that all the kinds of representations we are concerned with are compositional. To a first approximation, a representation is compositional iff its syntactic structure and semantic content are both determined by the syntactic structure and semantic content of its parts. Compositionality is required by any serious theory of linguistic and/or mental representations because both thought and language are productive and systematic, and that is intelligible only on the assumption of their compositionality. I suppose everybody knows this story, so I won't elaborate.

2.1 Discursive representations

The sentences of natural languages are the paradigms: here again the outlines are familiar. Every expression is a finite arrangement of constituents that are themselves either primitive or complex. Each complex constituent is a finite arrangement of "lexical" primitives (words, near enough). Lexical primitives have their syntactic and semantic properties intrinsically. Roughly, a word is a triple consisting of a bundle of orthographical/phonological features, a bundle of syntactic features, and a bundle of semantic features: these are enumerated by the word's "entry" in the "lexicon" of the language. A discursive representation in L is *syntactically* compositional iff its syntactic analysis is exhaustively determined by the grammar of L together with the syntactic analysis of its lexical primitives. A discursive representation is *semantically compositional* iff its semantic interpretation is exhaustively determined by its syntax together with the semantic interpretations of its lexical primitives. Consider, for example, sentence (1). Its syntactic structure is (more or less) as shown in (2), and its semantic interpretation is (more or less) *John loves Mary*:

1   John loves Mary
2   (John)NP (loves Mary)VP

The syntax and semantics of the sentence are determined by such facts as that "John" is a noun and denotes *John*, that "loves" is a verb and denotes the relation *X loves Y*, and that "Mary" is a noun and denotes *Mary*. Further details are available upon application at your local department of linguistics.

What matters for us is this: the semantic interpretation of a sentence (*mutatis mutandis*, of any discursive representation) depends exhaustively on the way that properties of its lexical primitives interact with properties of its constituent structure, and *not every part of a discursive representation is ipso facto one of its constituents*. So, for example, "John," "Mary," and "loves Mary" are among the constituents of (1) according to the analysis (2). But "John loves" is not, and nor is "John... Mary." This is part and parcel of the fact that neither the semantic interpretation of "John loves" nor the semantic interpretation of "John... Mary" contributes to determining the semantic interpretation of "John loves Mary"; in fact, neither of them *has* a semantic interpretation in that sentence (though, of course, each of the lexical primitives they contain does). I'll say: the constituents of a discursive representation are those of its parts that are recognized by its *canonical decomposition*. According to me, it is *having a canonical decomposition* that distinguishes discursive representations from iconic ones.

2.2 Iconic representations

Pictures are paradigms (but see the caveats to follow). I suppose that pictures, like sentences, have a compositional semantics. Their principle of compositionality is this:

Picture Principle: If P is a picture of X, then parts of P are pictures of parts of X.

But pictures and the like differ from sentences and the like in that icons don't have canonical decompositions; they have *interpretable parts,* but they don't have *constituents.* Or, if you prefer, all the parts of a picture are *ipso facto* among its constituents; icons are compositional according to the Picture Principle whichever way you carve them up. Take a picture of a person, cut it into parts however you like; still, each picture-part pictures a person-part. And the whole that you have if you reassemble all the picture's parts is a picture of the whole person that the parts are pictures of parts of.

So, then, in everything that follows, a representation that has no canonical decomposition is an icon. I will argue (quite soon now) that iconic representations lack a number of the characteristic features of conceptualizations, so the question we started with, "Could there be unconceptualized mental representations?", can be swapped for the question "Are any mental representations iconic?" And that, finally, is a question on which empirical evidence can be brought to bear.

2.3 Iconicity and individuation

So far, iconic representations are typically semantically evaluable (they are typically *of* this or that). But they have no canonical decompositions, which is to say, they have no constituent structure; which is to say that, however they are sliced, there is no distinction between their *canonical* parts and their *mere* parts. Here's another way to put this: an icon is a homogeneous kind of symbol from both the syntactic and the semantic point of view. Each of its parts *ipso facto* gets a semantic interpretation according to the same rule of interpretation that applies to each of the others (viz. according to the Picture Principle).

But none of that is true of discursive representations. Only a specifiable subset of the parts of a discursive symbol are syntactic or semantic constituents, and it is thus far open that the various constituents of a discursive representation may contribute in *different* ways to determining the semantics of their hosts. Our paradigms, the sentences of a natural language, are clearly structurally heterogeneous in this respect. Considered syntactically, they contain: nouns, verbs, adjectives, noun phrases, verb phrases, prepositional phrases, and so on. Considered semantically, they contain: singular terms, descriptions, predicates, and an apparatus of logical terms such as quantifiers, variables, connectives, and so on once again. Correspondingly, both the rules that distinguish sentential constituents from mere sentential parts and the rules that compose the interpretation of sentential expressions from the interpretation of their constituents turn out to be disconcertingly complex and hard to state; linguists have thus far had only very partial success in formulating either. Compare the unarcane apparatus that sufficed to formulate the Picture Principle.

Because they decompose into syntactically and semantically heterogeneous constituents, discursive representations can have logical forms (maybe all discursive representations that can express truths have them). By contrast, because they decompose into syntactically and semantically homogeneous parts, iconic representations don't have logical forms. I take that to be truistic. The logical form of a symbol is supposed to make its compositional structure explicit, viz. to make explicit the contribution that each of the interpreted parts contributes to the interpretation of the whole symbol. But icons don't *have* logical forms: each part of an interpreted iconic symbol contributes to the interpretation in the same way as each of the others.

We are now about to see that discursive symbols have a galaxy of representational properties that icons don't: properties that are, in fact, the characteristic marks of conceptualization. That's largely *because,* discursive representations being semantically and syntactically heterogeneous, their various constituents can contribute in different ways to determining the content of their hosts: singular terms contribute in one way, predicates contribute in quite another way, and logical constants in still another. But the Picture Principle says that every part of an icon contributes to its interpretation in the same way: it pictures part of what the icon does. In consequence, icons can't express (for example) the distinction between negative propositions and affirmative ones which turns (*inter alia*) on distinctions among logical constants. Likewise, they can't express quantified propositions, or hypothetical propositions, or modal propositions. They can't even express predication, since that requires (*inter alia*) distinguishing terms that contribute individuals from terms that contribute sets (or properties, or whatever).

For reasons that are quite closely related, whereas discursive representations typically carry ontological commitments, iconic representations don't. In particular, discursive representations do, but iconic ones do not, impose *principles of individuation* on the domains in which they are interpreted. I don't want to talk about this at length because I'm scared to. So it would help enormously if you'll just let me assume that what individuals a system of representation is ontologically committed to depends on the apparatus of quantifiers, variables, singular terms, and sortal predicates to which it has access. To a first approximation, systems of representation are committed to the individuals over which they quantify; conversely, if the available representations don't include quantifiers (or classifiers or something of the sort), then there won't be principles of individuation for whatever it is that the representations are of. Since iconic representations lack that sort of apparatus, there is no right answer to the question "which things (how many things) does this iconic symbol represent?" (Didn't Quine say something of that sort? I hope he did; I would so like to be in respectable company for a change.)

To be sure, a photograph may show three giraffes in the veldt, but it likewise shows: a family of giraffes; and an odd number of Granny's favorite creatures; and a number of Granny's favorite odd creatures; and a piece of veldt that is inhabited by any or all of these. No doubt, we usually can agree about how to interpret the ontology of such a photograph; we do so in light of whatever project we happen to have in hand. But that isn't the relevant consideration for present purposes: what matters to us is that the discursive symbol "three giraffes in the veldt" specifies a scene relative to such concepts as THREE, GIRAFFES, IN, and THE VELDT. A fortiori, a mind that lacks these concepts cannot use that symbol to represent the scene. Contrast iconic representation: you can, of course, see three giraffes in the veldt without having GIRAFFE, etc. Nor do you need those concepts to make a picture of three giraffes in the veldt; a camera and film will suffice.

Equivalently (more or less): the context "iconically represents…" like the contexts "sees…," "describes…," "points at…," "and "photographs…" all are transparent to the substitution of coextensive descriptions. But "discursively represents…" is like "sees as," and "describes as…" always has an opaque reading (which in fact it usually prefers). According to RTM, that's because *seeing as*… and *describing as*…, like other acts of conceptualization, operate by subsuming distal things under the concept that is expressed by the predicate of some mental representation. It is entirely in the spirit of RTM that "conceptualizing" and "predicating" are two ways of talking about much the same thing. So if conceptualization requires the apparatus of predication, and if iconic representations *ipso facto* lack such apparatus, then it follows that iconic representations are *ipso facto* non-conceptual. Which is just what I've been telling you for the last many pages.[1]

Brief review: we started with conceptualized v. unconceptualized representations. We swapped that for *representing as* v. *representing tout court*, which we then swapped for iconic v. discursive representation. This allowed us to swap the question whether there are unconceptualized mental representations (in particular, whether there is a perceptual given) for the question whether any mental representations are iconic. I then suggested that (because they lack logical form) iconic representations don't provide principles of individuation for their domains of interpretation. This suggests a final metamorphosis: "Are there unconceptualized representations?" becomes "Are there mental phenomena in which representation and individuation are dissociated?" If there are, then that is prima facie evidence of non-conceptual mental representation.

Well, is there such evidence? To begin with, if you want to test a theory, you need (what used to be called) "correlating definitions." Here is one: it is a rule of thumb that, all else being equal, the "psychological complexity" of a discursive representation (for example, the amount of memory it takes to store it or to process it) is a function of the number of individuals whose properties it independently specifies. I shall call this the "item effect."

Consider, as it might be, phone books. They specify properties of individuals (their numbers and addresses), and they are explicit as to both the individuals and the properties. All sorts of things follow: the phone books of big cities are generally bigger than the phone books of small cities; and they take up more shelf space; and it takes longer to look up an arbitrary number in a big phone book than in a small one; and it is harder to memorize (or even to copy) the contents of a big phone book than those of a small one; and so forth. This is all because the representations in phone books are discursive, hence conceptualized; they presuppose the possession and employment of such concepts as X'S NAME IS "Y" and PHONE P HAS THE NUMBER N. Lists, like sentences, are paradigms of discursive representation. They exhibit effects of their content (it is the number that is listed for John that you proceed to dial in consequence of looking his number up), and they also exhibit an effect of the number of items they contain.

---

[1] I can imagine a line of objection that runs like this: "You connect intentionality with conceptualization, and you say that iconic representation is *ipso facto* unconceptualized. So it ought to follow that there is no such thing as iconic *representation as*. But that's wrong; a green picture of a tree represents the tree that it pictures as green. Doesn't it?" What is wanted here is a more extensive discussion of iconic representation than I have the time or talent for, but here is the short answer: a green picture of a tree is one thing; a picture of a green tree is another; and a picture that represents a tree as green is yet a third. None of the three entails any of the others, which is to say that iconic representation per se cannot distinguish among them. You need conceptualization for that; in particular, you need the concept GREEN TREE.

Compare photographs: a photograph of sixty giraffes takes no more space in your album (or on the screen) than a photograph of six giraffes. For that matter, it takes no more space than a photograph of no giraffes (the one that you made when you forgot to take the lens cap off). Photographs are time-sensitive (very old ones are generally more degraded than very new ones) but they aren't item-sensitive. This is hardly surprising in light of the preceding discussion: iconic representations don't individuate; they don't represent individuals *as* individuals. A fortiori, nothing about them depends on the number of individuals that they represent.

3 Some Data at Last

Can we find, in the perceptual psychology literature, indications of a mode of representation that exhibits typical effects of iconicity; in particular, a mode of representation that *fails* to yield an item effect? If we can, then it is in the cards that such representations are unconceptualized, hence that there is a perceptual given.

In fact, relevant examples are the stock in trade of intro-level cognitive science texts. The basic idea is that perceptual information undergoes several sorts of processes (typically in more or less serial order) in the course of its progress from representation on the surface of a transducer (e.g., on the retina) to representation in long-term memory. Some of the earliest of these processes operate on representations that are stored in an "echoic" buffer (EB) and these representations are widely believed to be iconic.

Two consequences of their presumed iconicity should be stressed, since both suggest possible experimental investigations.

First, since iconic representations are unconceptualized, they do not individuate items that they represent; so representations in EB ought not to produce item effects. Second, qua unconceptualized, iconic representations can't express properties whose recognition requires perceptual inferences. So, in the case of vision, icons register the sorts of properties that photographs do (two-dimensional shape, shading, color, and so forth) but not "object" properties such as *being an animal* (or a fortiori, *being a cat belonging to Granny*).

Correspondingly, in the case of auditory perception, icons in EB should register the sorts of properties that show in a spectrogram (frequency, amplitude, duration), but not whether the distal sound is a rendering of "Lillibullero." For present purposes, if you have turned up a mental representation that doesn't individuate and isn't inferred, that is good reason to think what you've turned up is an icon.

Bearing all that in mind, let's start with an anecdote by way of building intuitions. So: there I am, seated at the keyboard, working hard on a piece for *Mind and Language* (or whatever); at the moment, I vacillate between a semicolon and a comma. A clock begins to chime. "Chime, chime, chime," the clock says. At first I ignore this, but then it seizes my attention. "I wonder what it may be o'clock," I say to myself (it being my habit to address myself in a sort of pig Georgian). What happens next is the point of interest: I commence to count the chimes, including the ones that I hadn't previously noticed. Strikingly (so, anyhow, the phenomenology goes) it's not just that I say to myself "There have been three chimes so far"; rather it's that I *count* the chimes that I hadn't till now attended to: "One chime, two chimes, three chimes," I think, thereby subsuming each chime under the sortal concept A CHIME. Four more chimes follow and I duly add them to get the total. I think: "It must be 6:30" (the clock in the hall runs half an hour fast).

Notice that one's ability to do this trick is time-bound; it lasts only for perhaps a second or two, so you can't count the unattended chimes that you heard yesterday. A psychologist might well conclude: *There's a brief interval during which an iconic (hence unconceptualized) representation of the chiming is held in EB. Within this interval, you can conceptualize (hence individuate, hence count) the chimes more or less at will. After that the trace decays and you've lost your chance.* I think he'd probably be right to so conclude. And I think that, in so concluding, he would postulate a perceptual given.

Prima facie objection: But clearly there *is* an item limit on the buffer. You may be able to count two or three chimes retrospectively, but I'll bet you can't do fifteen.

First reply (in passing): Temporal effects can mimic item effects so they must be controlled for. Suppose representations in EB last two seconds and it takes the clock sixty seconds to chime fifteen times. You will "lose" the last eleven chimes in such a sequence. This is not, however, an effect of the number of stimulus items that can be stored in EB; it's just an interaction between the temporal duration of the stimulus and the temporal capacities of the buffer.

Second reply (more interesting): It's not because the buffer is item-limited that you can't count up to fifteen retrospectively. Rather (once you control for the rate of temporal decay) it seems that how much you can put in the buffer actually is relatively unconstrained. It's not *representing* many chimes that's hard, it's *counting* them. For counting requires individuation, and individuation requires conceptualization, and it's independently plausible that conceptualizing costs.

There are data that suggest that this is indeed the right diagnosis. Some of the most convincing come from a deservedly famous series of experiments by George Sperling (1960). These findings are richer than I have space to summarize, but they support a pervasive phenomenological intuition: "When complex stimuli consisting of a number of letters are tachistoscopically presented, observers enigmatically insist that they have seen more than they can remember afterwards, that is, [more than they can] report afterwards." In the experiment, "the observer behaves as though the physical stimulus were still present when it is not (that is, after it has been removed) and... his behavior in the absence of the stimulus remains a function of the same variables of visual stimulation as it is in its presence." The critical experimental finding was that, queried just after the stimulus was turned off, though the subject could report only three of the letters he'd seen, he could report *any* three of them. So it appears there is a very short-term visual memory of which the capacity is, at a minimum, considerably greater than what S is able to read out of it. Apparently it is the cost of conceptualizing information in this memory, rather than the number of items that the memory is able to register, that bounds the subject's performance.

Notice that, though the Sperling results argue that the content of representations in EB is unconceptualized, these representations must of course *have* content; in particular, they must contain a content from which the categorization of an unattended stimulus (for example, a count of the chimes) can be recovered. That they do is crucial to explaining why the subject is accurate more often than chance. But, equally, the content they contain must not be *conceptual* content since, if it were, then there ought to be an item effect; which, apparently, there isn't. The long and short is: if "a given" is what is unconceptualized but nonetheless semantically contentful, it is thus far plausible that the representations in EB qualify as given.

But I do want to emphasize the "thus far" part. The argument I have set out is empirical through and through; it rather suggests that there is iconic representation in perception, but it certainly doesn't demonstrate that there is. Demonstrations are ever so much nicer than suggestions, of course; their level of confidence is so much higher. But there isn't one either pro or con in the present sort of case. Nor will there be. Since the issue about what kinds of mental representations there are is empirical, so too are the considerations that resolve it.

But I also want to emphasize that Sperling's study, though particularly elegant, is only one of a plethora of straws in the wind, all of which appear to be blowing in much the same direction. Effects of content without item effects are quite easy to find when you know where to look. I wonder why so many philosophers are so resistant to looking there.

4 Conclusion

I think there is quite likely a perceptual given. In any case, it would seem that the issue is empirical, so whether there's a given is, to that extent, no philosopher's business. On the other hand, if in fact there is a given, that should be of professional concern to philosophers who argue a priori that there can't be, that all content has to be conceptualized. Those philosophers are now required to sketch an alternative explanation of the sorts of empirical findings I've been gesturing toward. I am not holding my breath.

But does it matter philosophically in any other way? Does it, in particular, matter to epistemology? I have two reflections, both of which return us to considerations I raised earlier in the paper.

First epistemological reflection: If the given is supposed to be what ultimately grounds explicit justifications of perceptual inferences, then it must be both non-inferential and introspectible (as, indeed, foundationalist epistemologies have generally assumed). But then the empirical evidence is very strongly that there is no given: it seems to be a sort of iron law, one that holds in just about every case I've heard of, that what can be introspected is *always* the product of inferences (though the inferences are typically sub-personal and encapsulated). Contrapositively, what is a plausible candidate for *not* being inferred is almost never available to introspection. In particular, all the perceptual representations that are accessible to consciousness exhibit constancy effects and, by pretty general consensus, constancy effects are the products of inferences. You cannot, for example, see the retinal color of a thing (i.e. the color of the light the thing actually reflects to the eye); inferences that correct for background, distance, illumination, and so forth are automatic, mandatory, and *prior* to introspective access. You see oranges as orange even when the light is dim; that's because what you see is the retinal color *as corrected for* the effects of the intensity of the ambient illumination. Such considerations suggest, pretty strongly I think, that the given doesn't do what foundational epistemology wants it to: it doesn't provide a kind of representation that is both insensitive to contextual bias and available for conscious report. Well, if what is given turns out not to support a certain kind of epistemology, that does not argue against there being a given; it just argues against that kind of epistemology.

I wonder, sometimes, whether our current epistemology has quite caught up with the Freudian revolution in psychology: there is every sort of evidence that a great deal of the reasoning involved in the fixation of quotidian perceptual beliefs is unconscious, hence unavailable for report by the reasoner. That being so, the residual options for epistemology are to say either that most of our perceptual beliefs are unjustified or that much of what justifies our perceptual judgments isn't conscious. I'm unclear that much turns on which of these epistemology chooses.

Second epistemological reflection: It is often suggested, especially by philosophers in the Sellars tradition (such as Brandom, McDowell, and Davidson in some of his moods) that unconceptualized representations can't be what ground perceptual judgments because justification is a relation among *contents,* and whatever is unconceptualized thereby *lacks* content. The (putative) consequences of this (putative) truth are horrific. They include the principled impossibility of a "naturalized" epistemology; indeed, the principled isolation of "the realm of causes" from the "realm of reasons" quite generally. Thus McDowell says that causal explanations of perceptual judgments of the kind that psychologists seek can at best provide "exculpations where we wanted justifications."[2]

---

[2] McDowell, J. (1994), *Mind and World*, Harvard University Press.

This is, to be sure, a long question; but I do hate a priori arguments that such and such a kind of discourse can't be naturalized; and "realm"-talk makes my skin crawl. So I can't resist a couple of brief comments.

First, discussions about whether any representational content is given shouldn't just take for granted all content is *ipso facto* conceptualized. Not if, as I've been trying to convince you, there is a plausible case for preconceptual, iconic representation. On that assumption the (putative) truism that justification is a relation among the contents of representations does *not* entail that justification is a relation among *conceptualized* contents. Accordingly, the question that needs settling is whether the content of an unconceptualized representation might be the datum that grounds (i.e. makes rational) a perceptual judgment.

Well, I'm damned if I see why it can't be. A picture of three giraffes in the veldt carries information about there being three giraffes in the veldt. (Since "carries information about..." is extensional, it carries information about all sorts of other things too, of course. But so what?) Somebody who has the concepts GIRAFFE, THREE, VELDT, and so on (and *only* somebody who does) is *ipso facto* in a position to see the picture *as* showing three giraffes in the veldt, and hence to recover that information from the picture. All that being so, his reason for believing that there are three giraffes may well be that the picture shows three of them. His *reason*, notice; not his mere exculpation. As far as I can see, none of this is under threat from the consideration that judgment requires conceptualization.

Judgment requires conceptualization even if (as I suppose) *representation* doesn't; and, of course, there's no conceptualization without concepts. The question *how* (for example, by what computational processes) iconic representations might get conceptualized is, of course, very hard and the answer is unknown for practically any of the interesting cases. On the way of looking at things of which I've been trying to convince you, that is a large part of what the psychology of perception is about.

But, so far as I can see, there is nothing to preclude a story about how ironically carried information might function to ground a perceptual judgment. *Ground*, not just *cause*. I note in passing that I know no reason to suppose that such a story must have to assume that the required concepts are *constituted*, even in part, by rules for their application to iconic representations; or, indeed, that they are constituted, even in part, by *any* rules for applying them. There aren't, I shouldn't think, any *criteria* for applying GIRAFFE to giraffes; which is to say that perceptual inferences about giraffes don't have to ground in a priori truths. I take this to be a virtue of the story I've been telling.

I'll end with a brief methodological homily. I don't see that the epistemology of perception can simply ignore the empirical question how perception works. Quite generally, justifying a belief cannot require a thinker to do such-and-such unless the thinker has the kind of mind that *can* do such-and-such. (It cannot require him to introspectively access the preconceptual grounds of his beliefs unless he has the kind of mind that *has* introspective access to the preconceptual grounds of belief.) I've heard it said that how perception works doesn't matter to epistemologists because theirs is a normative not a descriptive enterprise. But how could one be bound by norms that one is, in point of nomological necessity, unable to satisfy? And what is the conceivable interest, even to epistemologists, of norms that don't bind us?

Reference

Sperling, G. (1960). "The information available in brief visual presentations," *Psychological Monographs*, 74, 1–29.

Introduction to Ned Block's Lecture

Ted Honderich

Ned Block studied at Harvard University and then taught next door at the Massachusetts Institute of Technology, and went on to be professor in the departments of philosophy and psychology and also in the Centre for Neural Science at New York University. A further and yet greater distinction is that he has not been at all converted by his locales to functionalism, the idea that what you are thinking or feeling at this moment is what is just a certain effect and cause, no matter what else is true or not true of it.

Block provides and considers a kind of evidence against two claims or theories about your seeing or otherwise perceiving something, say a red circle on a piece of paper. One theory is that you are somehow in a direct connection with the thing. The other is that there is something else in the story—something that just represents or stands for the red circle, in something like the way of a word or name. More particularly, what Block calls the phenomenal character of your perceiving, maybe better called your consciousness in the perceiving, is not what it is taken to be by the claims or theories of direct or naïve realism or those of representationism.

Rather, your phenomenal consciousness is or is a matter of what another philosopher in a superior way called *mental paint*—whose existence he then went on to deny. To allow this mental paint is to suppose your consciousness is or is a matter of a private inner thing that somehow *resembles* the red round thing on the paper, something somewhat like what used to be called a sense-datum, and at least some of what have more recently been called qualia. Block does say he is explaining your consciousness in a mentalistic way, by way of *mental* objects or qualities, unlike the way of naïve or direct realism or common ideas of representations.

The evidence against direct realism and representationism, and for his theory, in plain words open to being misunderstood or misconstrued, is that if you *look steadily* at something, go on fixing your eyes there, but just *think* of one part of what you are seeing, that part now looks different from the others in a new way. Get just a bit of the evidence for yourself. Try it for a start with Figure 5.2A. Keep looking steadily at a square dot but *attend to* one of the disks—engage in thinking of one of the disks. That disk, if you're like me, now looks different from before. So there's mental paint.

There is more experimental evidence put together, having to do with other cases of attention and differences in the way things look. These complications are needed in order to defend the theory of mental paint further as against those of direct realism or representationism. If you are or have been a student only of philosophy, you are likely to be among those who have to work at keeping a hold on things in the lecture, the psychology. Still, you will not need help in getting a hold on the whole general line of argument.

This is that there are changes in the look of things, differences in what we can call perceptual consciousness. These attention-changes, as we can call them, have to have a certain explanation. In the case of the first lot of evidence, they can't be explained by the disk on the paper itself, which didn't change, and in particular they can't be explained by direct connection with it. And they also can't be explained by any difference in representation of the disk. So they have to be explained by way of the theory of mental paint. That theory has to replace the other theories.

Block says in an abstract of his lecture that in virtue of what you have heard he is a mentalist, a propounder/defender of *mentalism*. Evidently this is not to say that he is not a physicalist. It is not to say that he is among the contemporary defenders of the outlook that brain and mind, brain and consciousness, are so different that the second must not be physical. If you are persuaded by the use of the evidence having to do with attention and its effects, what account are we going to give of the difference?

Bernard Williams' lecture in this book is about mainstream philosophy as a humanistic discipline. Philosophy is said to be what tries to make sense of our life, sometimes as an extension of science, but usually not. This philosophy is not scientism, not something assimilated to the aims and manners of science, not aspiring to an absolute, objective, or universal view, and is in a way historical. I leave it to you, reader, to consider the extent to which the present lecture is not mainstream philosophy as conceived, whether or how much this matters, whether or not any departure from that philosophy was a good idea, what light this lecture throws on Williams' lecture.

There is also a simpler question. The whole tradition of private entities in perceptual consciousness, from Locke's *ideas* in the 17th century to Ayer's sense data and a lot of people's qualia in the 20th century, has fallen into doubt. In a sentence, the tradition makes our seeing rooms and desks like just seeing them on television. To what extent, if any, does this apply to mental paint?

5

Attention and Mental Paint

Ned Block

1. Introduction

Are phenomenological characters of perception—e.g. what it is like to experience redness or roundness—philosophically reducible to or philosophically grounded in the redness or roundness of the objects one sees or to representations of redness or roundness? If there is no such reduction, then there can be said to be mental paint.[1] The mental paint issue cross-cuts the metaphysical dispute between physicalism and dualism. I am friendly to reductive physicalism in the sense of a *scientific* reduction of phenomenological qualities to biological properties of the brain, a reduction thesis comparable to the "micro-reduction" of water to H_2O, light to electromagnetic waves, and heat to molecular kinetic energy (Nagel, 1961; Oppenheim & Putnam, 1958), where micro-reduction is a reduction of properties of a whole to conglomerations of properties of the parts of that whole. Though I am open to reductive physicalism in that sense, I reject any *philosophical* reduction of the phenomenological qualities of perception to properties of objects such as redness or roundness or representations of redness or roundness and in this I am in agreement with some dualists (Burge, 2005; Chalmers, 2004). Philosophers may disagree about what the difference is exactly between scientific reduction and philosophical reduction. Perhaps it is the difference between an a posteriori reduction and an a priori reduction. I will not be discussing this issue further here.

One aim of this paper is to argue that philosophical reductions of phenomenological properties to direct awareness of properties of objects or representations of those properties are wrong. A second aim is to present evidence for some surprising

---

[1] I am not assuming that if there is mental paint, it is non-relational ("intrinsic") or has no representational aspect. Since I favor physicalism, I allow that mental paint may be a relational neural property. To avoid misunderstanding: I do not take the claim of mental paint to entail that there is anything red or round in the head when one veridically sees a red or round thing in the world as when red pigment in a painting represents a red barn.

phenomena involving attention that can be explained better with mental paint than without it. A third aim is to argue that certain kinds of indeterminacy in perception can be accommodated in terms of an indeterminacy in representational content without any corresponding indeterminacy in phenomenology.

It has been widely recognized that shifts of attention can affect the phenomenology of perception (Block, 1995; Chalmers, 2004; James, 1890; Macpherson, 2006; Nickel, 2007; Peacocke, 1993). What is controversial is whether such attentional changes in the phenomenology of perception can be accounted for in terms of what properties one is directly aware of or what properties one's phenomenological state represents. The dialectic of this paper starts with a preliminary claim that a difference in attention can produce a difference in phenomenology without any difference in what properties one is directly aware of or what properties one's experience represents. More specifically, two non-illusory percepts of the same feature of an object can differ in respect of, for example, perceived size or contrast. Later, I will suggest that indeterminate contents or awareness of indeterminate properties can accommodate the phenomena, but that experience is not indeterminate in the way it would have to be to save direct realism or representationism.

This may seem paradoxical: two percepts can differ in respect of say perceived size or perceived contrast, yet neither be illusory. How can that be? By way of understanding why there is no paradox, it might be useful to consider, briefly, loudness. Loudness— the perceived intensity of a sound[2]—is a function of a number of variables, aside from actual intensity, namely frequency, bandwidth, and the duration of the sound. Although loudness in some sense presents intensity and is experienced as presenting intensity, the same intensity can sound differentially loud depending on other variables. Analogously, although perceived size presents actual size, perceived size is a function not only of the actual size but of other variables, notably the distribution of attention. Just as there can be two phenomenally different but non-illusory presentations of the same sound intensity, there can be two phenomenally different but non-illusory presentations of the same size. Despite this analogy between perceived size and loudness, there are some disanalogies between the two cases that will be mentioned later.

I will argue that empirical facts concerning attention point in a direction incompatible with direct realism, and then move to arguing that the same points conflict with forms of representationism like that advocated by Alex Byrne, Peter Carruthers, Fred Dretske, Gilbert Harman, Chris Hill, William Lycan, Adam Pautz, John Searle, and Michael Tye[3] according to which the phenomenal character of perception is or

---

[2] The *American Heritage Dictionary* (3rd edition) defines "loud" as "characterized by high volume and intensity."

[3] Byrne, 2001; Carruthers, 2000; Dretske, 1995; Harman, 1990; Hill, 2006, 2009; Lycan, 1996; Pautz, 2010; Searle, 1983; Tye, 1995, 2000, 2009. Closely related views: Anscombe, 1965; Armstrong, 1968; Pitcher, 1970. I am not counting as representationist points of view such as that of Tyler Burge (2003) and David Chalmers (2004) in which modes of presentation are explicitly characterized in phenomenal terms or views such as that of Sydney Shoemaker (1994, 2001, 2003) and Chalmers (2006) in which the properties

supervenes on its representational content (how it represents the world to be). Similar points apply to Colin McGinn's "cluster of properties" view (1999, p. 319) and Mark Johnston's (2004) "sensory profiles" account. In previous papers, I have argued that the phenomenal character of perception goes beyond its representational content. Here the argument is importantly different: that there is something about the representational content of perception (and direct awareness) that is actually incompatible with the phenomenal character of perception. The paper will end with a brief discussion of a respect in which the mental paint view argued for here is less radical than what I have argued for previously.

But first, I will briefly characterize the direct realist and representationist opposition and the sense in which these views reject and I embrace mental paint.

2. Direct Realism and Representationism

According to direct realism, the phenomenal character of perceptual experience is "object-involving" in the following sense: an experience of the redness of the tomato depends for its existence and individuation on the tomato and (on some versions) its color. Any experience, even a possible experience, that is of a different tomato or no tomato or of a tomato that is not red is not an experience with that particular phenomenal character. Thus (surprisingly, counterintuitively) even an experience of a perfect duplicate of the tomato is bound to be different in phenomenal character.

This claim is often justified by appeal to introspection. C. D. Broad (1951) famously said: "In its purely phenomenological aspect seeing is ostensibly saltatory. It seems to leap the spatial gap between the percipient's body and a remote region of space. Then, again, it is ostensibly prehensive of the surfaces of distant bodies as coloured and extended... It is a natural, if paradoxical, way of speaking to say that seeing seems to 'bring one into direct contact with remote objects' and to reveal their shapes and colours." (Quoted in Fish, 2009; Hellie, 2007.) This "openness to the world" seems to be expressed by Martin Heidegger (1977, p. 156): "Much closer to us than any sensations are the things themselves. We hear the door slam in the house and never hear acoustic sensations or mere sounds." (Quoted in Smith, 2002.)

G. E. Moore's (1903) idea of the diaphanousness of experience is taken to combine the positive claim of openness with the negative claim that one cannot be aware of the experiences themselves (Crane, 2006; Martin, 2002; Siewart, 2003; Stoljar, 2004). Moore says "... the moment we try to fix our attention upon consciousness and to see what, distinctly, it is, it seems to vanish: it seems as if we had before us a mere emptiness. When we try to introspect the sensation of blue, all we can see is the blue; the other element is as if

attributed by perception are characterized phenomenally. There is a case for counting Daniel Dennett (1991) as a representationist as well, given his picture of the phenomenal character of perception in terms of the contents of perceptual judgments and beliefs that one is disposed to form.

it were diaphanous..."[4] I accept the positive introspective claim of openness. However, I will be arguing that, ironically, when combined with facts of attention, it dooms the very direct realist and representationist perspectives that it has been used to support.[5]

The object-involving view of perceptual experience is often explained in terms of constitution. As Bill Brewer (2004) puts it, "the subjective qualities of experience... are constituted by the actual spatial distribution of the various displays as these are accessible to the subject." John Campbell (2002, p. 116) describes a similar constitution view, according to which "the phenomenal character of your experience, as you look around the room, is constituted by the actual layout of the room itself: which particular objects are there, their intrinsic properties, such as colour and shape, and how they are arranged in relation to one another and to you." The point of direct realism is to capture the phenomenological differences among different percepts in terms of the world, specifically the direct pickup of worldly objects, properties, and relations rather than any *mental ways* of perceiving those items that go beyond the objects and properties that are perceived. Note that the difference between a percept as of green and a percept as of red can be acknowledged by all sides to be *normally caused* by the difference between red and green in the world. The controversial issue is whether this relation is constitutive rather than causal.

The second of the two views opposed to mental paint is representationism. Representationism (also called "representationalism" and "intentionalism") assumes that perceptual experiences have accuracy conditions (Siegel, 2008a) and holds (in one form) that the phenomenal character of experiences can be identified with the representational contents defined by those conditions (Tye, 1995). Or alternatively, what it is for a subject to have a certain phenomenal character is to have a certain representational content (Byrne, 2001; Crane, 2007). Representationism is sometimes described as a supervenience doctrine: phenomenal character supervenes on representational content (no difference in phenomenal character without a difference in representational content). As has often been noted (Kim, 1991; McLaughlin, 1995), supervenience is too weak a relation to ground a form of reductionism. My case against representationism depends on a version of it in which phenomenal character is determined by or flows from representational content rather than merely supervening on it.

---

    [4] As is less often noted, Moore follows this remark with what in my view is an equally significant truth, "Yet it can be distinguished if we look attentively enough, and know that there is something to look for." See Kind, 2003; Stoljar, 2004.
    [5] It is worth noting that this use of introspection allows for introspective determination of a highly theoretical conclusion. Benj Hellie (2006, 2007) makes the reasoning explicit (2007, p. 267): "If a judgment ascribes a property to an experience, and that judgment is the result of expert phenomenological study under ideal circumstances, then that property is among the experience's phenomenal characters." Ideal circumstances are familiar: not drunk, taken time, etc. Anyone who has read the writings of the highly trained expert practitioners of introspectionist psychology of the 19th century such as Wundt and Kulpe will be reluctant to accept such a principle. Phenomenological judgments are *the highly fallible starting point* (Block, 2007a) of any inquiry into consciousness.

On certain views of the content of perception (for example, Tye, 2009), representationism can be a version of direct realism—for example, if the contents of perception are just the objects and properties perceived rather than something more like a proposition. Confusingly, the term "representationalism" is used for what I call representationism and also used for indirect or representational realism, the view that one is aware of the apple only by being directly aware of something mental, for example a sense datum.[6] The mental paint view I will be defending here is opposed to representational realism, so it rejects representationalism in both senses of the term.

If we hold that a veridical perceptual state is individuated by what it is a direct awareness of, we may be led to the disjunctivist view (Fish, 2009; Hinton, 1973; Martin, 2002; McDowell, 1982; Putnam, 1999; Snowdon, 1979–80) that veridical, illusory, and hallucinatory cases share "no positive mental characteristics other than their epistemological properties of not being knowably different from some veridical perception" (Martin, 2004, p. 82). This is an epistemic conception of hallucination (Siegel, 2008b) in that no further mental properties are supposed to underlie the indiscriminability. (See Susanna Siegel's (2008b) critique.) Tyler Burge (2005) has refuted disjunctivism in a way that suggests that the direct realist intuition and the disjunctivist view that grows from it derive ultimately from a type/token error. Burge points out (see also Burge, 1991; Siegel, 2008a) that particular (datable) *token* perceptual states could be said to have object-involving contents (contents individuated in relation to actual existing things). For after all the veridicality condition of my percept of the whiteness of this page is that this page itself—not some other qualitatively similar page—is white. Since my perception could not have that content without the existence and presence of that particular page, the perceptual content could be described as object-involving. But as Burge notes, token perceptual states may be object-involving in this way even though there are *non-object-involving perceptual types* that apply both to the veridical perception of this page and equally to indistinguishable illusory perceptual states. These non-object-involving types would constitute a mental similarity among indistinguishable veridical and non-veridical perceptions.

I won't be discussing disjunctivism explicitly in this paper except in a few side remarks such as that of the last paragraph.

3. Selective Attention

I say that facts about attention point away from direct realism and representationism. But there are some attentional phenomena that direct realism and representationism are well equipped to accommodate.

---

[6] For this reason, "representationism" is a better term than "representationalism" for the view that phenomenal character is representational content. See Wright and Robinson (Robinson, 2008; Wright, 2008).

It is well known that differences in attention can make for differences in which aspects of the environment the subject is aware of. Many people have noticed what is often called the "cocktail party effect" (Cherry, 1953) in which people at a cocktail party focus on one conversation while at least partially losing conscious awareness of other conversations. Colin Cherry tested this idea using the "dichotic listening" paradigm in which subjects wearing headphones are instructed to listen to, say, the left channel and ignore the right. Such subjects were often unable to tell what language the speech in the unattended channel was in or even whether the speech was forwards or backwards. Later work showed that at least some information from the unattended channel was processed to a high level unconsciously, but still it was at least partially gated out of conscious awareness.

The reader can experience an example of selective attention via Figure 5.1. Attending to the face makes the house recede, phenomenally speaking, and conversely for attending to the house.

According to direct realism, one role of selective attention is to shift within a single scene from direct awareness of some properties to direct awareness of other properties (Campbell, 2002). So direct realism can easily accommodate the role of attention in selecting some objects, locations, and properties rather than others. A similar point can be made using Christopher Peacocke's (1992) adaptation of Ernst Mach's (1959) famous example: one can see a 45° tilted square either as a tilted square or as an

Figure 5.1 Attending to the face rather than the house changes the phenomenal character of experience. From (Tong et al., 1998), where it was used for a different purpose.

upright diamond. (See also the discussion in Macpherson, 2006.) The direct realist can accommodate the phenomenal difference by noting that the actual layout instantiates *both* properties and one's awareness of the layout is constituted by which of the actually instantiated properties are the ones that are selected by attention and are the properties the perceiver is directly aware of.

What I am calling direct realism is often called naïve realism (Smith, 2002), but the more naïve form of the view is that the phenomenal character of your experience as you look around the room is constituted by the actual objects and properties instantiated in the room, including their spatial locations and relations to you. This view leaves no room for two observers at the same location to have different experiences and so does not allow for the role just described for selective attention. Unfortunately, statements of direct realism often do not distinguish sharply between this genuinely naïve form of realism and what I am calling direct realism.[7]

David Chalmers (2004) notes that if one shifts attention back and forth between two pinpoint red lights, one's phenomenology changes. He mentions, however, that the change in phenomenology may be treatable as a representational change in which one's experience represents with varying specificity or else represents salience.[8] (I will be discussing salience later. For now, I will just mention that the direct realist may prefer not to allow that we are directly aware of salience, since salience is mental.) The world certainly contains properties of varying levels of abstractness, specificity or determinacy—for example, red in addition to vermilion and crimson—and changing attention can be a matter of changing which properties one is directly aware of.

Alex Byrne (cited in Tye, 2005, 2006) has noted that a grid of 9 dots in a 3 by 3 matrix can be seen either as 3 rows or as 3 columns, and arguably these shifts are at least in part a matter of shifting attention. Michael Tye (2005, 2006) replies that the experiential change is a matter of change of which properties are represented in the experience. When we see the square/diamond as a square, we visually represent its symmetry about an axis that bisects two sides, whereas when we see it as a regular diamond, we represent its symmetry about an axis that connects two angles. In the case of Byrne's matrix, we can represent 3 rows or 3 columns and that makes a phenomenal difference. (The difference may involve attention to one axis of symmetry rather than another.) Opinions differ as to the adequacy of these replies. (See Macpherson (2006); and see Nickel (2007) for a version of the Byrne example that may be less susceptible to Tye's reply.) But I will assume for the sake of argument that selection of the sort discussed can save direct realism (and representationism) from these problems.

---

[7] See Campbell (2002), p. 114–5, 116, 119 for formulations that do not do enough to distinguish naïve realism from direct realism. Tim Crane (2006) ascribes this view to Campbell and others, and with some justification expresses it as "the phenomenal character of a genuine perception is determined by how the perceived world is." Of course on that formulation there is no room for phenomenal character to be modulated by selective attention.

[8] I have also claimed (1995, p. 241) that "attention makes the experience more fine-grained" (2007b, p. 192).

Both realism and representationism have an "anti-mentalistic" feel to them, and it is important to get a bit clearer about it. We should distinguish between two questions a theory of conscious experience may wish to answer: (1) What is the difference—constitutively rather than causally—between consciously perceiving red and green? (2) What is the difference between conscious perception (say, as of green) and unconscious perception (as of green)? *The direct realist and the representationist are opposed to any appeal to conscious mental properties in the answer to the first question but not the second.* The answer to the first question for the direct realist is: the difference between red and green; that is, the difference between the two colors in the world; and for the representationist it is: the difference between representing red and representing green. Direct awareness and *conscious personal-level mental representation* come into the second question, not the first—for we can perceive (and represent) red and green and other properties unconsciously and sub-personally.[9]

The representationist view of the difference between perception of red and green is the same for both conscious and unconscious perception, namely the difference between representing red and representing green. Representationists differ among themselves in answering the second question. Tye (1995) says that unconscious perceptual representations differ from conscious representations in that the unconscious ones are not appropriately poised for use by the cognitive system. Lycan (1996) combines this sort of functionalism with an appeal to higher-order states.[10] On both views, representation comes into the answer to the first question but not the second.

As mentioned, the direct realist answer to the second question is: direct awareness; that is, the difference between conscious and unconscious perception of a face is the presence/absence of direct awareness of the face. A question may have occurred to the reader: what is the direct realist account of unconscious perception? Suppose the direct realist says unconscious perception of red is a matter of perceptual representation of red without direct awareness of it. But that answer rather undermines the opposition of direct realists to conscious representation. I have never seen a direct realist discussion of this issue, even a brief one. It is one more sign of the profound disconnect between direct realism and the science of perception (Burge, 2005), especially since most conscious perception also involves unconscious perception (Debner & Jacoby, 1994; Jacoby & Whitehouse, 1989).

The upshot then is that opposition to mental paint centers on the first rather than the second question. What the mental paint view denies is that the difference between

---

[9] For example, a "subliminal" presentation of an angry face can affect skin conductance and heart rate without the subject having any conscious inkling of what he or she has seen and similar results are obtained with angry faces in the blind field of a blindsight subject (de Gelder, Morris, & Dolan, 2005). An unconscious presentation of a photograph "primes" both a photograph and the name of an "associated" person. For example, a photograph of Princess Diana made English subjects of the 1990s faster in recognizing a picture and the name of Prince Charles (Block & Young, 1996; Young, 1994a, 1994b).

[10] As Daniel Stoljar (2007) notes, representationism is only plausible as a reductionist view to the extent that unreduced consciousness does not sneak into the representation relation.

conscious perception of red and of green is just the difference between red and green or representing red and representing green.

This point will figure in what follows because the direct realist response to the points I will be making about attention may be to appeal to attentive vs inattentive direct awareness or more generally to degrees of attentive direct awareness. Similarly, the representationist may want to appeal to degrees of attentive representation. What I will be arguing is that these moves are not true to the phenomena because the effect of attention on phenomenology is to change perceived contrast, perceived size, perceived hue saturation, and so on for certain other perceived properties. That is, the difference between one degree of attentive direct awareness and another is experienced by the subject as a difference in specific phenomenological properties such as perceived size or perceived hue saturation. I will argue that this puts the direct realist in a box—the direct realist has to say either that the subject is experiencing an illusion (an option I claim to be able to close off) or that the real properties of objects that the subject is directly aware of are changing—another option that I claim to close off.

This point may be thought to be fatal to direct realism while at the same time rescuing representationism, since the representationist can respond by postulating a representational content that corresponds to the change in perceived contrast, perceived size, perceived hue, and so on. However, representationists cannot postulate contents at will; rather the contents they appeal to must be grounded in normal veridical perception. And I will argue that the move just canvassed fails that test.

But before I get to these points, I will mention an attentional phenomenon that does *not* require mental paint. I regard selection as what happens when because of the joint effect of amplifying some representations and suppressing others, some things that could be seen are not seen. Other attentional phenomena are non-selectional.

4. Non-selective Attention 1

There are many convincing examples of attention changing appearance in a way that does not involve selecting some properties and de-selecting others. The effect I will be appealing to requires a small amount of practice in moving one's attention without changing fixation, but once one manages this it is a strong effect.

To get the effect, fixate (that is: aim your eyes at) any one of the 4 squarish dots in Figure 5.2A. Then move your attention around from one disk to another without moving your eyes. This appears to be much easier for some people than others. Still, every one of sixteen observers in Peter Tse's (2005) experiment said that the attended disk darkened and that they could darken a circle by shifting their attention to it. Tse argues convincingly that the visual system constructs the interpretation which minimizes the number of transparent (or translucent) layers seen. I won't go through the reasoning, but the reader can see one piece of evidence that seeing the disks as transparent is necessary for the effect by noting that the effect does not work for the

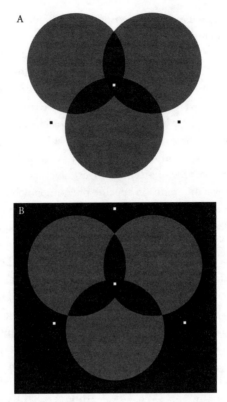

Figure 5.2 The Tse Illusion. In A, you can alter the brightness of a disk by attending to it while keeping your eyes fixated on one of the dots. This does not work for B.

stimulus in Figure 5.2B. (Zero of sixteen subjects reported darkening disks in that experiment.) Because the background of B is seen as black, the disks do not look like transparent or translucent disks. Because the effect depends on seeing the disks—non-veridically—as translucent, it could be argued that it is an illusion. The effect involves grouping and is selective in that sense, but it is not selective in the sense described in the last section, the sense that lends itself so easily to treatment by the direct realist.

I mention the Tse Illusion here for three reasons. First, in case any holdouts denied that change of voluntary attention can change phenomenology, this example should put that view to rest for once and for all. Second, it is useful by way of contrast to the next phenomenon I will be presenting to see why this phenomenon does not pose an immediately obvious problem for direct realism or representationism. The reason is that it is an illusion, both for the reason just mentioned and for the following reason: the three disks are really equally bright and what the moving of attention does is make one of them, illusorily, darker. Direct realism says that in veridical perception one is directly aware of actually instantiated properties, and that view is not challenged by an illusion. (Later, I will be discussing one direct realist attempt to provide a theory of illusion.) The representationist's representational contents are grounded in veridical perception and those contents can misrepresent in illusion so they will have no problem with this case.

Finally, as I mentioned, moving attention independently of fixation takes practice, and I hope the reader's practice with Figure 5.2 will allow a better appreciation of Figure 5.4 to come.

5. Non-selective Attention 2

I will now present the evidence that supports my challenge to direct realism and representationism. Let me go over the empirical facts that I will be appealing to.

1. As I mentioned in connection with Figure 5.2, when one's eyes are pointed straight at a thing or a place, one is said to be "fixating" it. However, and this is fact number one, one can consciously see something without fixating it, as when in Figure 5.2 one fixates one of the dots but nonetheless sees disks that one is not fixating. (I add "consciously" here to make it clear that I am not talking about subliminal perception or other sorts of unconscious perception. I will omit the word "consciously" in what follows, but talk of seeing in this paper should be understood as conscious seeing, unless otherwise indicated.) Sometimes we speak of this connection as looking at something out of the corner of one's eye.

2. One can see something without focally attending to it as well as without fixating it.

3. Most importantly: focal attention *changes* perceptual qualities such as perceived contrast, perceived color saturation, perceived object size, perceived spatial frequency (a measure of stripe density), perceived gap size, perceived speed, and perceived flicker rate. As with most results concerning consciousness, the experimental evidence for this conclusion has some loose ends that I will describe. Terminological note: contrast,[11] saturation, size, spatial frequency, gap size, and flicker rate are objective properties of objects or events. When I talk of perceptual qualities such as perceived contrast, perceived saturation, etc., I mean the relevant phenomenological qualities of the perceptual states that ground the perceiver's knowledge of objective contrast, saturation, etc.

---

[11] There are a number of somewhat different notions of contrast used for different purposes; the reader can think of contrast in terms of the higher luminance (of the lighter areas) minus the lower luminance divided by the average luminance. Luminance is itself an objective property though one that takes into account the response of an idealized human eye.

4. Attentional effects, both excitatory and suppressive, pervade the visual field (Datta & DeYoe, 2009; Downing & Pinker, 1985; Hopf et al., 2006).

The first three of these points were appreciated by William James (1890, p. 425): "... to some extent the relative intensity of two sensations may be changed when one of them is attended to and the other not." Although he emphasizes attention to sensations in this passage, the examples James uses to illustrate it include distributions of attention to colors and sounds in the environment. Hermann Ebbinghaus (1908a, 1908b) appears to have had a similar view. James also recognizes that "The subject is one which would well repay exact experiment, if methods could be devised," something that has now been done in experimental psychology, notably by Marisa Carrasco and her colleagues. The experiments to be described provide strong evidence for the claim that the phenomenal appearance of a thing depends on how much attention is allocated to it.

Figure 5.3 diagrams one of Carrasco's paradigms (Carrasco, 2009; Carrasco, Ling, & Read, 2004). The subject is instructed to look at the "fixation point" throughout each trial, never moving the eyes. (Obedience is often checked with an infra-red camera, but in any case in most versions of Carrasco's paradigm for involuntary attention there is not enough time for the subject's eyes to move.) The fixation point is presented for

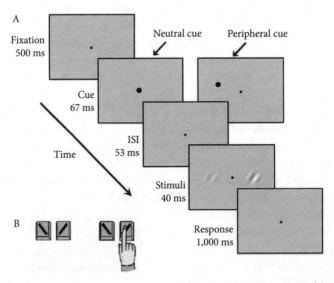

Figure 5.3 This diagram of an experiment reported in Carrasco, Ling, & Read (2004) is to be read from left to right, starting with the presentation of a fixation point for half a second that the subject is supposed to look at and ending with the fixation point, at which time the subject is supposed to respond, either by pressing one of the pair of keys on the left or one of the pair of keys on the right (pictured in the lower right-hand corner). ISI = interstimulus interval. The subject's task is to report the orientation of the grid-like patch (called a Gabor patch). Further details are presented in the text.

half a second, then a dot can appear (randomly) on the left, right, or center. The subject is instructed to ignore the dot and informed that the dot does not indicate or predict the orientation or side of the higher-contrast stimulus. However, low-level attention mechanisms ensure that the subject cannot ignore the dot. The results of the experiment reveal that a dot on one side attracts the subject's attention to that side. The subject then is shown another brief fixation point, then two "Gabor patches," small grids (made up of sinusoidal luminance stripes) each of which can face in one of two directions. The subject's task is to report the orientation of the Gabor patch that is higher in contrast (see footnote 11 for a definition of "contrast") by pressing one of the keys pictured in the lower right of Figure 5.3. The subject is supposed to press one of the keys on the left if the left Gabor patch is higher in contrast and one of the keys on the right if the right Gabor patch is higher in contrast. The subject is prepared for this judgment by being shown examples of comparisons of contrast. (If the subject is to judge e.g. color saturation, the subject is shown examples of differential color saturation.) The idea of the procedure is to avoid bias by placing the contrast judgment at one level of remove from what the subject is officially judging, namely angle. Of course the experimenter is interested in the apparent contrast, not the angle.

The result is that if an attended Gabor patch is slightly lower in actual contrast, attention can boost its apparent contrast to the point of apparent equality of contrast between the two patches. (This effect no doubt involves decreased apparent contrast of the less attended patch.) If the two Gabor patches are the same in actual contrast, an attended patch looks higher in contrast. Carrasco was able to map out the effect quantitatively for a wide range of contrasts. In Figure 5.4, the square dot between the two patches is a fixation point. If one is attending to the fixation point, one can still

Figure 5.4 The Gabor patch on the left has 22% contrast. The patch on the right has 28% contrast. A 6% contrast difference is easy to detect as the viewer can confirm. The effect described in the text is one in which involuntary attention attracted to the left increases the apparent contrast of the 22% patch (and decreases apparent contrast of the 28% patch) to the point of subjective equality between the two patches. With a bit of practice, one can voluntarily shift attention to the left or to the right and experience the increase from this diagram.

see both Gabor patches. (Try it!) The patch on the left looks lower in contrast than the one on the right, a veridical perception. However, if one is attending to the patch on the left, that patch looks equal in contrast to the patch on the right. The combination of increased attention to the left patch and decreased attention to the right patch makes for a 6-point boost in apparent contrast to the left figure relative to the right in Figure 5.4. (The boost effect increases with increasing average contrast.)

Figure 5.5 reports four comparisons of the sort just discussed. For example: if the subject fixates the upper-right square dot, and attends to the dot, the Gabor patch on the left of the fixation point (6% contrast) looks, veridically, to be lower in contrast than the one on the right; but if the subject attends to the 6% contrast patch it looks equal to the 8.5% contrast patch. So at this level of contrast, attention is worth 2.5 points of contrast. An especially interesting comparison is that on the upper left because a 3.5% patch is invisible if one is not attending to it. So, fixating the square dot on the upper left, the difference between attending to the left and attending elsewhere makes for a difference between seeing the patch and not seeing it.

The kind of attention involved here is involuntary, attracted by the appearance of a dot, but Carrasco and her colleagues have recently shown (Liu, Abrams, & Carrasco, 2009) that the same effect occurs with voluntary attention. Subjects were asked to fixate on a cross and to attend to the right if the right side of the cross thickened. Likewise for the left. Although voluntary attention is deployed much more slowly than involuntary attention, the boost to perceived contrast was about the same as for involuntary attention.

Interestingly, some perceptible features showed the effect and others did not. For example, color saturation shows the effect but hue does not. The effect works for gap size (Gobell & Carrasco, 2005), size of moving objects, flicker rate, and spatial

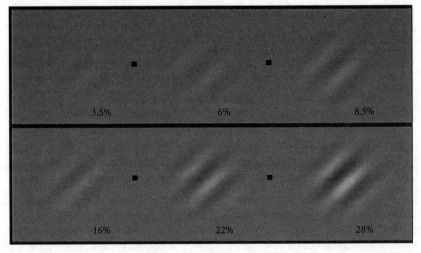

Figure 5.5 The previous figure comes from the lower right of this diagram.

frequency (more stripes in a Gabor patch of a given size constitute a higher spatial frequency). Further, building on earlier work (Golla et al., 2004; Shiu & Pashler, 1995), Carrasco and her colleagues showed (Montagna, Pestilli, & Carrasco, 2009) that attention increases acuity at the attended location. One of the underlying neural mechanisms of this fundamental feature of vision appears to be that attention shrinks the relevant receptive fields of neurons in the visual system, the receptive field of a neuron being the area of space that the neuron responds to (see references in Montagna, Pestilli, & Carrasco, 2009).

6. The Effect is Perceptual

Although there has been some controversy over what exactly these results show (Anton-Erxleben, Abrams, & Carrasco, 2010; Carrasco, Fuller, & Ling, 2008; Prinzmetal, Long, & Leonhardt, 2008; Schneider, 2006; Schneider & Komlos, 2008), it has been settled beyond any reasonable doubt that the effect is a genuine perceptual effect rather than any kind of cognitive effect. To begin, consider the idea that there is a cognitive bias to categorize the side where the dot appears as higher in contrast or that there is a tendency to find the orientation of the cued patch easier to judge. Both are made improbable by the fact that the boost to the attended side persisted *to the same degree* even when the instruction was to report the orientation of the *lower*-contrast patch rather than the *higher*-contrast patch (i.e. the ISI or interstimulus interval). Further, the attentional boost disappeared when the temporal gap between the dot and the patch was increased from 53 ms to 500 ms, which is what one would expect from the decay of transient attention in a perceptual effect but not what one would expect if a slow cognitive effect is governing the result.

Attention has in general been shown to operate via a number of neural effects in the perceptual system. Attention to a stimulus boosts the firing rate of neurons that respond to that spatial area and suppresses the firing rate of neurons that respond to other spatial areas. Further, the degree of enhancement and suppression reflects the degree of attention (Chen et al., 2008; Kastner, 2009; Reynolds, 2008). In general, increasing attention has a similar effect in the visual cortex as increasing contrast itself.

This picture is further supported by purely psychological experiments. One impressive psychological effect involves something called the "tilt aftereffect": if one looks at a visible tilted grating for, say, one minute, then gratings presented immediately afterward that are close in orientation to the original grating appear somewhat rotated away from the original grating. One version is diagrammed in Figure 5.6. The subject looks at the tilted grating in Figure 5.6A for a period, say one minute. When the subject looks at the vertical grating of Figure 5.6B, it will look slightly tilted in a counter-clockwise direction as depicted in an exaggerated form in Figure 5.6C. The explanation is to be found in the perceptual phenomenon known as "adaptation,"

A

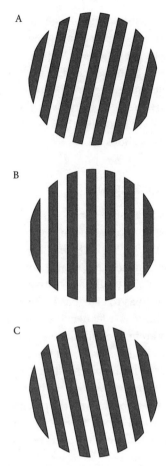

B

C

Figure 5.6 If the subject adapts to A (by looking at it for a minute), then looks at the vertical grating in B, it will look slightly tilted to the left as depicted in an exaggerated form in C.

present in all or virtually all sensory systems. In the first few minutes of exposure to a stimulus, receptor response decreases to the orientation, contrast, direction of motion, and other perceptual parameters of the stimulus, decreasing the perceptual performance on subsequent stimuli with respect to these parameters (Sèries, Stocker, & Simoncelli, 2009). In the case of tilt, receptors sensitive to the orientation of the stimulus undergo a raising of the threshold of activation. When the subject adapts to 5.6A, then looks at the vertical bars (in B), receptors that register a slight tilt to the right are firing more weakly than receptors that register a slight tilt to the left, making the vertical bars look tilted to the left.

One interesting feature of adaptation to a grating is that within limits, a higher-contrast grating raises the threshold for firing more and, further, that raised threshold lasts longer than would be produced by adaptation to a lower-contrast grating

(Langley, 2002). So, within limits, the higher the contrast of A, the bigger and longer lasting the effect on the tilt depicted in C. Ling & Carrasco (2006) compared with the increased size and length of the tilt after-effect accomplished by increasing the contrast of the adapter grating with the increased size and length of the tilt after-effect accomplished by *directing voluntary sustained attention to the adapter grating* (for periods up to 16 seconds). They found that attention to a 70% contrast grating increased the size and length of the tilt after-effect just the same as if the actual contrast of the grating had been increased between 11% and 14%. (Different subjects showed slightly different sizes of effect.) That is, a 70% grating plus focal attention had the equivalent adapting effect to an 81%–84% grating without focal attention. Increasing the contrast of a particular orientation of a grating has a benefit in making that orientation easier to see, but then after a few seconds it has a cost in making that orientation harder to see because of adaptation. And so Ling and Carrasco were able to show that sustained attention confers a benefit in the first few seconds, then a cost. The article is called "When sustained attention impairs perception" because it demonstrates, surprisingly, that a focally attended stimulus can be harder to see (after a few seconds) because of adaptation. The upshot is that since the attentional effect on perceived contrast affects adaptation, it is a perceptual effect.[12]

Another study I find impressive in demonstrating the perceptual nature of the effect involves the basic Carrasco paradigm with one major change: attention is cued by a sound on one side or the other instead of by a visible event (Störmer, McDonald, & Hillyard, 2009). A sound cue rather than a visual cue also vitiates the allegation that the effect is due to a sensory interaction (Schneider, 2006). Using this paradigm with some other minor changes, Störmer et al. got slightly smaller effects than Carrasco (5% rather than 6% elevation of perceived contrast at the 22% level). They found that the effect correlated with increased activity in the first stages of visual processing (using a brain imaging technique involving a mesh of wires on the scalp). Further, the increase in cortical activity occurred in the same cortical areas found to be sensitive to actual differences in contrast in the stimuli. And the larger the cortical effect, the larger the effect on subjects' judgments of increased contrast.

---

[12] Philosophers have been interested in the question of whether vision represents only properties like shape, size, contrast, color, and texture (Prinz, 2006) or whether vision also represents "high-level" properties such as facial expression, causation, or number (Siegel, 2006). (The same issue can be put in direct realist terms: are we visually directly aware of facial expression, causation, number?) There is, however, a powerful line of evidence that philosophers engaged in this debate have not noticed as far as I know: whether perception of a property shows *adaptation* of the sort described in the text. A very strong argument for supposing that vision represents facial expression is that if subjects look at an angry face for one minute, then at a mixed face that has some aspects of both anger and fear, subjects report that the mixed face looks scared. But if subjects start off staring at a scared face for one minute, then they say the mixed face looks mainly angry (Martinez-Conde & Macknik, 2010).

Moving to numerosity, the apparent numerosity of a display is increased if one stares at a low-numerosity display for one minute, and apparent numerosity is decreased if one stares at a high-numerosity display for one minute. This is strong evidence that we visually represent numerosity (Burr & Ross, 2008).

To sum up: there are strong reasons to suppose that the effects of attention on contrast documented by Carrasco and her colleagues are perceptual.

Where are we? Does the attended Gabor patch look to be higher in contrast as a result of the attention or not? The upshot of the studies I have been talking about is that the effect of attention on perceived contrast is a perceptual effect, not a cognitive effect or due to a response bias. So what? Given that the effect is perceptual, one can ask whether it is a *conscious* perceptual effect or an unconscious effect or has both a conscious and an unconscious component. One way to get evidence on whether an effect is conscious is to ask the subjects. That works for the Tse Illusion mentioned earlier and indicated in Figure 5.2. But there is a problem that will be familiar to anyone who has thought about experimental work on consciousness: one cannot simply ask subjects to compare an attended with an unattended stimulus since the question itself would induce attention to the supposedly unattended stimulus.

There has been controversy about the issue of whether or to what extent the Carrasco effect is a conscious effect (though the participants are not always as clear as they should be that this is the issue they are discussing), centering around methodological problems involved in asking subjects to make same/different judgments as opposed to "forced choice" judgments in which subjects indicate which item is higher on a given parameter (Schneider, 2006; Schneider & Komlos, 2008; Turatto, Vescovi, & Valsecchi, 2007). This issue has now been resolved by Anton-Erxleben, Abrams, & Carrasco (2010) which explores the methodological issues involved in same/different judgments, showing that when properly done, the perceptual effect can be demonstrated with both methodologies.

However, the possibility still exists that the effect, though perceptual, is partly unconscious. In order to control the subjects' attention and eye movements, experimenters have tended to use very brief stimuli (40 ms–100 ms), which may decrease the conscious component of the effect relative to the unconscious component.

We can get a bit of illumination on this issue using a different paradigm. There is considerable evidence that when events are simultaneous, attention to one of them can make it appear to occur before the other (Spence & Parise, 2010; Stelmach & Herdman, 1991; Van Der Burg et al., 2008).[13] Stelmach & Herdman showed subjects a screen containing 3 sets of 4 dots arranged in a square. They asked the subjects to attend to the left, or alternatively to the right, or to the center, always fixating the central square. Dots then appeared inside the 4-dot outline in the leftmost square and the rightmost square. The dots were sometimes simultaneous and other times slightly asynchronous (separated by a brief period). In one experiment, subjects were asked to choose which dot appeared earlier. This was a forced choice between left earlier and right earlier with no option for saying they occurred simultaneously. They found that the dot on the attended side was perceived to occur about 40 ms

---

[13] Titchener's (1908, p. 251) "law of prior entry" said "the object of attention comes to consciousness more quickly than the objects which we are not attending to." (Quoted in Spence & Parise, 2010.)

earlier than the other dot. For example, the subjects' point of maximum temporal uncertainty—that is, when they were unable to discriminate which came first—came when the dot on the unattended side led by about 40 ms. Then the experimenters added a third possible response—simultaneity. They found that when attention was to the center, subjects tended to judge simultaneity accurately, but when they attended to either the right or to the left, their judgments of simultaneity dropped precipitously both in absolute number (35% to 4%) and although they trended in the direction of the earlier judgments, the results were weak. This result suggests that there is a substantial unconscious component to the forced choice result. But what about a conscious component?

The experimenters then asked the subjects to adjust the difference between times of appearance of the dots in 5 ms increments. They were allowed to go back and forth as many times as they wished until they were satisfied that the dots appeared simultaneously. I really like this procedure because it allows for subjects to make *considered* phenomenological judgments. Anyone who has been a subject in an experiment in which brief stimuli have to be compared knows that subjects are often uncertain—the stimulus goes by so fast the subjects often feel as if their responses are partly a matter of guessing. Allowing the subjects to try the judgment repeatedly with the ability to change the timing is a way of boosting the credibility of the conscious source of the judgment.

The result was that subjects regarded the attended side as simultaneous with the unattended side when the unattended side led by about 40 ms. The authors give a model of subjects' behavior which I won't describe, but the upshot for our purposes is that same/different judgments provide a less adequate indicator of conscious perceptual state than other methods such as the ones described that indicated the 40 ms difference.

The issue of the size of a conscious effect for these very brief stimuli can, however, be sidestepped because the attentional effect is visible in the sample stimuli printed on the page. You can see it yourself using Figure 5.4! In the case of a one-off illusion like the Tse Illusion, the scientific community accepts the illusion because 16 subjects all said they got it and because the reviewers for *Vision Research* got it, but for a general phenomenon—attention alters perceived contrast—journals have a different perspective.

In what follows, I will simply assume that attention does in fact affect consciously perceived contrast, gap size, etc., as Carrasco's paradigm suggests.

Is the phenomenal effect of attention a matter of salience or vividness rather than perceived contrast? First, as the Stelmach experiment just described shows, attention can affect perceived simultaneity as well as contrast. And as I also mentioned, perceived gap size, speed, flicker rate, speed, color saturation, and spatial frequency are also affected. The attended item looks bigger, faster, earlier, more saturated, stripier. No doubt increased salience is a result of these changes, but it is not a substitute.

7. The Argument

How can the opponents of mental paint explain these results? I'll start with the issue as it affects direct realism, though as we will see, the arguments are similar for representationism. Let us begin by assuming that there is no relevant illusion; that is, that the two different percepts of the 22% patch in Figure 5.4 (the patch on the left) are both veridical or at least non-illusory. I will argue that on the assumption of no illusion, direct realism has no reasonable way of accommodating the results. Then I will argue that there is no relevant illusion.

It will be useful to run the entire argument with respect to Figure 5.4 (and a slight modification of it in Figure 5.7). Let me first review the facts. The subject's eyeballs are pointed at the fixation point in the center and in the Carrasco experiments described earlier, the subject attends either to the fixation point or to the figure on the left. (Let's ignore the cases in which the subject attends to the right.) When the subject attends to the fixation point, the experience of the *relative* contrasts—that the figure on the right has higher contrast—is veridical. When the subject attends to the figure on the left, the contrast of the figure on the left looks—non-veridically—to be the same in contrast as the figure on the right. There is no difference in the spatial position of the subject with respect to the two patches and no difference in the state of the sense organs or the relation between the sense organs and the layout. The difference between these two percepts of the 22% patch is entirely mental.

Consider the subject's perceptual experience of the 22% patch itself (the one on the left) in the two cases (rather than the perceptual experience of the comparison between the two patches). You may wonder whether the effect of attention really applies to a single patch as opposed to a comparison, where there is competition for the viewer's attention. Carrasco (Carrasco, Cigdem, & Eckstein, 2000) shows that the increase in sensitivity that underlies the effects reported occurs—though slightly decreased in magnitude—for a *single* Gabor patch rather than two competing patches.[14] *To repeat: we are talking about the percept of the 22% Gabor patch itself, not the comparative percept.* In the two cases (attention to the left, attention to the center) there are two different phenomenal experiences of the same item with the same relevant instantiated property, i.e. 22% contrast, yet the experiences are different. This is the challenge to direct realism. Attentively seeing and less attentively seeing the same thing—the 22% patch—are experiences that differ phenomenally but not in the item seen or in its instantiated properties.

Earlier, I mentioned cases in which opponents of mental paint appealed to differences in actually instantiated properties selected by attention, e.g. face vs house in Figure 5.1, axes of symmetry in the square/diamond case, rows vs columns in the

---

[14] Of course the methodology used cannot be the same as the experiments described since with a one-item stimulus there cannot be two items to compare. She (Yeshurun & Carrasco, 1999) gets similar results for gap size.

matrix case. It is not obvious how any such selection of properties can apply here, but it is worth considering whether there are properties in the display of different levels of specificity, grain, or determinacy that could be appealed to (cf. Chalmers, 2004, and Tye, 2005, 2006). For example, any scarlet patch is also red, and perhaps a perceiver can have different experiences of the same color patch depending on which is attended to, red or scarlet. A shift between awareness of red and awareness of scarlet might be phenomenologically significant. In the case of contrast, one could take the corresponding determinable/determinate relation to be, for example, that between medium-low contrast and 22% contrast. However, the results cannot be explained by appeal to a shift between direct awareness of 22% contrast in one case and medium-low contrast in another. For the subject experiences the difference as a difference in contrast *at the same level*, for example as a higher specific contrast or specific size, rather than as a move to a more generic or abstract level of contrast or size.

There is a related objection in which the two percepts involve different ranges of vagueness. I will take that up in due course.

Another line of objection would be to suppose that the subject is directly aware of the focus of attention in the layout, and since the focus of attention shifts, so does the phenomenology. In speaking of the focus of attention, I am indicating the thing or area of space that is attended to, and suggesting that it can be seen as a property of the layout. I think that allowing awareness of such mind-dependent properties of the layout would be a significant concession in direct realist thinking. Direct realists often try to capture aspects of appearance by appeal to a variety of types of relations to the subject. But these are normally characterized non-mentally. (For example, Campbell's 2002 book mentions spatial relations and jaundice. Noë (2004) treats appearances as spatial projections on a plane perpendicular to the line of sight.) Relations to a focus of attention or to a center of salience might fit the letter but not the spirit of these views. Recall the summaries quoted earlier by Brewer ("the subjective qualities of experience... are constituted by the actual spatial distribution of the various displays as these are accessible to the subject") and Campbell ("the phenomenal character of your experience, as you look around the room, is constituted by the actual layout of the room itself: which particular objects are there, their intrinsic properties, such as colour and shape, and how they are arranged in relation to one another and to you"). It would be as if they were allowing one kind of mental paint, attentional mental paint.

A better form of the idea for the direct realist would be to think of attention as coming into the direct awareness relation itself. But this idea in either of its forms will not help the direct realist, for a highly significant reason, one that I will be returning to again and again. Recall that subjects experience the effects of attention as alterations of perceived contrast, earliness, size, speed, flicker rate, and spatial frequency. Appealing to direct awareness of the focus of attention or, alternatively, attentional vs less attentional awareness of the patch is inadequate to explaining that phenomenology. Attending makes the item attended look, for example, *bigger*, so it is inadequate to say that it looks more attended to even if it *does* look more attended to. The same point applies to salience conceived as a phenomenal property of the layout—as mentioned earlier. It is certainly true that increases in perceived earliness, size, flicker rate, spatial frequency, and contrast bring with them an increase in salience. But looking bigger is not *just* a matter of looking more salient even if it *involves* looking more salient.

Earlier I said that the positive thesis of Moorean transparency was important to my case. This is one place where it comes in. The effect of attention is experienced in terms of appearance of contrast, speed, size, color saturation, etc. Attended things look bigger, faster, more saturated, and higher in contrast even if they also look more attended and more salient.

So far, I have been bracketing the issue that is most significant, whether one or both experiences of the 22% patch are illusory. Just what this comes to and how it avoids the problem depend on the direct realist's theory of illusion, which is the topic of the next section.

The discussion to follow concerns the question of whether there is an illusory percept of the 22% patch when the subject attends to the fixation point—or, alternatively, to the 22% patch itself. I always mean the issue of whether there is an illusory percept of the 22% patch (not the other patch). As before, I am ignoring the cases in which the 28% patch is attended, and I will speak of the attended patch and the unattended patch for brevity when what I really have in mind is the more attended vs less attended patch. There are a number of different views that finger one or the other patch as seen illusorily. The percept of the unattended patch can be accused of being illusory, or the percept of the unattended patch can be exonerated, the percept of the attended patch being accused instead.

There is a straightforward problem with both views, namely that they only make sense on what one might call a "steady spotlight" model of attention and that model is false. The model has both a spatial and a temporal dimension. I'll start with the spatial aspect, the idea of attention as a spotlight (Posner, Snyder, & Davidson, 1980). The spotlight model was known to be oversimple in the 1980s because it was shown that attentional effects are substantial far from the center of one's attentional field, but it was thought that attentional effects could be thought of in terms of a "gradient of attention" (Downing & Pinker, 1985), which would be compatible with a fuzzy spotlight. However, more recent work shows that the spotlight model is in far worse shape than previously thought. One basic failure is that there are two attentional fields, an excitatory field and a suppressive field. A second basic failure is that both fields are quite large and irregular (Datta & DeYoe, 2009; Hopf et al., 2006). How large? Hopf et al. show an excitatory effect from targets in one quadrant of the visual field (varying in strength) over perhaps half of the visual cortex and a suppressive field, also quite variable, that is only slightly smaller. Datta & DeYoe were able to tell which of 18 areas subjects were attending to with 100% accuracy just by eyeballing the scans, but for some areas, attention spread radially for distances up to more than half the width of the stimulus grid, which itself occupied 56° of visual angle. (The fovea, the central high-density part of the retina, responds to only about 2° of visual angle.) Datta & DeYoe note that "… attention is actively modulating visual processing throughout the field of view, not just in the local vicinity of the target" (2009, p. 1044). They suggest that the replacement of the spotlight metaphor by the "gradient of attention" metaphor is inadequate, and we should think in terms of the "landscape of attention."

That was the spatial point. The temporal point is that attentional resources available to the supposed spotlight are to some extent shared among other aspects of perception, for example other modalities, and with executive control mechanisms (Brand-D'Abrescia & Lavie, 2008) and cognition. Lavie and her colleagues have demonstrated many kinds of cases in which demanding cognitive or perceptual tasks siphon attention away from other perceptual tasks. One experiment (Cartwright-Finch & Lavie, 2007) contrasted a difficult perceptual task (Which arm of a cross is longer?) with an easy perceptual task (Which arm of a cross is green?) In the harder task, subjects were much less likely to consciously see an unexpected stimulus—so-called "inattentional blindness." To take an example more connected to everyday life, talking on a cell phone can foment "inattentional blindness" (Scholl et al., 2003; Strayer, Drews, & Johnston, 2003). It is as if electricity for the spotlight shares limited power with the air conditioning and public address systems, causing brownout for one if the other is making more demands.

You may object "OK, so there are borderline cases and the borderline is more uneven and larger and more varying in time than one might have thought. So what?" This response seriously underestimates the problem for the idea that there is any distribution or level of attention that entails either veridicality in normal circumstances or illusion. The problem for this view is that there is no way to pick which distribution of attentional resources engenders veridical perception and which engenders illusion.

For concreteness, let us consider the claim that when one attends to the fixation point, one's percept of the 22% patch is illusory, but when one attends to the patch itself, one's percept of it is (normally) veridical. Is it the absolute value of attention that is supposed to be crucial to attention making for veridicality? It can't be the absolute value since that would have the consequence that if the subject were speaking on a cell phone, *nothing* would be veridically perceived! So the claim must be based on relative allocation of attention. But the points about the landscape of attention show that many points in the visual field will be very close in the amount of attention allocated to them as the supposed focus of attention. How could these very small differences be—in normal circumstances—the difference between veridicality and illusion? An arbitrary cutoff—which some have proposed for baldness—would make no sense for veridicality.

To avoid misunderstanding: I agree that the terms "veridical" and "illusory" are as vague and context relative as many other terms. And I also agree that we can use

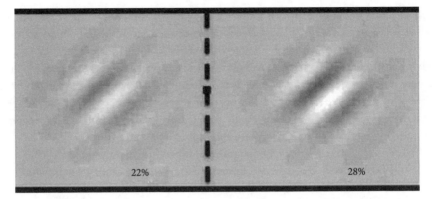

Figure 5.7 Every point on the dashed line is equidistant from the two Gabor patches.

the phrase "attend to" in an acceptable but loose and context-relative way. My point is rather that the claim that only the attended patch is seen veridically requires a non-context-relative kind of veridicality that cannot be justified.

In my view, these points count decisively against any illusion proposal, but I will mention one other point briefly. Consider the proposal that the supposed attentional spotlight engenders illusion. One motivation for this idea is that areas that are differentially attended are sometimes seen in an illusory manner as in the Tse Illusion mentioned earlier. Also, veridical comparison depends on the supposed spotlight of attention being in between the items compared, not directly on them. However, this advantage would apply to any point equidistant between the items being compared: in the example of the two patches, attending to *any point on the vertical line through the fixation point* in Figure 5.4, as shown in Figure 5.7. Every point on that line is equidistant between the 22% and the 28% patch and within the zone in which one can still see both (if the diagram is the right distance away from the eyes), so every point on that line is one such that attending to it might be predicted to yield a veridical comparison. Yet these different percepts of the 22% patch itself—the ones in which one is attending to different points on the line—*would be different phenomenologically from one another*, and so the refutation would be regenerated. Attending to the different points on that line would yield different phenomenal experiences of the 22% patch that are equally veridical. And that is the very situation that led to the problem for views opposed to mental paint in the first place.

If one wants to compare two patches, one does best for the supposed spotlight of attention to be aimed at a point equidistant from the two of them (unless someone has a handy map of one's landscape of attention), but one cannot conclude that only then do the patches look the way they actually are, since the way they look will depend on *which* of the points that are equidistant from them one chooses to attend to. The vertical line through the square dot in the middle may contain a myriad of such points.

Given the landscape of attention, there may be points on that line or elsewhere that yield correct comparisons but are phenomenally different from one another.

The facts about the visual system discussed here are not oddities but rather are closely related to the evolutionary purpose of perceptual systems, which is to get information about the world that is relevant to the organisms' other purposes, which of course include acting (Churchland, Ramachandran, & Sejnowski, 1994). Attention is attracted by movement or change in the environment. This "exogenous" attention is transient and involuntary and happens much faster than the eyes can move, so the experimental situation described earlier in which attention is directed somewhat differently from fixation is a common occurrence. The evolutionary point of the increased acuity and contrast at the attended location is to get more information about what is at that location. Because the effect of increasing acuity at one point inevitably reduces acuity at another (Montagna, Pestilli, & Carrasco (2009) say: "There was no benefit without a cost"), there is no way of making all perceptual comparisons accurate at once. Still, as Carrasco (2006) shows, the increased contrast sensitivity at the locus of attention improves performance on a variety of tasks. (See also Treue, 2004.)

These points are directly relevant to disjunctivism, as can be brought out by comparing the attended 22% patch with the seen but unattended 28% patch. There is at least one well-defined mental property in common to these two percepts, perceived contrast. Neither of these individual percepts (as opposed to the comparative percepts) are illusory but that same perceived contrast will be shared by various kinds of illusions as well. (See Burge's (2005) Proximality Principle.) The disjunctivists who claim "no common mental factor" are flouting what perceptual science tells us about the case.

It might be thought that the way to decide whether attended (or alternatively unattended) items are seen illusorily would be to consult behavioral tests of veridical perception. Since the heady and methodologically suspect days of the New Look in perception (Bruner & Goodman, 1947), there have been studies that have been taken to suggest that desired objects look closer. Recently, Emily Balcetis and David Dunning (2010) have used a variety of behavioral tests to argue for this conclusion. Most interestingly, when subjects toss a bean bag at objects that differ in subjects' conative attitudes towards them they tend to come up shorter for objects to which they have a positive conative attitude.

Attended objects look larger, so one might speculate as follows: (1) desired objects are more likely to be attended; (2) they look larger and therefore closer; so (3) the phenomenon is grounded in illusory perception of attended objects. If so, the argument I gave still stands, since, you will recall, even if the attended object is seen illusorily, the point is reinstated by *comparing one unattended object with another*. (See the discussion connected with Figure 5.7.)

However, I think more would have to be done to show that the "bean bag" test taps a genuine conscious perceptual phenomenon. In the case of the Carrasco phenomenon, I indicated some of the kinds of evidence that show it is a genuine perceptual effect. (For example, it affects perceptual adaptation.) The behavioral measures just mentioned do not reach that kind of standard of evidence and there have been some dramatic cases recently in which such effects appear to reflect "judgmental biases that result from the social, not physical, demands of the experimental context" (Durgin et al., 2009, p. 964).

Finally, to conclude this part of the discussion of illusion, I described a number of the alternatives just discussed as unmotivated (for example the idea of drawing an arbitrary cutoff of illusion, a border between illusion and veridicality). These proposals are unmotivated—unless one of your motivations is saving direct realism! I will be satisfied if my argument convinces a neutral reader.

8. The Direct Realist Account of Illusion

The points made in the last section count against an illusion in the attentional phenomena I have been talking about independently of any particular theory of illusion. (Recall that I am talking about the perception of an individual patch, not the illusory comparative percept.) But the point is strengthened when one sees just how implausible any direct realist theory of illusion would have to be.

I find direct realists evasive on the topic of illusion, but Bill Brewer (2004, 2008) has advanced a straightforward positive account of illusion from a direct realist perspective. Brewer's view (2008, p. 172) is that all perception, including illusory perception, is veridical perception *of something*. According to Brewer, in illusory perception, the something is a similarity to a situation which is not the one the subject is viewing. "Illusions are simply cases in which the direct object of experience has such visually relevant similarities with paradigms of a kind of which it is not in fact an instance." Consider the Müller-Lyer illusion: two lines (one with arrowhead endings, the other with reverse arrowheads) are actually equal in length but look unequal. Brewer's account is that the subject is directly aware of an actually instantiated property, the similarity between the equal lines and *other lines that are not present but are actually unequal*. As Brewer puts it (p. 176): "Suppose that someone has the diagram visually presented to her, from head-on, and in good lighting conditions, with eyes open and a normally functioning visual system. According to OV [Brewer's version of direct realism—the 'object view'], the core subjective character of her visual experience is simply constituted by that diagram itself. From that viewpoint, and given the circumstances of perception, it has visually relevant similarities with a paradigm pair of unequal lines at different depths. In this sense, the concept of inequality in length is intelligibly applicable to its main lines: the lines look unequal in length."

But what is that visually relevant similarity or similarities that a pair of equal lines has to a pair of unequal lines? *Of course the direct realist cannot say it is that they look the same*, since that would be to reintroduce unreduced phenomenology. It might help to see just how empty Brewer's proposal is to consider Wittgenstein's

(Rhees, 1968; Wittgenstein, 1993) supposition—far short of an inverted spectrum—that someone might wake up and find that red things look blue and vice versa.[15] The person Wittgenstein is imagining is having an illusory experience: red things look blue. On Brewer's account, he is seeing the visually relevant similarity or similarities between red and (paradigms of) blue. What are those similarities? Red and blue are both colors, they are both primary colors, and they are both colors of many flags and of Superman's costume, but none of these similarities will help Brewer's case. It is very difficult to see how to spell out that similarity between red and blue without appealing to how things look or to a representational content involving a representation of blue. In my view, direct realism is an unstable position for which there is no good account of illusion, whose motivations better support representationism, a subject to which I now return.

9. Representationism and Vagueness

As you will recall, representationism holds that the phenomenal character of a perceptual state is or is determined by its representational content. Representationism has an obvious advantage over direct realism: it has a better account of illusion. If a man has the phenomenology of seeing his wife as a hat (Sacks, 1985), he sees his wife, visually representing her as a hat. Direct realists see representationism as scanting "openness to the world," but as I mentioned I am doubtful about such theoretical introspections. Representationism has another major advantage over direct realism, an account of the difference between conscious and unconscious perceptual representation that gets to first base. The very "openness to the world" that direct realists like in an account of conscious perceptual representation makes it difficult to see what their account of unconscious perception could be, as noted earlier, whereas for representationism, the difference lies in some aspect of function.

My argument against direct realism was based on the fact that the way the 22% patch looks depends on where the subject is attending, so there can be more than one phenomenal character of experience of the same instantiated properties, even if nothing about the environment or the non-mental relations between the subject and the environment differs. An advocate of representationism might suppose that even if my argument vanquishes direct realism, representationism escapes unharmed, since the representationist can simply say that different distributions of attention to the same layout yield different representational contents: if an attended item looks bigger, faster, higher in contrast, higher in saturation, more stripy, or earlier, the

[15] "Consider this case: someone says 'it's queer/I can't understand it/, I see everything red blue today and vice versa.' We answer 'it must look queer!'" He says it does and, e.g., goes on to say how cold the glowing coal looks and how warm the clear (blue) sky. I think we should under these or similar circumst[ances] be incl[ined] to say that he saw red what we saw [blue]. And again we should say that we know that he means by the words 'blue' and 'red' what we do as he has always used them as we do."

representationist can, it may seem, handle that fact simply by adjusting the representational contents. The great strength of representationism after all is its ability to handle appearances in representational terms.

A similar point might be made on behalf of Colin McGinn's (1999) and Mark Johnston's (2004) views of the phenomenology of perception, views that combine elements of both representationism and direct realism. According to McGinn, the phenomenology of perception is determined by a "cluster of properties" ascribed by the percept. The same role is given to Johnston's "sensible profiles," which are structured properties. These views are more like representationism than direct realism in one respect: McGinn and Johnston do not require that the cluster of properties/ sensible profiles be actually *instantiated*. The phenomenal character of the visual experience of the man who mistook his wife for a hat could be captured by uninstantiated properties/profiles involving a hat shape, color, texture, etc. And a hallucinator and a veridical perceiver could be aware of the same cluster of properties/ sensible profiles, uninstantiated in one case, instantiated in the other, and thus have identical experiences. So McGinn and Johnston could give a response similar to the representationist response just mentioned: different distributions of attention can involve the same object, the 22% patch, but awareness of different clusters of properties/sensible profiles, and these different items could be said to explain the different phenomenologies.[16]

However, if I am right that none of the different percepts of the 22% patch are illusory, these proposals fall flat. Representationists are not free to postulate representational contents at will so as to reflect appearances—rather *these contents have to be grounded in veridical perception*. If the representationist says that changing the distribution of attention changes the representational contents (cluster of properties/ sensible profiles) without changing or selecting any different property of the actual layout, the upshot is that at least one of those representational contents is illusory, and if my argument against illusion is right, that claim is wrong. In short, if there is no illusion in either of the two percepts of the 22% patch, the extra degree of freedom buys the representationist nothing.

However, the representationist has a resource in addition to content: there is also the *mode* of the representation (Crane, 2007). A belief and a desire can have the same content—e.g. that world peace obtains, but with different relations to that content. Similarly there may be different modes of representation in perception. One might, for example, hold that vision and audition are such different modes. As mentioned in a slightly different form with respect to direct realism, the mode of representation could be more or

---

[16] McGinn's and Johnston's views do have the same problem as direct realism in accommodating unconscious perception though, since as with direct realism, their views do not allow for different relations to the clusters of properties/sensible profiles. The common flaw is a "one factor" account, a special direct relation to a cluster of properties/structured properties that is supposed to reflect openness to the world. By contrast, the representationist can appeal both to the representation relation and to the function of the representation.

less attentive, more or less determinate, more or less specific, more or less vivid, more or less salient. What is the difference between indeterminacy in mode and indeterminacy in content? We can get some illumination by considering a recent dispute.

An objection to representationism that has been much discussed (Block, 1996, 2003; Boghossian & Velleman, 1989; Peacocke, 1993; Tye, 1995, 2002) is that there is a phenomenal difference between blurry vision as of something, say a movie, whose lines may be clear and crisp, and (the contrasting case) a clear and crisp visual experience of a blurry movie—even when the same colors, shapes, and textures are represented with the same degrees of determinacy. The first could be produced by taking off one's glasses in a normal movie theater, the second by defocusing the projector while the viewers keep their glasses on. Tye (2002) regards the difference as one between experience *indeterminately representing* (glasses are off) and having an *indeterminate content* (glasses are on but the movie is blurred). One could argue about whether these categories are exactly right, but they will do for the analogy. The glasses off case (indeterminately representing) is a matter of indeterminacy in mode, whereas the glasses on case is a matter of indeterminacy in content. The point of the analogy is that in both cases, indeterminacy of mode and indeterminacy of content, there is the same attribution to points of space of light and dark and color. If we were to capture these two different percepts in terms of digital pixel arrays, the pixel arrays appropriate to the two cases could be exactly the same. The phenomenal difference consists in whether the blur captured in the pixels is attributed to the display or to the mode of perception.

Now consider a specific proposal for accommodating the experimental results in terms of indeterminacy. One option would be to regard the contents that differ but are equally veridical as having different *ranges of indeterminacy that include 22%*. So in the case of attending to the fixation point (in which case you will recall the 22% patch looks less contrasty than the 28% patch), the content of the percept of the 22% patch might be, say, 16%–28% contrast, whereas in the case of attending to the 22% patch itself (in which case you will recall it looks equal to the 28% patch), the content might be a higher range in which 22% is at one end, say, 22%–34% contrast. (Specific numbers are useful for concreteness. Since attention shifts perceived contrast at this level by about 6%, I am imagining that there is an "uncertainty" of plus or minus 6%.) Thus both representational contents would be veridical—since they both attribute a range that *includes the true contrast, 22%*—and they would also be different. The idea here is that the change of representational content imposed by a change of attention is the equivalent of seeing different indeterminate contrast levels. In the case of McGinn's and Johnston's versions, the clusters/profiles would include 16%–28% contrast in one case, and 22%–34% in the other.[17]

The problem with this proposal is that if the phenomenology of perception flows from representational content, then indeterminacy in content would have to be

---

[17] I am indebted in this paragraph to discussion with Christopher Peacocke.

reflected in an indeterminacy of *look*. But there need be no such indeterminacy. The Gabor patches used in the contrast experiments are designed to transition between light and dark in a smooth way, but this is not necessary for attentional effects and is not true of many other stimuli. For example, some size stimuli are shaped like the letter "C," where the relevant parameter is the distance from tip to tip. These are not in any reasonable sense fuzzy stimuli, but the subject sees the gap size as bigger if attended. Attention makes attended items bigger, faster, more contrasty, more saturated, and—in the case of events—earlier, as I have repeatedly noted. These effects do not depend on—and are not reflections of—any sort of fuzziness.

The representationist may retort that the point is not that the contents are fuzzy or represented indeterminately but that they are abstract relative to other contents, as determinables are to determinates, for example as red is to scarlet. But this line of thought runs into the following difficulty: the variation of 6% due to attention is way above the "just noticeable difference" threshold, which for stimuli at these levels is approximately 2%. (Or so I am told. In any case, just looking at the stimuli in Figure 5.4 shows that the difference is easily detectable. And you may recall that in the discussion of the tilt aftereffect, there was evidence that at higher levels of contrast, the increase due to attention was as much as 14%.) The point is that there is no single "look" that something has if it is 22% plus or minus 6% in contrast. By analogy, consider the supposition that something looks as follows: rectangular or triangular or circular. That disjunctive predicate does not describe *one* way that something can look—at least not in normal perceptual circumstances.

Now I have been considering an indeterminacy in content rather than mode. But the same point applies to both! Consider the cinema case just flagged. The mode version of the case (glasses off) and the content version (glasses on, but projector defocused) involve the same level of "fuzziness."

Versions of all these points apply equally to direct realism. The direct realist can suppose that we are directly aware of an indeterminate property of objects, one that is constituted by a range of contrasts, a higher range when one attends than when one does not attend. My objection to direct realism is that direct awareness of an indeterminate property or indeterminate direct awareness of a non-indeterminate property would have to be realized in perception either in the form of a phenomenal indeterminacy or in the form of a disjunctive awareness that does not correspond to any particular look.

To avoid misunderstanding: I like the vagueness proposal as a theory of *the representational content of perception*. What I insist on is that this representational content does not capture the phenomenology of perception.

I am happy with the vagueness proposal so long as the phenomenology is treated as a *mode of presentation of that representational content*. Thus the percept of the 22% patch when one attends to it could be said to have a representational content a major component of which is something like this: <That; 22%–34%>. (Burge (2010) argues persuasively that the content of perception should be understood demonstratively rather than propositionally.) *What I am arguing against is that this content is determinative of the phenomenology of the perception.* As I mentioned at the outset of the paper, in previous publications I have argued that the phenomenology of perception goes beyond its representational content, but here I am arguing for something a bit different, that the representational content of perception cannot determine the phenomenology of perception.

Of course representationists often emphasize that their view is that one kind of content of perceptual states (e.g. non-conceptual content) is determinative of phenomenology even if there are other types of content that are not so determinative. So the argument could be regarded as a challenge to representationists to put up or shut up: what kind of content of perception could determine the phenomenology of perception yet not have the problem just described?[18]

On my story, one could describe the perceptual content of the percept of the 22% patch when one is attending to it this way: *{Phenomenal component P; Referential component: <That; 22%–34%>}.* That is, the percept has both a phenomenal mode of presentation (Burge, 2003; Chalmers, 2004) and a representational content. (Elsewhere (2003, 2007c), I claim to have shown that the phenomenal mode does not supervene on the representational content or conversely.)

I said that the 22% patch attended (i.e. with more attention) is the same in perceived contrast as the 28% patch unattended (i.e. with less attention). And on the proposal that I have just been considering, both would be captured by *{Phenomenal component P; Referential component: <That; 22%–34%>}* where P is the same for both percepts. "Wait—how could that be? How could the percept of the 22% patch attended be exactly the same as the 28% patch unattended? Since the two patches are in fact different, at least one of those perceptions must be illusory!" This conclusion does not follow. One reason is the one already mentioned: that the actual contrast of both patches lies within the specified range. One is 22% and the other is 28%, both of which are in the range of 22%–34%. But there is another factor that has not come up yet in my discussion.

The change invoked by changing attention does not *look like a change in the world*—at least not to me. Take a look at Figure 5.4, fixating on the fixation point and moving your attention around. It does not look as if anything is *really* changing in contrast. That is, these changes don't have what Burge (2009) calls the phenomenology of objectivity. The change looks unreal (to me). Its unreality is similar to the unreality in the way an afterimage grows and shrinks as the surface you project it on moves further away or closer. If you look at a colored shape for two minutes and then look at a piece of paper, you see an afterimage as of the same shape in the complementary color. As you move the paper further away, the afterimage grows. (See any textbook on Emmert's Law, which describes this change of size.) But its growth

---

[18] The challenge concerns determination rather than the weaker supervenience relation.

looks somehow unreal or unobjective (cf. Masrour, 2010). The subjective unreality of these changes has not as far as I know received any empirical investigation. The subjective unreality of the effect of attention was noted by William James. He said (1890, p. 426) "… whatever changes the feeling of attention may bring we charge, as it were, to the attentions' account, and still perceive and conceive the object as the same… The intensification which may be brought about by attention seems never to lead us astray." James quotes Gustav Fechner (1882) (in English) saying, similarly, that when one increases attention, one "feels the increase as that of his own conscious activity turned upon the thing."[19] The upshot is that it is a mistake to treat the change in phenomenology wrought by the change in attention as equivalent in its effect on phenomenology of a change in contrast in the world.

If I am right that the distribution of attention does not produce an illusory percept of any single patch, whether attention is focused on that patch, on the fixation point, or on the other patch, then the visual system must in some way track where attention is focused and this information must be in some way reflected in the phenomenology of perception. Intuitively, it seems that this information is realized visually in the phenomena described, although it could be realized phenomenally in some other way. (Subjects can be wrong about which modality is the source of perceptual information.) If it is visual, then there is something phenomenally different between the way the attended 22% patch looks and the way the unattended 28% patch looks, even if they are the same in perceived contrast.

Let us think of the attentional tracking as a little voice that says where attention is directed and also that the range of contrasts attributed to the world should be adjusted to reflect reality because of that distribution of attention. Then we could think of the percept of the 22% patch attended as *{Phenomenal component P; Referential component: <That; 22%–34%>, Little Voice component: attended, so adjust downward}* whereas the percept of the 28% patch unattended might be *{Phenomenal component P; Referential component: <That; 22%–34%>, Little Voice component: unattended, so adjust upward}.* Further research might lead to evidence that the little voice should be partly absorbed into the phenomenal component or the representational component or both.

Many experiments on perception in effect encourage the subject to judge appearance. If subjects are asked to judge size in afterimages at different distances, apparent size will be reflected in the judgments. A different kind of experimental paradigm— say betting—might encourage a focus on reality instead of appearance.

At the beginning of the paper I mentioned an apparent paradox: two percepts can differ in respect of perceived contrast, size, etc., yet neither be illusory. I mentioned

---

[19] This point is noted by Geoffrey Lee (2009) in criticizing the transparency thesis with regard to temporal phenomenology. He says that moving our attention just does not seem like an external change. The same point is made in an unpublished paper by Sebastian Watzl. My point and the use of the quotations from James and Fechner are independent of Lee, Masrour, and Watzl.

that although loudness presents sound intensity, loudness is a function not only of intensity but also frequency, bandwidth, and duration. Two sounds of different intensities can sound the same in loudness and two sounds of the same intensity can sound different in loudness. One might wonder why there isn't a dimension of perceived size (or contrast or speed or saturation or earliness) that bears the same relation to actual size as loudness bears to actual intensity. Part of the answer is that it would not be very fruitful to project such an evanescent aspect of experience onto the world. That is a functional explanation but there is a more proximate explanation: the auditory system is built to register loudness and that is revealed in the fact that there is loudness constancy. A sound maintains its loudness as you move closer to the source and as its intensity increases. But the phenomena I have been describing involving attention have a kind of *anti-constancy* in that the perceived size changes even when the actual size is constant. A similar point applies to the behavior of afterimages as indexed in Emmert's Law. I would be surprised if this anti-constancy feature were not related to the subject's sense that these changes are not objective, and this idea fits with Burge's (2009) view of perceptual objectivity as grounded in constancies.

10. Mental Paint

I have argued elsewhere that the inverted spectrum (and other related thought experiments) supports mental paint. (These arguments are presented in (1990, 1999, 2003) and in a version I am much happier with, in (2007c).) The view of mental paint argued for here is in one respect much less radical than the one argued for in those papers.

If things we both call "red" (and think of as red) look to you the way things we both call "green" (and think of as green) look to me, then we have phenomenal qualities that represent ripe tomatoes as red, but do so very differently: your mental paint represents differently than mine. Further, we can have experiences that are the same in respect of mental paint, but represent differently, for example when I am looking at a red thing and you are looking at a green thing. The relation between mental paint and representational content is many-many.

However, the argument presented here does not allege any *extensional* gap between mental paint and representational content. I have not exhibited a case of same representational content/different phenomenology or same phenomenology/different representational content. I did present the argument as *roughly* having that form at the outset, but the final view just presented is that vague representational contents may be right. The focus here has been on a different kind of gap between mental paint and representational content: that to cope with attention, perceptual representation must be vague in content or mode in a way that the phenomenology of perception need not be.

Ironically, what sinks direct realism and representationism is the very aspect of perception that advocates of these views often take as their founding insight, the positive thesis of Moorean diaphanousness. Shifting attention makes items in the world look, non-illusorily, different in contrast, size, saturation, stripiness, speed, and (for events) time of occurrence. In order to cope with that fact, anti-mental paint views are forced to postulate kinds of vagueness that are not reflected in ways the world looks to be.

References

Anscombe, G. E. M. (1965). The Intentionality of Sensation: a Grammatical Feature. In R. J. Butler (Ed.), *Analytical Philosophy: First Series*. Oxford: Blackwell.

Anton-Erxleben, K., Abrams, J., & Carrasco, M. (2010). Evaluating comparative and equality judgments in contrast perception: Attention alters appearance. *Journal of Vision* 10 (11), 1–22.

Armstrong, D. M. (1968). The headless woman and the defense of materialism. *Analysis, 29*, 48–9.

Balcetis, E. & Dunning, D. (2010). Wishful seeing: Desired objects are seen as closer. *Psychological Science, 21*, 147–52.

Block, N. (1990). Inverted Earth. In J. Tomberlin (Ed.), *Philosophical Perspectives 4*. Atascadero, CA: Ridgeview.

Block, N. (1995). On a confusion about a function of consciousness. *Behavioral and Brain Sciences, 18*(2), 227–47.

Block, N. (1996). Mental Paint and Mental Latex. *Philosophical Issues, 7,* 19–49.

Block, N. (1999). Sexism, Racism, Ageism and the Nature of Consciousness. *Philosophical Topics, 26*(1 & 2).

Block, N. (2003). Mental Paint. In M. Hahn & B. Ramberg (Eds), *Reflections and Replies: Essays on the Philosophy of Tyler Burge* (pp. 165–200). Cambridge, MA: MIT Press.

Block, N. (2007a). Consciousness, accessibility, and the mesh between psychology and neuro-science. *Behavioral and Brain Sciences, 30*, 481–548.

Block, N. (2007b). *Functionalism, Consciousness and Representation*. Cambridge, MA: MIT Press.

Block, N. (2007c). Wittgenstein and Qualia. *Philosophical Perspectives, 21*(1), 73–115.

Block, N. & Young, A. (1996). Consciousness. In V. Bruce (Ed.), *Unsolved Mysteries of the Mind* (pp.149–79). Hove: Erlbaum.

Boghossian, P. & Velleman, J. D. (1989). Color as a secondary quality. *Mind, 98*, 81–103.

Brand-D'Abrescia, M. & Lavie, N. (2008). Task coordination between and within sensory modalities: Effects on distraction. *Perception & Psychophysics, 70*(3), 508–15.

Brewer, B. (2004). Realism and the Nature of Perceptual Experience. *Philosophical Issues, 14*, 61–77.

Brewer, B. (2008). How to Account for Illusion. In A. Haddock & F. Macpherson (Eds), *Disjunctivism: Perception, Action, Knowledge*. Oxford: Oxford University Press.

Broad, C. D. (1951). Some Elementary Reflexions on Sense-Perception. *Philosophy, 27*(100), 3–17.

Bruner, J. & Goodman, C. C. (1947). Value and need as organizing factors in perception. *Journal of Abnormal and Social Psychology, 42*, 33–44.

Burge, T. (1991). Vision and Intentional Content. In E. LePore & R. van Gulick (Eds), *John Searle and his Critics* (pp. 195–213). Oxford: Blackwell.

Burge, T. (2003). Qualia and Intentional Content: Reply to Block. In M. Hahn & B. Ramberg (Eds), *Reflections and Replies: Essays on the Philosophy of Tyler Burge* (pp. 405–16). Cambridge, MA: MIT Press.

Burge, T. (2005). Disjunctivism and Perceptual Psychology. *Philosophical Topics*, 33(1), 1–78.

Burge, T. (2009). Perceptual Objectivity. *Philosophical Review*, 118(3), 285–324.

Burge, T. (2010). *Origins of Objectivity*. Oxford: Oxford University Press.

Burr, D. & Ross, J. (2008). A Visual Sense of Number. *Current Biology*, 18, 425–8.

Byrne, A. (2001). Intentionalism Defended. *The Philosophical Review*, 110, 199–240.

Campbell, J. (2002). *Reference and Consciousness*. Oxford: Oxford University Press.

Carrasco, M. (2006). Covert attention increases contrast sensitivity: psychophysical, neuro-physiological and neuroimaging studies. In S. Martinez-Conde, S. L. Macknik, L. Martinez, J.-M. Alonso, & P. U. Tse (Eds), *Progress in Brain Research, Vol. 154: Visual Perception, Part 1*. The Netherlands: Elsevier.

Carrasco, M. (2009). Attention, cognitive models of. In P. Wilken, T. Bayne, & A. Cleeremans (Eds), *Oxford Companion to Consciousness*. Oxford: Oxford University Press.

Carrasco, M., Cigdem, P.-T., & Eckstein, M. (2000). Spatial covert attention increases contrast sensitivity across the CSF: support for signal enhancement. *Vision Research*, 40, 1203–15.

Carrasco, M., Fuller, S., & Ling, S. (2008). Transient attention does increase perceived contrast of suprathreshold stimuli: A reply to Prinzmetal, Long and Leonhardt (2008). *Perception and Psychophysics*, 70(7), 1151–64.

Carrasco, M., Ling, S., & Read, S. (2004). Attention alters appearance. *Nature Neuroscience*, 7, 308–13.

Carruthers, P. (2000). *Phenomenal Consciousness: A Naturalistic Theory*. Cambridge: Cambridge University Press.

Cartwright-Finch, U. & Lavie, N. (2007). The role of perceptual load in inattentional blindness. *Cognition*, 102, 321–40.

Chalmers, D. (2004). The Representational Character of Experience. In B. Leiter (Ed.), *The Future for Philosophy*. Oxford: Oxford University Press.

Chalmers, D. (2006). Perception and the Fall from Eden. In T. Gendler & J. Hawthorne (Eds), *Perceptual Experience*. Oxford: Oxford University Press.

Chen, Y., Martinez-Conde, S., Macknik, S. L., Bereshpolova, Y., Swadlow, H. A., & Alonso, J.-M. (2008). Task difficulty modulates the activity of specific neuronal populations in primary visual cortex. *Nature Neuroscience*, 11(8), 974–82.

Cherry, E. C. (1953). Some experiments on the recognition of speech, with one and with two ears. *Journal of the Acoustical Society of America*, 25, 975–9.

Churchland, P. S., Ramachandran, V. S., & Sejnowski, T. (1994). A critique of pure vision. In C. Koch & J. Davis (Eds), *Large-scale neuronal theories of the brain*. Cambridge, MA: MIT Press.

Crane, T. (2006). Is there a perceptual relation? In T. Gendler & J. Hawthorne (Eds), *Perceptual Experience* (pp. 126–46). Oxford: Oxford University Press.

Crane, T. (2007). Intentionalism. In A. Beckermann & B. McLaughlin (Eds), *Oxford Handbook to the Philosophy of Mind*. Oxford: Oxford University Press.

Datta, R. & DeYoe, E. (2009). I know where you are secretly attending! The topography of human visual attention revealed with fMRI. *Vision Research, 49*, 1037–44.

de Gelder, B., Morris, J. S., & Dolan, R. J. (2005). Unconscious fear influences emotional awareness of faces and voices. *Proceedings of the National Academy of Sciences, 102*(51), 18682–87.

Debner, J. A. & Jacoby, L. L. (1994). Unconscious perception: Attention, awareness and control. *Journal of Experimental Psychology: Learning, Memory and Cognition, 20*, 304–17.

Dennett, D. C. (1991). *Consciousness Explained.* Boston: Little, Brown.

Downing, C. J. & Pinker, S. (1985). The spatial structure of visual attention. In M. Posner & O. S. M. Marin (Eds), *Attention and Performance XI* (pp. 171–87). London: Erlbaum.

Dretske, F. (1995). *Naturalizing the Mind.* Cambridge, MA: MIT Press.

Durgin, F. H., Baird, J. A., Greenburg, M., Russell, R., Shaughnessy, K., & Waymouth, S. (2009). Who is being deceived? The experimental demands of wearing a backpack. *Psychonomic Bulletin & Review, 16*(5), 964–9.

Ebbinghaus, H. (1908a). *Abriss der Psychologie.* Leipzig: Veit & Co.

Ebbinghaus, H. (1908b). *Psychology: An Elementary Text-book.* Boston: Heath.

Fechner, G. (1882). *Revision der Hauptpuncte der Psychophysik.* Leipzig: Breitkopf und Härtel.

Fish, W. (2009). *Perception, Hallucination and Illusion.* Oxford: Oxford University Press.

Gobell, J. & Carrasco, M. (2005). Attention alters the appearance of spatial frequency and gap effect. *Psychological Science, 16*, 644–51.

Golla, H., Ignashchenkova, A., Haarmeier, T., & Thier, P. (2004). Improvement of visual acuity by spatial cueing: a comparative study in human and non-human primates. *Vision Research, 44*(13), 1589–600.

Harman, G. (1990). The Intrinsic Quality of Experience. *Philosophical Perspectives, 4*, 31–52.

Heidegger, M. (1977). The Origin of the Work of Art. In D. F. Krell (Ed.), *Martin Heidegger: Basic Writings.* New York: Harper and Row.

Hellie, B. (2006). Beyond Phenomenal Naiveté. *The Philosophers' Imprint, 6*(2), 1–24.

Hellie, B. (2007). Factive Phenomenal Characters. *Philosophical Perspectives, 21*(1), 259–306.

Hill, C. S. (2006). Perceptual Consciousness: How it Opens Directly onto the World, Preferring the World to the Mind. In U. Kriegel & K. Williford (Eds), *Consciousness and Self-Reference* (pp. 249–72). Cambridge, MA: MIT Press.

Hill, C. S. (2009). *Consciousness.* Cambridge: Cambridge University Press.

Hinton, J. M. (1973). *Experiences.* Oxford: Oxford University Press.

Hopf, J.-M., Boehler, C. N., Luck, S. J., Tsotsos, J. K., Heinze, H.-J., & Schoenfeld, M. A. (2006). Direct neurophysiological evidence for spatial suppression surrounding the focus of attention in vision. *Proceedings of the National Academy of Sciences, 103*(4), 1053–58.

Jacoby, L. L. & Whitehouse, K. (1989). An illusion of memory: false recognition influenced by unconscious perception. *Journal of Experimental Psychology: General, 118*, 126–35.

James, W. (1890). *Principles of Psychology.* New York: Henry Holt.

Johnston, M. (2004). The Obscure Object of Hallucination. *Philosophical Studies, 120*, 113–83.

Kastner, S. (2009). Attention, neural basis of. In T. Bayne, A. Cleeremans, & P. Wilken (Eds), *The Oxford Companion to Consciousness.* Oxford: Oxford University Press.

Kim, J. (1991). Supervenience as a philosophical concept. *Metaphilosophy, 21*, 1–27.

Kind, A. (2003). What's so Transparent about Transparency? *Philosophical Studies, 115*(3), 225–44.

Langley, K. (2002). A parametric account of contrast adaptation on contrast perception. *Spatial Vision*, 16(1), 77–93.

Lee, G. (2009). *"Inner Time" in Consciousness and the Passing of Time*. New York University PhD Thesis, New York.

Ling, S. & Carrasco, M. (2006). When sustained attention impairs perception. *Nature Neuroscience*, 9(10), 1243–45.

Liu, T., Abrams, J., & Carrasco, M. (2009). Voluntary Attention Enhances Contrast Appearance. *Psychological Science*, 20(3), 354–62.

Lycan, W. G. (1996). *Consciousness and Experience*. Cambridge, MA: MIT Press.

Lycan, W. G. (2001). The Case for Phenomenal Externalism. *Philosophical Perspectives*, 15, 17–35.

Mach, E. (1959). *The Analysis of Sensations*. LaSalle: Open Court.

Macpherson, F. (2006). Ambiguous Figures and the Content of Experience. *Nous*, 40(1), 82–117.

Martin, M. G. F. (2002). The Transparency of Experience. *Mind and Language*, 17, 376–425.

Martin, M. G. F. (2004). The Limits of Self-Awareness. *Philosophical Studies*, 120, 37–89.

Martinez-Conde, S. & Macknik, S. L. (2010). What's In a Face? *Scientific American Mind*, 20(1), 26–36.

Masrour, F. (2010). Phenomenal Objectivity and Phenomenal Intentionality: in Defense of a Kantian Account. In T. Horgan & U. Kriegel (Eds), *The Phenomenal Intentionality Research Program*. Oxford: Oxford University Press.

McDowell, J. (1982). Criteria, Defeasibility and Knowledge. *Proceedings of the British Academy*, 455–79.

McGinn, C. (1999). *Knowledge and Reality*. Oxford: Oxford University Press.

McLaughlin, B. P. (1995). Varieties of supervenience. In E. Savellos & U. Yalcin (Eds), *Supervenience: New Essays*. Cambridge: Cambridge University Press.

Montagna, B., Pestilli, F., & Carrasco, M. (2009). Attention trades off spatial acuity. *Vision Research*, 49, 735–45.

Moore, G. E. (1903). The Refutation of Idealism. *Mind*, 12, 433–53.

Nagel, E. (1961). *The Structure of Science: Problems in the Logic of Scientific Explanation*. New York: Harcourt, Brace & World.

Nickel, B. (2007). Against Intentionalism. *Philosophical Studies*, 136(3), 279–304.

Noë, A. (2004). *Action in Perception*. Cambridge, MA: MIT Press.

Oppenheim, P. & Putnam, H. (1958). The Unity of Science as a Working Hypothesis. In H. Feigl, M. Scriven, & G. Maxwell (Eds), *Concepts, Theories and the Mind-Body Problem: Minnesota Studies in Philosophy of Science* (Vol. 2, pp. 3–36). Minneapolis: University of Minnesota Press.

Pautz, A. (2010). Why Explain Visual Experience in terms of Content? In B. Nanay (Ed.), *Perceiving the World: New Essays on Perception*. New York: Oxford University Press.

Peacocke, C. (1992). *A Study of Concepts*. Cambridge, MA: MIT Press.

Peacocke, C. (1993). Review of M. Tye, The Imagery Debate. *Philosophy of Science*, 60, 675–7.

Pitcher, G. (1970). *A Theory of Perception*. Princeton: Princeton University Press.

Posner, M., Snyder, C., & Davidson, B. (1980). Attention and the detection of signals. *Journal of Experimental Psychology: General*, 109, 160–74.

Prinz, J. J. (2006). Beyond Appearances: The Content of Perception and Sensation. In T. Gendler & J. Hawthorne (Eds), *Perceptual Experience* (pp. 434–59). Oxford: Oxford University Press.

Prinzmetal, W., Long, V., & Leonhardt, J. (2008). Involuntary attention and brightness contrast. *Perception and Psychophysics, 70*, 1139–50.

Putnam, H. (1999). *The Threefold Cord: Mind, Body and World.* New York: Columbia University Press.

Reynolds, J. H. (2008). Mapping the microcircuitry of attention. *Nature Neuroscience, 11*(9), 861.

Rhees, R. (1968). Notes for Lectures on "Private Experience" and "Sense Data": Note on the Text. *The Philosophical Review, 77*(3), 271–5.

Robinson, H. (2008). Why Frank Should not have Jilted Mary. In E. Wright (Ed.), *The Case for Qualia* (pp. 223–46). Cambridge, MA: MIT Press.

Sacks, O. (1985). *The Man who Mistook his Wife for a Hat.* New York: Touchstone: Simon & Schuster.

Schneider, K. A. (2006). Does attention alter appearance? *Perception and Psychophysics, 68*, 800–14.

Schneider, K. A. & Komlos, M. (2008). Attention biases decisions but does not alter appearance. *Journal of Vision, 8*(15), 1–10.

Scholl, B. J., Noles, N. S., Pasheva, V., & Sussman, R. (2003). Talking on a cellular telephone dramatically increases "sustained inattentional blindness". *Journal of Vision, 3*(9): 156.

Searle, J. R. (1983). *Intentionality.* Cambridge: Cambridge University Press.

Sèries, P., Stocker, A. A., & Simoncelli, E. (2009). Is the Homunculus "Aware" of Sensory Adaptation? *Neural Computation, 21*, 1–33.

Shiu, L.-P. & Pashler, H. (1995). Spatial attention and vernier acuity. *Vision Research, 35*, 337–43.

Shoemaker, S. (1994). Self-knowledge and "inner sense". *Philosophy and Phenomenological Research, 54*, 249–314.

Shoemaker, S. (2001). Introspection and Phenomenal Character. *Philosophical Topics, 28*(2), 247–73.

Shoemaker, S. (2003). Content, Character and Color. *Philosophical Issues, 13*, 253–78.

Siegel, S. (2006). Which Properties are Represented in Perception? In T. Gendler & J. Hawthorne (Eds), *Perceptual Experience* (pp. 481–503). Oxford: Oxford University Press.

Siegel, S. (2008a). The Contents of Perception. In E. N. Zalta (Ed.), *The Stanford Encyclopedia of Philosophy* (Vol. Winter, 2008). Stanford: Center for the Study of Language and Information.

Siegel, S. (2008b). The Epistemic Conception of Hallucination. In A. Haddock & F. Macpherson (Eds), *Disjunctivism: Perception, Action and Knowledge.* Oxford: Oxford University Press.

Siewart, C. (2003). Is Experience Transparent? *Philosophical Studies, 117*, 15–41.

Smith, A. D. (2002). *The Problem of Perception.* Cambridge, MA: Harvard University Press.

Snowdon, P. F. (1979–80). Perception, Vision and Causation. *Proceedings of the Aristotelian Society, 81*, 175–92.

Spence, C. & Parise, C. (2010). Prior-entry: A review. *Consciousness and Cognition, 19*(1), 364–79.

Stelmach, L. B. & Herdman, C. M. (1991). Directed Attention and Perception of Temporal Order. *Journal of Experimental Psychology: Human Perception and Performance, 17*(2), 539–50.

Stoljar, D. (2004). The Argument from Diaphanousness. In M. Ezcurdia, R. Stainton, & C. Viger (Eds), *New Essays in the Philosophy of Language and Mind* (Vol. Supplemental volume of *The Canadian Journal of Philosophy*, pp. 341–90). Calgary: University of Calgary Press.

Stoljar, D. (2007). Consequences of intentionalism. *Erkenntnis, 66*(1–2), 247–70.

Störmer, V., McDonald, J., & Hillyard, S. A. (2009). Cross-modal cueing of attention alters appearance and early cortical processing of visual stimuli. *Proceedings of the National Academy of Sciences, 106*(52), 22456–61.

Strayer, D. L., Drews, F. A., & Johnston, W. A. (2003). Cell phone-induced failures of visual attention during simulated driving. *Journal of Experimental Psychology: Applied, 9,* 23–32.

Titchener, E. B. (1908). *Lectures on the elementary psychology of feeling and attention.* New York: Macmillan.

Tong, F., Nakayama, K., Vaughan, J. T., & Kanwisher, N. (1998). Binocular Rivalry and Visual Awareness in Human Extrastriate Cortex. *Neuron, 21*(4), 753–9.

Treue, S. (2004). Perceptual enhancement of contrast by attention. *Trends in Cognitive Sciences, 8*(10), 435–7.

Tse, P. U. (2005). Voluntary attention modulates the brightness of overlapping transparent surfaces. *Vision Research, 45,* 1095–98.

Turatto, M., Vescovi, M., & Valsecchi, M. (2007). Attention makes moving objects be perceived to move faster. *Vision Research, 47,* 166–78.

Tye, M. (1995). *Ten Problems of Consciousness.* Cambridge, MA: MIT Press.

Tye, M. (2000). *Consciousness, Color, and Content.* Cambridge, MA: MIT Press.

Tye, M. (2002). Representationalism and the Transparency of Experience. *Nous, 36*(1), 137–51.

Tye, M. (2005). On the Nonconceptual Content of Experience. In M. E. Reicher & J. C. Marek (Eds), *Experience and Analysis.* Wien: Obvahpt.

Tye, M. (2006). Nonconceptual Content, Richness, and Fineness of Grain. In T. Gendler & J. Hawthorne (Eds), *Perceptual Experience.* Oxford: Oxford University Press.

Tye, M. (2009). *Consciousness Revisited.* Cambridge, MA: MIT Press.

Van Der Burg, E., Olivers, C. N. L., Bronkhorst, A. W., & Theeuwes, J. (2008). Audiovisual events capture attention: Evidence from temporal order judgments. *Journal of Vision, 8*(5), 1–10.

Wittgenstein, L. (1993). Notes for Lectures on "Private Experience" and "Sense Data". In J. Klagge & A. Normann (Eds), *Ludwig Wittgenstein: Philosophical Occasions 1912–1951.* Indianapolis: Hackett Publishing Company.

Wright, E. (2008). Introduction. In E. Wright (Ed.), *The Case for Qualia* (pp. 1–42). Cambridge, MA: MIT Press.

Yeshurun, Y. & Carrasco, M. (1999). Spatial attention improves performance in spatial resolution tasks. *Vision Research, 39,* 293–306.

Young, A. (1994a). Neuropsychology of awareness. In M. Kappinen & A. Revonsuo (Eds), *The Neuropsychology of Higher Vision: Collected Tutorial Essays.* Hillside, NJ: Erlbaum.

Young, A. (1994b). Recognition and reality. In E. Critchley (Ed.), *Neurological boundaries of reality.* London: Farrand Press.

Introduction to John McDowell's Lecture

Ted Honderich

John McDowell came from the University College of Rhodesia and Nyasaland to New College in Oxford as a Rhodes Scholar. In due course he became a Fellow of University College Oxford, and then moved to the philosophy department at the University of Pittsburgh. He has written widely—in all of the philosophies of mind and language, ancient philosophy, metaphysics, epistemology, and metaethics. He is an independent thinker in the tradition of the later Wittgenstein among others and in connection with the Oxford philosopher Gareth Evans, whose posthumous book he edited. His own fruitful books and papers have been much discussed.

Waiting for the traffic light to change, we intend to cross the street when that happens, and when it does, we then intend differently what we do—cross. So we or most of us have the habit of distinguishing what we may call *intentions for the future*, as McDowell calls them, or forward-looking or inactive intentions, from *intentions in action* as he calls them—which latter things presumably are what have also been called active intentions, volitions, initiations, and traditionally willings—all of which do not require something called *the will*, a separate faculty of mind, which has been discarded along with other such faculties. John Searle is one philosopher among us who gives and develops such a distinction between intentions.

In place of these two things McDowell puts one, or in a sense puts one. An intention for the future itself *becomes* or turns into an intention in action. The two make up one continuant. Also, he explains, that the latter phase is said to change its *shape* as the action goes forward does not make for other than the whole intention that is one thing.

Much that is at least new and arresting is said of the intention in action. It is said, to take an example that may be unfamiliar, that the intention does not relate *de re* but rather *de dicto* to the action it is in. The difference between *de re* and *de dicto*, which is to say between being about a *thing* and being about a *representation*, all has to do with representations or propositional attitudes, including beliefs, desires, statements, sentences—and intentions.

It is a matter, surely, of several different differences. But just take the philosopher Quine's example of a desire. *I want a boat* can mean either that I want a particular one, maybe that particular thing that I tried unsuccessfully to buy yesterday, or that I want some boat, one of the things that are boats, any of the items that are of that kind or fall under that term as I use it. So, to get back to intentions, I take it we are to understand that the intention in action is not about just that particular action.

Leaving aside much more that is said of the new view of intention, including the matters of keeping track of time and the succession of shapes, it is presented as having a number of recommendations over the old view. It is more natural, familiar, not a theory but rather a spelling out of ways we learn to think and talk about intentionality, and simpler.

It is also an extension of the admired account of intention of the late London philosopher Brian O'Shaughnessy. In particular this is an account of intention that is in accord with his general *dual aspect* view of the mind, an account in the tradition of many predecessors, including Spinoza. In intentionally engaging in *bodily* action, the action's intentional character is an *aspect* or manifestation of or a perspective on an underlying state or reality, and in O'Shaughnessy's case and McDowell's apparently something that is also *bodily* through and through.

I myself wonder about the question of whether in the lecture there is a dependence on an explicit principle of counting depended on that can be made explicit—of when two things are two parts of one thing or instead two things. No doubt that is worked on in the challenging part of philosophy that is mereology. I wonder too about what is implicit in the lecture, that what it says of intending does what Wittgenstein recommended, which is that good philosophy 'leaves everything as it is'. Has philosophy not changed our conceptions of ourselves? In what fundamental way did Plato, Descartes, Hume, Kant, and the rest leave everything as it is?

I cannot say I myself have been wholly converted from my own form of the ordinary view of intentions. But the reasonable intention of even a fine lecture cannot conceivably be conversion of all parties. The aim, first, is to make you really think. This one does.

6

Some Remarks on Intention in Action

John McDowell

1. PHILOSOPHERS SOMETIMES TREAT "intention in action" as a technical term.[1] But a concept expressible with that phrase can be easily made out to be no more than part of common sense. I want to sketch a way of conceiving intention in action that we can be in command of just by being familiar with relevant regions of our ordinary language.

2. TO BEGIN ISOLATING SOMETHING we might mean by "intention in action," we can distinguish it from intention for the future. An intention in action is an intention that is in the course of getting executed, so it is contemporaneous with doing whatever it is an intention to do. In that respect an intention in action stands in contrast with a prior intention, an intention to do such-and-such at some future time. A prior intention pre-dates the action that is its execution, if indeed there is any such action, as there will not be if the person who has the intention is prevented or changes her mind or forgets.

One can do something intentionally without having had a prior intention to do it. One can act intentionally on the spur of the moment. But we can ask: when doing something intentionally *is* doing something one had a prior intention to do, how does the prior intention relate to the intention in action we implicitly acknowledge when we say the doing is intentional? I am going to begin working up to a picture of intention in action by considering an answer to this question given by John Searle. I think Searle's answer is helpful as a contrast to a different picture that I want to recommend.

On Searle's account, intentions in action are new items that a prior intention starts to generate when the time to execute it comes. Prior intentions and intentions

---

[1] Robert B. Brandom hyphenates it into a single word, which implies that he is not treating it as a bit of ordinary language; see *Making It Explicit: Reasoning, Representing, and Discursive Commitment* (Cambridge, MA: Harvard University Press, 1994). John Searle also hyphenates it in *Rationality in Action* (Cambridge, MA: MIT Press, 2001). In *Intentionality* (Cambridge: Cambridge University Press, 1983), he left it as three words.

in action are different even apart from the difference in their temporal relation to stretches of activity. A prior intention has as its object an action, doing such-and-such at some future time. But an intention in action, generated by the prior intention at its due time, has as its object not the action the agent is embarking on, but something Searle conceives as a component of it.

Consider, for instance, an intention harbored by someone standing on a kerb: the intention to cross the street when the light turns green. On Searle's account, when she sees the light turn green, that intention—a prior intention, an intention for the future—starts to *generate* intentions in action. The object of the intention for the future is crossing the street; the objects of the intentions in action that it generates are the limb movements that need to happen if the person is to cross the street. As those limb movements begin, she begins crossing the street. If all goes well, she gets to the other side, thereby completing an action of crossing the street. On Searle's account, the action is a causally structured complex: its components are, first, the intentions in action that the prior intention began to generate when the agent saw the light turn green, and, second, the limb movements on which the intentions in action are targeted, which the intentions in action will have caused.

I think it is clear that this is a bit of philosophical theory, not a spelling out of ways we learn to think just by learning to talk about acting intentionally. And I do not think Searle would dispute that. He would say there are philosophical purposes for which his theory is needed. I am not going to try to assess this claim directly. I have cited Searle's theory only as a foil, to bring into relief a different answer to the question how intentions in action are related to intentions for the future. I would claim that the different answer is more natural, and if that is right, it cannot be irrelevant to the philosophical purposes for which Searle thinks we need his theory. But I am not going to attend to that for its own sake.

On this different account, when one sees the light turn green and starts crossing the street, it is not that an intention for the future starts to generate new items, intentions in action as Searle conceives them. Rather, what was an intention for the future *becomes* an intention in action. When one starts to do something one had a prior intention to do, say crossing the street, one's intention, now in action, is still directed at crossing the street, not at the limb movements that need to happen if one is to do that. In saying what the prior intention was an intention to do, one mentions a time: when the light turns green, in my example. When its time comes, what was a prior intention takes a new shape as an intention in action, provided the agent does not forget the intention, knows the time has come, is not prevented from acting accordingly, and does not change her mind.

What were prior intentions become intentions in action, on this picture, through the operation of an ability to keep track of time. My street-crossing case involves a very simple instance of that ability. One determines the time for acting as the time at which a recognizable thing is going to happen: one's intention is to cross the street when the light turns green. When that recognizable thing happens and the subject recognizes that the time has come, the intention becomes an intention in action. That is just another way to say she starts doing what she intended, and still intends, to do.

Of course the ability to keep track of time has more sophisticated forms also. And of course its relevance to a subject's psychological history is not restricted to the way intentions persist through time. The ability to keep track of time is operative whenever one keeps hold of time-specific thoughts as time passes. For instance, one can retain for a while a bit of knowledge one could express, when one acquired it, by saying "The light is turning green." One needs to express it differently later, perhaps by saying "The light turned green a while ago." It is the *same* bit of knowledge, persisting through the passage of time, that needs to be expressed in these different ways. Just so, it is the *same* intention, persisting through the passage of time, that alters from being an intention for the future to being an intention in action when its time comes, provided that it does not lapse through change of mind or forgetfulness, and provided that the agent knows its time has come and is not prevented from acting.[2]

3. OBJECTING TO SEARLE'S CONCEPTION of how intentions in action relate to intentions for the future, Brian O'Shaughnessy points out that at any moment while one is, say, intentionally crossing a street, one has an intention that is still directed at the future. At any time during the crossing, one intends to go on crossing from the point one has reached to the other side.[3]

This intention, the intention to go on crossing, is not an intention in action in Searle's sense. This intention has as its object a prospective action: going from the point one has reached to the other side of the street. In contrast, the intentions in action that are operative in intentionally going on crossing, as Searle sees things, are supposed to have as their objects the limb movements that need to happen if one is to do that, items that are not themselves actions but that Searle conceives as components of actions.

In response to O'Shaughnessy, Searle acknowledges that after one has embarked on doing something one had a prior intention to do, an intention for the future persists into the time during which one is doing whatever it is. There is an ever-shrinking residue of the original prior intention, present throughout the time of acting as an intention whose object is still in the future: in my example, an intention whose object at any time is to go from the point one has reached to the other side of the street. (Searle writes of "the remains of the prior intention."[4]) But Searle still distinguishes

    [2] On keeping track of time, see Gareth Evans, *The Varieties of Reference* (Oxford: Clarendon Press, 1982), especially 192–6.
    [3] See O'Shaughnessy, "Searle's Theory of Action," in *John Searle and His Critics*, ed. Ernest Lepore and Robert Van Gulick (Oxford: Blackwell, 1991), 271–88. O'Shaughnessy works with an example involving an intention to swim across the Channel from Dover to Calais. But the structure is the same, and I shall stay with my example of crossing a street.
    [4] See Searle's "Response: The Background of Intentionality and Action," in *John Searle and His Critics*, ed. Ernest Lepore and Robert Van Gulick (Oxford: Blackwell, 1991), 298.

this shrinking residue of the prior intention from the intentions in action that bring about the limb movements required for executing it. When one realizes that the time determined for acting by the original prior intention has come (when one sees the light turn green, in my example), the intention that was the prior intention starts to generate, directly, suitable intentions in action, and thereby indirectly to generate suitable limb movements. Thereafter, persisting in its increasingly residual form, it goes on indirectly generating limb movements, by directly generating intentions in action, as one goes on crossing the street.[5]

And this picture presumably applies also where there was no prior intention. Throughout an intentional street-crossing, even if there was no prior intention to cross the street, there must be an intention of the sort that, where there was a prior intention, Searle conceives as a shrinking residue of it: an intention directed, at each moment, towards an action that is still in the future, going from the point one has reached to the other side. Searle's picture must be that, whether or not there was a prior intention, intentionally crossing a street involves a shrinking intention for the future that progressively discharges itself by generating intentions in action that in turn generate suitable limb movements.

That is quite complex. Consider, in contrast, the simplicity of the alternative picture I described. On my alternative picture, when one is intentionally doing something that one had a prior intention to do, one's intention in action is what the prior intention *became* when the time it determined for action arrived. When its time comes and the agent knows it, the intention, provided it is not thwarted and does not lapse through change of mind or forgetfulness, takes on the new shape of an intention that has begun to express itself in action. And now the phenomenon O'Shaughnessy points to, the directedness towards a diminishingly future stretch of action, falls straightforwardly into place. It is just what one would expect of a persisting intention that has become an intention in action because its time has come, and that continues to be operative in the acting in which it expresses itself. Similarly with an intention that is at work in doing something on the spur of the moment—an intention that begins its career as an intention in action, rather than becoming an intention in action after a phase in which it is an intention for the future.

To make sense of how a prior intention becomes an intention that has begun to be executed, I invoked the ability to keep track of time. The present point is that an intention that is being executed persists, directed at a diminishing future, through the time it takes to do whatever it is. To make sense of that we need, not the ability to keep track of time, but the ability to keep track of how one's action is progressing. Unless one is keeping track of how far one has come, one cannot intelligibly intend to go on from there to the other side of the street.

O'Shaughnessy draws more distinctions than I am envisaging here. In his view, there is an overarching intention of crossing the street, which may or may not have

---

[5] See Searle's "Response," 298; see also *Rationality in Action*, 50–1.

previously been an intention for the future, but which, in either case, persists in its entirety after one has begun crossing the street, though more and more of the street-crossing it is directed at recedes into the past as one goes on crossing. And there is *in addition* a continuum of intentions for the future, one for any instant during the period in which one is crossing the street, directed at progressively less extensive completions of the crossing. O'Shaughnessy conceives these future-directed intentions as caused by the overarching persisting intention of crossing the street, and so as distinct from it.[6]

With this continuum of future-directed intentions, O'Shaughnessy addresses the phenomenon Searle aims to accommodate by envisaging a single shrinking intention, perhaps a residue of what was a prior intention, intelligibly shifting in its future-directed content as one makes progress in one's action. But O'Shaughnessy's conception of the overarching intention of crossing the street seems enough to accommodate that phenomenon. Unlike Searle's shrinking intention for the future, O'Shaughnessy's overarching intention stays, as it were, the same size. It has, throughout, the whole intended street-crossing as its object. The extent of its directedness at the future shrinks, but shrinkage in its projected future is expansion in how much achievement lies behind it. And as far as I can see, this picture of the persisting overarching intention leaves unmotivated O'Shaughnessy's idea that there is *also* a continuum of future-directed intentions, each directed at a different remainder of the street-crossing, caused by the overarching intention and hence distinct from it. The shifting future-directedness is just what is to be expected of the overarching intention itself, as it progressively finds expression in crossing the street. Instead of the multiple intentions O'Shaughnessy invokes, with their orientation towards smaller and smaller continuations of what one is doing into the future, we need only consider successive shapes taken by a persisting intention in action.

The general form of the shifting future-directedness of intention in action is this: one intends to do whatever is needed in order to finish doing what one is doing. In the street-crossing example this idea functions in a particularly simple way. At any time in the course of crossing the street, what one still needs to do is to go on from the point one has reached to the other side of the street. But the same structure fits projects with more complex shapes, such as baking a cake or building a house. In these cases, when we spell out what is required if one is to finish doing what one is doing, at a moment at which one is some way into doing it, we need to introduce things to do with more complex relations to what one has already done. Having beaten the eggs, one needs to fold in the four, and so on until the cake is baked. But the idea of going on until one has finished doing what one is doing still fits, for the content of the diminishingly future-directed intention that, on the picture I am recommending, an intention in action is.

---

[6] See O'Shaughnessy, "Searle's Theory of Action," 274–5.

4. ROBERT BRANDOM says intentions in action are special among intentions in being able to be directed at particular actions.[7] Going further in the same direction, George Wilson specifies intentions in action as intentions directed *de re* at particular actions.[8]

But it may be true of one that one is crossing a street though one is not going to cross the street; perhaps halfway over one is going to be knocked down by a bus.[9] One's intention in action may be correctly specifiable by saying "I am crossing the street," even if one is not going to make it to the other side. So there may never be a relevant particular action of the sort that figures in the specification of one's intention in action—for instance a street-crossing. There may be no action for it to be directed *de re* at.

Reality comes to contain, as it were, a particular action of the type describable as "my crossing the street" only when it gets to be true to say "I have crossed the street." But by then the time for the relevant intention of crossing the street to be an intention in action is over. (The relevant intention; of course I may have embarked on another intentional street-crossing.) When an intention of crossing the street is an intention in action, it has behind it, at any point, a stretch of action with the particularity that comes with completion, signaled by the truth of a claim in the perfect tense: one has moved to *here* (to put it in a way that requires imagining oneself engaged in the action). But an intention that is still in action also looks forward to a stretch of action that may never emerge into reality as a particular achievement: moving from *here* to the other side. By the time there is a particular action of crossing the street for a thought of crossing the street to be directed at, one has crossed the street, and it is too late for the thought to have the nature of an intention. So there is no coherent way to suppose that it is particular actions that intentions in action are *in*. It must be wrong to think directedness at particular actions is the distinctive mark of intentions in action.[10]

I have framed the conception of the reality of particular actions that threatens the Brandom/Wilson doctrine in terms of a mode of thought to which tenses matter. Actions are a species of events. And I am urging an asymmetry between things that have happened, which I am allowing as particulars, and things that are going to happen, or things that are happening, which I am not.

Now someone may want to object that from a tenseless perspective there would be no warrant for this asymmetry.

    [7] Brandom, *Making It Explicit*, 258.

    [8] See George M. Wilson, *The Intentionality of Human Action* (Stanford: Stanford University Press, 1989).

    [9] See G. E. M. Anscombe, *Intention* (Oxford: Blackwell, 1957), 39. The logical point here is not special to intentional action; as Anscombe remarks, it may be true of something that it is falling over though it never falls over (perhaps someone catches it before it can be said to have fallen over).

    [10] Wilson argues that his conception of intentions in action is needed in order to account for the logical form of various ordinary ways of talking about people doing things intentionally. What I am urging commits me to rejecting his arguments, but I shall not try to do that here.

Particular substances come into reality when they are, say, born or made. They depart from reality when they die or are destroyed. In contrast, it is natural to say that, like events of other sorts, particular actions, once they have acquired their particularity, have the kind of reality that is appropriate to events from then on. They become part of history—in a slightly peculiar, but intelligible, sense in which history can include events that have been forgotten. But in spite of this contrast, an asymmetry that corresponds to the one I am urging for events shows up for substances. Particular substances do not lose their particularity when they go out of existence— one can say, of a particular substance, that *it* no longer exists; whereas things in the category of substance that do not yet exist are not yet the particulars that, as we may awkwardly say, they are going to be. Thinking ourselves into a tenseless perspective cannot require us to hold that, when we revert to the perspective of a thinker in time, we need to distinguish two different logical forms for, say, "I am baking a cake," one in which a particular cake is in question and one in which that is not so, though at the time when one might say such a thing one cannot tell which of the two forms one's saying has. Suppose I am baking a cake. Perhaps a God's-eye view, from outside the temporal unfolding of events, has in its scope a cake that is going to result from my cake-baking. It will be a particular cake, certainly; after all, there is no other kind of cake, as Frege might have said. But it cannot be right to suppose that if that is so, then "I am baking a cake"—something intelligible only at a time-bound perspective—has a relational form, amounting to "There is a cake that I am baking," and if not, not. What one says when one says "I am baking a cake" is not proved false if no cake results from one's activities. (Consider "I was baking a cake, but I was interrupted.") And this independence of the statement's truth from a requirement that there be a cake that is going to come into existence must characterize a form such a saying has even if a cake *is* going to come into existence as a result of the activities described by the person who says it. It cannot be necessary to wait and see whether one's cake-baking is going to be successful before one can know what logical form to attribute to one's statement, "I am baking a cake."

It is true that after one has brought one's cake-baking to a successful conclusion, one can say "This is the cake that I was baking." But we must not take that to supply the instance that made it true earlier to say "I am baking a cake," construed as equivalent to "There is a cake that I am baking"—as if, when the cake comes into existence, one gets to be in a position to follow up something amounting to "There is a cake that I am baking...," after an interval, with "... namely this one."

Just so, at the time-bound perspective at which one might say "I am crossing the street," the logical form of what one is saying cannot await a determination by what is going to happen—so that "I am crossing the street" relates me to a particular action of crossing the street if there is going to be one (that is, if I am going to get to the other side), and not if not. The logical form of "I am crossing the street" must be determinable from the time-bound perspective at which alone it so much as makes sense. And that requires us to say that such a statement does not relate me to a particular action, even if I am going to get across the street. But I am assuming that "I am crossing the street" exemplifies the appropriate form for expressing my intention in action when I am crossing the street. So it must be wrong to suppose that its being an intention in action consists in the presence of a *de re* relation to a particular action.

While one is performing an action of a sort constituted by a terminus—like crossing a street, which is not complete until one has reached the other side—one is engaging in various activities: perhaps moving one's legs in a certain way, or walking *simpliciter* rather than from somewhere to somewhere.[11] Activities occupy time in a different way from actions. As soon as one has embarked on an activity, the activity is all there, in a way that is indicated by the fact that one can attribute it with a use of the perfect tense: as soon as one is walking, one has walked. (Of course this does not imply that the current stretch of walking is over.) Since the activity is all there at any moment, we can, if we like, conceive it as an object, a *res*. And then it seems harmless to characterize a shape taken by one's intention in action, at any time in one's progress across the street, as the intention, concerning one's current relevant activity, that it contribute suitably to crossing the street. That is as close as we can get to the Brandom/Wilson doctrine. Intention in action can be seen as relating *de re* to relevant activity. But that is not to say that intention in action relates *de re* to the action it is in.[12]

5. AS I SAID, O'Shaughnessy countenances, besides the overarching intention of crossing the street (to stay with my example), a continuum of exclusively future-directed intentions, one for each moment in crossing. I suggested a simplification: instead of those distinct and multiple future-directed intentions, consider the diminishingly future-directed aspect of the persisting overarching intention itself.

Now O'Shaughnessy also envisages another set of intentions that would figure in someone's crossing a street: intentions directed at moving one's limbs in the necessary ways.[13] The idea is that these intentions reflect motor skills—not just the ability to make the movements needed for the routine exercise of a skill such as walking, but sometimes a more finely tuned responsiveness to circumstances, as when one puts a foot down carefully to compensate for an unevenness in the surface.

Here we are closer to Searle's intentions in action than anything so far has brought us. But as O'Shaughnessy insists, these intentions are still distinct from intentions in action in Searle's sense. An intention in action in Searle's sense has as its object a limb's moving thus and so, whereas an intention of this kind has as its object one's moving the limb thus and so.

---

[11] There are issues about whether by abstracting from the whence and the whither one can arrive at a concept of walking *simpliciter* that is a concept of activity as opposed to action, but I shall simply barge past them. I am using the idea only to exemplify a general structural point.

[12] In this section my pervasive and deep indebtedness to Michael Thompson's "Naive Action Theory" (Part Two of *Life and Action: Elementary Structures of Practice and Practical Thought* (Cambridge, MA: Harvard University Press, 2008)) is especially palpable.

[13] See O'Shaughnessy, "Searle's Theory of Action," 278.

Here too I see no need to multiply intentions as O'Shaughnessy does. O'Shaughnessy conceives these detailed motor intentions as generated by the overarching intention, the intention to cross the street in our example, and so distinct from it. But we need not follow him in this. We can see motor intentions, rather, as shapes taken by the overarching intention as it expresses itself. In the picture as we already have it, persisting intentions change their shape from being intentions purely for the future to being intentions in action, when a subject recognizes that the time for acting has come. And once they have taken on the guise of intentions in action, they change to having less in prospect and more behind them of what they are intentions to do, as an agent makes progress in a project. In the same spirit, we can say that these same intentions, intentions to do things like crossing streets, change from one determinate short-term motor shape to another as they express themselves in acting.

Motor skills are anyway presupposed by the very idea of intentions to do things like crossing streets. But in making their role explicit, I have added a third item to the background against which the shifting career of a persisting intention is intelligible. I was already appealing to the ability to retain thoughts through the passage of time, and the ability to keep track of the progress of actions. The third item is the ability to move one's limbs as executing one's intentions requires. These are all things on which the changes of shape undergone by an intention to do something like crossing a street depend.

We need to avoid a certain implausibility in spelling out the idea of short-term motor shapes taken by intentions to do things like crossing streets. One's limb movements in walking are surely not intentional under descriptions that involve the specifics of what one does at a given moment with one's hips and knees. Normally competent walkers do not know what they do when they walk at that level of description. What we can say is, perhaps, that one's movements are intentional under specifications like "moving as walking requires," or perhaps "moving as stepping over that obstacle requires." Ordinary competence in walking determines which movements, described in terms of what one does at the relevant joints, conform to such specifications; that determination is not a task for the practical thinking that intention belongs to.

6. I HAVE DIVERGED from O'Shaughnessy in rejecting the multiplicity of intentions that figures in his picture. I want to differ from him in another way as well. O'Shaughnessy does not allow the title "intention in action" to any of the intentions he countenances. He thinks there is something wrong with the very idea of an intention in action. I have been working with the thought that we might refuse to count as intentions in action the items Searle applies that label to, intentions whose objects are that one's limbs should move in certain ways, but that we might apply the label to different candidates: in particular, to the persisting overarching intentions that O'Shaughnessy himself acknowledges. But O'Shaughnessy would have no sympathy with that.

O'Shaughnessy's scepticism about intention in action is in the first instance directed against the way Searle uses the notion. With intentions in action as Searle conceives them, it is not just that they are not prior to the actions they are said to be in. That would not be objectionable by O'Shaughnessy's lights. Searle's intentions in action are supposed to be in the actions in another sense besides that merely temporal one: they are supposed to be components of them. And O'Shaughnessy finds it unintelligible that anything deserving to be conceived as an intention might, as he puts it, "actually enter the precincts of the action itself."[14]

The implications of this are more general than hostility to Searle's idea that an intention might be in an action by being a component of it. If we accept O'Shaughnessy's prohibition on intentions entering the precincts of action, we have to suppose that the intention of crossing a street—to fix on the single item to which I have suggested we can reduce the multiplicity of contemporaneous intentions he countenances—relates to someone's crossing the street only from outside. Compare, perhaps, how an intention that a tree should fall might be conceived as relating to the tree's falling, if the intention is realized in one's sawing through the tree's trunk with the result that it falls. I do not want to defend Searle's idea that intention might be in action by being a component of it. But I want to resist any suggestion that the relation between intention and action is appropriately modeled on the relation between an intention operative in sawing through a tree's trunk and the falling of the tree, understood in such a way that—to echo O'Shaughnessy—the intention does not enter the precincts of the falling.[15] I want to urge that the intention of crossing a street, conceived in the Protean shape-shifting way I have recommended, should not be conceived as related to one's crossing the street only from outside.

I shall spell this out by exploiting another region of O'Shaughnessy's thinking.

In his groundbreaking work on the will, O'Shaughnessy presents a dual aspect conception of physical, or bodily, action.[16] Acting physically is exercising motor capacities. And exercising a motor capacity is as such a bodily phenomenon. But according to the dual aspect conception, it is also psychological, and not just in an isolable component but through and through. A psychological concept, expressible by "willing," applies not to some supposed psychic initiating occurrence, but to the relevant bodily goings-on, those describable as a subject's exercising a motor capacity, in their

[14] O'Shaughnessy, "Searle's Theory of Action," 282.

[15] I put it like this to leave room for ultimately querying the idea that the intention does not enter the precincts of the falling. I am going to urge that intention informs, and so enters into the precincts of, at least one's moving of one's limbs when one engages in bodily action. But why should this exteriorization of intention stop at the boundaries of one's body? Why not say my intention informs my felling of the tree? And then, by way of an identification of the tree's falling with my felling it, we get to the thought that my intention informs the tree's falling. (This note is a beginning on a response to a proposal by Anton Ford.)

[16] See O'Shaughnessy, The Will: A Dual Aspect Theory, 2 vols, (Cambridge: Cambridge University Press, 1980). There is a helpful brief statement of the dual aspect conception in the opening pages of O'Shaughnessy's paper "The Epistemology of Physical Action," in Agency and Self-Awareness, ed. Johannes Roessler and Naomi Eilan (Oxford: Clarendon Press, 2003), 345–57.

entirety. Willing is not something that causally initiates bodily acting and perhaps supervises it from outside. Willing is in the acting, not in the sense that willing is part of an action, but in the sense that "willing" is a characterization of the acting itself, apt for capturing its psychological aspect.

Now O'Shaughnessy is impressed by the thought that willing, so conceived, belongs to animal life in general, whereas intending does not. Intending is not universal in animals. O'Shaughnessy marks the restriction by saying that intention can be attributed only to animals whose behavior is future-directed in a certain distinctive way. Consider a cat slinking along, belly to ground and with whiskers twitching, in a way that can be explained by saying it is stalking a bird. That explanation implicitly invokes a projected future in which the bird has been caught.[17] "It's stalking a bird" answers a version of the question "Why?" in terms of which G. E. M. Anscombe famously isolates intentional action. In fact this example of the attribution of intention to animals other than human beings is Anscombe's own.[18]

So the concept of intention has a more restricted application than the concept of willing, even before we consider the special form in which the concept of intention applies to agents who are responsive to the question "Why?"—as the bird-stalking cat of course is not. O'Shaughnessy accommodates this distinction between intending and willing by holding that intending is *additional* to the willing that just is acting conceived in a way that focuses on its psychological aspect. Intending belongs to a higher region of the psychological. Intending is not merely psychological but mental. Intending causally initiates willing—that is, acting—and supervises it from outside its precincts.

We certainly have to acknowledge that the idea of intending is different from the idea of willing plain and simple, willing as it is found in animals that do not have intention. But do we have to agree with O'Shaughnessy that intending is additional to willing? Why not conceive intention in action as a special form taken by willing, in animals that are at least, as we might put it, proto-rational? That would allow us to go further than O'Shaughnessy does with the dual aspect conception of bodily action, as both physical through and through and psychological through and through. If intention in action is a species of willing, then, like the willing plain and simple to which O'Shaughnessy restricts the concept of willing, it can be in action, not in the Searle-like sense that it is a component in actions, but in an O'Shaughnessy-like sense, that it just *is* acting, characterized in a way that captures a now more sophisticated psychological aspect that this kind of acting has.

It may seem a problem for this proposal that willing in O'Shaughnessy's sense just is acting. In contrast, intending makes its appearance not only in the form of intention in action, but also—in rational animals—in the form of intention purely for the future. Intention purely for the future cannot be just what willing is: that is, acting,

---

[17] On the future-directedness of intention, see O'Shaughnessy, *The Will*, 2:303–30.
[18] See Anscombe, *Intention*, 86–7.

characterized in a way that brings out its psychological aspect. But surely intention in the course of being acted on should be just what intention purely for the future is except that its time is present.

But everything depends on the direction in which we take that equation. We might think it requires us to base a conception of intention in action on an independently intelligible conception of intention purely for the future. That would threaten the possibility of supposing that intention in action is a species of willing—that it just is acting, on the part of an animal that is at least proto-rational, but described so as to highlight its psychological aspect. But we do better to centre our conception of intention in general on intention in action, and frame our conception of intention purely for the future in a way that suits how intention in action is best understood.

Once intentions purely for the future are on the scene, we are concerned with rational animals, and we can say an intention is the kind of thing that can be arrived at by practical reasoning (though intentions need not be acquired like that). Practical reasoning can be for the future. I can reason about which bus to take tomorrow, and conclude by forming an intention to take the one that leaves at 8.28. But that should not dislodge us from holding that when practical reasoning is about what to do now, drawing the conclusion is acting, as Aristotle says. It would be better to say: drawing the conclusion is beginning to act.

Intention for the here and now is, if you like, a kind of thought. But it is practical in the sense that assenting to such a thought just is beginning to act in a certain way, for instance starting to cross a street; and continuing to assent—not revoking one's assent—is continuing to act, for instance continuing to cross the street. An intention for the future is, by all means, a thought of the same kind, apart from the time difference. But the way to accommodate that is not to distance intention for the here and now from acting, on the ground that intending purely for the future is not acting, but to conceive an intention for the future as a potential action biding its time. When its time comes, provided the agent knows its time has come and is not prevented, and provided she does not change her mind, it will become an instance of willing—that is, acting. On these lines we can sustain the extended version of the dual aspect conception that I was envisaging. We can say intention in action is the form that is taken, in intending animals, by willing, which we can conceive in an expanded version of O'Shaughnessy's way. Intention in action just is the acting that it is in, under a characterization that brings out its psychological aspect, a psychological aspect that is more sophisticated than the one captured by talk of willing plain and simple.

The picture of intention for the future as potential action biding its time is no more than an application, in the context of the extended dual aspect conception, of the idea I urged at the beginning of this lecture: that intentions for the future become intentions in action when their time comes, provided the agent knows the time has come, and is not prevented, and does not change her mind. According to the extended dual aspect conception, talk of intention in action is just talk of acting intentionally, framed so as to emphasize its psychological aspect. Since there can be intentions for the future, acting intentionally can be, though it need not be, the mature form of something that was already present before acting was underway. An intention for the future stands to the acting one engages in when one starts to execute it, or, equivalently, to the intention in action that it becomes at that point, as a caterpillar stands to the butterfly it becomes in metamorphosis.

7. I HAVE BEEN WORKING with an image of intentions as a kind of continuant whose instances change their shape as time passes.

The first kind of shape-shifting I considered was the shift from intention purely for the future to intention in action. That is what I have just proposed redescribing by saying that an intention purely for the future is an action in waiting, and it matures into an action in progress when its time comes. Action in waiting is something whose essential nature is that in due course, failing prevention or change of mind or losing track of time, it takes on the shape of action in progress.

The second kind of shape-shifting was in respect of how much of what an intention is an intention to do has been done and how much remains to do, and the third was in respect of the specifics of the (more or less) skilled bodily movements that an agent is engaging in at successive moments in intentionally doing something like crossing a street. Here my suggestion has been that to talk of an intention in action as a continuant that changes its shape as time passes is just a way of talking of the unfolding of an action intentionally undertaken. This should bring out that though the image of intentions as a kind of continuant is helpful for some purposes, it should not encourage us to conceive intentions as self-standing items; talk of intention is just talk of an aspect of behavior that manifests practical rationality, action that is underway or anticipated.

I want to end by stepping back and saying something, very briefly, about why we should be interested in the possibility of incorporating intention in action, contrary to O'Shaughnessy's own view, into a version of his dual aspect conception of bodily action.

As O'Shaughnessy notes, a capacity to move limbs at will is characteristic of animals in general; it is not special to rational animals. That can make it tempting, perhaps almost irresistible, to conceive facts about practical rationality at work—including the full-blown intentional character that a bit of behavior is marked out as having if its agent is responsive to Anscombe's question "Why?"—as just additional parts of the truth about bodily behavior, distinctive of the special case in which bodily behavior is engaged in by a rational animal. On this view, movings of limbs that are intentional are, in themselves, just what movings of limbs are in an ordinary animal, and the intentional character is extra to—it is natural to say "*behind*"—those goings-on, which in themselves have no more to do with rationality than bodily movements on the part of non-rational animals. And then it is overwhelmingly natural to cash out the image expressed by that use of "behind" like this: the operation of practical rationality that is registered by describing a bit of behavior as intentional is related to the agent's movings of her limbs as cause to effect. My extension of O'Shaughnessy's dual aspect conception yields a contrasting picture, in which intentional bodily behavior is itself informed by practical rationality, not just a result of its operations.

And such a conception seems clearly attractive. If rationality can be *in* bodily activity as opposed to behind it, we have a vivid contrast with a familiar picture according to which a person's mind occupies a more or less mysterious inner realm, concealed from the view of others. If physical activity can be rationality in action, as opposed to a mere result of exercises of rationality, we have a vivid contrast with the tendency to distance a person's body from the mind that is the seat of her rationality.

References

Anscombe, G. E. M. *Intention*. Oxford: Blackwell, 1957.

Brandom, Robert. *Making It Explicit: Reasoning, Representing, and Discursive Commitment*. Cambridge, MA: Harvard University Press, 1994.

Evans, Gareth. *The Varieties of Reference*. Oxford: Clarendon Press, 1982.

O'Shaughnessy, Brian. "The Epistemology of Physical Action." In *Agency and Self-Awareness*. Edited by Johannes Roessler and Naomi Eilan. Oxford: Clarendon Press, 2003.

O'Shaughnessy, Brian. "Searle's Theory of Action." In *John Searle and His Critics*. Edited by Ernest Lepore and Robert Van Gulick. Oxford: Blackwell, 1991.

O'Shaughnessy, Brian. *The Will: A Dual Aspect Theory*. 2 vols. Cambridge: Cambridge University Press, 1980.

Searle, John. *Intentionality*. Cambridge: Cambridge University Press, 1983.

Searle, John. *Rationality in Action*. Cambridge, MA: MIT Press, 2001.

Searle, John. "Response: The Background of Intentionality and Action." In *John Searle and His Critics*. Edited by Ernest Lepore and Robert Van Gulick. Oxford: Blackwell, 1991.

Thompson, Michael. *Life and Action: Elementary Structures of Practice and Practical Thought*. Cambridge, MA: Harvard University Press, 2008.

Wilson, George M. *The Intentionality of Human Action*. Stanford: Stanford University Press, 1989.

Introduction to Christine Korsgaard's Lecture

Ted Honderich

Christine Korsgaard was a student of philosophy and English literature in Illinois, then a philosophy graduate student at Harvard of the esteemed hypothetical social contract theorist John Rawls. She taught at other universities including Chicago, and then returned to a professorship at Harvard, where she has also served as head of department. She has the further distinction of being the first woman to give the John Locke lectures in Oxford.

God, you may suppose, could have created a completely happy universe, all that ever exists, with everybody and every animal in it happy—or he could have created a completely miserable universe, everybody and every animal in it miserable. But forget about religion if you want. You can just as well imagine and compare for yourself the completely happy universe and the completely miserable universe. You agree, don't you, that the first one would be an awful lot better, that it would be right to choose it if you could? But you will hear there is a problem or question about this choice.

It is not the usual sort of choice or judgement having to do with happiness, misery, and the like. With respect to this choice or judgement, in favour of the happy universe, all there ever is, there is *nobody* better off. The choice is not the usual choice between the same people or animals being either happy or instead miserable. It is between people and animals existing and being happy or miserable and those people not existing at all. You could say that in a certain sense nobody at all would be being *deprived* of happiness by the second choice. In a sense there is no comparison here.

And, moreover, there is the same situation with respect to the first choice. In short, *nobody's* life would be made better by that choice of the happy universe.

Further, there is the same kind of situation, it seems, about choosing between a universe of greater equality and a different universe of lesser equality. The question here, as in the first case, to put it differently, is why the first world would be better. Here too, you can say, there exists no one to whom it matters.

Korsgaard agrees that the first choices are right. So does she then agree that there is what can be called *impersonal good*? And, further, that what it means to say something is good for you, say, is that you *have* some impersonal good, that you stand to impersonal good in that way? She argues, on the contrary, that to begin with impersonal good is to make it impossible to say what the having consists in, what relation it names.

This leads to a discussion of what we *can* mean by saying that something is good for someone, how these are related to each other. Also to a discussion of what sorts of entities can be in this relation. The answer to the latter question depends on a particular way of thinking or philosophizing about coming to answers to questions about right and wrong—thinking of an imagined contract, thinking in or near the way proposed by Rawls in his *A Theory of Justice*. Thus in the end we are vindicated in thinking a world full of happy people is better than a world full of miserable ones, even if the people are different in the two cases, even if nobody and no animal is better off.

Questions arise about this thinking, one about desires or reasonable or natural desires—and hence about actually conscious beings, existing beings. Are these grounds of right and wrong, the stuff of the Principle of Humanity for example, conceivably an *immediate* means to rejecting the idea of impersonal goods? There is also the older question of whether imagined contract-making is not really an argument for right principles but rather something written into the contract-making tacitly from the start.

Korsgaard's is original work, work that depends on new assumptions and asks its own new questions. They may become familiar. Conceivably the new assumptions and questions may become as settled as those of earlier philosophers of whom we already know that they gave rise to the philosophical concerns to come. Who knows? Certainly the lecture is reminiscent of the progress of a Platonic lecture, otherwise known as a Platonic dialogue.

7

On Having a Good

Christine M. Korsgaard

1. Good for and Impersonal Goods

You are the kind of entity for whom things can be good or bad. This is one of the most important facts about you. It provides you with the grounds for taking a passionate interest in your own life, for you are deeply concerned that things should go well for you. Presumably, you also want to *do* well, but that may be in part because you think that doing well is good for you, and that your life would be impoverished if you did not.[1] But even if your interest in doing well is completely independent of any reference to your own condition, it probably depends on the thought that there are other entities, entities who are dependent upon you or affected by you, for whom things can be good or bad. It is only because there are entities like you, entities for whom things can be good or bad, that anything is important at all. If there were no entities for whom things can be good or bad, nothing would matter.

What I have just said may sound rather obvious, but in fact, it is controversial. Many philosophers believe that things can be good or bad without being good or bad *for* anyone or anything in particular. They think, for instance, that the world is a better place if it is full of happy people and animals than if it has no inhabitants at all, or only miserable ones. Or they think that it is better if wealth is distributed more equally than if some people are very rich and some very poor. If things like these are true, you might suppose, then there must be what are sometimes called 'impersonal' goods. Then you will probably think it is important that such goods should be realized, even though there is no one for whom they are good.

What I have just said may seem puzzling. Isn't it better if the world is full of happy people and animals, because it is better *for* those people and animals? And isn't it

---

[1] Actually, it follows from the view I defend in this paper that it is necessarily true that doing well is good for you, or at least that you cannot achieve your good without doing well. See section 5.

better if wealth is distributed equally, because it is better for the people who would otherwise be poor? The trouble with the first of those claims—that the world is better if it is full of happy people and animals because it is better for those people and animals—is that it is unclear that the world would be the worse for *those* people and animals, if they did not exist at all. Are all of the people and animals who never existed, and never will, in an unfortunate condition? Is that a bad thing for them? What a miserable place the world must be, if that is the case! But surely, you will reply, it is better if the world is full of happy people and animals than of miserable ones? But for whom is it better? If we are comparing two worlds containing the *same* inhabitants, in one of which those inhabitants are miserable and in one of which they are happy, the second world is clearly better for *them*. But suppose we are not comparing two worlds with the same inhabitants. If you are miserable, would it better *for you* if you were replaced by someone who is not? As for the second claim, of course it is better for the people who would otherwise be poor if wealth were distributed more equally. But by the same token, it would be worse for the people who would otherwise be rich.[2]

It seems, then, difficult to explain why we are tempted to think that a world full of happiness is better than a world full of misery, or that equitable distributions of wealth are better than lopsided ones, if we hang on to the intuition that things are only good or bad because they are good or bad for someone. On the other hand, it seems strange to suppose that these things matter, if there is no one to whom they matter.

There is another problem as well. Suppose things are good or bad independently of any entities for whom they are good or bad: that is, suppose that the notion of 'good' is conceptually prior to the notion of 'good-for'.[3] Then what does it mean to be an entity for whom things can be good or bad? Presumably, it means that you stand in some important relation to the goodness or badness of certain things, but what relation, exactly, is it? It cannot be simply that you are aware of these goods and evils, or perceive them, and appreciate their good or bad character. For even if the poor are very generous-minded, and are glad to think of the happy condition of the rich, they seem to stand in a different relation to the happy condition of the rich than the rich themselves do.

In order for something to be good *for* a certain person, you will want to reply, he has to be the one who *has* it. But that just raises the same question again. What relation are

---

[2] This may be false, of course: it may be better for each and every one of us to live in a world where wealth is more equally distributed. Being wealthier than others may corrupt your character so that you are less capable of genuine happiness, for instance. Or if you are good enough to be happy, knowing that you have more than your share may make you unhappy. But in that case equal distributions would be better for individuals, and the example would not, after all, pose a challenge to the idea that things must be good or bad for someone if they are good or bad at all.

[3] Many people seem to think that there are both personal and impersonal goods, and that there is *no* conceptual priority relation between them. I think this is a non-starter. Why do we call them both by

we talking about, when we talk about this 'having'?[4] The strange fact that we talk about moral matters in terms borrowed from economics—'value', 'obligation', 'owes', and so on—may lull us into supposing that we have some clear notion of ownership to work with in this case. But the notion of property-ownership will not help us out here, for to say that something is your property is to say that you may use it or enjoy it and that no one else may use it or enjoy it without your permission. But this is not what we mean when we say that your happiness is your *own* good. For even though the happiness of the rich is the good of the rich and not of the poor, the generous-minded among the poor are certainly free to enjoy the happiness of the rich if they can, and do not need the rich's permission for that.

There is a question, then, about what it means to have a good—to be the kind of being for whom things can be good or bad. There is also a question about which things can be the *kind* of entity for whom things can be good or bad. After all, one way out of the dilemmas I've just been discussing would be to suppose that something like 'containing happy people and animals' could be good for the universe itself, or, perhaps more plausibly, that equitable distributions could be good for the community. But if this way out of the dilemma does not work, or if it does not seem to correctly capture our reasons for favoring those things, then there are also questions about what, if anything, does explain why we favor those things. These are the questions I will investigate in this paper: questions about what it means to have a good, what kinds of entities can have one, and how we can explain those cases in which things seem to be good or bad without being good or bad for anyone in particular.

2. Why Having a Good Must Be Prior to Good

I will begin from the question what it means to be the kind of entity for whom things can be good or bad.[5] Essentially there are two possible views about this; in this section

the same name? Is it because it is impersonally good that the personal goods should be realized? If that is not always so—and presumably, it would not be—then why do we call the personal goods 'good' in those cases where it is not? One might adopt what Tim Scanlon calls a buck-passing theory of the good, and then try to argue that whether the good is personal or not depends on whether the reasons are personal or not. (See T. M. Scanlon, *What We Owe to Each Other* (Cambridge: Harvard University Press, 1998), Chapter 2, especially p 97ff.) But in my view, the question what it means to 'have' a reason gives rise to problems that are parallel to those that arise from the question what it means to 'have' a good. Later I will explain why I think 'having a good' is prior to the existence of 'goods'. Kantians believe that you have a reason when you have made something your maxim. In that case the condition of 'having a reason' is also prior to the existence of 'reasons'. For some relevant discussion, see my 'Valuing Our Humanity', §2, English version forthcoming. The paper is available in Spanish translation by Dulce María Grande in *Signos Filosóficos*, No. 26, July–December 2011.

   [4] See Christine M. Korsgaard, *The Sources of Normativity* (Cambridge: Cambridge University Press, 1996), §4.3.3, 146–47.
   [5] For another version of the argument of this section see Christine M. Korsgaard, 'The Relational Nature of the Good', forthcoming in *Oxford Studies in Metaethics*, Volume 8, ed. Russ Schafer-Landau (Oxford: Oxford University Press, 2013).

I will consider the first. The first view, which I have already mentioned and cast some doubt on, holds that some things are good or bad independently of their goodness or badness for anyone or anything in particular. Then to be the kind of entity for whom things can be good or bad is to be capable of standing in some particular relation to certain good or bad things. Focusing on aesthetic cases can make this option initially seem tempting. *La Traviata* or Van Gogh's *Starry Night* or the Taj Mahal are good things, and to be the kind of entity for whom these things can be good or bad is to be the kind of entity who is capable of appreciating exactly that fact about them. Because you are capable of appreciating aesthetic value, exposure to beauty is good for you, while having ugliness thrust upon you is bad. Because rabbits and squirrels are not capable of appreciating aesthetic value, or anyway not of the kind in question, operas and paintings and architectural masterpieces are nothing to them. The rabbit can appreciate the flavor and texture of a carrot, or the squirrel that of a nut, so these kinds of things can be good for such creatures. But isn't the experience of appreciation or enjoyment *itself* also a good thing for the creature who is capable of it? After all, isn't it better to enjoy than to suffer, or to appreciate than to be repulsed? But is that because a creature who is capable of appreciating things is also capable of appreciating his own appreciation, or enjoying his own enjoyment? But then are these second-order appreciations and enjoyments also good for the creature, and if so, what makes them so? There is clearly no point in starting off on that endless regress. But that leaves us stuck where we were: if the capacity to appreciate or enjoy something is what makes it good for you, what makes appreciation and enjoyment themselves good for you?

We can see a pattern here. Many people find it natural to suppose that what makes something good for you is that it makes you happy. But they also suppose that your own happiness is a good thing for you. For it is surely better for you to be happy than sad. Is that because being happy makes you happy? This little conundrum may be what drives people to the ownership theory that I mentioned earlier: happiness, they say, is a good thing in itself, and what makes a bit of happiness good *for you* is that it is *yours*.

But, as I argued before, we then need to explicate what it means to say that the happiness is *yours*. What relation is that? As I said before, it is not the ordinary ownership relation, the relation of standing in normative control over the *use* of a thing. It also seems odd to analogize happiness to property for other reasons. Could there be unowned bits of happiness lying around, the way there were once unowned bits of real estate?[6] Following John Locke, shall we say that you may lay claim to a piece of happiness, only if you make sure you leave enough and as good for others?[7] From a moral point of view, it might be pleasant to believe that, but declining a piece of

---

[6] I've worded it this way because, strictly speaking, there is no *property* that is not someone's property, any more than there is happiness that is not someone's happiness. Property is a relational notion. But it does in a sense name a relation between two independently existing things.

[7] John Locke, *Second Treatise of Government* (Indianapolis: Hackett Publishing Company, 1980), Chapter V, Paragraph 33, 21.

happiness is not a way of ensuring that it is there for someone else.[8] All happiness is someone's happiness: the idea of happiness is an inherently relational idea. To say that your happiness is yours is not to say that you stand in a special relation to some piece of happiness that would otherwise be free-floating or belong to someone else. And if happiness is the good, that means that to say that something is good for you is not to say that you stand in a special relationship to something good that would otherwise be free-floating, or belong to someone else.

Now of course some people assert, and some deny, that happiness is the good. If this debate is about anything, the term 'happiness' must refer to something more specific than just 'whatever is good for someone'. Many people think it refers in particular to the quality of our experiences, and has something to do with their being pleasant rather than painful. Then people who deny that happiness is the good are protesting against the idea that all that matters is the quality of our experiences, while the people who think happiness *is* the good are convinced that unless we experience something, at least indirectly, it can have no impact on us whatever.

But we do not need to enter this familiar debate, for everything I said before about happiness can be said about pleasure. We can claim that what makes something good for you is that it provides you with pleasant experiences. But that cannot be what makes pleasant experiences *themselves* good for you. That little conundrum may drive us into an ownership theory of pleasure: pleasure is a good thing, and what makes it good for you is that it is yours. But then again, we have to ask what the ownership consists in. Here the tempting answer will be that you are the one who experiences it. But again, it is not as if there is some unexperienced pleasure lying around, and being the one who experiences it is laying some sort of a claim to it.[9] All pleasure is someone's pleasure: the idea of pleasure is an inherently relational idea. To say that your pleasure is yours is not to say that you stand in a special relation to some piece of pleasure. If pleasure were the good, that would mean that to say that something is good for you is not to say that you stand in a special relationship to something good. And while we are at it, experience is relational too: so to say that you are the one who has a certain experience is not to say that there is some experience to which you stand in a special relation. So what makes something your good cannot be that you are the one who experiences it.

I have been arguing that to say that something is your good cannot be to say that there is some good to which you stand in a special relation, a relation at which we gesture by saying that you are the one who 'has' that good. I can imagine someone

---

[8] Declining some *thing* that would make you happy can be a way of ensuring that *it* is there for someone else, of course, and if it would make that other person happy then this is a case where you can trade in your happiness to secure that of someone else. But that really is a very different point: it does not show that happiness is a good thing in itself like a piece of property that becomes good for you when you claim it for your own.

[9] If someone thanks you for doing something, and you reply, 'The pleasure is all mine', you are not saying something crassly selfish.

thinking that he can show that this *form* of argument *must* be wrong. Take the following comparison: If Aristotle is right in arguing that a dead hand is not really a hand at all, then every real hand must be someone's hand.[10] Yet, surely, we can still say that what makes something *your* hand is that you are the one who *has* it? But, no, actually we cannot, for there is still the problem of what the right kind of 'having' consists in. We can imagine all kinds of macabre ways in which you could 'have' a hand that would not make it *yours* in the sense we want here. Only when we hit on the right relation—the right kind of 'having'—would the hand really be, by Aristotle's criterion, a hand at all.[11] What this shows is that the condition of 'having a hand' is prior to the hand itself. So the important point here is not merely that everything that is good must be someone's good: it is that everything that is good must be related to someone in a particular way before it can really *be* something good at all. That shows that the condition of 'having a good' is prior to the good itself. That is why I am claiming that someone's being in a condition of having a good, or something's being good for someone, is prior to the good itself.

3. Two Senses of Good for You

I started from the claim that there are two possible views about what it is to be an entity who has a good. The first holds that some things are good or bad independently of their goodness or badness for anyone or anything in particular, and that to be the kind of entity for whom things can be good or bad is to be capable of standing in some particular relation to those good and bad things. We have now seen what is wrong with that theory. This brings us to the other view, which is that the notion of good-for is more fundamental than the notion of good, and that for something to be good is essentially for it to be related to someone in a particular way.

But before I can say what that particular way is, I need to distinguish two apparently different things we might mean when we say that something is good for someone. Suppose Alfred and Bertrand are competing for a position, and Alfred gets it. That, we say, is good for Alfred, but bad for Bertrand. To be clear here, I am not imagining that the position is one that Alfred and Bertrand want just because, say, it carries a salary. I'm imagining it as a coveted position, one in which a person might engage in worthwhile activity and distinguish himself at the same time, a position that might be the basis of a good life. When we use 'good for Alfred' in this kind of

[10] Aristotle, *Metaphysics* 7.10 1035b23–5: 'for it is not a finger in *any* state that is the finger of a living thing, but a dead finger is a finger only homonymously.' *Politics* 1.2 1253a20–5: 'if the whole body be destroyed, there will be no foot or hand, except homonymously, as we might speak of a stone hand; for when destroyed the hand will be no better than that.' *On the Soul* 2.1 412b20–2: 'when seeing is removed, the eye is no longer an eye, except in name—no more than the eye of a statue or a painted figure.' The translations are from *The Complete Works of Aristotle: The Revised Oxford Translation*, ed. Jonathan Barnes (Princeton: Princeton University Press, 1984).

[11] 'For it is not a hand in any state that is a part of man, but the hand which can fulfill its work, which therefore must be alive; if it is not alive, it is not a part.' Aristotle, *Metaphysics* 7.10 1036b30–2.

case, we are using it in the way I have been using it up until now in this paper. We mean that getting the position will be a source of pleasure for Alfred or will make him happy, or that it is part of things going well for him, or that it is part of what makes his life a good one for him. We mean to put Alfred's getting the position in the same category of things in which hedonists put pleasure and eudaimonists put happiness, the category of things that are good for their own sake or things that constitute such goods or contribute to them. To say that things are good in this sense is to mark their relation to things we might decide to pursue for their own sakes. So although the term isn't perfect for my purposes, I am going to call this the 'final' sense of good-for.[12]

On the other hand, when Alfred's mother informs him that broccoli is good for him, she does not mean to put broccoli in the same category in which hedonists put pleasure and eudaimonists put happiness. She does not mean that eating broccoli is part of the human good in the way that aesthetic experiences, happy marriages, and lives full of accomplishment and pleasure are part of the human good. She does not mean that either broccoli itself, or eating broccoli, is a final good. It is possible that that is true, I suppose, but nevertheless, it is not what she means. She means, more or less, that broccoli is healthy, and that it will make Alfred healthy. I am going to call this, for now anyway, the 'motherly' sense of good-for, as opposed to the final sense.

Now you may be tempted to think that the difference here is just a matter of degree, a question of how directly the thing benefits Alfred. Actually, there are two ways to hold this view. A crude sort of hedonist thinks that pleasure, thought of as some particular kind of sensation, is the final good, and everything else is related to that final good causally. In that case everything but pleasure itself is instrumental to the final good, and the difference of degree in question here is a matter of instrumental or causal distance. Eating broccoli causes you to be healthy, which makes you capable of engaging in certain other activities, which in turn cause the sensation of pleasure. A less crude hedonist, however, might think that the relationship between pleasure and activity is not one in which the activity causes a certain sensation, but one in which the pleasure is somehow a characteristic of the activities themselves.[13] Even so, this less crude hedonist might think that the difference between the way in which the pleasurable activities are good for you and the way in which broccoli is good for you is a matter of the directness of the benefit. Dancing a waltz with a handsome partner is the sort of thing that constitutes the good for you directly, while eating broccoli is good for you too but less directly: it promotes your health, which equips you for

---

[12] 'Final' is a slightly misleading name, since it turns out that both ends and means can be good in the way that I am trying to identify here. As will become clear, I mean goods that seem or can seem worthy of pursuit from the agent's point of view, whether for their own sake or for the sake of something else, something that is a final good in the more ordinary sense. Nevertheless, in what follows I will sometimes use 'final' in the more ordinary sense, to refer to goods sought for their own sake. I don't think this will cause any confusion.

[13] See Aristotle's discussions in the *Nicomachean Ethics* at 7.11–12 and 10.1–5.

enjoying such activities as dancing waltzes with handsome partners, as well of course as helping you to ward off pain.

But there are two problems with the idea that what we have here is simply a difference of degree in the directness of the benefit. The first is that the kinds of theories that make this way of thinking seem natural are exactly the ones that landed us in the quagmire we have just left behind: they leave nothing for the claim that pleasure or pleasurable activities or happiness are *themselves* good for you to mean. On this theory, we would have to identify a final good as the thing that is most directly related to—well, to what?—to your final good, of course—and so we would get stuck in a circle.

So let's grant that the difference between saying that getting the job is good for Alfred in the final sense and saying that broccoli is good for Alfred in the motherly sense is not just a matter of how directly the thing in question benefits Alfred. What then is the difference? You might be tempted to say that even though we have not yet figured out quite what we mean when we say that something is good for Alfred in the final sense, it is still clear enough what we mean when we say that something is good for Alfred in the motherly sense. We mean that it is instrumental—that it *promotes* some final good that is valued for its own sake. That is what Alfred's mother is saying about eating broccoli.

I don't think that is right, however, and this brings me to the second problem. According to the theory on offer, eating broccoli promotes Alfred's health, and Alfred's health in turn promotes his ability to engage in the kinds of activities that somehow directly constitute his final good. Keep in mind that the question is not merely whether all of that is true, but rather whether that is what Alfred's mother is saying when she says that broccoli is good for him. That's what doesn't seem right to me. For suppose that Alfred's lover has left him to take up with Bertrand, and Alfred is feeling suicidal. 'Eat your broccoli,' his mother urges. 'It's good for you.' According to the theory on offer, Alfred should say, 'No, it isn't. Since all I want to do is die, the benefits of eating broccoli are completely irrelevant to me, or maybe they are even bad, since they will tend to keep me alive.' But of course, that's not what Alfred is actually going to say. What he actually is going to say is, 'Yes, but I don't care.'

Perhaps you think this is just because Alfred is not sufficiently reflective, and the use of the phrase 'good for you' to mean something like 'promotes your health' is so well established, idiomatically, that he fails to question the suitability of the claim to his own case. A more philosophical Alfred *would* say the first thing: that his mother has made a wrong calculation about what will benefit him. But in my view the second Alfred, the more likely Alfred, has got it right. Alfred is not explaining to his mother that she has made an error in calculation. He is declaring that, being in despair, he does not care about himself, and so does not care about what is good for him. 'Good for you' in the motherly sense of 'broccoli is good for you' *does* mean something like 'promotes your health', not something like 'indirectly promotes your final good'.

The only problem is that 'promotes your health' is a little too specific, even for the motherly use of the phrase. For one thing, even in the motherly sense, we often generalize the idea to include psychological health, as when we say, 'It is precisely because you are so depressed that it would be good for you to get out and see people more.' Even in the motherly sense, we sometimes generalize the idea even further to include moral and spiritual health, as when we say, for instance, 'You have been so successful that it is really good for you to be taken down a peg now and then.'

But the problem is not merely that the proposed definition of the motherly sense of 'good for you' as 'promotes your health' might be taken to be limited to physical health. It is also that—or so I claim—we can use the phrase in the motherly sense to talk about things that are not good by way of promoting, or at least not *merely* by way of promoting, anything at all. This point is a little harder to motivate, but let me give it a try. For one thing, I think that we sometimes say, in the same spirit as Alfred's mother, that it is good for people to enjoy themselves sometimes, or to contemplate natural beauty, or to go to museums to appreciate art or to learn something about the world they live in. That is to say, we sometimes recommend these things, not as things that would be good for people in the sense of making them happy, but in the sense of being somehow healthy. Yet these things are not mere means that promote some other state.

Well, you may reply, that is no problem. Many things are both means and ends. When we say that these things are good for people in the same spirit in which Alfred's mother says that broccoli is good for Alfred, we mean that they promote people's psychological, moral, and spiritual health, and so are means. But when we say that they are good for people in the spirit in which we said that it was good for Alfred but bad for Bertrand that Alfred got the position, we mean they are also ends. The motherly use of good-for applies to the means to various kinds of health, while the final use of good-for applies to ends, which, as it happens, sometimes coincide with the means to various kinds of health.

But I don't think it's quite that simple. For consider that in the resulting story, it is good for people to enjoy themselves sometimes, contemplate natural beauty, go to museums to appreciate art and learn something about the world they live in, so that they achieve a state we call 'health', which in turn promotes their ability to enjoy themselves sometimes, contemplate natural beauty, and go to museums to appreciate art or learn something about the world they live in. What sort of a merry-go-round, you might ask, are we on here?

The answer, of course, is that it is the same sort of merry-go-round that the classical Greek philosophers, at least Plato and Aristotle, thought we were on with respect to the moral virtues. What the practice of moral virtue makes us capable of, according to Plato and Aristotle, is virtuous activity itself. In fact for this very reason, Plato and Aristotle frequently compared moral virtue to health.

This comparison will help us to see that the problem rests in the characterization of health as a means. In *The Practice of Value*, Joseph Raz suggests at one point that health is a means to personal survival.[14] No one survives, of course, but I suppose we could view health as a means to an extended life. Few people, however, wish for an extended life unless they can be assured of a reasonable degree of health. Do we then want health as a means to living a reasonably healthy life? Taking our cue from virtue, we can see that the right thing to say here is not that health is valued as a means to an extended life but rather that it is valued as the excellence, or the goodness, of your physical life.

There are two reasons why this is the right thing to say. One is that it is very nearly a tautology to say that good health will extend your life, and claims about means are not normally tautologies.[15] Although obviously health does not guarantee the extension of life—you can always get hit by a meteorite—we should not call a condition 'healthy' if it did not tend to maintain or extend life. The other is that it explains the pair of judgments I just mentioned—that people try to be healthy in order to extend their lives but only if their lives will be healthy ones. The explanation is simply that people want to extend reasonably good physical lives but do not usually want to extend bad ones unless there is some special reason. For of course health *can* be a means to something in particular—if you want to survive long enough to finish writing your masterpiece, or to raise a late-born child to adulthood, say—but that thought is most natural when you have come to regard your physical life *itself* as a means to something in particular, to some other aspect of your life. But in the ordinary case, we do not think of health as a means to something, but rather as simply one form of the goodness of your life, namely the goodness of your physical life. When we generalize the motherly use of 'good for you' to broader forms of life, to the psychological and the spiritual and the moral, then we are talking about the goodness of your life quite generally. In the motherly sense, when we say that something is good for you, we mean that it either causes or constitutes your overall well-functioning, in some dimension of life.

So does this mean that I am after all suggesting that there is no difference between the final use of 'good for you' and the motherly use of 'good for you', no difference between what Alfred's mother is saying when she says broccoli is good for him and what we are saying when we say that getting the position is good for him? Not quite. What I am suggesting is that the final sense and the motherly sense of 'good for you' mention the same set of facts, but from two different perspectives. From one of these perspectives, we view Alfred as a functional system; that is, an entity whose parts and lesser systems all contribute to the achievement of some end or ends, in some cases

---

[14]   Raz, J. *The Practice of Value* (Oxford: Clarendon Press, 2003), 16. Of course Raz grants that one may value health for other reasons as well. See my commentary on his remarks at 77–81 of that volume for background to the thoughts here.

[15]   If we generalize the instrumental relation to include the constitutive one, then there are cases where claims about means are tautologies, namely where there is a necessary constituent. It is a tautology that your vote is needed if the end is 100% voter turnout, say. Some philosophers also think that performing an action is, tautologously, a means to the performance of that action.

simply to the maintenance or continuation of that functional system itself. From the other, we view the things that are good for Alfred from Alfred's own point of view. It is because these two perspectives can come together that there is such a thing as the good. Let me explain.

4. Goodness and Functional Systems

The association of the idea of the good with the idea of a functional system goes back at least to Plato and Aristotle. To say that something is a good X, they believed, is to say that it has the properties that enable it to perform its function well.[16] Here we are using 'good' in an ordinary evaluative sense: a good knife is sharp; a good car is safe and gets good gas mileage; a good teacher is patient and attentive; a good watchdog is fierce and loyal. A living thing just as such may also be viewed as a functional system, as Aristotle taught us: we can view its function as a kind of self-maintenance, or survival and reproduction, or as leading the life characteristic of its kind. We are viewing the living thing as that kind of functional system when we evaluate its condition as healthy or not.

But it is not merely the case that functional systems are the sort of thing that can be evaluatively good or bad; it also appears to follow from the way in which functional systems can be good or bad that things can be good or bad *for* them, in the motherly sense. Being driven once in a while is good for a car, while low-quality gasoline is bad for it. Earthworms and rain are good for the soil, and fresh air and exercise are good for both you and your dog. If something is a functional system, the properties that enable it to perform its function well are the properties that make it a good one, and the conditions that tend to promote and protect those properties are good for it. So functional systems, by their very nature, have a good. They have a good in the motherly sense of having a good—the sense in which broccoli is good for Alfred. Now recall that I said that the motherly sense could be extended to talk about things that affect a person or an animal's psychological health, or a person's moral and spiritual condition. When we say, 'you have been so successful, it is really good for you to be taken down a peg now and then', are we thinking of the person as a functional system? I think we are. The implication is that the build-up of self-satisfaction may eventually clog the person's moral arteries so much that it will interfere with his ability to keep on doing as well as he has.

If the idea of being good for something is linked to the idea of a functional system, where does the idea of a functional system come from? Does it name something we encounter in experience, a substance like water or a property like blue? It would seem not, for the idea is too deeply rooted in the way we see the world for that. I cannot treat this topic properly here, but let me gesture at the very large issues that I have

---

[16] For Aristotle, see especially *Nicomachean Ethics* 1.7; for Plato see *Republic* Book I, 352d–354b.

in mind. Aristotle thought that for a thing to be unified in the way that a thing has to be unified in order to count as a thing at all—that is, an *ousia* (οὐσία), or a substance—is for it to be a kind of functional system.[17] This makes the idea a basic metaphysical one. In the *Critique of Judgment*, Kant suggests, speaking a bit roughly, that the exercise of reflective judgment—the kind of judgment we use to form concepts of the kinds of things that there are, as opposed to the kind we use to place objects under concepts we already have—anyway, reflective judgment, or concept formation, involves interpreting some things as functional systems within the manifold of experience. Kant's idea is really the same as Aristotle's, with the characteristic Kantian twist of making the principle of substantial unity, functional unity, one that emanates outward from us rather than one that we encounter in nature.[18] If these ideas are right, then the idea of a functional system is roughly what Plato called the Form of the Good, the organizing principle at the basis of all objects or of our ways of conceptualizing them. Except, of course, for the fact that something is not good absolutely simply by virtue of being a functional system, even a functional system that is good or perfect of its kind. After all, a nuclear bomb or an assassin may be perfect of its kind. But a functional system is still the form of something, if what I've just said is right—it is the form of *having a good*.

5. Goodness and Agency

Now that's still having a good in what I have been calling the motherly sense— the sense in which 'good for you' means something like 'enables you to function well'. So now I'm going to switch from calling that good for you in the 'motherly' sense to calling it good for you in the 'functional sense'. Something is good for you in the functional sense if it maintains, promotes, or enhances your functioning. In order to get at 'good for you' in the final sense, we need to talk about another way in which we use the concept of the good. In my paper, 'Realism and Constructivism in Twentieth-Century Moral Philosophy', I argue that we use normative concepts to mark out schematically the solutions to certain kinds of problems which we have to solve.[19] I take my cue from John Rawls, who argued that we use the concept of 'justice' to mark out the solution to the problem of how the benefits and burdens of social cooperation are to be distributed. 'Justice' is our word for whatever solves that problem, and philosophers who argue about what justice is are arguing about how that problem ought to be solved.[20]

---

[17] I defend this claim in 'Aristotle's Function Argument' in Christine M. Korsgaard, *The Constitution of Agency* (Oxford: Oxford University Press, 2008).

[18] For further discussion, see Christine M. Korsgaard, *Self-Constitution: Agency, Identity, and Integrity* (Oxford: Oxford University Press, 2009), Chapter 2.

[19] In Korsgaard, *The Constitution of Agency*.

[20] Among other things, this solves the problem about what philosophers who define justice completely differently are disagreeing *about*.

Now the fact that we are reflective agents who do not automatically do what desire and instinct prompt us to do also confronts us with problems. For as a reflective agent, you cannot treat the bare fact that something attracts you as a reason to try to *go for it* without further ado. Nor can you treat the fact that an act would promote some end you've decided to go for as settling the question what you should *do*, for the act that promotes your end might not be, in various ways, worth it. There might be prudential or moral costs. So we have to have some way of making these decisions, some procedure or principle to follow. These two problems are the problems of the good and the right respectively—the problem of what to go for, and the problem of what to do. They are not of course completely independent, because you cannot actually decide to go for something without first deciding that that there's some *way* of going for it—that is, some act that would promote or achieve it—that you might conceivably find it worth deciding to do.[21] But of course you also cannot even generate some candidate actions to consider without first settling on some things you might like to go for. So insofar as we are agents, we are faced with these two interlocking problems. I want you to keep in mind that the two problems are interlocking, because that will matter later on.

Why do we use the same word—'good'—when we are talking about the success of functional systems and when we are talking about the things we've decided to go for? There seems to be a curious sort of interdependence between two ideas at work here, the idea of a functional system and the idea of an agent. When we regard an object as a functional system, we are regarding it rather as if it were a kind of agent, and the purpose that it serves as if it were an end that it had decided to go for. It is as if behind our division of the world into objects lurked a form of primitive animism, a determination to view the world as being full of agents like ourselves.

But then again, when we view ourselves as agents, we view ourselves in turn as functional systems.[22] For to be an agent is to be essentially subject to a standard of success and failure, and to be subject to a standard of success and failure in the very same way that a functional system is. Here's what I have in mind. A functional system—let's say a machine—is designed to achieve a certain end. If it does not achieve its end, we say that it has failed. You were late this morning, you say, apologetically, because your alarm clock broke down and failed to go off. But to be successful, it is not enough that your alarm clock goes off from any cause whatever. If the alarm rings because a sudden jolt of electricity happens to break a spring which accidentally hits the mechanism that sets off the alarm at 7:00 a.m. precisely, it is not a good clock.

---

[21] That is what Kant called 'the paradox of method' and Rawls called 'the priority of the right'. For Kant, see *The Critique of Practical Reason* (translated by Mary Gregor for Cambridge: Cambridge University Press, 1997), 5:63; for Rawls, *A Theory of Justice*, 2nd ed. (Cambridge, MA: Harvard University Press, 1999), 27–8.

[22] The remarks that follow are borrowed from 'The Normative Constitution of Agency' (forthcoming in *Rational and Social Agency: Essays on the Philosophy of Michael Bratman*, ed. Manual Vargas and Gideon Yaffe (New York: Oxford University Press), §1.3.

A functional system, to be successful, has to be *the kind of thing* that reliably achieves its end.

In the same way, the kind of success that we associate with agency is not exhausted by the idea of the agent actually bringing the end about, since an agent who brought about his end only accidentally—say by a deviant causal pathway—would have failed as an agent. If I fire my gun wildly astray, but the bullet ricochets off a cast-iron fence and happens to hit the target in exactly the spot that I intended, I have not made a good shot. Indeed, once I understand the causal situation, I should feel that I have been the beneficiary of a lucky accident, that is: that *I* didn't really *do* anything at all. To be successful in action is not merely to do something that brings about your end. To be successful in action is to make yourself into *the kind of thing* that reliably achieves that end.[23]

So to regard yourself as an agent is to regard yourself as a functional system, and to regard yourself as a functional system is to regard yourself as having a good, in the functional sense of good. But now it is not *only* the functional sense of good. For if you regard the thing you aim at as a final good—that is, as something worth going for—then you regard the things that promote it, your own condition included, as good in that way too. An agent necessarily values his own efficacy, and therefore necessarily values his own functional good as an aspect of his final good.

6. Why Some Things Have a Good in the Final Sense

One more step is necessary.[24] When we regard an organism as a functional system, we regard its end as being, as I said earlier, something along these lines: to maintain itself, to survive and reproduce, or to live the life characteristic of its kind. The end of an organism is, in a sense, simply to be and to continue being what it is, or as I have put it elsewhere, to constitute itself.[25]

Now if the organism is an agent—roughly speaking, an animal or a person—the way that she constitutes herself is in part by having conscious states that track, at least roughly and defeasibly, what is good or bad for her in the functional sense. An animal that has any chance of surviving must feel hungry when she needs food, fear in the face of predators and threats, and pain in the face of conditions that are damaging to

---

[23] Our self-consciousness about our agential success and failure is thus the source of the first primitive normative thoughts that leads us to the idea of well-functioning and from there to normative thought more generally. Notice the close tie this provides between normative thought and the first-person perspective. And notice too that a failure of efficacy is not the only route to the idea of a failure of one's agency; a failure of autonomy provides another such route. See *Self-Constitution*, §5.1. I am indebted here to discussion with Alan Code.

[24] For another version of the argument of this section, see 'The Origin of the Good and Our Animal Nature', forthcoming in *Problems of Goodness: New Essays on Metaethics*, ed. Bastian Reichardt.

[25] Korsgaard, *Self-Constitution*, especially §2.2.

her. She must *perceive* what is good for her in the functional sense as attractive and what is bad for her in the functional sense as aversive, and those perceptions must determine what she decides to go for and what to avoid.[26] If the organism is a rational agent, then she will do some of this consciously, using the word 'good' to designate the things that are good for her in the functional sense when she decides to go for them. She *conceives* the things that are good for her to be good things in the final sense, and as such she decides to go for them.

Before I said that the motherly or what I am now calling the functional sense of good for you and the final sense of good for you name the same set of facts from two different perspectives. In one, we view the entity as a functional system, and in the other, we view the things that are good for the entity from the entity's own point of view. I have now explained why that is so. Animals *perceive*, and rational animals also *conceive*, what is good for them as something to go for, and so as what is good for them in the final sense too. What is functionally good for them, in the broad sense I have been describing, is also good from their point of view, and so is their final good.[27]

Now let me avert some possible confusions. First, I am not claiming that anything that seems good from your point of view is therefore actually good for you, in either the functional or the final sense. We are highly imperfect functional systems, and therefore we can get it wrong: what seems good to us may not be good for us after all. Importantly, because you are a functional system that works *by* tracking your own good through perception and thought, when you do get it wrong you are malfunctioning. The very fact that you don't know what's good for you is, in a way, a large part of *what* is wrong.

Second, I am not claiming that the final good for people is survival and reproduction, or simple self-maintenance, or even to lead a healthy life of our kind. That is, I am not claiming that, unless we take a capacious view of what is involved in self-maintenance, or in leading a healthy life of our kind. For first of all, recall that I have argued that even the functional sense of good-for extends to things that both promote and constitute our psychological, moral, and spiritual health as well as our physical health. Second (or maybe this is the same), elsewhere I have argued that the human project of self-constitution involves the adoption and maintenance of what I call 'practical identities', 'the roles and relationships in terms of which we value ourselves and find our lives worth living and our actions worth undertaking'.[28] For us, the functional sense of good-for and therefore the final sense too will include whatever promotes and constitutes our practical identities.[29] Formally speaking, my view

---

[26] Korsgaard, *Self-Constitution*, §6.1.2.

[27] Notice an important consequence of this story: valuing is prior to value. It is because there are things that necessarily strike agents as things to go for that there are final goods.

[28] I introduce the notion of practical identity in *The Sources of Normativity*, 101. For further discussion, see *Self-Constitution*, §1.4.

[29] This is why 'final' isn't a great word here (see note 12): because this sense of good also encompasses the things that promote the things we decide to pursue for their own sakes.

is a rather obvious one: that the human good is being able to make something valuable or worthwhile of ourselves.[30]

Nor, thirdly, am I saying that the things that promote and constitute our practical identities are good only *because* they promote and constitute our practical identities, and so only good in a vaguely instrumental sense. That would be the same mistake as thinking the things that promote and constitute health are instrumental because they promote survival. Like health, the successful maintenance of our practical identities is the excellence of our lives. The things that promote and constitute the maintenance of our practical identities are final goods because, as self-constituting beings, we see them as things to go for.

7. The Problem Cases

I have argued that having a good cannot just be a matter of standing in a special relation to something that is, as it were, already independently good. Just as nothing counts as a hand unless it is related to the nervous system of an animal in a quite particular way, so nothing counts as a good until it is related to an agent in a quite particular way. An animal whose nervous system makes it possible to wiggle his fingers without manipulating them externally has a hand. An entity whose functional organization involves her tending to that very functional organization—that is, looking after it through action—has a good, in the final sense of good. These claims are parallel: hands and final goods are artifacts of these relationships.

On this account, what most obviously has a good are individual people and animals. Since those *are* the things that most obviously have a good, I take that to be a virtue of the account. We can now have many arguments about what sorts of things count as agents and what would be good for them. But according to my account everything that has a good is an agent, and everything good is, necessarily, some agent's good. This brings us back finally to the problem cases I mentioned at the outset. It seems hard to explain why we are tempted by the idea that a universe full of happy people and animals is better than a universe full of miserable ones, since if the people and animals involved in the two cases are *different* people and animals, then there is no one for whom it is better. It seems hard to explain why we are tempted by the idea that a society in which wealth is distributed more equally is better, since although it is plainly better for some people, who would otherwise be poor, it is also plainly worse for others, who would otherwise be rich. Obviously these are not the only problem cases. But I will end by discussing these two cases, to give you a sense of how I think we should handle these issues.

---

[30] That is, the human good is carrying out the particularly normative form of self-constitution particular to our kind, the rational kind. What gives content to 'valuable' here? First, in *Self-Constitution* I argued that morality is necessary for successful self-constitution. I also describe the way thoughts about value more generally can get a footing in *Self-Constitution*, §10.1.4.

As I mentioned early on, one way to approach the problem of the two universes would be to try to make it out that the universe is itself the kind of agent for whom things can be good or bad. Then perhaps it is better *for* the universe if it is full of happy people and animals than if it is full of miserable ones? During his science television series *Cosmos*, Carl Sagan at one point suggested rather impressively that humanity represents the way in which the universe comes to know itself.[31] It's a pretty thought, although I'm not sure a Kantian can accept it. But never mind that. Could the idea that we somehow count as the consciousness of the universe give us grounds for thinking of the universe as an agent for whom things can be good or bad?

Obviously there are some difficulties here. One is that even if we did think so, it is not clear why it would be better for the universe to be full of happy people and animals, unless we also think its function is to support happy life.[32] More importantly, though, when we have the thought that the universe full of miserable life is not as good as the universe full of happy life, it is not because we are sympathizing with the *universe*. It is because we are sympathizing with the people and animals who are in the universe, and we find the thought of their happiness pleasing. In fact, that in itself is already part of the explanation of why we tend to think that the universe full of happy life is better. For you should notice that on the account of the good that I have given, sympathy plays an essential role in the way the concept functions. According to my account, we arrive at the idea of the final good when we look at the world in the way that a certain kind of entity—one that functions by tracking its own functional good through perception and thought—looks at the world. That means that any thoughts I have about what is good for you are essentially sympathetic. But it is not that we are pleased when we sympathize with happy people and animals *because* we believe independently of sympathy that their happiness is a good thing. If we believed that, we could be pleased by it without the aid of sympathy. Rather, they necessarily regard their happiness, or more properly speaking the conditions that constitute it, as something to go for, something worthy of pursuit. And then when we sympathize with them, we regard their happiness, and the things that constitute it, that way too.[33] That's why we see it as good.[34]

The larger point I am trying to make here is that we cannot completely divorce thoughts about the good from thoughts about what to go for, given that the original home of the concept is, so to speak, in the deliberative standpoint. That's why I asked you to keep in mind, earlier, the way in which the problems named by 'the right' and

---

[31] Quoted on the Carl Sagan website at http://www.carlsagan.com/.

[32] Sagan's idea that we are the consciousness of the universe would explain the temptation to think that, I suppose.

[33] The 'or rather, the conditions which constitute it' is there because I am among those who don't believe that people characteristically pursue happiness. I believe we pursue projects we think are worthwhile, and are happy when we are succeeding in promoting or realizing those projects. Saying that people pursue happiness is, at best, shorthand.

[34] This is another manifestation of the fact that valuing is prior to value.

'the good' are interlocking. For I think we will find the answer to the question we are asking now in that fact.

When we think about the comparison between the goodness of two universes, it is impossible not to import thoughts about which of the two we would bring into existence were we in the position of the creator and therefore faced with that choice. If we were, I think we all agree, we would certainly bring into existence the universe full of happy people and animals if we could. But that's not because it contains more happiness and happiness is impersonally good. It's because if you are the creator, then it is *right*—that is, it is your duty—to do as well as you can for *whomever* you create. So the universe full of happy people and animals is not exactly more worthy of choice because it is better. Rather, it is better—and yes, in my view we *do* get that conclusion—because it is more worthy of choice. But this is not to say that there is no one for whom it is better, and that no thought of the good guides the choice. The happier universe is better for *whomever gets created*. But in order to explain why 'whomever gets created' is the right way to single out the beneficiary of the choice in this case, we have to appeal to the deliberative context in which the choice is made, including any duties inherent in that deliberative context.

When we are deciding to have children or enacting legislation that will affect population, we are also in the position of a creator. That is why it makes perfect sense to say, for instance, that it will be better to have a child later when you are in better circumstances, even though there is no genetically identifiable child for whom that is better. Your duty as a prospective parent is to do as well as you can for whatever child you have, not for some genetically identifiable individual who does not yet exist and may never do so. Notice also that Parfit's famous repugnant conclusion—the conclusion that we must keep adding to the population until the conditions created by the crowding destroy the value of life, making it not worth living—is blocked by these arguments.[35] The world is not better with more total happiness in it, because there is no one for whom it is better, nor do we owe it to non-existent people to bring them into existence so that they can have a little fun. Our duty, when we are settling population policy, is to the future inhabitants of the planet, *whoever they are*.

As for equitable distributions, there are two important things to say about them, but they come to the same thing. The first is modeled exactly on what I said about the two universes. More equitable distributions, like universes full of happy people and animals, are better because they are more worthy of choice, in the context in which one chooses a system of distribution, which is when one is setting up a basic structure for society. In order to learn why the more equitable distribution is more worthy of

---

[35] Parfit first introduced the repugnant conclusion in Chapter 17 of *Reasons and Persons* (Oxford: Clarendon Press, 1984). The argument in the text bears generally against puzzles arising from the 'non-identity' problem—cases in which we can apparently do better by producing a better state of affairs for a genetically different individual. These cases may be thought to support the idea of impersonal goods. I am arguing instead that it is not always right to identify the beneficiaries of action in terms of their genetic identities.

choice, all you have to do now is read John Rawls' *Theory of Justice*, to find out why in these circumstances a more equitable distribution is the one that would be chosen.[36] Here, as in the case of the two universes, the choice is governed by thoughts about what is better for someone. First, the parties in the original position make the choice asking what, under the veil of ignorance, will be better for themselves. But that is only a step along the way. The more important point is that we readers who make the thought experiment of entering the original position are undertaking to make the choice in the way that will be best for a citizen of a liberal society considered merely as such. Again, the context of the choice explains why that is the beneficiary we should be thinking of in this kind of case.

The other thing to say is that the political state, unlike the universe, is a kind of agent—indeed, according to my own arguments in *Self-Constitution*, a self-constituting one.[37] We might think that there are all kinds of ways in which the state, considered simply as such, is better off if there are more equitable distributions. More equitable distributions support a middle class, with all the benefits to stability and culture that a middle class is supposed to provide. In the end, I think that this comes to the same thing, though. The benefits of stability and culture ultimately accrue to the citizen, considered just as such. In both arguments, the beneficiary of the state is the representative citizen, and we look to what is good for her. But the reason we do so is because it is to her that the arrangements of the state must be justified, and not to some genetically identifiable individual. The state has no good of its own that is not the good of the representative citizen.

This is not to say that there are not other kinds of collective agents that do have such a good; say, corporations or universities or clubs. But it is a particularly important point to make about the state. The state's interests can come into conflict with yours, considering you as a private individual. But they cannot come into conflict with yours, considering you as a representative citizen. That there should be occasion to sacrifice the citizen for the good of the state is a logical impossibility.

8. Conclusion: Everything Good is Good for Someone

In this paper I have argued that the concept of someone's having a good is prior to the concept of something's being good—just as the concept of having a hand is prior to the concept of something's being a hand. An agent is the sort of thing that has a final good, because an agent necessarily regards her own well-functioning as something to go for. I think it follows that everything that is good in the final sense must be good for

---

[36] In fact, the reason why I keep using 'more equitable' rather than 'equal' is because I think a distribution according to Rawls' Difference Principle (the principle of choosing the distribution that is the best for the worst off) is preferable to a strictly egalitarian one. See *A Theory of Justice*, Chapters 2 and 3.

[37] See *Self-Constitution*, Chapter 7.

someone. Using the case of the two universes, I've tried to indicate how I would handle cases in which our intuitions might seem to be ones that we can explain only by appeal to impersonal goods. What's really happening in these cases is not that we are appealing to impersonal goods, but rather that the designation of the relevant beneficiaries is given by the nature of the choice that is being made. Where there was really no choice between the universe full of happy inhabitants and the universe full of miserable ones, there would be no fact about which one was better—but then, because the question raised by the concept of the good is the question what to go for, there would also be no occasion for making the judgment. I believe that these arguments vindicate the existential claim I started out from: the only reason why anything matters is because the world contains entities *for* whom things can be good or bad.

Introduction to T. M. Scanlon's Lecture

Ted Honderich

Tim Scanlon teaches at Harvard, having previously done so at Princeton. Before then he was a student of mathematical logic and in particular proof theory as well as philosophy at Princeton and Harvard and for a year in Oxford. He has principally been known as a successor to John Rawls and such different predecessors as Jean-Jacques Rousseau and Immanuel Kant, but makes his own use of the shared idea of a hypothetical or imagined social contract, of which you heard in Christine Korsgaard's lecture.

For Scanlon, to speak without qualification, an action is wrong if it would be disallowed by a set of principles that no one could reflect on together with others and then reject as a basis for general agreement. He is definitely not talking about the general Principle of Utility or the general Principle of Humanity against lives of distress or suffering. Nor are the principles the political attitudes of liberalism or conservatism. It was indeed supposed, in my view with reason, that Rawls' method of deriving his own two principles of justice and of allowable socio-economic differences already presupposed those very principles. We are to accept that there is no such circularity in Scanlon's story.

His contract line of argument is bound up with the subject of *reasons* and their weights, his concern in this lecture. But this subject is taken forward on its own, without explicit reference to a social contract. Reasons in his wide sense include moral judgements such as your judgement the other evening that a man was treating his wife badly, didn't care about it, and was cruel and heartless. But reasons in the wide sense also include reasons for actions having to do with self-interest, and also reasons for beliefs, and reasons for anything else. They include reasons for what *is* to be done, where that final question comes after settling the questions of what ought to be done and what is in someone's or something's interest. So reasons have to do with all of what can be called the *normative* in a wide sense.

Reasons are propositions we can come to know and whose general nature is explicable. Evidently the idea is that we come to understand the species that is moral judgements only by understanding the genus of which they are a species. Reasons in this sense are not feelings, attitudes, or inclinations. Reasons in this sense are *not* in the category of desires and cannot be reduced to desires. To see moral judgements as in the category of reasons is thus to leave behind the moral philosophy of some decades ago, in particular the metaethics that took moral judgements to be exactly of the order of desires—or to be imperatival utterances owed to desires. We thus also leave behind a whole tradition including David Hume's curiously unrestrained declaration in the 18th century that reason is and ought to be the slave of the passions.

Reasons are indeed truths, a special category of truths somehow owed to thinking and living with others. They are owed to reflection that includes others and their views and is a process that, like Rawls', issues in what can be called reflective equilibrium. Evidently they are not in either of the traditional two categories of truths of fact, spoken of in terms of correspondence to fact, and truths of logic or meaning, having to do with entailment, validity, and so on. Further, that these reasons are truths rather than desires definitely doesn't stop them from their having some special grip on us, from their being motivating, moving us to action. If the nature of these reasons is puzzling, if their way of existing is a question, it can be dealt with or approached, as the matter of the existence of numbers can be dealt with but not in the same way.

This *reasons fundamentalism* necessarily also includes consideration of other matters listed near the beginning of the lecture, including the supervenience of reasons on ordinary facts, our way of knowing reasons, and their truth being a matter of common sense. What is said indeed brings to mind two other lecturers in this volume, Christine Korsgaard and Simon Blackburn. The first is, so to speak, in the same or a nearby world. The second is not.

I find some of this view, reasons fundamentalism, elusive, as lesser propositions offered by me and other struggling philosophers are found elusive. Great philosophers also come to mind, including Kant, certainly not consistently pellucid. Clearly it is possible for us to be seized by ideas that may in fact be discoveries or necessary constructions but also be unable to fit the rest of the world around them clearly. Maybe great originality is always this way. In the present case there is help in a book edited by Wallace, Kumar, and Freeman—*Reasons and Recognition: Essays in the Philosophy of T. M. Scanlon.*

For other questions, and more than questions, proceed to Simon Blackburn's lecture. And from it, to continue your inquiry, proceed back to this one.

8

Reasons Fundamentalism

T. M. Scanlon

1. Contemporary metaethics differs in two important ways from the metaethics of the 1950s and 1960s, and even the later 1970s, when John Mackie wrote *Ethics: Inventing Right and Wrong*. In that earlier period, discussion in metaethics focused almost entirely on morality: on the proper interpretation of claims about moral right and wrong, and other forms of moral evaluation. Today, although morality is still much discussed, a significant part of the debate concerns practical reasoning and normativity more generally: reasons for action, and, even more broadly, reasons for belief and other attitudes, which are increasingly recognized as normative, and as raising questions of the same nature as those about reasons for action.

The metaethics of the mid-twentieth century also focused on the question of *motivation*. With respect to morality in particular, the question was how agents can be motivated by their moral judgments. In *The Possibility of Altruism*, Thomas Nagel was attacking the prevailing Humean orthodoxy, and he considered requirements of ethics and prudence to be rational requirements. But he nonetheless presented the problem he was addressing as a problem about motivation. Thus he wrote, "I conceive of ethics as a branch of psychology. My claims concern its foundation, or ultimate motivational basis."[1] Today, although motivation is still mentioned, questions are also likely to be put in terms of *reasons*. With respect to morality, the question is when and why it is true that a person has a reason to do what will benefit him or her in the future, or to do what morality requires.

It may be tendentious for me to say that metaethics as a field has undergone these two changes. Perhaps they are only changes in my own thinking, or the thinking of those I talk with most frequently. But, whatever may be said about the field as a whole, my approach in this lecture will fall on the second side of each of these dichotomies: my focus will be on normativity in general, treating morality as a special case,

---

[1] Thomas Nagel, *The Possibility of Altruism* (Oxford: Oxford University Press, 1970), p. 3.

and I will be concerned centrally with the idea of a reason—mainly with the idea of a reason for action.

I believe that truths about reasons are fundamental in two senses. First, they are not reducible to or identifiable with truths of other kinds, such as truths about the natural world of physical objects, causes, and effects. Second, their normativity cannot be explained in other terms. So I am what might be called a Reasons Fundamentalist. There are also two further ways in which reasons might be fundamental. Reasons might be the only fundamental elements of the normative domain, other normative notions such as *good* and *ought* being analyzable in terms of reasons. Second, the normative domain might just *be* the domain of claims about reasons. I am inclined to believe that reasons are indeed fundamental in these two further ways. But these beliefs are controversial, and I will set them aside in what follows. The Reasons Fundamentalism that I will be discussing is just the thesis that reasons are fundamental in the first two ways I have mentioned.

2. The idea that there are truths about reasons for action is strongly supported by common sense. Consider, for example, the following claims.

(1) For a person in control of a fast moving automobile, the fact that the car will injure and perhaps kill a pedestrian if the wheel is not turned is a reason to turn the wheel.

(2) The fact that a person's child has died is a reason for that person to feel sad.

(3) The fact that it would be enjoyable to listen to some very engaging music, moving one's body gently in time with it, is a reason to do this, or to continue doing it.

These things seem, to me at least, obviously true. But the philosophical thesis that these are irreducibly normative truths may seem unsatisfactory, because it leaves unexplained many things that need explaining. Consider the following questions.

Relational Character: Reasons are reasons *for* an agent. How is this relational character to be understood?

Determinate Truth Values: Are statements about reasons true or false, independent of our opinions about them? Does the idea that there are irreducibly normative truths of this kind have unacceptable metaphysical implications?

Supervenience: How are facts about reasons related to facts, about what occurs, and what causes what, in the natural world? Normative facts are not entailed by such natural facts, but at least many normative facts depend on non-normative facts: they vary when non-normative facts vary and cannot vary as long as non-normative facts remain the same. This seems puzzling, and in need of explanation.

Knowledge: If there are irreducibly normative facts about reasons, how can we come to know such facts?

Practical significance: Judgments about reasons play a different role than other beliefs—such as beliefs about the natural world—in practical reasoning and in the explanation of action. How can they play this role if they are beliefs?

Strength: Reasons have varying strengths. The reason to turn the wheel of the car, for example, is a stronger reason than the reason to go on listening to enjoyable music: the fact that turning the wheel to avoid hitting the pedestrian would interfere with one's enjoyment of the music on the radio is not a sufficient reason not to turn it. So there is a question about what this strength amounts to.

Optionality: Some reasons seem to be "optional": they are merely considerations it makes sense to treat as reasons. Whereas other considerations are non-optional: they provide reasons that should be taken into account, whether or not they are conclusive. The pleasure of listening to music, in the example I just gave, is an optional reason—merely something it makes sense to count as a reason if one decides to do so. Whereas, at least in most circumstances, the fact that doing X would substantially reduce one's risk of an early death is a non-optional reason to do X, whether or not it is conclusive in a given case.

3. All of these questions might seem to be answered by an account of reasons that bases them on desires, such as

(4) X has a reason to do A just in case doing A would promote the fulfillment of some desire that X has.

or

(5) X has reason to do A if doing A would promote the fulfillment of a desire that X would have if X were fully aware of the relevant non-normative facts and thinking clearly.

Views of this kind explain the relational character of reasons: reasons are *reasons for* a person who has the relevant desire, or would have such a desire if fully informed and thinking clearly. They might also seem to account for the phenomenon of strength: desires have varying strengths, that is to say, varying motivational power, and a desire theory might hold that one reason is stronger than another just in case the desire on which it is based is stronger in this motivational sense. The fact that some reasons are optional might also be explained by saying that they are reasons for doing something *if you desire or want to do so*, and the idea that some reasons are non-optional would thus be the idea that there are some things that promote the fulfillment of desires that everyone has (or everyone who is fully informed about his or her situation and thinking clearly).

There also might seem to be no difficulty explaining how we can know what reasons we have according to a view of this kind, since we can, at least sometimes, know what we desire, or would desire under certain conditions, and what would fulfill those desires. And we can explain how reasons can motivate, since desires motivate a person to do what would promote their fulfillment, and a person who has a reason to do something has a desire that that action would promote the fulfillment of.

Finally, a desire theory might claim to explain the phenomenon of supervenience. At one level, this seems obvious: if the reasons for action that people have are a function of natural facts about their desires and what will promote their fulfillment, then as long as these natural facts remain unchanged, people's reasons for action will remain the same as well.

The ability to explain these aspects of reasons is, I believe, a large part of what makes desire-based accounts appealing. There are, however, well-known difficulties with accounts of this kind. Some of these difficulties concern the counterintuitive implications of desire theories about what reasons people have. Does a person really have a reason to do what will fulfill any desire he or she has, no matter how foolish? Does the reason the driver has to turn the car really depend on his or her having a desire that would be fulfilled by doing this? These problems might be lessened by shifting from actual desires to informed desires, and making suitable assumptions about what people would desire if fully informed. But this move brings problems of its own for the desire view's account of motivation, since it is less obvious that people are always motivated by the fact that an action would promote the fulfillment of desires if these are desires that they do not have, but only would have under different conditions.

I believe that substantive objections of this kind count strongly against desire theories of reasons. But I want to set these objections aside for the moment, and instead consider what may seem to be a deeper objection, which claims that the explanatory potential of these theories is in an important respect illusory. The illusion arises from the fact that desire theories can be understood in two very different ways, and statements of these theories often do not clearly distinguish between them.

One way in which it is natural to understand desire theories is as substantive normative claims about what reasons people have. It may be quite plausible (in many cases) to say that people have reason to do what will promote the satisfaction of their desires. This normative thesis could explain some features of reasons for action, such as the relational nature of such reasons, and their strength, in the ways I have mentioned. (Although the idea that the strength of a reason to do something is proportional to its motivational effectiveness does not seem very plausible.) But since a normative desire theory is itself just a very general normative claim, it does not seem to address many of the other questions I have listed.

If there are serious metaphysical problems about the idea of irreducibly normative truths, a normative desire theory would not respond to these worries because it is itself a normative truth of this kind. Nor would a normative desire theory provide a general explanation of how we can come to know normative truths. It simply makes a general substantive claim about reasons for action—that we have reason to do whatever satisfies our desires—which, if true, leaves us only with the empirical problem of figuring out which actions will do this. In the same way, the thesis that the only thing we have reason to do is to get as much money as possible would leave us just with the problem of figuring out how to get rich. It would not solve the problem of how we can come to know normative truths, but would simply offer one such truth, which it claims we know. These points might be summed up by saying that normative desire theories are not rivals to Reasons Fundamentalism but are quite compatible with it. Perhaps they even presuppose it.

An alternative interpretation of a desire theory would take that theory to offer a reductive claim about what it *is* for someone to have a reason, rather than a normative claim about the reasons for action, according to which for p to be a reason for an agent to do a just is for the truth of p to help explain how doing a would promote the satisfaction of some desire that the agent has.[2]

Interpreted in this way, a desire theory might provide answers to some of the questions I have listed. It would respond to metaphysical worries about irreducibly normative truths by holding that facts about reasons for action are just a kind of natural fact. And it would respond to epistemological worries as well, by holding that we can come to know truths about reasons for action through the usual kinds of empirical inquiry.

The question, however, would be whether identifying facts about reasons with non-normative facts would explain reasons or eliminate their normativity. The "action guiding" force of reasons, on such a theory, would seem to be purely causal and explanatory. If the fact that one has a strong reason not to do a (and no countervailing reason to do a) is just a natural fact about what will satisfy one's desires, then this fact might explain one's failure to do a. But it does not explain why believing that one has such a reason (believing that this natural fact obtains) can make it irrational for one to do a.

A reductive desire theorist might reply, as Mark Schroeder does, that all normativity is to be understood in terms of the idea of a reason. So if it is true that *a person's having a reason just consists in some fact about that person's desires and what will promote them*, a reductive desire theory preserves normativity, since it preserves the idea of a reason.[3] So the question is whether this reductive claim should be accepted. I myself believe that this claim is refuted by the evident lack of intrinsic normative significance of facts about desires. But simply asserting that this is so may seem to lead to a standoff. To move beyond this standoff, one needs to consider and assess the evidence offered in support of the reductive thesis. In Schroeder's case, much depends on his claim that facts about desires, rather than, say, about what a person would enjoy, are the best explanation of the reasons that one person (who likes dancing) has to go to a party where there will be dancing (as compared to the reasons of another person, who does not like to dance).[4] This claim does not strike me as plausible but pursuing the matter here would take me too far afield.[5]

    [2] As Mark Schroeder argues in *Slaves of the Passions* (Oxford: Oxford University Press, 2007).
    [3] See Schroeder, *Slaves of the Passions*, pp. 79–83.
    [4] Schroeder, *Slaves of the Passions*, Chapters 1 and 8.
    [5] I discuss the matter further in *Being Realistic about Reasons* (Oxford: Oxford University Press, 2014). Lecture 2.

It seems, then, that desire theories face a dilemma: either they begin with a normative claim about reasons for action, in which case they do not explain the features of reasons that may seem puzzling; or else they make a reductive claim, which eliminates normativity altogether. This raises two questions. The first is whether there is any way of understanding the appeal of a desire theory that avoids this dilemma. The second is whether explanations of the kind offered by normative desire theories are as unsatisfactory as they seem. I believe that a normative desire theory is unsatisfactory, but not for the reasons I have just been discussing—not because of its lack of explanatory depth.[6]

4. A different way of explaining truths about reasons holds that reasons can be grounded in an idea of rationality. A rationality-based account has the following general form:

(6) The fact that p is a reason for a person to do a when and because rationality requires such a person to count this fact in favor of doing a.

The right-hand side of this formula employs the idea of a reason—the idea of counting a consideration *in favor of* an action. But what it employs is just the idea of an agent's *treating* something as a reason. It thus involves no appeal to conclusions (arrived at independently) about what reasons people actually have. The work in this formula is done instead by the concept of rationality, which is taken to support such conclusions.

There is a familiar sense of "rational" in which the rational thing to do is just the thing that is required or supported by the reasons one has or, perhaps, by the reasons one would have, if one's other beliefs were true. People use "rational" in this sense when, for example, they claim that it is rational to do what is in one's self interest (or would be in one's self interest if one's other beliefs were true). Such a thesis does not explain claims about reasons in terms of rationality, but rather presupposes, or asserts, claims about what reasons people have.

A rationality-based account of reasons would be trivial, and fail in its aim of explaining the idea of a reason for action, if it appealed to a notion of rationality of this sort. So an account of reasons of the kind I am considering must employ a conception of rationality that does not consist of or depend on a substantive conception of the reasons people have.

In a Kantian theory, which is the most familiar view of this type, the fundamental claim is that the Categorical Imperative is a condition of rationality. The claim is that anyone who sees him or herself as a rational agent must, on pain of irrationality, see the Categorical Imperative as the fundamental principle of practical reasoning. A consideration p is a reason for an agent to do a, according to this theory, if a failure to count this fact as a reason to do a would be incompatible with the Categorical Imperative. So far, this seems to cover only moral reasons, broadly construed.

---

[6] For further discussion, see *Being Realistic about Reasons*, Lecture 4.

Christine Korsgaard's version of a Kantian view extends this by adding that the fact that p is a reason for an agent to do a if failing to see it as such a reason is incompatible with some "practical identity" that the agent has adopted (and adopting that identity is itself compatible with the Categorical Imperative).[7]

Consider now how a view that bases claims about reasons on requirements of rationality might explain some of the puzzling features of reasons that I mentioned above. A view of this kind can explain what I called above the relational character of facts about reasons, since such facts are, on this view, facts about what an agent can (consistent with rationality) treat as a reason. It can also explain what makes claims about reasons correct when they are correct: they are correct if they do indeed follow from requirements of rationality. We can know what reasons we have, on such an account, because we can know what rationality requires, and insofar as we are rational we will be moved to do what we have reason to do. The "strength" of reasons can be explained in what might be called a "top down" fashion, in contrast to the "bottom up" explanation offered by a desire theory. It is not that reasons "come with" particular strengths, as they would on a desire-based view. Rather, one consideration is a stronger reason than another if it would be irrational to refrain from doing what the former reason counts in favor of because the latter reason counts against so acting.

It is less clear how a rationality-based view should explain the optional character of some reasons. But I will leave this aside for now in order to consider what has been seen as one of the main advantages of such a view over rival accounts, such as Reasons Fundamentalism.

This concerns what Christine Korsgaard calls "The Normative Question," of how reasons acquire their normative force or, as she sometimes puts it, how reasons "get a grip on" an agent. A view of the kind I am calling Reasons Fundamentalism, which takes there to be facts about which things are reasons, cannot, she says, give a satisfactory answer to this question. If a consideration's being a reason for a person is just another fact about the world, she says, then the person could still be perfectly indifferent to this fact.[8]

What kind of grip is in question here? If it were the "grip" of authority that moral conclusions are thought to have over us, then this could be intelligibly explained by offering reasons to do what morality requires. But the move from morality to reasons in general rules out such an answer. The authority of conclusions about reasons for action cannot be explained by giving a further reason since the same question would arise over again about this reason.

We might say that the Normative Question is a question of motivation. But here we need to distinguish several different issues. On the one hand, there is the question of

---

[7] See Christine Korsgaard, *The Sources of Normativity* (Cambridge: Cambridge University Press, 1996), esp. pp. 102–7, 239–42. For a non-Kantian view that bases reasons on rationality see Joshua Gert, *Brute Rationality: Normativity and Human Action* (Cambridge: Cambridge University Press, 2007).

[8] Korsgaard, *The Sources of Normativity*, pp. 44–6.

how a person can be motivated by the thought that some fact is a reason for action if this thought is a mere belief that something is the case. This is the problem coming down to us from Hume. I believe that, as I will argue in Lecture 3, the idea of rational agency provides an answer to this question, which might be called the internal question of motivation. I will not discuss this question here, however, since I do not believe it is the question that Korsgaard has in mind.

A second way of understanding Korsgaard's Normative Question in terms of motivation would be to see it as what might be called an external question of motivation—a question about how the fact that p is a reason for an agent to do a, if it is just a fact, could get the agent to accept that p is a reason to do a and treat it as such. The agent could simply deny that it is a reason. If he did, what could we say to him? A Reasons Fundamentalist, Korsgaard might say, would simply insist that p is after all a reason, and that is all there is to it.[9] This is obviously not going to move the person who denies it.

The challenge here is not, I think, correctly described as a question of motivation if that is understood to mean a question that might be answered by a psychological explanation of how a person could be moved to respond to a fact in a certain way. The problem is not a matter of motivation in this psychological sense, but rather of something more like normative authority. The question is not how an agent might come to respond to the fact that p is a reason for her to do a, by accepting that it is a reason, but rather a question of why, if she does have these reasons, she *must* so respond. That is why she calls it "the *normative* question."

Korsgaard is quite correct about what a Reasons Fundamentalist, or at least *this* Reasons Fundamentalist, would say in a situation of the kind she imagines. According to a Reasons Fundamentalist, the relation that holds between an agent and a consideration X in such a situation just *is* the relation of p's *being a reason for that agent to do a*. The "grip" that this has on the agent just is this relation: *being a reason for* him or her (or, in the strongest cases, a conclusive reason).[10] As Korsgaard puts it, quite correctly, a Reasons Fundamentalist "insists on the irreducible character of normativity."[11] The fundamental disagreement here concerns whether some further explanation can and should be given of why the agent in this situation *must* treat p as a reason.

Korsgaard believes that in order to explain the force of this "must," we have to find something *about the agent* in virtue of which she must accept that p is a reason for her to do a. Whatever plays this role can't just be another truth about what reasons the person has, or else the whole problem would begin again. But in order to have normative force,

[9] Korsgaard, *The Sources of Normativity*, p. 38.
[10] For a similar statement see R. Jay Wallace, "Normativity and the Will," in his *Normativity and the Will: Selected Essays on Moral Psychology and Practical Reason* (Oxford: Oxford University Press, 2006), pp. 75–6.
[11] Korsgaard, *The Sources of Normativity*, p. 32.

the explanation we are looking for can't just be a psychological principle. It follows that the problem can be solved only by finding a kind of normativity—some grounding for a "must"—that does not start from a claim about which things are reasons. Korsgaard finds this in the idea of rational agency itself. As she puts it, "Kantians believe that the source of the normativity of moral claims must be found in the agent's own will..."[12] I believe that what she here says explicitly about moral claims is in her view true of all claims about reasons. Claims about moral requirements are grounded in things that an agent must accept insofar as she sees herself as acting at all. Other reasons are things that an agent "must" see as reasons in virtue of some more specific identity that she has.

5. The idea that claims about the reasons an agent has must be grounded in something that is already true of that agent (or of that agent's own attitudes) is shared by a surprisingly wide range of views, many of them not at all Kantian. I am tempted to say, although it would no doubt be an exaggeration, that it is shared by almost all those who believe in normative reasons but are not Reasons Fundamentalists.

Consider, for example, Gilbert Harman's view.[13] Harman writes that an agent's reasons for action must follow from his or her "goals, desires or intentions." He does not put it this way, but it seems in the spirit of his view to add that claims about reasons that are not so based fail to "get a grip on the agent." I believe that something similar might be said by proponents of desire-based views more generally, such as Bernard Williams' view that the only valid claims about reasons are what he calls internal reason statements—that is, claims about what could be reached by a sound deliberative route from the agent's actual subjective motivational set.[14]

Williams' idea of a "sound deliberative route" allows that a consideration can be a reason for an agent even though the agent is not presently motivated by that consideration. It is enough that being so motivated has the right kind of connection with the agent's present attitudes. This connection might be described in terms of motivation, but it seems to me at base a *normative* connection, as indicated in the fact that what is in question is a *sound* deliberative route.[15] What the soundness of this route does is to ground the reason normatively in something to which the agent is already committed, thereby making it something the agent cannot deny without irrationality.

Another claim that Williams once made may be relevant here. Arguing against proponents of "external" reasons, he said that there are many criticisms that might be brought against a man who treats his wife badly and does not care at all about

[12] Korsgaard, *The Sources of Normativity*, p. 19.

[13] As expressed in Gilbert Harman, "Moral Relativism Defended," *Philosophical Review* 84 (1975), pp. 3–22.

[14] See his "Internal and External Reasons" in Bernard Williams, *Moral Luck* (Cambridge: Cambridge University Press, 1981), pp. 101–13.

[15] I said earlier in discussing desire-based views that the move from an actual desire account to one based on informed desires might involve sacrificing the connection with motivation that is one of the hallmarks of desire theories. The fact that desire theorists are not troubled by this move may support the point I am making—that what may be described as motivation is actually a matter of rational connection.

this—he may be cruel, heartless, and so on, and it might be better if he were not like this. But a defender of "external reasons" statements, Williams said, wants to go beyond this and say that the man is *irrational* if he fails to recognize that he has a reason to treat his wife differently.[16] A defender of external reasons need not make this claim, as Williams later recognized.[17] But I conjecture that Williams made the claim in the first place because he himself believed that claims about reasons must "get a grip on the agent" in a way that would ground a charge of irrationality if the agent ignored these reasons. He therefore thought that his opponent would want to claim this as well.

A similar thought seems to be what draws Michael Smith, in *The Moral Problem*, to identify reasons with what a person would desire for him or herself if fully rational.[18] The fact that the reason is determined by what *that person* would desire if fully rational (fully informed, thinking clearly, and so on) ensures a connection with the agent him or herself, perhaps close enough to make it irrational for the person to reject the reason. As Smith has said more recently, "If morality requires some limited form of altruism then... the principle of limited altruism is a principle... on all fours with *modus ponens* and *modus tollens* and the principle of means-ends."[19] Here again, the idea seems to be that claims about the reasons an agent has, if correct, must be claims that the agent cannot deny without irrationality.

The idea of grounding claims about an agent's reasons in attitudes that that agent already holds may derive some of its appeal from the dialectical context in which argument about reasons for action is imagined to take place. In Williams' example of the man who sees no reason to treat his wife better, the context is an instance of what Gilbert Harman calls "external reasoning," a context in which two people are arguing about what reasons for action one of them has.[20] In such a context, facts about one party's actual attitudes (as opposed to the merits of the content of those attitudes) have a particular salience. It is an obvious dialectical advantage to be able to "get a grip" on your opponent by saying: "But you accept that... and it follows from this that the fact that *p* counts in favor of *phi*-ing."

It is noteworthy, I think, that much of Williams' discussion in "Internal and External Reasons" involves cases in which one person is trying to force some other person to agree that he has a reason to act in a certain way. (The example just

<hr/>

[16] Williams, "Internal and External Reasons," p. 110. Korsgaard makes a similar suggestion about what a realist might claim in "Acting for a Reason," in *The Constitution of Agency* (Oxford: Oxford University Press, 2008) p. 213.

[17] In "Replies," in J. E. J. Altham and Ross Harrison, *World, Mind, and Ethics: Essays on the Ethical Philosophy of Bernard Williams* (Cambridge: Cambridge University Press, 1995), p. 192.

[18] Michael Smith, *The Moral Problem* (Oxford: Blackwell Publishers, 1994), pp. 151ff.

[19] Michael Smith, "Objectivity and Moral Realism: On the Significance of the Phenomenology of Moral Experience," in *Ethics and the A Priori: Selected Essays on Moral Psychology and Meta-ethics* (Cambridge: Cambridge University Press, 2004), p. 250.

[20] Gilbert Harman, "Notes on Practical Reasoning," www.princeton.edu/~harman/Papers/SPAWN.pdf, p. 3.

mentioned, of the man who treats his wife badly, is a case in point; the Owen Wingrave example is another.[21] These are, I think, typical.) Part of Korsgaard's argument early in *The Sources of Normativity* assumes a similar dialectical situation. She imagines two people disagreeing about whether something is a reason for a certain action, and she observes that it is mere reiterative stone-kicking for one party to say, in the face of the other's denial, "But it just *is* a reason!"[22] A much more effective response would be to come up with an argument that begins from something that the other party accepts, or cannot deny on pain of irrationality.

But what it takes for a claim to be correct need not be the same as what it takes for the claim to be one that one's opponent in argument cannot consistently deny. These two things are certainly different with respect to claims about empirical facts, and I believe they are also different with respect to claims about reasons, which is the matter at issue. That they are different is strongly suggested when we shift to what Harman calls a case of "internal reasoning," which is reasoning about what reasons one has oneself. In this case, the mere fact that one cannot consistently reject a claim about reasons given that one has some desire, intention, or other attitude does not itself settle the matter. One can always ask oneself why one should have these attitudes—whether they can be justified in the relevant way. From the agent's own point of view his or her own attitudes are largely transparent to the subject matter under consideration.

Korsgaard recognizes, indeed emphasizes, the possibility of this kind of reflective "stepping back" when one is thinking about what reasons one has. In such a situation, she says, a person must keep on asking "why" until she comes to a point at which it is "impossible, unnecessary or incoherent to ask why again."[23] This is what she calls the search for the unconditioned. But, leaving aside whether it is possible to find an unconditioned starting point for reasoning about what reasons one has (a starting point that does not itself involve some substantive judgment about reasons), must we always seek such a starting point? The claim that we must continue stepping back until it is "impossible, unnecessary or incoherent to ask why again" would be much less plausible without the disjunct "unnecessary." But when is it unnecessary to ask any further? I would say that this depends on the substantive merits of the answer one has reached—on whether this answer is clearly correct, or whether there is any reason to doubt it.

Grounding claims about reasons in claims about rationality (that is to say, claims about what is required to avoid *irrationality*) thus has greatest appeal in the case of external reasoning. In internal reasoning what comes to the fore are substantive conclusions about the subject matter being dealt with—in this case reasons about what to do. There is a reversal here that may at first seem surprising, but should not be so.

---

[21] Williams, "Internal and External Reasons," p. 106.
[22] Korsgaard, *The Sources of Normativity*, p. 38ff.
[23] Korsgaard, *The Sources of Normativity*, p. 33.

Claims about irrationality are in one sense more internal than substantive claims about reasons. As John Broome says, they depend only on the contents of the subject's own mind.[24] But such claims are not as relevant in internal reasoning as in the external variety, and it is the point of view of internal reasoning that is primary in an investigation of reasons and normativity. From this point of view the question of how reasons "get a grip on one" properly disappears. There is only the question: what reasons do I have?

6. If my arguments are accepted, then Reasons Fundamentalism is the most defensible of the three accounts of reasons I have considered. But this should be of only limited comfort to the Reasons Fundamentalist. His view is left standing, but it is also left holding the bag of claims about the relation "being a reason for," claims which may strike many as quite implausible and in need of explanation. But how implausible are they, and what kind of explanation do they call for?

I said that the relation "being a reason for" might be thought puzzling. But from a normative point of view—the point of view we take up when we are deciding what to do, and asking what reasons we have, claims like (1)–(3) with which I began are not puzzling. They seem obviously correct. And if, when I ask how there could be such a thing as this relation of being a reason for, that is to say, how these things could be reasons, and stand in the normative relations I asserted, this again does not seem puzzling. Is it puzzling how the fact that turning the steering wheel is necessary in order to avoid killing someone could be a reason to turn the wheel? As a normative question, this is not puzzling.

The puzzle, if there is one, arises only when I take a more philosophical stance and, stepping outside "the normative point of view" ask what kind of truths these are. Here, I think, we are bound to be frustrated. The correct response, I believe, is simply that they are normative truths (truths about what reasons we have). To accept this answer is to reject the puzzlement. If instead we try to place normative facts "in the world" by identifying them with facts of some other kind, then, as in the case of Reductive Desire Theories, we will deprive them of their normativity.

But even if we accept that irreducibly normative truths do not commit us to special entities of any kind, it may as I have said remain puzzling why these truths supervene on natural (physical and psychological) truths. We should notice, however, that the claim that they do supervene is just another normative claim: a claim about the kind of considerations that provide reasons. So if any explanation of this fact can be offered, it will be a normative explanation, rather than a metaphysical one.[25]

Arguably, the same is true of the question of how we can come to know normative truths. If these truths described a metaphysical realm apart from us, then there would be a question how we could "get in touch with this realm." But truths about

---

[24] John Broome, "Does Rationality Consist in Responding Correctly to Reasons?" *Journal of Moral Philosophy* 4 (2007), pp. 349–74.
[25] For further discussion see *Being Realistic about Reasons*, Lecture 2.

reasons are not truths about such a realm any more than mathematical truths are. So the question of how we can discover these truths is the question about what forms of normative reasoning are good reasoning, and thus, in itself, a normative question.

Less controversially, the problems of explaining the strength of reasons and the possibility of optional reasons are also ones that require normative solutions. I am not saying that these matters are not puzzling; only that they are of an essentially normative character.[26]

If I am correct about this, then it would be a mistake to object to normative versions of desire theory on the ground that the solutions they offer to the problems of supervenience, strength, knowledge, and optionality are insufficiently deep. Desire-based answers to these puzzles may, as I believe, be unsatisfactory, but it is not because these answers are themselves normative. That is the only kind of answer we should expect.

Things are different, however, when it comes to explaining the special role that normative beliefs play within our practical thinking. The kind of explanation of the "significance" of conclusions about reasons that is asked for here cannot be one that would be provided by giving a reason, since this would just be more of the talk that is supposed to be explained. So what is being asked for is some more "external" explanation of the content of claims about reasons and the nature of the activity of thinking about what reasons we have.

The problem, as it comes down to us from Hume, is how a person can be motivated by the thought that something is a reason for action if this thought is a mere belief that something is the case. Non-cognitivists might maintain that this cannot be explained as long as normative judgments are understood as a kind of belief. Accepting a claim about reasons, they insist, must instead be something like accepting an imperative. As Hare said long ago, an imperative is the only kind of judgment that is logically linked with action.[27] But the link in question here, between, say, accepting that X is a good reason for doing A and being disposed to do A, is not a matter of *logic*. Rather, it is a matter of rationality. It is part of being a rational agent that accepting a judgment about the reasons one has generally leads to, and can explain, one's behaving in certain ways—forming or not forming certain intentions, performing or not performing certain actions, and accepting or not accepting other propositions.[28]

This description of the matter has the right dual character. On the one hand it refers to, or presupposes the possibility of, a causal explanation. A rational agent, at least the human ones we know of, is a physical organism that is so constituted that relations of causation at the physical level produce certain patterns at the level of thought and behavior. On the other hand, the description also has the appropriate rationalizing

---

[26] For a thoughtful normative explanation of the optionality of some reasons, see Joseph Raz, *Engaging Reason* (Oxford: Oxford University Press, 1999), pp. 94–105. I discuss the matter further in *Being Realistic about Reasons*, Lecture 5.

[27] R. M. Hare, *The Language of Morals* (Oxford: Oxford University Press, 1952), pp. 20, 171–2.

[28] See *Being Realistic about Reasons*, Lecture 3.

character: the agent is not only caused, for example, to move his or her limbs in a certain way, but will, insofar as he or she is rational, see this movement as making sense in the light of, and guided by, certain aims.

So the idea of rationality, rather than serving a normative function, grounding claims about the reasons people have, serves an explanatory function, explaining the link between the acceptance of a reason and subsequent intentions and actions—a role that might otherwise be played by desire or, in expressivist views, by imperatives or some other non-cognitive attitude.

Introduction to Simon Blackburn's Lecture

Ted Honderich

Back in the 1950s, there was still the following old idea about moral judgements and reasons for them, and talk of right and wrong and moral language generally: they are a matter of *truths*—if somehow intuited truths rather than ones got in plain ways, say by just the meanings of words or the evidence of your eyes. There was also the following younger idea: moral judgements and so on are only a matter of the expressings of emotion or desire, related to *Boo!* and *Hurrah!* and *Shut the door!* This idea was subsequently included in what is called *expressivism*. In the course of time the first idea, of morality as truths, intuited or otherwise, acquired from elsewhere in philosophy the name of *realism*. And so the opposed expressivist idea became *anti-realism*.

To this bundle were then added marriages or anyway cohabitations, one being the formidable work of Professor Simon Blackburn. It was carried forward in the course of his learning in Cambridge and then his teaching in Oxford, the University of North Carolina, and Cambridge. He is also the maker of the best short philosophical dictionary, has been the editor of the leading philosophical journal *Mind*, and is a humanist.

The lecture is original work, though maybe prompted by what it mentions, David Hume's opinion in the eighteenth century that our moral carry-on, what he called our *sense* as distinct from our *reason*, is or has 'a productive faculty'. This faculty, in 'gilding and staining all natural objects with... colours, borrowed from internal sentiment, raises in a manner a new creation'. At least part of this seems to be that in thinking about our feelings we are committed to accepting the existence of some sort of fact out in the world, a causal disposition to our feelings, something about which there are truths.

Blackburn's *quasi-realism*, like so much else in new philosophy, is such that there is disagreement as to what it does come to or has to come to, not to mention claims that it is inconsistent. It also has both opponents of its factual or realist side and opponents of its expressive side. In his Royal Institute lecture, he concerns himself with the latter adversaries.

They are philosophers resistant to the role assigned to emotion, desire, and the like—say *attitudes* in general. These opponents depend instead on the role of what they take to be facts in morality expressed by *reasons*. With morality, for Blackburn, this supposed *majesty* of reason is denied. Things are a lot more complicated. *Slavery is wrong* is at least more a matter of what are called movements of the mind rather than facts, despite the facts in the world to which the attitudes are related.

There are more particular propositions. We are reassured that the given account of reasons has the upshot, denied by some adversaries, that dogs have reasons. There is examination of the relevance of the superior view that an attitude taken as a disposition to do something is not in itself a reason for the thing. There is consideration of the objection that what seems to be the identification of reasons with attitudes faces the fact that we can always open the question of whether an attitude is defensible or the like. There is close examination of the idea that the rationality of means-end reasoning, choosing an effective and not self-defeating means to an end, is separate from the play of attitudes. There is acute examination of a supposed paradox about murdering someone gently.

I myself have been forcefully reminded by the lecture that of course both attitudes and factual beliefs enter into my carry-on about right and wrong, my actual judgements. Still, are there things that can be called moral truths, anyway one, this being the Principle of Humanity? It incorporates or rests on fundamental human desires, great goods, our shared human nature. Against this brave tendency about a moral truth, it is clear that quasi-realism is a challenge.

This kind of fecund uncertainty is a common enough experience in good lecture halls. Most lectures worth sitting through add questions to your life, questions about the lecture. In this case, as others, get the lecturer's books—Blackburn's *Essays in Quasi-Realism* (1993), *Ruling Passions* (1998), and *Being Good* (2003).

9

The Majesty of Reason

Simon Blackburn

I. Introduction

In this paper I contemplate two phenomena that have impressed theorists concerned with the domain of reasons and of what is now called 'normativity'.[1] One is the much-discussed 'externality' of reasons. According to this, reasons are just there, anyway. They exist whether or not agents take any notice of them. They do not only exist in the light of contingent desires or mere inclinations. They are 'external' not 'internal'. They bear on us, even when through ignorance or wickedness we take no notice of them. They thus very conspicuously shine the lights of objectivity, and independence, and even necessity. By basking in this light, ethics is rescued from the slough of sentiment and preference, and regains the dignity denied to it by theorists such as Hobbes or Hume, Williams, Gibbard, or myself. Hence, many contemporary philosophers compete to stress and to extol the external nature of reasons, their shining objectivity.[2]

The other phenomenon is that of the inescapable 'normativity' of means-ends reasoning. Here the irrationality of intending an end but failing to intend the means is a different shining beacon. It is that of pure practical reason in operation: an indisputable norm, again showing a sublime indifference to whatever weaknesses people actually have, and ideally fitted to provide a Trojan horse for inserting rationality

---

[1] I should say that I have misgivings about the term, and usually find myself wanting to put inverted commas around it. I believe Fodor has said that 'cows go "moo", but philosophers go "norm"', and I incline to agree.

[2] Broome, J. 2004. 'Reasons', in R. J. Wallace *et al.* (eds), *Reason and Value: Themes from the Moral Philosophy of Joseph Raz*, Oxford: Clarendon Press, 28–55; Dancy, J. 2000. *Practical Reality*, New York: Oxford University Press; Nagel, T. 1970. *The Possibility of Altruism*, Princeton: Princeton University Press; Parfit, D. 1997. 'Reason and Motivation', *Proceedings of the Aristotelian Society*, Supplementary Volume 71, 99–130; Raz, J. 1975. *Practical Reason and Norms*, London: Hutchinson & Co. Ltd; Raz, J. 2003. *The Practice of Value*, Oxford: Clarendon Press; Schafer-Landau, R. 2003. *Moral Realism: A Defence*, New York: Oxford University Press; Wallace, R. J. 1999. 'Three Conceptions of Rational Agency', *Ethical Theory and Moral Practice*, 2, 217–42.

into practical life. If the means-end principle is both unmistakably practical and yet the darling child of rationality itself, then other principles of consistency or of humanity, or of universalizing the maxims of our action, can perhaps follow through the breach in the Humean citadel that it has spearheaded. And so we get the dazzling prospect that if people who choose badly are choosing against reason, then this can be seen to be a special and grave defect. It would locate the kind of fault they are indulging. It would give us, the people of reason, a special lever with which to dislodge their vices. Being able to herd knaves and villains in a compound reserved for those who trespass against reason and rationality therefore represents definite progress.

It is sad to have to spoil the party, but I fear that these apotheoses of reason contain much less than meets the eye. Ethics is given no new light, nor is its armoury in the least strengthened, nor is its status beyond anything dreamed of by Hume remotely established, by these contemporary enthusiasms. In fact, the massive amount of work that has gone into the coronation of reason has been almost entirely misdirected.

II. Moving the Mind

Clearly we should not start by being deluded by the noun, thinking of reason as a kind of magical faculty or structure. We should start with the relation. Reasons are reasons *for* something: the primary datum is relational. The field of the relation is less clear, or rather more diffuse. Propositions are reasons for propositions, facts are reasons for intentions and desires, some intentions are reasons for others. Actions have reasons and one action may be another person's reason for a different action. But corresponding to each of these and other relations there is a potential movement of the mind, a movement *guided* by the first mental state, and *issuing* in the second, when the reason is accepted or operative. So when we talk in the abstract of one proposition being a reason for another, or a fact being a reason for a norm or decision, the field is one of abstract representations corresponding to potential movements of a mind so guided. The movement in question might be one from one cognitive state or a true belief state to another: this is when we talk of theoretical reason. Or it might be one from the apprehension of a fact about a situation to an action or a desire or the formation of a motive or intention: this is when we talk of practical reason. We can also include movements that have action itself as their terminus, if we wish. A movement might also be that from a plan or an intention, or the supposition that a policy is settled, coupled with belief about the means that are open, to the postulation or adoption of a strategy for realizing the intention. A particular movement of the mind might therefore consist in Sally noticing that there is a mouse under the chair and inferring that the cat is somewhere around, or noticing that her scratching the blackboard is distressing Molly and then, guided by this thought, supposing she should continue.

The notion of guidance is intended to suggest the difference between taking one thing as a reason for another, and being subject to some kind of free association in which one thing leads to another, but not by a process of reasoning. It is the difference between thinking that a restaurant is expensive, and for that reason going elsewhere, and finding (either consciously or unconsciously) that the restaurant reminds you of an evening long ago with your mother-in-law, and finding yourself going elsewhere. Since the relationship between reasoning and causes of behaviour is puzzling, it may be hard to say in what the difference consists, and there will certainly be cases that are neither clearly one nor the other. Psychologists in Newcastle found that in weeks when a picture of eyes looking at subjects was added as a kind of banner headline to a poster indicating suggested prices for coffee, in a communal coffee room, the amount stumped up in the honesty box went up by nearly three times compared with weeks when a neutral image of flowers was substituted.[3] Is this a case of free association between a cue suggestive of being watched, leading to an unconscious fear of exposure, or is it a case of unconscious reasoning, triggered by that same cue, from the possibility of being watched to feeling you should not be a free rider?

A related distinction holds between movements with which the agent himself is comfortable, or which he endorses, and movements that the agent either does not consciously know about, or might wish away. This is close to Gibbard's distinction between accepting a norm and being in the grip of one.[4] Thus someone in the grip of a fetish or a compulsion might be said not to have a reason for doing what he does, but only find himself caused to do it, as if by some outside force. But he could equally be said to have had a reason for acting as he did. Plato's Leontius, who had a shameful thing about recently executed corpses, found himself sufficiently gripped by the consideration that there were corpses to be seen to go and see them.[5] He may have felt as if he were doing so 'almost' against his own will. But we can properly say that he had his reason for going. What we will not say is that the fact that there are recently executed corpses somewhere is *actually* a reason for going and looking, unless we wish to commend the process, for instance to medical students. For the purposes of this paper I shall mostly be concerned with conscious sensitivity to the starting point and to its tendency to steer the movement of mind in question, rather than with subliminal or subdoxastic forces which may or may not be counted as giving reasons.

By an abstract representation I mean simply that we can leave out mention of actual agents and their actual states of mind, and contemplate the guidance purely in the abstract, considered as a relation between truths, or one between truths and possible intentions or desires. We can say, for instance, that the fact that an action

[3] Bateson, M., Nettle, D., and Roberts, G. 2006. 'Cues of being watched enhance cooperation in a real-world setting', *Biology Letters*, 2, 412–4.

[4] Gibbard, Allan. 1990. *Wise Choices, Apt Feelings*, Cambridge, Massachusetts: Harvard University Press.

[5] Plato, *Republic*, 439e.

is distressing people is a reason for desisting, or the fact that there is a dead mouse under the chair is a reason for inferring that there is a cat around. It is often difficult to frame such abstract relations without a *ceteris paribus* clause, since the particular circumstances of particular cases may nullify the reason. If you keep a pet mink a dead mouse may not be a reason for inferring the presence of a cat, and if someone has no business being distressed because what you are doing is harmless, there may perhaps be no reason to desist. Nevertheless the abstract generalization may be a useful general guide, even when it is liable to exceptions.

Some philosophers insist that the actual and potential movements of the mind must start from genuine cognitions, or even facts. I shall mostly defer to this usage, in which a false belief or a misapprehension does not provide a reason for anything. We might say that it does not provide a *real* reason for anything, although unfortunately some people take it to do so. I do not entirely like the stipulation, since it forces us to say that people who through little or no fault of their own misapprehended the facts and inferred or acted accordingly had no good reason, or no real reason, for what they did. And that sounds harsh, for they may not have been at all irrational, after all. They certainly had *their* reasons for what they did, and they may have acted well in the light of them. The general who is misinformed by a normally reliable source about the disposition of enemy troops, but who then plans well accordingly, is only unfairly accused of having had no reason for what he did, unlike the one who has proper information and then thoroughly botches his plans. The second might be court-martialled for acting irrationally or for no reason, but surely not the first. Similarly the victim of hallucination taking himself to perceive a rat in the drawer acts reasonably enough in then shutting it, although his movement of mind does not start with apprehension of a fact. However, nothing important hinges on this stipulation in what follows and we could in these cases follow the course of saying that there were after all 'factive' reasons in play: not the fact of the enemy troops being thus-and-so, nor the fact of the rat's proximity, for these were not facts, but the fact that the informant reported as he did, or the fact that it looked as if there were a rat there. Similarly, in the Newcastle case we cannot say that the subjects reasoned from the fact of being watched, but we might choose to say that they reasoned from the fact that there is a possibility of being watched.

Of course aims and intentions as well as apprehensions provide reasons. Sally's reason for scratching on the blackboard may be to annoy Molly. If we say, as no doubt we should, that this was a bad reason, what we say is unfortunately ambiguous between negatively evaluating Sally's intention, and negatively evaluating the means she adopted to realize it, for instance if we approve of Sally's mischief but Molly was unfortunately out of earshot. It is important to distinguish these since they impute quite different faults to Sally. It would matter, for instance, if we are wondering whether to employ Sally to annoy Molly in the future.

When we say that the field of reason is that of movements of the mind, we must include *failures* to move as the kind of thing which excites verdicts of reasonable or the reverse. Gordon may be unreasonable in ignoring Jack's interventions, or failing to pick up Molly's signs of distress. This is just an instance of the way in which more generally we criticize failures to act as well as positive actions.

So what are we saying about the actual or potential guidance of the mind? We say that p is a reason for q or that the fact of x is a reason for doing y when we think it is good to infer q from p, or to be moved towards doing y upon apprehending x. By invoking the relation we *commend* or *endorse* the kind of guidance of the mind that it indicates. Molly's distress is therefore a reason for Sally to stop scratching the blackboard. Movement from apprehension of that distress to her stopping would be a good movement of Sally's mind. It would be good even if in fact Sally does not know about Molly's distress, or does not care a jot about it, or is actively enjoying it. It would be good even if Sally could not implement it, perhaps because of some kind of ingrained insensitivity or some equally ingrained and immovable determination to ignore or humiliate Molly. The reason for Sally to stop is just there anyway—it is Molly's distress—and Sally, or a slightly improved version of Sally, can apprehend it by normal perception. But this does not imply that she needs nothing more to apprehend it *as* a reason for stopping. She may or may not be guided by it. If she is, we say she is being reasonable, by way of commending her.

III. A Blind Alley

An agent's blindness or malformation may prevent a good reason for a movement from being *her* reason for doing anything. When we describe *her* reason, we are simply producing a fact about her and the explanation of her states—the way her mind was guided. It has nothing to do with how it would have been good for her to be guided. When agents not only are not moved but cannot be moved in the right direction, they are still liable to criticism, and this is the sense in which reasons are external. This in turn means that there is absolutely no need to follow Bernard Williams' regrettable move of making the contingent profiles of *actual* concern of an agent determine what is to be said in the context of evaluation. This is so even if, like Williams, we expand the domain of an agent's actual concerns to include an idealized set of concerns, the ones to which they could deliberate in ways they themselves approve. Thus when Williams considers an agent who is a confirmed wife-beater and who has not got sufficient internal resources to deliberate to a better way of being, he finds it difficult to judge that there is good reason for him to stop.[6] I say instead that there is no difficulty here. There is indeed good reason—excellent reason—for him to stop. *He* sees no reason to stop, and perhaps his mind is too corrupt or impoverished ever to be guided in that way, or even for him to comprehend improvement in this

---

[6] Williams, B. 1995. 'Internal Reasons and the Obscurity of Blame' in *Making Sense of Humanity*, Cambridge: Cambridge University Press, 191.

respect. Nevertheless, it would be better if he did. Some may be optimistic enough to suppose that all human beings have enough resources within them to come to adopt, as their reason for acting, anything which actually is a reason for acting. It is a nice, pious, hope, but our language and our thoughts are far from presupposing that at the outset. There need be no optimistic assumption that any agent can be moved by any reason.

With this understood, this whole debate between 'internalists' and 'externalists' in the theory of reason collapses. Externalists were right that reasons are just there anyway, for the starting points of guidances of the mind are there anyway— i.e. regardless of whether particular people notice them, or could bring themselves to move in good directions because of them. But this is an entirely hollow victory, for internalists remain right that it is only in the light of the contingent ways we are that we can instance movements, and just as obviously it is only in the light of the contingent ways we are that we commend and endorse them. So the phenomenon is of no interest to the debate between Humeans in the theory of motivation and value, and others.

IV. Kinds of Guidance

We should notice that it is the *kind* of guidance that we are commending, not its end-point nor its consequences. It may be a pity that Sally came to believe that the cat was around, because her project was to decapitate it, although her reason for believing it was the perfectly good one that there was a dead mouse under the table. It may be good that Cedric brought Sally flowers on her birthday, even if his reason for doing so was the bad one that they would exacerbate her allergies. You can move in a bad way but get to truths, and to doing the right thing or the fortunate thing. And conversely, you can move well, but be moving to falsehoods, and to doing the wrong thing or the unfortunate thing, although we should accept that there are some destinations so bad that nothing could count as a good journey ending up with them: an intention to commit genocide, for instance.

In the case of theoretical reason, our sense of how truths relate to each other gives us our standards for good or bad movements. Of course, it is not entirely easy to describe the relations behind these standards. But we know the general pattern. The premise p makes q more probable, or q provides the best explanation of p or the simplest or only plausible explanation of p. The gold standard, of course, is that p could not be true without q being true, but few movements of the mind are guided by relations that meet the gold standard, except in logic lecture rooms and mathematics classes. In most cases we have to settle for less, or, if we use the modal term it may be because we are operating under a tacit contextual assumption that some possibilities are too outlandish or irrelevant to take into consideration. When we settle for less, we may only want to say that in the circumstances p was a good enough reason for assuming q, and here the circumstances may determine not only the probability of *q* being false, but the gravity of getting it wrong and the cost of investigating further. It may only correspond to a good movement of the mind if nothing much hangs on it. This touches upon the relation between alethic standards and pragmatic ones, an area in which there is a clear difference between the 'right' kind of reason for believing something, and the 'wrong' kind of reason, such as the advantage in doing so. A similar distinction arises in practical reasoning, where it hinges on the difference between a reason for admiring something, which is on account of the way it merits or deserves admiration, and an extraneous or 'wrong' kind of reason, such as strategic or political reasons for doing the same. The difference lies in the kind of movement of the mind in question. If we are egging someone on to admire something because it will be politic to do so, we are not commending the kind of movement that takes in only the relevant properties the thing possesses—those we take to be indicators of merit—and is guided to admiration on their account. It is if, but only if, we were prepared to commend this kind of movement we would say that the thing merits or deserves admiration. But if we see advantage in admiring it, for instance in becoming one of the club or sneaking a financial return, we are only hoping for a particular endpoint, and the only movement of the mind that is commended is one that takes account of the advantage and sets about gaining it. In the alethic case there are deep issues here, going to the heart of pragmatism, about the connections between success in action on the one hand and a general cognitive ability to represent the world on the other. However, they do not concern us in this paper.

In the case of practical reason, the widest standards are those for evaluation in general. In saying that Molly's being in distress is a reason for Sally to desist, I commend or endorse or express approval of the movement of mind in which Sally takes in Molly's distress and as a result desists. This is entering an ethical judgement. I will have my own reasons for it: I hold that things go better if people are guided like this. If I go further and say that it is a decisive reason or a compulsory reason for Sally to desist, then I do not merely commend the movement, but insist upon it or regard it as compulsory, and stand ready to censure Sally if she fails to move the the the appropriate way.

In standard cases of succumbing to temptation, we can be described, albeit unhelpfully, as being unreasonable. Seeing the situation as it is, and judging which action is best to perform given how things stand, and then doing the other thing, will generally (although not always) be an instance of a bad or inferior movement of the mind; that is, a case of being unreasonable.

If life were simple, the virtue of reason would simply be a matter of moving well, one dyadic relation at a time. But of course it is not. Many considerations clamour for attention; many movements which would otherwise be good are nullified or outweighed by others. The *phronimos* or person of judgement and practical reason needs not only sensitivity to reasons one at a time, but a capacity to amalgamate them, weigh them, and prioritize them. The better he does this, the more reasonable we allow him to be.

Since movements of the mind, in the generous sense we have given ourselves, occupy so much of the territory of ethics, it should be little surprise that Scanlon's project of 'buck passing', or seeing talk of good and bad, right and wrong, obligation and trespass, as verdicts entered in terms of 'reasons', might be feasible.[7] Nor is it surprising that Michael Smith can urge the sovereignty of the ideally rational self, since this will just be the self whose mind moves exactly as it should.[8] But of course, the takeover is merely nominal. For all we are given are moves within the ethical. We are not provided any independent methodology, or independent underwriting of the ethical as a domain. The suggestion we have been following out tells us nothing about the authority of these verdicts on good or bad practical movements of the mind. It merely uses the judgements themselves. If, for instance, we were troubled by objectivity before, we will be troubled by it after. For in spite of any contrary appearance, this talk of reasons imports no new standards and no new buttress for whatever standards we deploy.

V. Unkindness to Animals

Derek Parfit writes that 'Other animals can be motivated by desires and beliefs. Only we can understand and respond to reasons.'[9] But we now see that this is not so. That there is a snake in the path is an excellent reason for me to step aside. But it is also an excellent reason for my dog to step aside, and the dog will probably do so every bit as quickly as me. The dog responds to the reason with an alacrity more than matching my own. Parfit had earlier said, correctly, that 'reasons for acting are facts that count in favour of some act' (121), and on this occasion the dog understood and responded smartly to one of those, the fact that counted in favour of jumping aside, just as I did.

Parfit probably did not intend to deny, as he actually did, that the dog responds to reasons. The tenor of his discussion, as of many others, is that we ourselves are not just responding to the presence of the snake, but to some 'normative feature' of the snake or in other words a further evaluative or deontic fact about the situation of its being in the path, a halo or nimbus of normativity beatifying the union between the presence of the snake and a subsequent sidestep, a radiance to which Parfit, but not the dog, can respond, and in which he can beautifully bask. Needless to say, this is pure fantasy. The position of the snake can be quite sufficient to set one's legs racing. We do not need to respond to anything more or anything different; indeed, since speed is probably of the essence, we need not do so. There is no time for extra processing.

---

[7] Scanlon, T. M. 1998. *What We Owe to Each Other*, Cambridge, Massachusetts: Belknap Press.

[8] I do not in this paper highlight any differences between 'rational' and 'reasonable'. Pruned of theoretical accretions I think they come to little more than, as Edward Craig once put it to me, being reasonable just means being reasonably rational.

[9] Parfit, D. 1997. 'Reason and Motivation', *Proceedings of the Aristotelian Society*, Supplementary Volume 71, 127.

And since stepping aside is highly appropriate, this is a good movement of the mind, and equally so for the dog. We could, if we wish, give *some* meaning to saying that we, but not the dog, see the snake as a reason to jump aside. If this is to mean more than that we are disposed so to act, a property we share with the dog, it must be along the lines of our satisfaction with the movement, or willingness to endorse it and recommend it for similar occasions, or in other words our own positive valuation of our own conduct. This is all that separates Parfit, basking, from the dog. If we put them in the negative and said rather that we do not regret the movement or feel ashamed of it, or inclined to apologize for it, then once again the dog and we are on all fours, since it too feels no regret or tendency to apologize. Perhaps a young mongoose would feel some proto-version of these emotions, were its sidestep derided for cowardice by its mongoose mentors. But not the dog, and we share everything essential to walking with equal safety through the forest. Hence, there is nothing about our thoughts conducted in terms of reasons that affords any evidence at all for speciesist intuitions.

Do we gain anything by subscribing to the thesis that if an agent has a reason to do something and is properly aware that the reason obtains, then they must be motivated to do it 'on pain of irrationality'?[10] First, notice that it is not very apparent how severe this pain is: Sally and her mischievous ilk can evidently put up with it quite contentedly. If we want to improve Sally by threatening pain, it had better be of a different sort. And most people find it sufficient to call children like Sally naughty, insensitive, mischievous, careless, callous, or even wicked, while after all it was the pain the snake might cause rather than any other imagined pain that explained our sidestep. We thought 'Oh heavens, it might bite me' rather than 'Oh heavens, how horrid to be irrational'. The invocation of irrationality is not an improvement, but an abstraction that washes out the interesting textures or particular contours of individual cases of vice and virtue. We would of course like Sally's mind to move in better ways. We would like her to take Molly's distress to guide her more reliably, and in the reverse way than it evidently does at present. We have familiar devices of persuasion and argument. 'How would you like it if Molly did the same to you?' we might ask. Perhaps Sally does not mind the sound of fingernails on the blackboard, but Molly can reciprocate by playing her bagpipes, which annoys Sally just as much. Sally wouldn't like it at all. We hope that thinking about that will motivate her to stop. But it may not. She can gamble on the kind and forgiving Molly not playing her bagpipes, or gamble on her parents stopping her if she does. Or, she can expect Molly to play her bagpipes, and be getting her own strike in first. Or, she can usually beat Molly in a fight. Or, she knows she may have to pay for her fun later, but still finds it irresistible to be naughty now. So we might try rubbing Sally's nose in Molly's distress, hoping to activate empathy or pity, and thence remorse and a better frame of mind. But perhaps we fail. It was, after all, the prospect of Molly's distress that excited Sally's mischief in

---

[10] Wallace, R. J. 1999. 'Three Conceptions of Rational Agency', *Ethical Theory and Moral Practice*, 2, 218.

the first place. Suggesting that it is Sally's 'rationality' that is at fault now looks simply like a *deformation professionelle* that afflicts moral philosophers, rather than an open road to new proofs of Sally's wrongness, or new therapies for bringing her back to the straight and narrow. It is in this vein that Bernard Williams scoffed at that *ignis fatuus* of moral philosophy 'the argument that will stop them in their tracks when they come to take you away'.

VI. The Authority of Reason

A problem area that now clears up nicely is that of the 'authority' of reason, a problem some writers have found in 'Humean' proposals about motivation and desire. In the leading paper on this theme, Warren Quinn urged that there is a basic issue between rationalists such as himself, and 'subjectivists' or 'noncognitivists'.[11] Although I disown the labels, he clearly has in mind expressivist and in general naturalistic approaches to ethics of the kind that I favour. He writes that:

The basic issue here is more fundamental: whether pro- and con-attitudes conceived as functional states that dispose us to act have any power to rationalize those acts.

He points out that bizarre, pointless, functional states (such as a disposition to switch on any radio that I find not to be on) do not 'give me even a *prima facie* reason to turn on radios'. The disposition may explain how I am, but by itself it cannot make any resulting act of turning on a random radio sensible. And after rejecting any attempt to invoke higher-order states, such as pro- or con-attitudes to the having of this first-order disposition, to help with this problem, he concludes that in themselves dispositions such as tendencies to try to obtain things or to feel pained by things do not 'rationalize' choices. Even choices of means to given ends are not rationalized unless the ends themselves are, and only a genuine cognition of the objects of choice as 'good' could do that. Parfit enthusiastically takes the same line.

It seems strange to say that a movement towards, say, eating a proffered piece of pie is not 'rationalized' by my occurrent hunger, so we need to take a closer look at this line of thought. First of all, which movement of the mind is in question? One proposal would be that it is from an awareness of a desire to a tendency to satisfy the desire. But that is not the typical case. When acting on a desire we are not typically self-reflective, taking a fact about ourselves as our starting point.[12] Rather, we take in a fact about our situation, and our desires are functional states manifested in the relationship between the fact we apprehend, and the tendency towards action which

---

[11] Quinn, W. 1995. 'Putting Rationality in its Place' in Hursthouse, Lawrence and Quinn (eds), *Virtues and Reasons: Philippa Foot and Moral Theory*, Oxford: Oxford University Press.

[12] In *Ruling Passions*, I call this the 'leading, characteristic mistake of a whole generation of theorists wanting to go beyond Hume', and ten years later I can add around a third of a new generation. See *Ruling Passions*, Oxford: Oxford University Press, 1998, 254.

results. As the desire for food, hunger is manifested in the way in which a tendency to take the pie issues from and is guided by an awareness that it is being proffered. Does the desire, then, 'rationalize' the tendency? It explains it, in whichever way dispositions may be said to explain their manifestations. But Quinn is indeed right that it does not by itself show that the movement of mind is either good or bad, admirable or despicable, and so does not fund evaluative talk in terms of reason or rationality. That is not its job. However, all that shows is that Quinn's demand that desire *should* validate or rationalize choice was entirely misplaced. To enter on the enterprise of arguing that a movement of the mind was a good one is a different business. To do this one has to step back, and see if one can fit the movement into whichever practices in the area one endorses, or at least shares or understands or accepts as immune to criticism. The compulsive, oddball desire, such as the addiction to turning silent radios on, is pointless, and potentially costly and irritating. So of course we are not inclined to endorse the movement of the mind from awareness of a silent radio to the motivation to turn it on, that manifests the compulsion.

Quinn and Parfit may have thought that if particular desires cannot 'rationalize' themselves, then nothing in our conative dispositions, taken as a whole, could do so either: the picture is that the Humean world is one with 'normativity' bleached out of it. This would be a dangerous form of argument, whose weakness is more familiar from discussions of coherentism and foundationalism as they apply to cognitive states. While many writers accept that a belief cannot validate itself, they tend to suppose that its membership of a sufficiently coherent set may do so. Or, if other things than beliefs are allowed into the justificatory pool, they may include things like processes and actions, such as the engagement of perceptual processes in causal interaction with the world, or the experiences resulting from such engagement. If this begins to paint a satisfactory picture of cognitive justification—which it had better do because it is really the only game in town—then a parallel story can do a parallel job for practical dispositions, first invoking a whole matrix of surrounding dispositions, and then potentially invoking experience of the way those dispositions stand the test of time, as they are tried out in human practice. These together provide the only tribunal that a single desire could ever face. In other words, although we can stand apart from any particular desire or disposition, and consider the good of it in the light of other desires and dispositions, taken as a whole, there is no process of standing back from all of them at once, any more than there is in the case of belief.

Someone with Quinn's orientation might try urging that so long as this is 'just us', it can only tell us what we actually value, but not what *is* of value. But little is gained by denigrating the only methods we use, or could use. Insisting upon a wholesale cleavage between 'fact' and 'value' at this point would not so much be protecting the autonomy of the normative world as making it on the one hand immune to awareness, and on the other hand of no conceivable interest. It is in fact only philosophers' illusions, not valuations and norms, that are bleached out of the Humean world.

VII. Open Questions

Nevertheless, the contemporary enthusiasm for reasons suggests that, in many minds, the substitution of the sovereignty of the good by the sovereignty of reasons is to be not just a change of idiom, but a change of regime. It is to open the way to a new dawn of philosophy, a new dispensation, and new philosophical territory to occupy and explore. It is important therefore to consider the view that by moving onto the territory of reason we are, actually, moving. I suggest that the only remaining temptation to think this arises because of the possibility of an 'open question' akin to Moore's famous open question about goodness. However, in this application this question opens not between goodness and some natural property, but between reason and goodness. Thus if everything I have said is true, a critic may complain, how can there be the open and difficult question of whether it is always reasonable to be good? How can there be an issue, for instance, of whether reason might sometimes demand a sacrifice of goodness, in favour of such competing candidates as self-interest? How could we so much as worry whether reason stands on the side of prudence and self-interest, or on the side of justice or benevolence or the common good?

The question is very real, and fertilizes the idea of reason as a particular kind of authority, a self-standing normative structure magnificent enough to be used to measure and assay even the claims of virtue themselves. But I want to explain this open question differently.

For since 'reasonable' and its clan are general terms of commendation, like other such terms they can take on a particular cast. They can be confined to commendation within a subset of possible dimensions. This happens whenever we talk of 'good for (the economy, the crops)' or 'good from (the point of view of the banks, the farmers)', and in the same way we talk of reasons of state, economic reasons, reasons of health, personal reasons, or strategic reasons. In chapter XVIII of *The Prince* Machiavelli notoriously claims that the Prince sometimes has overwhelming reason to behave cruelly and inhumanely, treacherously and in bad faith. In short, he must behave badly. The dimension within which the commendation is given is simply that of his own survival, and Machiavelli notoriously thinks that when that competes with conventional goodness not only does it win in men's actual conduct, but it is necessary that it should. Here what the Prince has most reason to do is not what is best: the movement of mind that is commended may be crafty, deceitful, treacherous, and inhumane. He has to be these things (while appearing not to be) in order to survive.

All this is in accord with our proposal. The point is that the crafty and strategic movement of mind is indeed *commended*. It may not be being commended in conventional terms—that is why Machiavelli prompted such shock and gained his dark reputation—but it is commendation within what he regarded as the most important dimensions of statecraft, namely survival and success. The example generalizes. Whenever anyone describes a potential conflict between reason and virtue, what we find is that reasons are restricted to within a dimension, and the question is whether wider, more humane virtues of justice or benevolence need curtailing because of the insistent demands of that dimension.

So we can open the question whether it is always reasonable to be good, not because reason is an autonomous lawgiver at some unspecified distance from the good, whose injunctions have their own authority, yet ones that may conflict with the injunctions of virtue or obligation. We open it, for instance, when we explicitly or implicitly worry about the old and uneasy conflict between self-interest and the other-regarding virtues. In an ideal world, perhaps, we could commend each without ever ranking them, for they march in step. But in the real world, and in spite of the optimism of some classical philosophers, any coincidence between them is a fragile business; servants of the world are not necessarily good trustees of their own interests, and indeed it is a political achievement to bring them into anything resembling an alignment. Machiavelli thought that in the Italy of his time, no such alignment obtained; hence, reasons of state had to trump better-known virtues, and the ideal prince had better be aware of that ugly fact.

To solve this we cannot appeal to the autonomous court of reason. We can only walk around our own moral and ethical thought, and then campaign for whatever resolution appeals to us.

VIII. Means and Ends

We now turn to the much-discussed issue of means-ends reasoning, which is so frequently paraded as a prize specimen of 'practical rationality', a normative constraint of almost divine authority, and even a Trojan horse to insert into the citadel of naturalism. If Humean naturalism cannot even account for the majesty of this norm, then it is indeed in trouble.

It may be worth remarking that Kant did not think of it like that. Kant thought it is *analytic* that if we will the end we will what is known to be the only means to it:

In the volition of an object as my effect, my causality as acting cause, that is, the use of means, is already thought, and the imperative extracts the concept of actions necessary to this end merely from the concept of a volition of this end...when I know that only by such an action can the proposed effect take place it is an analytic proposition that if I fully will the effect I also will the action requisite to it; for it is one and the same thing to represent something as an effect possible by me in a certain way and to represent myself as acting in this way with respect to it.[13]

One can see why he might have thought that if we consider the problem of interpretation offered by the agent who might at first sight seem to intend (which I shall use as synonymous with 'will') an end, yet shows little or no inclination to adopt what he knows to be necessary means. It is at least plausible that we cannot be sure *where he*

---

[13] Kant, I. 1785. *Groundwork of the Metaphysics of Morals*, Royal Prussian Academy Edition IV, 417.

stands on the issue.[14] Does he really intend to meet me for golf, if he said he would, but has not bothered to collect his clubs or put gas in his car? Perhaps he said so, but if he is comfortably resting in front of the TV as the necessary time ticks away, interpretation falters. Kant only says that if we *fully* will the end we intend the means, and that seems about right. Our friend's intention may be half-hearted; or his knowledge of the necessary means may be insufficiently robust, as when he knows that the time at which he might have got himself to the course has gone, but 'hopes that something might turn up'. What is clear is that we cannot rely on him; we do not know where he stands on the project of playing golf, and perhaps he does not either, and probably there is no determinate reality about where he does stand. Socially he is a thundering nuisance, since on the basis of his apparently sincere say-so, we turn up, only to find he is not going to be there.

A norm of action is something to which we can conform, or fail to conform. But if Kant is right then there is a difficulty about failing to conform to the 'norm' of means-ends rationality. It cannot be done. There is, however, a cluster of very closely related norms, and indeed our errant golf partner exhibits what it is to fail to conform to them. He is a nuisance, as already noticed. He is incapable of following through on apparent commitments, for communicating an intention on which the audience is likely to rely as normally undertaking a commitment. He is weak-willed, in the sense properly made prominent by Richard Holton, and that builds on Michael Bratman's path-breaking discussions of the virtue of diachronic consistency in aims.[15] All that is sufficiently serious, as we all know: 'No man, having put his hand to the plough, and turning back, is fit for the Kingdom of God.' But what remains unclear is whether there is a more specific 'norm' of means-ends rationality, against which he has trespassed, or against which anyone can trespass. It is here that Kant's doctrine stands in the way.

There is much to say about the logic of this area, but I shall be brief. First, a preliminary warning: we should notice something treacherous about our habit of introducing apparent reference to states of mind, such as desires or intentions, into the antecedent of such means-ends conditionals. In the context of deliberation, the most the conditional can easily be heard to mean is that if we are to *achieve* the end, we have to intend the means; that is, in a normal world in which the end is to be achieved, such-and-such is the plan to adopt. In the context of deliberation 'if we *want* him to come we have to write a letter', 'if we *would like* a good time we had better not go to Torremolinos', or 'if we *wish* to get home tonight we had better leave now' would normally be taken to have as antecedents *not* states of mind, but their satisfaction: we could equally or better have put it by saying that 'if he is to come...', 'if we are to have a good time...', or 'if we are to get home...' The reference to wants, intentions, or wishes

[14] I gratefully adopt this useful expression from Michael Bratman.
[15] Bratman, M. 1987. *Intention, Plans, and Practical Reason*, Cambridge, Massachusetts: Harvard University Press; Holton, R. 1999. 'Intention and Weakness of Will', *Journal of Philosophy*, **96**, 241–62.

is, in my view, an incidental way of indicating *why* we are interested in planning for those outcomes, rather than an integral way of specifying the condition in question itself. There is no inference, no movement of the mind, from the recognition of a state of mind itself to a demand or plan, but only an inference from the presumption that an end is to be achieved, to proposing a plan for achieving it. Such auxiliary mention of intentions, wants, or wishes may also get into the consequents of conditionals. I might say 'if you are to do the washing up, you will want to wear an apron' when I suppose that (a) you are to do the washing up, (b) you do not want to do it, and (c) you do not and will not want to wear an apron either. The conditional does not induce contradiction, because the mention of a want is incidental to its real content, which is to recommend that if you are to do the washing up, wear an apron.

The logic of the area is bedevilled by problems of 'factual detachment', made prominent in deontic logic by the paradox of gentle murder (Forrester's paradox). Consider the inference:

> If you murder someone, then you ought to murder them gently
> You murder someone
> Hence: you ought to murder them gently
> Hence: you ought to murder them.

The problem is how to interpret the first premise so that the conclusion does not follow, firstly by a simple application of modus ponens, and secondly by the principle that if a specific ought to occur then its generic ought to occur.

The solution is to consider closely the way we naturally formulate the conditional. We might better say: 'if you *are to* murder someone, you ought to do it gently'. The activity is one of *supposing* that the end is given, and then recommending means, and this is a quite different activity from that of assessing the pair of <ends/means> together.[16] *In the deliberative context*, the goal is being taken as given, just as in a three-horse race the advice to sell an evens bet on Canter if Galloper scratches only becomes 'live' or actable-upon if Galloper scratches. I think the best way of putting this is to say that the conditional proposes a plan: a plan of what has to be done or is best to be done either to bring about the nearest normal world in which the end is achieved, or to do something else in that world.[17] The question of whether it is a good idea to achieve this end simply does not enter in, any more than when we say 'if the giant slime is coming, flee for your lives!' we express any attitude either to the probability or the desirability of the giant slime coming, or of any complex that has this as a component. The English variant closest to the Latin is perhaps more perspicuous here: *when* you murder someone, you ought to murder them gently.

---

[16] I believe this was first made clear in Thomason, R. 1981. 'Deontic Logic and the Role of Freedom in Moral Deliberation' in R. Hilpinen (ed.), *New Studies in Deontic Logic*, Dordrecht: Reidel.
[17] I talk of the closest normal world, following Bonevac, D. 1998. 'Against Conditional Obligation', *Nous*, 32.

In the context of deliberation, the conditional 'if we murder someone, then we ought to do it gently' is a perfectly acceptable recommendation of a plan for the nearest normal world in which we are in fact to murder someone. Much better do it gently! The 'ought' of planning detaches. The plan is conditional upon an antecedent being something which *we are to do*: it is only when or if we are to murder someone that we should follow the plan to do it gently. This is most obvious when the murder is unavoidable or irrevocable: the assassins we employed are on their way and beyond recall, but we can somehow get a painkiller to the victim before they arrive, so that is what we ought to do.[18] But mere supposition or postulation of the end *takes us to the same deliberative context* as actual irrevocability. Incidentally, the consequent is detachable even if the murder is not irrevocable or inevitable; it may be still under consideration, and the consequent only detached, in the way that any consequent is detached in a formal argument, potentially en route to a reductio or a modus tollens. Finding that we have no way of murdering the victim gently, we might renege on the plan to murder him at all.

All this is the context of deliberation. To repeat, in that context, the conditional 'if we intend E we ought to do M' signals the endorsement of a plan of action M in the normal world in which we are to perform or bring about E. Nothing is said about whether it was a good idea or morally acceptable, or inevitable or anything else, to have the intention itself. A consequence of deliberations in which the conditional works just as conditionals normally do (sustaining modus ponens, opening the way to modus tollens) may be to make it clearer than before that we had better abandon the intention itself. And in that context, 'if we intend the end, then we ought to intend the means' is clearly a good principle. 'To get the closest normal world in which the end is to be achieved, plan on using the means.' Of course you should, and if Kant was right you must, on pain of forfeiting your claim genuinely to intend the end.

But this does not imply that when we switch to the different context, that of external judgement, we need to see anything good either about having the intention, or about using whichever means the intention requires if it is to be fulfilled. In the paradox of gentle murder the premise 'you murder someone' tells of a state of affairs, removing us from the context of deliberation and putting us into one of assessment of the whole state of affairs. And it will remain that you did something you ought not to have done: the conclusion no longer follows.

Although the language of reasons can be used carefully, so that the necessary distinctions are maintained, it makes it very easy to get all this wrong. Thus consider the question whether Iago's villainous intention to destroy Othello 'provides a reason' or 'provides a normative reason' for him to manufacture lies about Desdemona. We naturally recoil from saying that it does: we do not want to hear ourselves recommending anything about Iago's end, nor the means he adopts. On the other hand Iago

---

[18] Setiya, K. 2007. 'Cognitivism about Instrumental Reason', *Ethics*, 649–73.

does his planning impeccably; having turned his hand to the plough, he does not turn back, even if he is ploughing the wrong field. How are we to combine our out-and-out rejection of Iago's intention and its handmaidens, with acknowledgement of his abilities as a planner?

Fortunately, we have ample ways of saying what needs to be said. There are two terrible things to say about Iago: he had villainous ends in view, and he chose villainous means to execute them. There is one, perhaps grudging, good thing to say about him: he is an able planner. When he contemplated and intended the closest normal world in which he is to effect Othello's destruction, he planned efficiently and as it turns out successfully to bring it about. If we imagine instead an Iago who (at least apparently, if we remember Kant) intends Othello's destruction, but does little or nothing effective to execute it, then things are reversed. There is one bad thing to say about him—he is not an effective or efficient planner—and two slightly better things can be said than are to be said in the Shakespearean scenario: first that he does not set up Desdemona, and second that his intention to destroy Othello seems relatively insecure or half-hearted. It is a mistake to try to shoehorn all these, and perhaps more, distinctions into the one verdict on whether Iago did or did not have a 'normative reason' for his behaviour, or any part of it. The language simply will not bear the complexity of the distinction between the perspective of deliberation and that of external assessment, and it also encourages inattention to the crucial difference between description of Iago (given in terms of his reasons for doing one thing or another) and endorsement of one or another facet of the movements of his mind.

A conflation that assists in confusing this issue is that the conditional 'if we intend the end we ought to intend the means' can sound as if the antecedent locates a state of mind, and then it looks as if the issue is to be whether our having that state of mind provides some sort of reason for supposing that we 'ought', perhaps in some strong ethical sense, to intend the means. And that sounds in general outrageous: how can we bootstrap ourselves into having reasons, or even obligations, so easily?

But as already argued, in the context of deliberation the apparent reference to a state of mind is incidental. There is no inference from a state of mind to a plan, but only a supposition that something is to be done, to the conditional selection of a plan for doing it. And with this the appearance that means-ends rationality or means-ends normativity provide a problem for Humeans, a shining jewel that they cannot pick up, and hence that gives theorists an incentive to mine for others, disappears.

IX. The Plasticity of Reason

If we throw away attention to the particular nature of people's flaws, preferring a blanket diagnosis of 'unreasonable' or 'irrational' whenever their minds move in ways we think inferior, we not only lose important textures and distinctions, but we also lose most chances of engagement and improvement. For 'unreasonable' and still more 'irrational' not only function as general terms for denigrating the movement of people's minds. They usually have further, sinister connotations that the defect is irredeemable, that it is not sensitive to discursive pressure, that it licenses us to treat the subject as a patient or in other ways as beyond the human pale, or out of the game. Let us return to errant Sally. We can say, of course, that Sally is irrational or unreasonable—her mind is guided in bad ways. What we cannot do is invest the term with more interest than it gains from gesturing at the more specific and insightful descriptions of the particular flaws that infect Sally's character. But if we are to improve Sally, it is her particular flaws that need particular attention. We might want to cherish Sally a little more, be careful how we praise Molly when Sally is present, be more careful of providing opportunities for envy and jealousy, and so forth. In harsher climates, we might have wanted to frighten or bribe her. Whatever rationalists, intuitionists, realists, Kantians, or Platonists may say, these are the only tools anyone has. But using them, we may win in the end. Sally may not be irredeemable after all. For one implication of all this is that reason is every bit as pliable as sentiment.

Bibliography

Bateson, M., Nettle, D., and Roberts, G. 2006. 'Cues of being watched enhance cooperation in a real-world setting', *Biology Letters*, **2**, 412–4.

Bennett, Jonathan. 1974. 'The Conscience of Huckleberry Finn', *Philosophy*, **49**, No. 188.

Blackburn, Simon. 2005. 'Success Semantics' in Hallvard Lillehammer and D. H. Mellor (eds) *Ramsey's Legacy*, Oxford: Oxford University Press.

Bonevac, D. 1998. 'Against Conditional Obligation', *Noûs*, **32**:1.

Bratman, M. 1987. *Intention, Plans, and Practical Reason*, Cambridge, Massachusetts: Harvard University Press.

Broome, John. 2004. 'Reasons' in R. J. Wallace *et al.* (eds), *Reason and Value: Themes from the Moral Philosophy of Joseph Raz*, Oxford: Clarendon Press, 28–55.

Cowley, Christopher. 2005. 'A New Defence of Williams's Reasons-Internalism', *Philosophical Investigations*, **28**:4, 346–68.

Dancy, J. 2000. *Practical Reality*, New York: Oxford University Press.

Fitzpatrick, W. 2004. 'Reasons, Value, and Particular Agents: Normative Relevance without Motivational Internalism', *Mind*, **113**, 285–318.

Foot, P. R. 1978. 'Reasons for Action and Desires' in Joseph Raz (ed.), *Practical Reasoning*, Oxford: Oxford University Press, 178–84.

Grice, G. R. 1978. 'Motive and Reason' in Joseph Raz (ed.), *Practical Reasoning*, Oxford: Oxford University Press, 168–77.

Holton, R. 1999. 'Intention and Weakness of Will', *Journal of Philosophy*, **96**, 241–62.

Kant, I. 1785. Royal Prussian Academy Edition, IV, 417. Also H. J. Paton (ed.), *The Groundwork of the Metaphysic of Morals*, New York: Harper Row.

Korsgaard, C. 1986. 'Skepticism about Practical Reason', *Journal of Philosophy*, **83**, 5–25.

Korsgaard, C. 1996. *The Sources of Normativity*, Cambridge: Cambridge University Press.

Lewis, D. 1996. 'Elusive Knowledge', *Australasian Journal of Philosophy*, **74**.

Nagel, T. 1970. *The Possibility of Altruism*, Princeton: Princeton University Press; reprinted 1978.

Parfit, D. 1997. 'Reason and Motivation', *Proceedings of the Aristotelian Society*, Supplementary Volume 71, 99–130.

Plato. 2008. *Republic*, translated by R. Waterfield, Oxford: Oxford University Press.

Quinn, W. 1995. 'Putting Rationality in its Place' in Hursthouse, Lawrence, and Quinn (eds), *Virtues and Reasons: Philippa Foot and Moral Theory*, Oxford: Oxford University Press.

Raz, Joseph. 1975. *Practical Reason and Norms*, London: Hutchinson & Co. Ltd.

Raz, Joseph. (ed.) 1978. *Practical Reasoning*, Oxford: Oxford University Press.

Raz, Joseph. 2003. *The Practice of Value*, Oxford: Clarendon Press.

Scanlon, T. M. 1998. *What We Owe to Each Other*, Cambridge, Massachusetts: Belknap Press.

Setiya, K. 2004. 'Against Internalism', *Noûs*, 38, 266–98.

Setiya, K. 2007. 'Cognitivism about Instrumental Reason', *Ethics*, 649–73.

Shafer-Landau, R. 2003. *Moral Realism: A Defence*, New York: Oxford University Press.

Smith, M. 2004. *The Moral Problem*, Oxford: Blackwell.

Suikkanen, Jussi. 2004. 'Reasons and Value—In Defence of the Buck-Passing Account', *Ethical Theory and Moral Practice*, 7, 513–35.

Thomason, R. 1981. 'Deontic Logic and the Role of Freedom in Moral Deliberation' in R. Hilpinen (ed.), *New Studies in Deontic Logic*, Dordrecht: Reidel.

Wallace, R. J. 1999. 'Three Conceptions of Rational Agency', *Ethical Theory and Moral Practice*, 2, 217–42.

Wallace, R. J. 2002. 'Scanlon's Contractualism', *Ethics*, 112:3, 429–70.

Wallace, R. Jay et al. (eds). 2004. *Reason and Value: Themes from the Moral Philosophy of Joseph Raz*, Oxford: Clarendon Press.

Williams, B. 1979. 'Internal and External Reasons', reprinted in *Moral Luck*, Cambridge: Cambridge University Press, 1981, 101–13.

Williams, B. 1995. 'Internal Reasons and the Obscurity of Blame' in *Making Sense of Humanity*, Cambridge: Cambridge University Press.

Wong, D. 2006. 'Moral Reasons: Internal and External', *Philosophy and Phenomenological Research*, 72, 536–58.

Introduction to Mary Warnock's Lecture

Ted Honderich

Baroness Mary Warnock is known to philosophers mainly for the books *Ethics Since 1900* (1960), *Existentialism* (1970), *Imagination* (1976), *The Intelligent Person's Guide to Ethics* (1998), *An Intelligent Person's Guide to Ethics* (2004), and *Dishonest to God: On Keeping Religion Out of Politics* (2010). She has taught in the Oxford and Cambridge women's colleges Lady Margaret Hall, St Hugh's College, and Girton College. She is known to the wider world for public service having to do with reasoned committee reports bearing her name, on human embryos, euthanasia, education, and animal experimentation. It has been said, by me, truly, that she gives the great and the good a good name.

What is natural and what isn't? What is unnatural or against nature? And what follows from the answer about what is to be done?

There have been religiously inclined conceptions of nature, as in the case of Prince Charles connected with organic farming. It has been opined that we need always to go with the grain of nature. There have also been politically or indeed morally inclined conceptions in the case of reactions on behalf of Indian peasants and other reactions to genetically modified non-replicating and otherwise objectionable seeds. Heidegger, who did not ever reject his Nazi past or at any rate connections, objected to the technology that commodifies what should instead be our *dwelling* in nature. Bernard Williams concerned himself with an intrinsic good of nature. There have also been our widely shared and indeed common ideas and feelings about nature of a Romantic kind—vernal woods and our experience and poetry of them.

It is Warnock's inclination to ask for more in objections having to do with the unnatural in connection with developments in science and technology. She remarks that we need to depend not on principles of sensibility, for example, but on principles of sense. We need these principles with respect to dark anticipations at the present time that are like earlier anticipations that had to do with Hiroshima and the discovery of DNA. We need to think more about *human* reproductive cloning in particular. We need to think more in our new situation that began with the cloning of Dolly the sheep.

Put aside what is quite different, therapeutic cloning, in short a use of cells in treatment. Perhaps instructively, not much objection to this having to do with the unnatural is made—unnatural in some sense though it obviously is. What are we to think about human reproductive cloning? It wouldn't be natural in any sense that comes to mind quickly, would it, for a child to come into the world by non-sexual means? A child, that is, who as a result of biotechnology inherits its makeup from only one person rather than two, a child having a genetic inheritance from only that one person.

Suppose that you do agree—do give the *natural* answer in some sense—that the fact of the child's having only one parent in the given sense wouldn't be natural in some sense. Is that a moral argument against it? That is the principal particular question considered in the lecture. It is an impressively reflective instance of the genre of applied ethics, which began to have that name in about 1982.

If this question of morality or more clearly of right and wrong can be introduced by way of considerations of legality, it is as certainly different from legality, as needs to be asserted regularly. One thing is easy enough about this reproductive cloning. In the foreseeable future of science, this will be wrong. It will be wrong on the simple and great ground of risks to the cloned child—clear enough just on the small facts of the life of Dolly the sheep, who had things wrong with her.

But suppose the day comes when there are not those risks. Can we now say that human cloning will still be wrong on the ground of being unnatural? There are weak considerations here, one being that the cloned child would be being denied a human right to personal identity. There is the stronger consideration of possible consequences with respect to the general good or bad of society, anticipated in Aldous Huxley's *Brave New World*.

It is argued by Mary Warnock, with respect to whether any cloned child would suffer, that here too an answer must be speculative. It is remarked by her that we would in a way be being natural in taking benefit from the cloning researchers, who like all of us are part of human nature. You will need to consider for yourself her philosophically judicious words.

Is it the gravamen of the lecture that considerations of the natural are in serious thinking unlikely to outweigh or even be challenges to a reflective and contentful principle of right and wrong? You could look into the question by way of what was mentioned earlier, that intelligent person's guide to ethics.

10

What Is Natural?
And Should We Care?

Mary Warnock

In the present climate of rapidly developing biotechnology we repeatedly hear demands to call a halt. Science, we are told, is going too fast. Neither our moral sense nor our sense of order and familiarity in the world can keep up. Even scientists sometimes advocate caution, and those who are not scientists beg biologists not to do things that are 'unnatural' or 'against nature'. In what follows, I want to consider some of the various meanings that may be attached to such appeals. Should they be taken seriously? Does the designation of something as 'unnatural' constitute a moral argument against it? This is a complicated problem of cultural meaning; but it is of more than theoretical importance. For the moral beliefs of non-scientists are increasingly held to have a proper place in determining public policy with regard to the regulation of science. It is thought that politicians must take such beliefs into account in deciding what science may or may not be permitted. It is therefore essential to examine this element in popular moral thought to see whether it contains anything of substance.

In the *Treatise of Human Nature*, when looking for the 'general principles upon which our notions of morals might be founded', David Hume raised the question whether such principles were connected with Nature. But he went on to remark that this depends what we understand by Nature (*Treatise* Book III, part I, section II) 'than which', as he said, 'there is not a word more ambiguous and equivocal'. Pointing out that the natural may be opposed to the unusual or to the artificial (a dichotomy of which he famously makes use in his analysis of the virtues) he also notes that it may be opposed to the miraculous, in which case, as he agreeably says, 'every event that has ever happened in the world, excepting those miracles on which our religion is founded', is natural. In this sense whatever biotechnology can do, however hitherto unthought of, is natural. No law of nature is breached by their procedures. Rather those who manage to do new things, such as making a clone of a whole animal, are discovering new laws unknown before, governing, for example, how cells divide and differentiate. Yet, in the layman's pejorative sense, there could surely be few things as unnatural as nonsexual reproduction. For despite Hume's apparently neutral observations, it has to be acknowledged that whatever is the opposite of 'natural' readily takes on a sense of something suspect, not to be trusted. Think of 'artificial silk', that widely despised material of the 1930s. Or, of course, 'unnatural vice'. Unnatural here does not mean simply unusual, still less miraculous.

It is this layman's pejorative sense that needs to be examined, for it is this sense that expresses the attitude of the non-scientist towards biotechnology. Let us look for a start at the Reith Lectures of the year 2000, for the first time a series of lectures from different speakers, each followed by a public debate. The title of the series was *Respect for the Earth* (published in paperback in 2000 by the BBC and Profile Books Ltd).

Among the contributors was the Prince of Wales, whose words have been widely quoted. He spoke from a broadly theistic position, though he acknowledged that those who did not accept the traditional idea of God could nevertheless share his view. I think that, as a matter of fact, it is at least much easier for lay people to make their point against the biologists if they do believe in God, or are at least prepared to use the concept of God as a kind of metaphor. At any rate, the Prince said 'it is because of our inability or refusal to accept the existence of a Guiding Hand that nature has come to be regarded as a system that can be engineered for our own convenience, or as a nuisance to be evaded and manipulated, and in which anything that happens can be fixed by technology and human ingenuity.' He allowed that the idea of stewardship, that human beings have a God-given and sacred duty to look after Nature, though part of the Judaeo-Christian culture, has been held, explicitly or implicitly, by many who do not subscribe to the idea of a divine creator. The stewardship idea was confirmed in a pronouncement from the Vatican in December 2001 which stated that 'man has a right and a duty to act within and on the created order, making use of other creatures to create the final goal of all creation: the glory of God through the promotion of Man'. So the steward does not look after Nature for its sake, but for his own. Following Fritz Schumacher, the Prince drew a distinction between the science of understanding and the science of manipulation. He called upon biologists to seek, if they wished, to try to understand Nature, but not to attempt to intervene in it. He asked that scientists show a greater respect for the genius of Nature's designs, being careful to 'use science to understand how nature works, not to change what nature is, as we do when genetic manipulation seeks to transform a process of biological evolution into something altogether different'. And finally he spoke eloquently about the need to 'work with the grain of nature' to improve agricultural techniques that have 'stood the test of time', rather than attempt a genetic revolution by means of the genetic modification of seeds or crops. Here speaks the voice of those who are emotionally devoted to organic farming, or those who see genetically modified food as a threat regardless of whether there are any proven dangers in any specific GM food. Such people very often slip into the language of theology. They may not wish to prove the existence of God by an appeal to the beauties and intricacies of Nature, but they take for granted that evidence of the hand of God and the Natural are one and the same. Think of Pope's *Essay on Man* (Epistle III, lines 147–48), where he expresses this common eighteenth-century view:

> 'Nor think in NATURE'S STATE they blindly trod
> The state of Nature was the reign of God'

In another contribution to the Reith Lectures, an Indian woman, Dr Vandava Shiva, a director of the Research Foundation for Science, Technology and Ecology at New Delhi, spoke passionately about the way that globalization and the sale of GM seeds to Indian farmers has impoverished farming, and destroyed the ancient tradition of women's contribution to biodiversity. Women used to grow vegetables and herbs in their gardens, to feed their families; and they used to sell produce at local markets, thus ensuring the continuity of crops grown from natural seed. They have now been side-lined, and driven out of business. The patenting of new seed by international companies, forcing farmers to buy new seed each year, has driven these farmers into terminal poverty and suicide. In the general discussion after the lectures, she was praised by some for her appeal to the ancient wisdom of women and the land, but criticized by others for her assumption that Indian farmers had no choice but to buy the new GM seeds marketed by international companies; and criticized by others again for her patronizing belief that the peasant-farmer way of life should be preferred to any possible increase in affluence and civilization. Leaving on one side the specific problems of poverty in India, what emerges here is a strong political rather than religious element in the preference for the 'natural' over the 'unnatural'. And as a matter of fact this has always been so.

Even the theistic words of the Prince of Wales are, after all, extraordinarily close to those of Edmund Burke, who, in his *Reflections on the Revolution in France*, argued that the elevation of Reason brought about by the Enlightenment answered to 'abstract systems of the human mind rather than the truths of Nature'. 'By a constitutional policy', he wrote, 'working after the pattern of Nature, we receive, we hold, we transmit our government and our privileges in the same manner in which we enjoy and transmit our property and our lives.' He is speaking of the British system of government; but he could equally well have been speaking of our traditional system of land-ownership and farming.

Again, Heidegger, who increasingly towards the end of his life became preoccupied with the revelation of True Being to be found in what he called 'dwelling' (wohnet), regards modern technology as a possibly fatal threat to this revelation of truth. In his *Discourse on Thinking* (1955) he said 'We can say "yes" to the unavoidable use of technological objects, and we can at the same time say "no" insofar as we do not permit them to claim us exclusively and thus to warp, confuse and finally lay waste to our essence.' Modern technology, he argues, turns everything into a commodity, what he calls a 'standing reserve'. When the Rhine is dammed so as to become a power-plant it becomes essentially a water-power supplier, deriving its essence from the power station, not from its existence simply as a river. Even if people still regard it as a river in a landscape, it is admired only by groups of tourists ordered to look at it by a travel agency, a commodity for use by the tourist trade. His ideal of dwelling is a farmhouse in the Black Forest, built some two hundred years ago as the dwelling of peasants. 'Here the self-sufficiency of the power to let earth and heaven, divinities and mortals, entering the simple oneness into things, ordered the house'. Here we may notice not mere nostalgia, but a strong whiff of folk-worship and the Fatherland, of belonging to one's ancestral past and the non-welcome of aliens. Commenting on this passage the critic Jonathan Bate (himself no stranger to the idea of 'dwelling' and the worship of the Earth) speaks of the disturbing connexion between ecologism and extreme right-wing politics which, he says, may be traced back into the nineteenth century to social Darwinism and 'the co-presence in the later work of John Ruskin of a prescient ecological awareness and an atavistic neo-feudalism.' Heidegger himself never repudiated his Nazi affiliations. And without recourse to accusations of Nazism, it is easy to recognize and indeed to understand the paradox which is rooted in romanticism, the longing for a private and sheltered sense of 'oneness' with nature, and a belief that such 'dwelling' reveals a profound truth which is, and should be, available to all.

And so it is extremely difficult in current discussions of genetic modification, especially of crops and cattle, those apparently essential props in the drama of natural country life, to separate those arguments that turn on the alleged intrinsic evils of the practice from those that rely on the supposedly harmful effects on the environment, and from those that are straightforwardly political. Arguments coming roughly from the Left turn into arguments against capitalism and its inevitable exploitation of the poor; those from the Right confuse what may be genuine fears with a kind of Golden-Ageism, a longing for a bygone time of small farms and self-sufficient peasants, keeping their places in a hierarchical society and believing in a beneficent Divine Order.

Of course to discover a close connexion between general environmental fears and political opinions is not to make any great discovery: everyone knows that a concern for the good of the environment that looks to benefit not only present but future generations (sustainable development) and a concern with social justice and the relief of poverty are both of them political aims, even if not always wholly compatible. But I believe it must be said that it is not only those whose political sympathies are with the Right who retain a longing for the idea of Nature left alone, a kind of hankering for Wilderness. We may not wish to share the values of Heidegger, but I believe there are few who do not, even if guiltily and secretly, share those of Wordsworth who, after all, in the Prelude described his wife, Mary, as 'Nature's Inmate', as having, that is, Nature as her Dwelling. The idea of Nature is for many of us haunted by the ideas of the imagination, of sublimity and the recognition of immortal longings in ourselves. And with these aesthetic ideas, causing us, in Kant's words, 'to reach out to that which can never be adequately expressed', a reaching out which is at the heart of all creative imagination and all art, goes a feeling of respect or love for Nature itself.

Bernard Williams has written about this (see, for example, 'Must a concern for the environment be centred on human beings?' in *Making Sense of Humanity,* Cambridge University Press, 1995); and so, more recently, has David Wiggins ('Respect for Nature' in *Proceedings of the Aristotelian Society,* New Series Vol. 100.2000). In his article, Wiggins refers to 'what we care about independently of our own interests but have difficulty in characterizing in such a way as to cause it to impinge on public policy proportionately to its importance' (Wiggins, p. 8). If we lament, with Heidegger, the disappearance of the Natural it is because, in Wiggins' words, we lament the disappearance 'of all sorts of things human beings have loved and delighted in, and might still in the future love or delight in, with the option to find indefinitely many other such things for whose loss we could scarcely imagine ourselves being compensated' (Wiggins, p. 10).

At the heart of the intrinsic value of Nature, and perhaps at the root of our love for it, is that we value it, and it does not care for us. We love it as we love another human being whom we know is not our slave. Mary Midgley in her book *Beast and Man* (Routledge, 1978) quotes from Iris Murdoch's *The Sovereignty of Good* (Gifford Lectures, 1970), where she describes the lifting of her spirits as she watches a hovering kestrel. Mary Midgley says 'If we found we were in Disneyland with plastic kestrels going up at carefully randomized intervals the entire point would be lost'. And she ends with these words 'We need the vast world, and it must be a world that does not need us... a world we did not programme, since only such a world is the proper object of wonder.' This wonder arises not only from the fact that the natural world long predates humanity, but, as we have learned to understand, its laws are discoverable and gradual in their operation. We did not make them. In the metaphor of religion 'It is He that hath made us and not we ourselves.' The Romantic idea of nature is something that we cannot, and most of us would not want to, disburden ourselves of. There is a sense of the word 'nature' in which nature is the source of our greatest pleasures and insights and which gives meaning to our lives.

Nevertheless I think we should resist the temptation to found a campaign against science on principles of sensibility rather than sense. So it is time to return to the fears that scientists are going too far against Nature. We must examine some of these fears to see whether they must be described as fears of the unnatural or whether they, or some of them, can be justified without reference to Nature and its grain; or, if not justified, then laid to rest.

There are those, such as Dr Barry Commoner in the United States who published a report on Genetically Modified Crops at the beginning of 2002, who believe that biologists have made an enormous mistake. What they plan to do by altering the genes of crops may or may not be 'unnatural'; what is certain, they hold, is that it will not work. For a plant's own genes will be disrupted by being modified, and therefore any artificially changed genetic system will inevitably give rise to unforeseen and unforeseeable consequences. This in turn will lead to economic disaster. Here, then, is an economic or utilitarian argument against genetic modification, which has no need to have recourse to the concept of Nature. Similarly, in this country there is an increasing tendency to encourage 'greener' methods of farming, on a smaller scale, contrary to the Common Agricultural Policy, which encourages quantity at the expense of quality. This sort of campaign, which the Prince of Wales incidentally strongly supports, is based on economic considerations rather than on the fear of interfering with the natural order.

But I shall say no more about the genetic modification of crops. For, though I believe this to be a subject of enormous importance, it is an area where it is extremely difficult to sift out the arguments whose centre is the idea of nature from those that are either economic or more broadly political. Instead I shall turn to some developments in medical research where protests against the unnatural are most frequently to be heard.

Nowhere has the fear of biological scientists been more articulate than in the matter of mammalian cloning. It is perhaps instructive, as a start, to compare this fear with the generally shared fear of the new developments in physics in the 1940s and 50s.

Non-scientists understood nothing of the research that had gone on into what was known as 'splitting the atom'. But the expression itself held terror. Was it not a contradiction? Was not the atom, as Lucretius had taught, the ultimate indivisible component of the physical world? Were not the laws of Nature being overturned? And then after Hiroshima in 1945, though many of us felt guiltily relieved that the war was over, we quickly realized that the destruction of 75,000 people by the dropping of a single bomb was something that could be repeated (and this tally of destruction took no account of the long-term damage to those who survived, the nature of which only gradually became clear). We were frightened of the future, seen starkly in terms of a choice between the survival and the elimination of the human race. It was this fear that lay behind the campaign to Ban the Bomb. Banning the Bomb turned more moderately into the policy of nuclear containment; and this was only a more up-to-date version of the kind of international programme for securing peace that had been familiar since the end of the First World War, though the stakes were higher. It was to be a matter of international negotiation, in the hope that everyone in the world would see that it was in their own interest to seek peace in a self-denying way. How much longer this policy is going to hold we cannot say, but for a longish time it worked and our fear more or less receded, while even non-scientists became accustomed to the thought that physics had changed since the days of Lucretius, and that the so-called atom was not an indivisible little lump of stuff.

The fears that lie behind the demand to inhibit the advances of the biological sciences by regulation and prohibition, though generally as anti-scientific as those fears half a century ago, are in some ways different. They are more moralistic. They are not fears of instant destruction but of more insidious and gradual changes whose outcome is harder to foresee or define. They are for the most part not fears that stem from the possible outrageous ambition and unscrupulousness of national leaders, but rather from the demands of an apparently insatiable market, ready to go to any lengths to have what have become known as Designer Babies, changing society, so the timid believe, in fundamental but unpredictable ways. Moreover our post-enlightenment reliance on the laws of nature seems more radically undermined by biotechnology even than it had been by our having to rethink our outdated ideas of the laws of physics.

The great symbol and expression of these biotech fears is to be found in Mary Shelley's *Frankenstein; or the new Prometheus*, published as long ago as 1818, in which she deliberately sought, as she said, to 'speak to the mysterious fears of our nature, and awake thrilling horror'. In this she certainly succeeded. The thrilling horror was of the misuse of technology to create a life that would be beyond control, and also deeply unhappy. This story is more myth than science-fiction, a deeply shared cultural myth that lives on into the twenty-first century.

The myth, like all myths, encapsulates something deeply rooted in human psychology. It catches the public attitude towards the life-sciences. As early as the 1920s, Julian Huxley foresaw the vast powers that biology was about to have at its disposal: 'At present', he wrote, 'we do not know how to produce genetic mutations, but the belief that we shall eventually be able to do so underlies our work; and once we have discovered the way, our knowledge of the laws of heredity will enable us to build up improved races of animals and plants as easily as the chemist now builds up every sort and kind of substance in the laboratory' (*Essays in Popular Science*, 1926). And then in 1932 came a new myth, giving body to this eugenic speculation, Huxley's younger brother Aldous' *Brave New World*, a myth which spoke as powerfully to our fears as Frankenstein, but depicting this time a world in which lives could be created and controlled by Government diktat, to serve supposedly Utopian ends (ending in equal unhappiness).

As soon as the discovery of DNA was known to the general public, in the early 1950s, speculation was rife as to whether new forms of life would be created, as Julian Huxley had predicted, by altering DNA. Frankenstein's monster and the brave new world were constantly invoked: the concept of genetic engineering had been born, and it went against the grain of a culture retaining many of the ideas of Nature learned in the century before, both the romantic idea of Nature as our dwelling, and the Darwinian idea of species, including the species Man, evolving gradually, according to the laws of natural selection, ideas which had on the whole settled down together to cohabit harmoniously in a largely secular world.

In the light of these past horrors, I want now to look at the public reaction to the prospect of human cloning, the latest in the line of things held to be 'against nature'.

Cloning is the form of nonsexual reproduction in which all the offspring are genetically identical to each other and to the parent from which they are derived. All the identical organisms are collectively a clone; and each individual in the group is a clone of all the others. Many plants, such as strawberries, for example, reproduce both sexually by seeds and also by putting out suckers and thus producing plants that are extensions or clones of the parent plant. (Human beings have of course long interfered with Nature by taking cuttings of plants to form clones.) Mammals as well as plants may clone naturally but by a quite different process, when a single embryo divides in the uterus to form identical twins (or, with two divisions, identical quadruplets). But it takes radical intervention to produce the clone of a mammal in any other way.

Research has been going on for many years to investigate the possibility of artificially cloning animals, with a view to providing a quick way to reproduce a particularly successful strain of cattle or sheep. Fifty years ago the biologist John Gurden took the nuclei out of frogs' eggs and transferred intestinal cells from an adult frog to replace the nuclei, and succeeded in producing tadpoles. However, these tadpoles did not develop into frogs. Later, using cells from tadpoles to replace the nucleus of the egg, he managed to produce tadpoles which matured. But it was easier to work with frogs and salamanders which have large eggs, and where fertilization takes place outside the body, than with mammals. Indeed for some time it was believed that mammalian cloning by nucleus-transfer was impossible. Then in 1997 the birth of Dolly was announced, the sheep who had been cloned from the cell of an adult sheep by scientists at the Roslin Institute, outside Edinburgh. This was a genuine break-through.

The method used was to take a mammary cell from an adult ewe (a Finn Dorset variety in this case) and culture it in the laboratory so that it multiplied. Meanwhile an egg was taken from another ewe (this time a Scottish Blackface) and its nucleus was extracted by means of a pipette. The whole cell of the first ewe was then inserted into the 'shell' of the enucleated egg, and the egg was exposed briefly to an electric current which made it fuse to form an embryo (known as a 'reconstructed embryo'). This embryo was a clone of the Finn Dorset sheep, though it still had a small amount of DNA belonging to the Scottish Blackface whose egg had been used. This was contained in the mitochondrial cells lining the 'shell' of her egg. These cells are few in number, but are significant, in that they can be the cause of serious illness if they mutate. They pass only through the female line. So Dolly, though a clone of the Finn Dorset sheep, had a few genes from the Scottish Blackface, and was thus not a strictly identical clone, as identical twins are. So far, only female mammals have been cloned.

Reconstructed embryos are extremely fragile and transferring them to the uterus of the surrogate mother who is to carry them to term is a matter of great difficulty. At the Roslin Institute, 277 reconstructed embryos were produced, and 29 of them, apparently in good condition, were transferred to 13 potential surrogates. But the result was only one viable lamb.

As soon as Dolly's birth was announced the inevitable question arose: If sheep, why not humans? Is there any reason, in principle, why human cloning should not be carried out? This would probably be the most radical intervention in the course of nature so far contemplated. After all, even in vitro fertilization, the forming of an embryo in the laboratory rather than in the human body (which Aldous Huxley had imagined, and seen as the end of the family), is the result of sperm fusing with egg; cloning, in contrast, does not involve sperm at all. It is a wholly new and manifestly 'unnatural' way of producing an embryo. Would it for this reason be intrinsically wrong?

In trying to answer this question, it is necessary to take some time to consider what has happened to cloning since the birth of Dolly, the first mammalian clone.

There is first an important distinction to be drawn between reproductive cloning and so-called therapeutic cloning. Reproductive cloning, as I have explained, results in the birth by surrogate of a clone animal, the result of cell nuclear transfer. Since 1997, many cloned animals have been born, some of them having had their genes engineered at the point of nuclear transfer. For example five cloned piglets have been produced with a type of genetic modification that may make possible the use of pig organs for human organ transplant without rejection. In humans reproductive cloning would have as its aim the nonsexual production of a complete human baby.

Therapeutic cloning, on the other hand, uses only the first part of the techniques of reproductive cloning. When an embryo is first formed, the cells which make it up are undifferentiated; that is, it is not yet determined how they will develop to become one of the 200 or so specific types of cell that make up the human body (though there is evidence that even at the earliest stage there is a difference between those cells that will be at the top and those that will be at the caudal end of the embryo as it develops). However, the undifferentiated stem cells of the embryo in the laboratory can be induced to differentiate into specific types of cell, and the cell-lines thus developed can reproduce themselves for ever. So cell-banks can be built up, for example of skin-cells, which, it is hoped, can be used for cell transplant. This would be more effective than organ transplant, and could be used for replacing damaged cells in the brain or the spinal cord, where organ transplant is not possible. At present scientists are only beginning to discover how cells start to differentiate or how they can be induced to differentiate into specific cell-types. It is for this research that cloned embryos are tools. It would defeat the purpose of research into the possibility of cell transplant if the embryo produced were allowed to develop beyond the stem-cell stage where the cells had begun to differentiate; that is, four or five days of embryo-life. In the UK, in accordance with the Human Fertilisation and Embryology Act 1990, embryos of less than 14 days' life may be used for research and then destroyed. The 1990 Act permitted this use only for purposes connected with fertility and infertility. The permitted use has now been extended in scope to cover 'therapeutic cloning'.

It was generally believed that permitting such research did not permit human reproductive cloning, which, it was thought, had been explicitly ruled out by the 1990 Act. However, in November 2001 a test case was brought to the High Court by a group opposed on moral grounds to any research using human embryos, and who were convinced that the Act did not rule out reproductive cloning. And on November 15th Mr Justice Crane found that embryos created by cell nuclear replacement were not covered by the Act, indeed that as the Act stood they should not count as embryos at all. For the relevant part of the Act refers to 'Live human embryos where fertilization is complete'. It should not therefore be taken to include embryos produced otherwise than by fertilization. Now in 1984, when the Report of the Committee of Inquiry was published on which the 1990 Act was based, creating an embryo by cell nuclear transfer was thought to be impossible. It was assumed that the only way to create an embryo was by fertilization of egg by sperm. So in the light of the then knowledge the words 'when fertilization is complete' were otiose, and indeed did not appear in the committee's Report, but only in the Act. If they had not been added in the Act, all embryos, however produced, would have been covered by the prohibition of cloning. But with the new method of producing embryos those produced otherwise than by fertilization were held by the judge to be, by implication, excluded from the prohibition.

As soon as this judgment was handed down, an excitable Italian, Professor Antinori, announced his intention of coming to England to avail himself of the loophole, with an English colleague and 200 women who, he claimed, had offered their services as surrogates. He boasted that there would be a cloned baby within a year. The Government were completely thrown by this threat, and rushed through legislation in the minimum possible time, to prohibit the insertion into a woman's uterus of an embryo created by cell nuclear replacement. This is now a criminal offence in the UK, as it is in most of Europe. Professor Antinori is continuing his experiments in, as far as is known, Kentucky.

But it is time to consider the morality as opposed to the legality of human reproductive cloning. For the foreseeable, and I believe for any imaginable future, the attempt to clone human beings would be morally wrong, on the grounds of risk and uncertainty. No one should be permitted to subject their fellow human beings to such risks, even if they have volunteered to become part of the trial. After all, those who desperately want children are genuinely desperate, and might be prepared to accept risks which in a more rational frame of mind they would see as unacceptable. Such people should not be exploited by inquisitive scientists or ambitious doctors. Apart from the vast numbers of embryos that were created in the attempt to produce Dolly, and the numbers of surrogates used (unthinkable if the subjects were human), it is not yet certain what effects cloning may have on the cloned offspring. Dolly was perfectly formed at birth, though rather large, but showed some signs of premature aging, was overweight and suffered from arthritis in all her legs. She died aged 6 in 2003. I think it quite probable that human reproductive cloning will never be attempted because of the inherent risks to the child. We shall know more of this as more clones of other mammals are produced. This moral argument has nothing directly to do with the unnaturalness of the method of producing the clone. It rests on a different principle altogether: that even consenting human beings should not be used for risky experimental purposes unless, I suppose, there are overwhelming reasons for doing so, such as national security. The desire of the subject to have a baby would never afford such an overwhelming reason.

This, however, can be seen as a pragmatic argument, though one, in my view, affording a strong moral case against cloning, as things are. But what of the principle? Supposing that it turned out in some distant future that in parts of the United States, or, say, China, there grew up, as is perhaps quite likely, a demand for human clones, and a desire on the part of scientists or even of governments to press ahead and be first in the field, and if some of the present risks had been overcome, should the cloning of human beings still be prohibited in this country? And if it should, would this be on the ground that cloning was unnatural? It is always difficult to evaluate moral arguments that are in this way hypothetical. In the nature of the case, one cannot tell what it would be like for the risks to be overcome, and it is not clear how valid a moral judgment can be, when it can have no basis in experience. But, as has frequently been observed, since natural clones in the form of identical twins exist and are not regarded with moral horror it cannot be the mere existence of human beings who share identical DNA that causes outrage. Thus, while some have argued that to be born a clone would be to be born without a basic human right, namely to have one's own personal identity, this must be nonsense. For no one believes that identical twins, being physiologically and spatially separate from each other, do not possess personal identity. Even Siamese twins are commonly thought to have separate identities.

Many objectors argue that it must necessarily be wrong to allow a child to be born who is not the offspring of an egg fertilized by sperm, and that to make a child by cell nuclear replacement would be to break the proper connection between the child and two parents of different gender. This is an argument that, indirectly, relies on the concept of nature. For certainly in nature mammals reproduce by the fertilization of egg by sperm, and it is natural for a child to be born thus.

So we are brought back to our original question. Does the fact that something can be intelligibly described as unnatural constitute a moral argument against it? Is the general consensus that to permit human cloning would be to subvert a natural law a sufficient ground for a public policy that would prohibit it? As so often, in the case of framing public policy, one needs to ascertain some facts, facts which here, in the nature of the case, are not available. The evidence on which to base a judgment of public morality would here have to be twofold. First, would the possibility of human cloning be prejudicial to the good of society? If the policy of cloning were widespread, and carried out under compulsion, by the will of Government, in the interests, let us say of purging society of undesirable elements, or of producing armies of obedient citizens, in the manner of Brave New World, then the answer would be 'yes'. Such a policy would be in the last degree harmful, even if, as in Huxley's myth, citizens were given drugs to keep them happy. No human would choose to live in such a society. But if cloning were permitted where, let us say, a couple wanted to start a family, but the man could produce no sperm, or the woman no eggs, then it seems to me that society would not be in any way damaged, any more than it is damaged by the provision of assisted reproduction for the infertile, on a case-by-case basis. Doubtless if everyone preferred to have their children by cloning then there would be a damaging diminution of the human gene pool over a period of time, or so it is argued. But if cloning were something which, like other assisted reproduction, were subject to regulation, and provided on medical grounds, then, at least in a society such as our own, accustomed to regulation and licensing, no harm to society as a whole need be foreseen.

The second kind of evidence needed would be whether or not the child who was a clone would suffer. Here again, the answer must be speculative. But at the present time we are becoming more tolerant of the idea of different kinds of families within which children may flourish. For example, it is widely debated whether homosexuals, male or female, should have access to assisted conception (by means of artificial insemination with donor sperm, or the use of a surrogate mother) if they wish to have and bring up a child. Such a birth would be one which resulted from no direct sexual involvement between mother and father, even though the embryo would have come into existence by means of fertilization rather than cell nuclear replacement. Many people hold that there is nothing morally wrong with such a birth; and indeed that the resulting child may flourish, if his parents are stable and loving. Would the process of cloning be so very different? The crucial thing is that, as soon as they are able to understand, children should know their origins and thus trust their parents. It is deception and concealment that is morally wrong and potentially damaging to children. No argument based on what is natural has any place here; and I cannot myself see that a family formed by cloning, if such a thing were ever feasible, would be very different. The fact that he came into existence through cell nuclear transfer rather than by fertilization need not make a radical difference to a child. Even the fact that she could foresee some respects in which she would inevitably take after her parent need not have too damaging an effect. As things are, children can often predict at least in part what they will be like physically when they are middle-aged. As for qualities of character, it is likely to be forever impossible to predict exactly what is and what is not an expression of shared genes; and if a child saw her mother displaying, let us say, extremes of bad temper, her own determination not to grow up like that might save her from doing so. No one, child or adult, is nothing except her genes. Moreover the environment in which a cloned child would grow up would be in many ways different from that of her parent clone, and this would help to form her. In short, I do not believe that a consideration of the good of the child should automatically rule out cloning in the hypothetical world in which it had become safe. We do not know enough to prohibit it on those grounds. But I believe that for many years each decision to make a clone, if it were ever safe, would have to be made in the light of the circumstances. However much techniques improve, cloning a mammal will always be a laborious and expensive procedure of uncertain outcome. Realistically, it is highly unlikely that it would ever be the preferred way of bringing a child into the world, unless perhaps, as some predict, a disastrous shortage of male sperm made its use necessary to keep humanity going.

To conclude, I have argued that a respect and love for Nature does not provide a valid argument against continued research in the biological sciences. To say this is not to belittle the richness of the concept of Nature. Nature has an intrinsic value, whether we think of it as the field of all our understanding of ourselves and other animals, and plants; or as the source of sometimes ineffable imaginative epiphanies. But we also value the power that the new biotechnology may have to provide medical science with the means to cure or alleviate conditions so far without remedy. We should not seek to bring these different values into conflict through a spurious link with what is Natural.

In any case, there is one sense in which the use of the new technology whether in agriculture or in medicine is far from contrary to the grain of Nature. For man is a part of Nature and his role in the natural world is to improve his environment and to try to ameliorate the ills that threaten the whole species. Hence arises both agriculture and medicine. Of course, as Plato knew, any techne can be used for good or ill; and biotech is no exception. But we have to decide what is for good or ill by other criteria than that of Nature itself, mostly, as is the way with decisions of public policy, by balancing risks against benefits. However difficult this balancing act may be, I believe we should be optimistic, and continue to do our best. It cannot be wrong to welcome the revolution in our ability to alleviate suffering, even if there is a great deal still to be done. We should be grateful to biological scientists, not suspicious of them; perhaps we should even complete Miranda's cry 'O Brave New World that has such people in't'.

Introduction to John Searle's Lecture

Ted Honderich

John Searle attended the University of Wisconsin-Madison and went to Oxford as a Rhodes Scholar. In and away from his base in the University of California at Berkeley, he has been the greatest adversary, surely a victorious adversary, of the philosophy and science of consciousness associated with the computer. Its general expression, as you have heard before now, is in the philosophical doctrine of functionalism. In sum, that is that your now being perceptually conscious or your thinking something or your wanting something is in its nature nothing more than an effect and cause of other things of which only such causal propositions are relevantly true. Searle's lucid books expounding an opposed philosophy include *Speech Acts* (1969), *Intentionality* (1983), *The Rediscovery of the Mind* (1992), *Mind, Language and Society* (1998), and *Freedom and Neurobiology* (2004).

In his lecture he brings the traditional problem of determinism and freedom together with his developed theory of mind and in particular consciousness. The lecture, which fully rewards the attention it requires, brings together at least the following ten propositions, several seemingly inconsistent, as he allows.

(1) Freedom is indeed a problem to be considered within responses to the large problem of the nature of consciousness. It was not adequately treated as a free-standing problem or a problem within morality, let alone religion. (2) Consciousness like all else is *somehow* physical. A principal reason for saying so is that it has physical effects, say arm movements. (3) Consciousness is *different* from the rest of the physical. In Searle's own view, it is a higher-level or systemic biological feature, related to its constituent neural facts in something like the way in which a wheel is related to its constituent molecules. (4) Epiphenomenalism, denying that consciousness itself has effects, such as the arm movements, is incredible.

(5) Both our tendency to determinism, our tendency to take it that there is complete evidence that every event has a sufficient or necessitating cause, that all events are

caused in this way, and our contrary tendency to what is called psychological inde-terminism, a sensing or experiencing or feeling that our decisions and choices could have been otherwise, that they were not effects—both of these tendencies are some-how to be explained. (6) As assumed by Searle here without discussion, we in our lives understand freedom to be *origination*, uncaused choices and decisions, often spoken of as free will, rather than *voluntariness*, choices and decisions not compelled or the like, which are quite consistent with determinism.

(7) Quantum physics proves an indeterminism is right—there are standardly uncaused events down in the microworld. There are *gaps* between events. So there is at least the possibility of our having the freedom of origination. (8) Our reasoning processes, true to our experiencing of them, in fact have those gaps in them, but they can explain our actions anyway—the gaps do not make for epiphenomenalism. There is *rational explanation* of our actions. (9) Our reasoning is bound up with our having or being entities that are selves or egos or rational agents in what is sometimes called a metaphysical sense, not unities of perceptions, thoughts, and feelings, as supposed by Hume and others, including Derek Parfit, the lecturer next to come in this volume. (10) The philosophical problems of determinism and freedom now dealt with, despite further questions and mysteries, leave us with only the problems of freedom in the science of neurobiology, which are far harder.

Determinism has in the past been a principal concern of mine. So I make bold to report my own continuing convictions about the above propositions of the lecture, some of which are thereby thrown into sharper relief.

(1) What is assumed about freedom and consciousness and (2) what may be believed about consciousness as somehow physical are both true. With respect to (3), consciousness is indeed really different somehow or other, but not in being a higher-level or systemic property, which is not its essential or principal distinction. Plainly there are other higher-level or systemic properties. (4) Epiphenomenalism is indeed incredible.

(5) We do need to accommodate to some extents both determinism and our con-trary tendency. (6) Surely we must not ignore the freedom of voluntariness in think-ing of our human condition. Doing so is a little benefit to Searle's thinking, but does not much affect his particular propositions about origination.

(7) An attitude contrary to Searle's is that interpretations or applications of the mathematics of quantum theory to reality are an admitted mess, including con-tradictions etc., and there is no macroworld evidence of real randomness. (8) So I myself remain unpersuaded of gaps inconsistent with determinism. (9) Selves of some kind, or anyway a fact of subjectivity or individuality, but not originating selves or egos or the like, must enter into an adequate theory of our existence. (10) I too suppose that the freedom problem is now one for science, but as a result of what can initially be clarified as *actual consciousness*. I doubt that the scientific problem is harder.

Is philosophy a little more passionate than science, and with more pique in it? I end here by saying that I am now dismayed by a journal article of mine against a predecessor of Searle's lecture, another journal article. I have learned more since, above all from a book I especially recommend to you. Searle's recent *Rationality in Action*, Searle in action again, which enlarges greatly on the lecture.

11

Free Will as a Problem in Neurobiology

John R. Searle

I. The Problem of Free Will

The persistence of the traditional free will problem in philosophy seems to me something of a scandal. After all these centuries of writing about free will, it does not seem to me that we have made very much progress. Is there some conceptual problem that we are unable to overcome? Is there some fact that we have simply ignored? Why is it that we have made so little advance over our philosophical ancestors?

Typically, when we encounter one of these problems that seems insoluble it has a certain logical form. On the one hand we have a belief or a set of beliefs that we feel we really cannot give up, but on the other hand we have another belief or set of beliefs that is inconsistent with the first set, and seems just as compelling as the first set. So, for example, in the old mind-body problem we have the belief that the world consists entirely of material particles in fields of force, but at the same time the world seems to contain consciousness, an immaterial phenomenon; and we cannot see how to put the immaterial together with the material into a coherent picture of the universe. In the old problem of sceptical epistemology, it seems, on the one hand, according to common sense, that we do have certain knowledge of many things in the world, and yet, on the other hand, if we really have such knowledge, we ought to be able to give a decisive answer to the sceptical arguments, such as 'How do we know we are not dreaming, are not a brain in a vat, are not being deceived by evil demons, etc.?' But we do not know how to give a conclusive answer to these sceptical challenges. In the case of free will the problem is that we think explanations of natural phenomena should be completely deterministic. The explanation of the Loma Prieta earthquake, for example, does not explain why it just happened to occur, it explains why it *had* to occur. Given the forces operating on the tectonic plates, there was no other possibility. But at the same time, when it comes to explaining a certain class of human behaviour, it seems that we typically have the experience of acting 'freely' or 'voluntarily' in a sense of these words that makes it impossible to have deterministic explanations. For example, it seems that when I voted for a particular candidate, and did so for a certain reason; well, all the same, I could have voted for the other candidate, all other conditions remaining the same. Given the causes operating on me, I did not *have* to vote for that candidate. So when I cite the reason as an explanation of my action I am not citing causally sufficient conditions. So we seem to have a contradiction. On the one hand we have the experience of freedom, and on the other hand we find it very hard to give up the view that because every event has a cause, and human actions are events, they must have sufficient causal explanations as much as earthquakes or rain storms.

When we at last overcome one of these intractable problems it often happens that we do so by showing that we had made a false presupposition. In the case of the mind-body problem, we had, I believe, a false presupposition in the very terminology in which we stated the problem. The terminology of mental and physical, of materialism and dualism, of spirit and flesh, contains a false presupposition that these must name mutually exclusive categories of reality—that our conscious states qua subjective, private, qualitative, etc, cannot be ordinary physical, biological features of our brain. Once we overcome that presupposition, the presupposition that the mental and the physical naively construed are mutually exclusive, then it seems to me we have a solution to the traditional mind-body problem. And here it is: All of our mental states are caused by neurobiological processes in the brain, and they are themselves realized in the brain as its higher-level or system features. So, for example, if you have a pain, your pain is caused by sequences of neuron firings, and the actual realization of the pain experience is in the brain.[1]

The solution to the philosophical mind-body problem seems to me not very difficult. However, the philosophical solution kicks the problem upstairs to neurobiology, where it leaves us with a very difficult neurobiological problem. How exactly does the brain do it, and how exactly are conscious states realized in the brain? What exactly are the neuronal processes that cause our conscious experiences, and how exactly are these conscious experiences realized in brain structures?

Perhaps we can make a similar transformation of the problem of free will. Perhaps if we analyse the problem sufficiently, and remove various philosophical confusions, we can see that the remaining problem is essentially a problem about how the brain works. In order to work toward that objective I need first to clarify a number of philosophical issues.

Let us begin by asking why we find the conviction of our own free will so difficult to abandon. I believe that this conviction arises from some pervasive features of

---

[1] I am assuming for the sake of this article that the right functional level for explaining mental phenomena is the level of neurons. It might turn out to be some other level—micro-tubules, synapses, neuronal maps, whole clouds of neurons, etc—but for the purposes of this article it does not matter what the right neurobiological explanatory level is, only that there is a neurobiological explanatory level.

conscious experience. If you consider ordinary conscious activities such as ordering a beer in a pub, or watching a movie, or trying to do your income tax, you discover that there is a striking difference between the passive character of perceptual consciousness, and the active character of what we might call 'volitional consciousness'. For example, if I am standing in a park looking at a tree, there is a sense in which it is not up to me what I experience. It is up to how the world is and how my perceptual apparatus is. But if I decide to walk away or raise my arm or scratch my head, then I find a feature of my experiences of free, voluntary actions that was not present in my perceptions. The feature is that I do not sense the antecedent causes of my action in the form of reasons, such as beliefs and desires, as setting causally sufficient conditions for the action; and, which is another way of saying the same thing, I sense alternative courses of action open to me.

You see this strikingly if you consider cases of rational decision making. I recently had to decide which candidate to vote for in a presidential election. Suppose for the sake of argument that I voted for George W. Bush. I had certain reasons for voting for Bush, and certain other reasons for not voting for Bush. But, interestingly, when I chose to vote for Bush on the basis of some of those reasons and not others, and later when I actually cast a vote for Bush in a voting booth, I did not sense the antecedent causes of my action as setting causally sufficient conditions. I did not sense the reasons for making the decision as causally sufficient to force the decision, and I did not sense the decision itself as causally sufficient to force the action. In typical cases of deliberating and acting, there is, in short, a gap, or a series of gaps between the causes of each stage in the processes of deliberating, deciding and acting, and the subsequent stages. If we probe more deeply we can see that the gap can be divided into different sorts of segments. There is a gap between the reasons for the decision and the making of the decision. There is a gap between the decision and the onset of the action, and for any extended action, such as when I am trying to learn German or to swim the English Channel, there is a gap between the onset of the action and its continuation to completion. In this respect, voluntary actions are quite different from perceptions. There is indeed a voluntaristic element in perception. I can, for example, choose to see the ambiguous figure either as a duck or a rabbit; but for the most part my perceptual experiences are causally fixed. That is why we have a problem of the freedom of the will, but we do not have a problem of the freedom of perception. The gap, as I have described it, is a feature of our conscious, voluntary activities. At each stage, the conscious states are not experienced as sufficient to compel the next conscious state. There is thus only one continuous experience of the gap but we can divide it into three different sorts of manifestations, as I did above. The gap is between one conscious state and the next, not between conscious states and bodily movements or between physical stimuli and conscious states.

This experience of free will is very compelling, and even those of us who think it is an illusion find that we cannot in practice act on the presupposition that it is an illusion. On the contrary, we have to act on the presupposition of freedom.

Imagine that you are in a restaurant and you are given a choice between veal and pork, and you have to make up your mind. You cannot refuse to exercise free will in such a case, because the refusal itself is only intelligible to you as a refusal, if you take it as an exercise of free will. So if you say to the waiter, 'Look, I am a determinist—que sera sera, I'll just wait and see what I order', that refusal to exercise free will is only intelligible to you as one of your actions if you take it to be an exercise of your free will. Kant pointed this out a long time ago. We cannot think away our free will. The conscious experiences of the gap give us the conviction of human freedom.

If we now turn to the opposing view and ask why we are so convinced of determinism, the arguments for determinism seem just as compelling as the arguments for free will. A basic feature of our relation to the world is that we find the world causally ordered. Natural phenomena in the world have causal explanations, and those causal explanations state causally sufficient conditions. Customarily, in philosophy, we put this point by saying that that every event has a cause. That formulation is, of course, much too crude to capture the complexity of the idea of causation that we are working with. But the basic idea is clear enough. In our dealings with nature we assume that everything that happens occurs as a result of antecedently sufficient causal conditions. And when we give an explanation by citing a cause, we assume that the cause we cite, *together with the rest of the context*, was sufficient to bring about the event we are explaining. In my earlier example of the earthquake, we assume that the event did not just happen to occur; in that situation it had to occur. In that context the causes were sufficient to determine the event.

An interesting change occurred in the early decades of the 20th century. At the most fundamental level of physics, nature turns out not to be in that way deterministic. We have come to accept at a quantum mechanical level explanations that are not deterministic. However, so far quantum indeterminism gives us no help with the free will problem because that indeterminism introduces randomness into the basic structure of the universe, and the hypothesis that some of our acts occur freely is not at all the same as the hypothesis that some of our acts occur at random. I will have more to say about this issue later.

There are a number of accounts that seem to explain consciousness and even free will in terms of quantum mechanics. I have never seen anything that was remotely convincing, but it is important for this discussion that we remember that as far as our actual theories of the universe are concerned, at the most fundamental level we have come to think that it is possible to have explanations of natural phenomena that are not deterministic. And that possibility will be important when we later discuss the problem of free will as a neurobiological problem.

It is important to emphasize that the problem of free will, as I have stated it, is a problem about a certain kind of human consciousness. Without the conscious experience of the gap—that is, without the conscious experience of the distinctive features of free, voluntary, rational actions—there would be no problem of free will. We have the conviction of our own free will because of certain features of our consciousness. The question is: Granted that we have the experience of freedom, is that experience valid or is it illusory? Does that experience correspond to something in reality beyond the experience itself? We have to assume that there are causal antecedents to our actions. The question is: Are those causal antecedents in every case sufficient to determine the action, or are there some cases where they are not sufficient, and if so how do we account for those cases?

Let us take stock of where we are. On the one hand we have the experience of freedom, which, as I have described it, is the experience of the gap. The gap between the antecedent causes of our free, voluntary decisions and actions, and the actual making of those decisions and the performance of those actions. On the other hand we have the presupposition, or the assumption, that nature is a matter of events occurring according to causally sufficient conditions, and we find it difficult to suppose that we could explain any phenomena without appealing to causally sufficient conditions.

For the purposes of the discussion that follows, I am going to assume that the experiences of the gap are psychologically valid. That is, I am going to assume that for many voluntary, free, rational human actions, the purely *psychological* antecedents of the action are not causally sufficient to determine the action. This occurred, for example, when I selected a candidate to vote for in the last American presidential election. I realize that a lot of people think that psychological determinism is true, and I have certainly not given a decisive refutation of it. Nonetheless, it seems to me we find the psychological experience of freedom so compelling that it would be absolutely astounding if it turned out that at the psychological level it was a massive illusion, that all of our behaviour was psychologically compulsive. There are arguments against psychological determinism, but I am not going to present them in this article. I am going to assume that psychological determinism is false, and that the real problem of determinism is not at the psychological level, but at a more fundamental neurobiological level.

Furthermore, there are several famous issues about free will that I will not discuss, and I mention them here only to set them on one side. I will have nothing to say about compatibilism, the view that free will and determinism are really consistent with each other. On the definitions of these terms that I am using, determinism and free will are not compatible. The thesis of determinism asserts that all actions are preceded by sufficient causal conditions that determine them. The thesis of free will asserts that some actions are not preceded by sufficient causal conditions. Free will so defined is the negation of determinism. No doubt there is a sense of these words where free will is compatible with determinism (when for example people march in the streets carrying signs that say 'Freedom Now' they are presumably not interested in physical or neurobiological laws), but that is not the sense of these terms that concerns me. I will also have nothing to say about moral responsibility. Perhaps there is some interesting connection between the problem of free will and the problem of moral responsibility, but if so I will have nothing to say about it in this article.

II. How Consciousness Can Move Bodies

Because the problem of free will is a problem about the causal facts concerning certain sorts of consciousness, we need to explain how consciousness in general can function causally to move our bodies. How can a state of human consciousness cause a bodily movement? One of the most common experiences in our lives is that of moving our bodies by our conscious efforts. For example, I now intentionally raise my arm, a conscious effort on my part, and lo and behold, the arm goes up. What could be more common? The fact that we find such a banal occurrence philosophically puzzling suggests that we are making a mistake. The mistake derives from our inherited commitment to the old Cartesian categories of the mental and the physical. Consciousness seems too weightless, ethereal and immaterial ever to move even one of our limbs. But as I tried to explain earlier, consciousness is a higher-level biological feature of the brain. To see how the higher-level feature of consciousness has physical effects, consider how higher-level features work in the case of metaphysically less puzzling phenomena.

To illustrate the relationships between higher-level, or system, features on the one hand, and micro-level phenomena on the other, I want to borrow an example from Roger Sperry.[2] Consider a wheel rolling downhill. The wheel is entirely made of molecules. The behaviour of the molecules causes the higher-level, or system, feature of solidity. Notice that the solidity affects the behaviour of the individual molecules. The trajectory of each molecule is affected by the behaviour of the entire solid wheel. But of course there is nothing there but molecules. The wheel consists entirely of molecules. So when we say the solidity functions causally in the behaviour of the wheel and in the behaviour of the individual molecules that compose the wheel, we are not saying that the solidity is something *in addition* to the molecules; rather it is just the *condition* that the molecules are in. But the feature of solidity is nonetheless a real feature, and it has real causal effects.

Of course there are many disanalogies between the relation of solidity to molecular behaviour, on one hand, and the relation of consciousness to neuronal behaviour, on the other. I will explain some of them later, but now I want to focus on the feature that we have just explored, and suggest that it applies to the relation of consciousness and the brain. The consciousness of the brain can have effects at the neuronal level even though there is nothing in the brain except neurons (with glial cells, neuro-transmitters, blood flow, and all the rest). And just as the behaviour of the molecules is causally constitutive of solidity, so the behaviour of the neurons is causally constitutive of consciousness. When we say that consciousness can move my body, what we are saying is that the neuronal structures move my body, but they move my body in the way they do because of the conscious state they are in. Consciousness is a feature of the brain in a way that solidity is a feature of the wheel. We are reluctant to

---

[2] Roger Sperry, 'A Modified Concept of Consciousness' (*Psychological Review*, 1969).

think of consciousness as just a biological feature of the brain, in part because of our dualistic tradition, but also because we tend to suppose that if consciousness is *irreducible* to neuronal behaviour then it must be something extra, something 'over and above' neuronal behaviour. And of course consciousness, unlike solidity, is not ontologically reducible to physical microstructures. This is not because it is some extra thing; rather it is because consciousness has a first-person, or subjective, ontology, and is thus not reducible to anything that has a third-person, or objective, ontology.[3]

In this brief discussion I have tried to explain how consciousness can have 'physical' causal consequences, and why there is nothing mysterious about that fact. My conscious intention-in-action causes my arm to go up. But of course, my conscious intention-in-action is a feature of my brain system, and as such at the level of the neurons it is constituted entirely by neuronal behaviour. There is no ontological reductionism in this account, because at no point are we denying that consciousness has an irreducible first-person ontology. But there is a causal reduction. Consciousness has no causal powers beyond the powers of the neuronal (and other neurobiological) structures.

III. The Structure of Rational Explanation

I said that the problem of free will is a problem about certain sorts of consciousness. If we look at the sorts of explanations that we give for actions which are manifestations of the gap—that is, actions which are expressions of our experience of free, rational decision making—we find that the experience of free will is reflected in the logical structure of action explanations. In a word, because of the gap, explanations that appeal to our rational decision-making processes are not deterministic in form in a way that typical explanations of natural phenomena are deterministic in form. To see how this is so, contrast the following three explanations:

1. I punched a hole in the ballot paper because I wanted to vote for Bush.
2. I got a bad headache because I wanted to vote for Bush.
3. The glass fell to the floor and broke because I accidentally knocked it off the table.

Of these examples, 1 and 2 look very similar in their syntactical structure, and they appear to be different from 3. I will argue, however, that 2 and 3 are the same in their underlying logical structure, and they both differ in this respect from 1. 3 is a standard causal explanation which states that one event or state caused another event or state. The logical form of 3 is simply: A caused B. But the form of 1 is quite different. We do not take statements of form 1 as implying that the event

³ For further discussion, see John R. Searle, *The Rediscovery of the Mind* (Cambridge, MA: MIT Press, 1992), especially Chapter 5.

described by the clause before 'because' had to occur, given the occurrence of the event described after the 'because' and the rest of the context. We do not take 1 as implying that my desire to vote for Bush was such as to force me to punch a hole in the ballot paper, that given my psychological state at the time, I could not have done otherwise. Explanations of this form may on occasion cite causally sufficient conditions, but the form of the explanation does not require such conditions. If we compare 1 and 3 with 2 it seems to me that 2, like 3, is a matter of causally sufficient conditions. The form of 2, like 3, is simply: A caused B. In that context, the state of my desiring to vote for Bush was causally sufficient for the event of my getting a headache.

But this feature of rational explanation leaves us with a puzzle, almost a contradiction. It seems that if the explanation does not give causally sufficient conditions, it cannot really explain anything, because it does not answer the question why one event occurred as opposed to another event, which was also causally possible given exactly the same antecedent conditions. I think answering that question is an important part of the discussion of free will, so I want to spend a little bit of time on it.

As a matter of their logical structure, explanations of voluntary human actions in terms of reasons are different from ordinary causal explanations. The logical form of ordinary causal explanations is simply that event A caused event B. Relative to specific contexts, we typically take such explanations as adequate because we assume that in that context, event A was causally sufficient for event B. Given the rest of the context, if A occurred then B had to occur. But the form of the explanation of human behaviour, where we say that a certain person performed act A by acting on reason R, has a different logical structure. It is not of the form 'A caused B'. I think you only understand that structure if you realize that it requires the postulation of a self or an ego. The logical form of the statement 'Agent S performed Act A because of reason R' is not of the form 'A caused B', it is of the form 'A self S performed action A, and in the performance of A, S acted on reason R'. The logical form, in short, of rational explanation is quite different from standard causal explanations. The form of the explanation is not to give causally sufficient conditions, but to cite the reason that the agent acted on.

But if that is right, then we have a peculiar result. It seems that rational action explanations require us to postulate the existence of an irreducible self, a rational agent, in addition to the sequence of events. Indeed, if we make explicit two further assumptions to those we have already been making, I think we can derive the existence of the self.

Assumption 1: Explanations in terms of reasons do not typically cite causally sufficient conditions

and

Assumption 2: Such explanations can be adequate explanations of actions.

How do I know that Assumption 2 is true? How do I know such explanations can be and often are adequate? Because in my own case I often know exactly what reasons I had for performing an action and I know that an explanation that cites those reasons is adequate, because I know that in acting I *acted on* those reasons and on those reasons alone. Of course we have to allow that there are all kinds of problems about the unconscious, self-deception, and all the rest of the unknown and unacknowledged reasons for action. But in the ideal case where I consciously act on a reason and am consciously aware of acting on a reason, the specification of the reason as the explanation of my action is perfectly adequate.

We have already been making a third assumption,

Assumption 3: Adequate causal explanations cite conditions that, relative to the context, are causally sufficient.

And this assumption just makes explicit the principle that if a causal statement is to explain an event, then the statement of the cause must cite a condition that in that particular context was sufficient to bring about the event to be explained. But from Assumptions 1 and 3 we can derive:

Conclusion 1: Construed as ordinary causal explanations, reason explanations are inadequate.

If we were to assume that reason explanations are ordinary causal explanations we would have a straight contradiction. To avoid the contradiction we have to conclude:

Conclusion 2: Reason explanations are not ordinary causal explanations. Though they have a causal component, their form is not A caused B.

That leaves us with a problem. How are we to explain the adequacy of these explanations if they have a causal component, and, nonetheless, are not standard causal explanations? I think the answer is not hard to find. The explanation does not give a sufficient cause of an event, rather it gives a specification of how a conscious rational self acted on a reason, how an agent made a reason effective by freely acting on it. But when spelled out, the logical form of such explanations requires that we postulate an irreducible, non-Humean self. Thus:

Conclusion 3: Reason explanations are adequate because they explain why a self acted in a certain way. They explain why a rational self acting in the gap, acted one way rather than another, by specifying the reason that the self acted on.

There are thus two avenues to the gap, an experiential and a linguistic. We experience ourselves acting freely in the gap, and this experience is reflected in the logical structure of explanations that we give for our actions. We experience ourselves acting as rational agents, and our linguistic practice of giving explanations reflects the gap (because the explanations do not cite causally sufficient conditions); and for their intelligibility these explanations require that we recognize that there must be an entity—a rational agent, a self, or an ego—that acts in the gap (because a Humean bundle of perceptions would not be enough to account for the adequacy of the explanations). The necessity of assuming the operation of an irreducible, non-Humean, self is a feature both of our actual experience of voluntary action and the practice that we have of explaining our voluntary actions by giving reasons.

Of course such explanations, like all explanations, allow for further questions about why those reasons were effective and not other reasons. That is, if I say that I voted for Bush because I wanted an improvement in the educational system, there is a further question, why did I want that improvement? And why was that reason more compelling to me than other reasons? I agree that such a demand for explanations can always be continued, but that is true of any explanation. Explanations, as Wittgenstein reminded us, have to stop somewhere, and there is nothing inadequate about saying that I voted for Bush because I wanted an improvement in the educational system. It does not show that my answer is inadequate to show that it admits of further questions.

I am here summarizing briefly a complex argument that I have spelled out in more detail in Chapter 3 of *Rationality in Action* (MIT Press, 2001). But the bare bones of the argument can be conveyed even in this brief summary: We have the first-person conscious experience of acting on reasons. We state these reasons for action in the form of explanations. The explanations are obviously quite adequate because we know in our own case that, in their ideal form, nothing further is required. But they cannot be adequate if they are treated as ordinary causal explanations because they do not pass the causal sufficiency test. They are not deterministic in their logical form as stated, and they are not deterministic in their interpretation. How can we account for these facts? To account for these explanations we must see that they are not of the form A caused B. They are of the form a rational self S performed act A, and in performing A, S acted on reason R. But that formulation requires the postulation of a self.

Conclusion 3 does not follow deductively from the assumptions. The argument as presented is a 'transcendental' argument, in one of Kant's senses of that term. Assume such and such facts and ask what are the conditions of possibility of these facts. I am claiming that the condition of possibility of the adequacy of rational explanations is the existence of an irreducible self, a rational agent, capable of acting on reasons.

Let us take stock again of where we are. We saw, first, that the problem of free will arises because of a special feature of a certain type of human consciousness, and we saw, second, that in order to explain our apparently free behaviour, we have to postulate an irreducible notion of the self. This, by the way, is typical of philosophy—in order to solve one problem you have to solve a bunch of others, but so far, I seem to have given you three problems for one. We started with the problem of free will, and we now have the problems of free will, of consciousness, and of the self, and they all seem to hang together.

IV. Free Will and the Brain

I now turn to the main question of this article: How could we treat the problem of free will as a neurobiological problem? And the assumption that I am making is that if free will is a genuine feature of the world and not merely an illusion, then it must have a neurobiological reality; there must be some feature of the brain that realizes free will. I said earlier that consciousness is a higher-level, or system, feature of the brain caused by the behaviour of lower-level elements, such as neurons and synapses. But if that is so, what would the behaviour of the neurons and the synapses have to be like if the conscious experience of free will were to be neurobiologically real?

I have said that the philosophical solution to the traditional mind-body problem is to point out that all of our conscious states are higher-level or systemic features of the brain, while being at the same time caused by lower-level micro-processes in the brain. At the system level we have consciousness, intentionality, decisions, and intentions. At the micro level we have neurons, synapses, and neurotransmitters. The features of the system level are caused by the behaviour of the micro-level elements, and are realized in the system composed of the micro-level elements. In the past I have described the set of causal relations between decision making and acting in terms of a parallelogram where at the top level we have decisions leading to intentions-in-action, and at the bottom level we have neuron firings causing more neuron firings. Such a picture gives us a parallelogram (Figure 11.1).

The question is, if we suppose there is a gap at the top level in the case of rational decision making, how might that gap be reflected at the neurobiological level? There are, after all, no gaps in the brain. In order to explore alternative hypotheses we need to consider an example.

A famous, if mythological, example is the judgment of Paris. Confronted with three beautiful Goddesses, Hera, Aphrodite, and Pallas Athena, Paris was required to deliberate and reach a decision as to which should receive the golden apple, inscribed

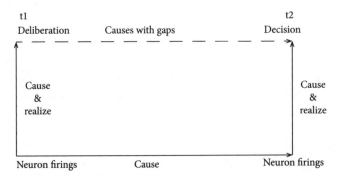

Figure 11.1 The neuron firings at the lower level cause the higher-level deliberation and decision, both of which are realized in the neuronal system. The metaphor of levels is graphically illustrated by a rectangle or parallelogram.

'For the fairest'. He was not to decide this by appraising their beauty but by choosing among the bribes each offered. Aphrodite promised that he would possess the most beautiful woman in the world, Athena that he would lead the Trojans to victory over the Greeks, and Hera offered to make him ruler of Europe and Asia. It is important that he has to make a decision as a result of deliberation. He does not just spontaneously react. We also assume that he was operating in the gap: He consciously felt a range of choices open to him; and his decision was not forced by lust, rage, or obsession. He made a free decision after deliberation.

We can suppose there was an instant when the period of reflection began, call it t_1, and that it lasted until he finally handed the apple to Aphrodite at t_2. In this example we will stipulate that there was no further stimulus input between t_1 and t_2. In that period he simply reflected on the merits and the demerits of the various offers. All the information on the basis of which he makes his decision is present in his brain at t_1, and the processes between t_1 and t_2 are simply a matter of deliberation leading to the choice of Aphrodite.

Using this example we can now state the problem of the freedom of the will with somewhat more precision than we have been able to do so far. If the total state of Paris' brain at t_1 is causally sufficient to determine the total state of his brain at t_2, in this and in other relevantly similar cases, then he has no free will. And what goes for Paris goes for all of us. If the state of his brain at t_1 is not causally sufficient to determine the subsequent states of his brain up to t_2, then, given certain assumptions about consciousness that I need to make clear, he does have free will. And again, what goes for Paris goes for all of us.

Why does it all come down to this? The answer is that the state of his brain immediately prior to t_2 is sufficient to determine the beginning of the muscle contractions that caused and realized his action of handing the apple to Aphrodite. Paris was a mortal man with neurons like the rest of us and as soon as the acetylcholine reached the axon end plates of his motor neurons, then, assuming the rest of his physiology was in order, his arm, with apple in hand, started to move toward Aphrodite by causal necessity. The problem of free will is whether the conscious thought processes in the brain, the processes that constitute the *experiences* of free will, are realized in a neurobiological system that is totally deterministic.

So we have two hypotheses, first that the state of the brain is causally sufficient, and second that it is not. Let us explore each in turn. On Hypothesis 1 let us suppose that the antecedently *insufficient* psychological conditions leading up to the choice of Aphrodite at t_2, the conditions that led us to the postulation of the gap, are matched at the lower neurobiological level by a sequence of neurobiological events each stage of which is causally *sufficient* for the next. On this hypothesis we would have a kind of neurobiological determinism corresponding to a psychological libertarianism. Paris has the experience of free will, but there is no genuine free will at the neurobiological level. I think most neurobiologists would feel that this is probably how the brain actually works, that we have the experience of free will but it is illusory; because the neuronal processes are causally sufficient to determine subsequent states of the brain, assuming there are no outside stimulus inputs or effects from the rest of the body. But this result is intellectually very unsatisfying because it gives us a form of epiphenomenalism. It says that our experience of freedom plays no causal or explanatory role in our behaviour. It is a complete illusion, because our behaviour is entirely fixed by the neurobiology that determines the muscle contractions. On this view evolution played a massive trick on us. Evolution gave us the illusion of freedom, but it is nothing more than that—an illusion.

I will say more about Hypothesis 1 later, but first let us turn to Hypothesis 2. On Hypothesis 2 we suppose that the absence of causally sufficient conditions at the psychological level is matched by an absence of causally sufficient conditions at the neurobiological level. Our problem is, what could that possibly mean? There are no gaps in the brain. In order to take seriously the hypothesis that the free will that is manifested in consciousness has a neurobiological reality, we have to explore the relation of consciousness to neurobiology a little more closely. Earlier I described consciousness as a higher-level feature of the brain system. The metaphor of higher and lower, though it is common in the literature (my own writings included), I think is misleading. It suggests that consciousness is, so to speak, like the varnish on the surface of the table; and that is wrong. The idea we are trying to express is that consciousness is a feature of the whole system. Consciousness is literally present throughout those portions of the brain where consciousness is created by and realized in neuronal activity. It is important to emphasize this point, because it runs contrary to our Cartesian heritage that says consciousness cannot have a spatial location: Consciousness is located in certain portions of the brain and functions causally, relative to those locations.

I explained earlier how consciousness could function causally, by giving an analogy between the consciousness of the brain and the solidity of the wheel, but if we carry that analysis a step further, we see that on Hypothesis 2 we have to suppose that the logical features of volitional consciousness of the entire system have effects on the elements on the system, even though the system is composed entirely of the elements, in the same way that the solidity of the wheel has effects on the molecules, even though the wheel is composed of molecules.

The point of the analogy was to remove the sense of mystery about how consciousness could affect neuronal behaviour (and thus move human bodies) by showing how, in unmysterious cases, a system feature can affect micro-level elements in a system composed entirely of the micro-level level elements, in which all causal powers are reducible to the causal powers of the micro-level elements. But of course any analogy goes only so far. The analogy: Solidity is to molecular behaviour as consciousness is to neuronal behaviour, is inadequate at, at least, two points. First, we take the wheel to be entirely deterministic, and the hypothesis we are examining now is that the conscious voluntary decision-making aspects of the brain are not deterministic. Second, the solidity of the wheel is ontologically reducible to the behaviour of the molecules, and not just causally reducible. In the case of consciousness, though we suppose that consciousness is causally reducible to the behaviour of the micro elements, we cannot make a similar ontological reduction for consciousness. This is because the first-person ontology of consciousness is not reducible to a third-person ontology.

So far then, in our preliminary formulation of Hypothesis 2 we have three claims. First, the state of the brain at t_1 is not causally sufficient to determine the state of the brain at t_2. Second, the movement from the state at t_1 to the state at t_2 can only be explained by features of the whole system, specifically by the operation of the conscious self. And third, all of the features of the conscious self at any given instant are entirely determined by the state of the micro elements, the neurons, etc at that instant. The systemic features are entirely fixed at any given instant by the micro elements, because, causally speaking, there is nothing there but the micro elements. The state of the neurons determines the state of consciousness. But any given state of neurons/consciousness is not causally sufficient for the next state. The passage from one state to the next is explained by the rational thought processes of the initial state of neurons/consciousness. At any instant the total state of consciousness is fixed by the behaviour of the neurons, but from one instant to the next the total state of the system is not causally sufficient to determine the next state. Free will, if it exists at all, is a phenomenon in time. Diagrammatically the best I can do is this (Figure 11.2).

I have stated both Hypothesis 1 and Hypothesis 2 very swiftly, and it is now time to go over them a bit more slowly to see what is involved.

V. Hypothesis 1. Epiphenomenalism

The best way to think of Hypothesis 1 is to think of it as an engineering problem. Imagine you are building a conscious robot. You build it in such a way that when confronted with choices it has the conscious experience of the gap. But you construct its hardware in such a way that each stage is determined by the preceding stages and

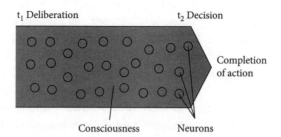

Figure 11.2 In this diagram, we avoid the metaphor of levels. Consciousness is a feature of the system, and the system is composed of neurons. The thesis of free will is that there are temporal stages of the system that do not determine the next temporal stage by causally sufficient conditions.

by the impact of outside stimuli. Each movement of the robot's body is entirely fixed by its internal states. Indeed, we already have a model for this part of the technology in traditional artificial intelligence. We simply put in computer programs that will give the robot an algorithmic solution to the problems posed by the input stimuli and the states of the system. On Hypothesis 1, Paris' judgment was preprogrammed in advance.

I have said that an objection to Hypothesis 1 is that it leads to epiphenomenalism. The distinctive features of conscious rational decision making would have no real influence in the universe. Paris' judgment, my behaviour and the robot's behaviour are all entirely causally determined by the activity going on at the micro-level. But, someone might challenge me, why is the supposition involved in Hypothesis 1 any more epiphenomenal than any other account of the relationship of consciousness to the physiological functioning of the human body?

I have claimed that once we abandon the traditional dualistic categories there is no mystery at all about how consciousness can function causally. It is simply a matter of a higher-level, or system, feature functioning causally. And, furthermore, the account that I gave does not postulate any causal over-determination. There are not two sets of causes, the consciousness and the neurons; there is just one set, described at different levels. Consciousness, to repeat, is just the state that the system of neurons is in, in the same way that solidity is just a state that the system of molecules is in. But now, on my own account, why should Hypothesis 1 imply epiphenomenalism any more than Hypothesis 2? The answer is this. Whether a feature is epiphenomenal depends on whether the *feature* itself functions causally. Thus there are many features of any event that are causally irrelevant. For example, it is a feature of the event where I accidentally knocked the glass off the table that I was wearing a blue shirt at the time. But the blue shirt was not a causally relevant aspect of the event. It is true to say, 'The man in the blue shirt knocked the glass off the table', but the blue shirt is epiphenomenal—it does not matter. So when we say of some feature of an event that it is epiphenomenal, what we are saying is that that feature played no causal role. The suggestion that I am making is that on Hypothesis 1 the essential feature of rational decision making, namely the experience of the gap—the experience of alternative possibilities open to us, the experience that the psychological antecedents of the action are not causally sufficient to compel the action, and the experience of the conscious thought processes where we make up our minds and then act—all of those features of the experience do not matter. They are irrelevant. The specific determinate forms of those features whereby we anguish over a decision and consider various reasons are as irrelevant as the blueness of my shirt when I knocked the glass over. The judgment of Paris was already determined by the antecedent state of Paris' neurons, regardless of all of his cogitations.

The mere fact that a system feature is fixed by the micro elements does not show that the system feature is epiphenomenal. On the contrary, we saw how consciousness could be fixed by neuronal behaviour and still not be epiphenomenal. To show that something is epiphenomenal, we have to show that the feature in question is not a causally relevant aspect in determining what happens. The epiphenomenalism in this case arises because the causal insufficiency of the experiences of the gap and the effort to resolve the insufficiency by making up our minds is simply not a causally relevant aspect in determining what actually happens. Our decision was already fixed by the state of our neurons even though we thought we were going through a conscious process of making up our minds among genuine alternatives, alternatives that were genuinely open to us, even given all of the causes.

Epiphenomenalism is sometimes said to be explained by counterfactuals. Multiple causes apart, the truth of 'Even if A had not occurred then B would still have occurred' is supposed to be the test for whether A is epiphenomenal. But this test is at best misleading. Assuming that both the experiences of the gap and the final decisions are fixed at the neuronal level, then if the experiences had not occurred the decision would not have occurred, or at least its occurrence would not have been guaranteed, because they are both caused by the same neuronal processes. So if one is absent the cause of the other must have been removed as well. But this does not show that the experiences were not epiphenomenal. The test for epiphenomenalism is not the truth of the counterfactual, but the reasons for its truth. The test for epiphenomenalism is whether the feature in question is a causally relevant aspect. On Hypothesis 1 the distinctive features of the gap and of rational decision making are causally irrelevant.

Well, what's wrong with epiphenomenalism? As we come to understand better how the brain works, it may turn out to be true. In the present state of our knowledge, the main objection to accepting epiphenomenalism is that it goes against everything we know about evolution. The processes of conscious rationality are such an important part of our lives, and above all such a biologically expensive part of our lives, that it would be unlike anything we know in evolution if a phenotype of this magnitude played no functional role at all in the life and survival of the organism. In humans and higher animals an enormous biological price is paid for conscious decision making, including everything from how the young are raised to the amount of blood flowing to the brain. To suppose that this plays no role in inclusive fitness is not like supposing the human appendix plays no role. It would be more like supposing that vision or digestion played no evolutionary role.

VI. Hypothesis 2. The Self, Consciousness, and Indeterminism

Hypothesis 1 is unattractive, but at least it is coherent and fits in with a lot of what we know about biology. The brain is an organ like any other and is as deterministic in its functioning as the heart or the liver. If we can imagine building a conscious machine then we can imagine building a conscious robot according to Hypothesis 1. But how would one treat Hypothesis 2 as an engineering problem? How would we build a conscious robot, where every feature of consciousness is entirely determined by the state of the micro elements, and at the same time the consciousness of the system functions causally in determining the next state of the system by processes that are not deterministic but are a matter of free decision making by a rational self, acting on reasons? So described, it does not sound like a promising project for Federal funding. The only reason for taking it seriously is that as far as we can tell from our own experiences of the gap, together with what we know about how the brain works, that is precisely the condition we are in. We are conscious robots whose states of consciousness are fixed by neuronal processes, and at the same time we sometimes proceed by nondeterministic conscious processes (hence neuronal processes) that are matters of our rational selves making decisions on reasons.

How could the brain work so as to satisfy all those conditions? Notice that I do not ask, 'How *does* the brain work so as to satisfy all those conditions?' because we don't know for a fact that it does satisfy the conditions, and if it does, we have no idea how it does so. At this point all we can do is describe various conditions that the brain would have to meet if Hypothesis 2 is true.

It seems to me there are three conditions, in ascending order of difficulty, and an account of brain functioning in accord with Hypothesis 2 would have to explain how the brain meets these conditions.

1. Consciousness, as caused by neuronal processes and realized in neuronal systems, functions causally in moving the body.

I have already explained in some detail how this is possible.

2. The brain causes and sustains the existence of a conscious self that is able to make rational decisions and carry them out in actions.

It is not enough that consciousness should have physical effects on the body. There are many such cases that have nothing to do with rational free actions, as when a man gets a stomach ache from worry, or throws up at a disgusting sight, or gets an erection from erotic thoughts. In addition to a neurobiological account of mental causation one needs a neurobiological account of the rational, volitional self. How does the brain create a self, how is the self realized in the brain, how does it function in deliberation, how does it arrive at decisions, and how does it initiate and sustain actions?

In the sense in which I introduced the notion of the self by the transcendental argument of section III, the self is not some extra entity; rather, in a very crude and oversimplified fashion, one can say that conscious agency plus conscious rationality = selfhood. So if you had an account of brain processes that explained how the brain produced the unified field of consciousness,[4] together with the experience of acting, and in addition how the brain produced conscious thought processes, in which the constraints of rationality are already built in as constitutive elements, you

---

[4] For the importance of the unified field, see John R. Searle, 'Consciousness', *Annual Review of Neuroscience*, 2000, Vol. 23, pp. 557–78.

would, so to speak, get the self for free. To spell this out in a little more detail, the elements necessary for an organism to have a self in my sense are first, it must have a unified field of consciousness; second, it must have the capacity for deliberating on reasons, and this involves not only cognitive capacities of perception and memory but the capacity for coordinating intentional states so as to arrive at rational decisions; and third, the organism must be capable of initiating and carrying out actions (in the old-time jargon, it must have 'volition' or 'agency').[5]

There is no additional metaphysical problem of the self. If you can show how the brain does all that—how it creates a unified field of consciousness capable of rational agency in the sense just explained, then you have solved the neurobiological problem of the self. Notice that, as far as the experiences are concerned, both Hypothesis 1 and Hypothesis 2 need to meet this condition. Indeed, any theory of brain function has to meet this condition, because we know that the brain gives us all these sorts of experiences. The difference between Hypothesis 1 and Hypothesis 2 is that on 1 rational agency is an illusion. We have the experience of rational agency but it makes no difference to the world.

3. The brain is such that the conscious self is able to make and carry out decisions in the gap, where neither decision nor action is determined in advance, by causally sufficient conditions, yet both are rationally explained by the reasons the agent is acting on.

This is the trickiest condition: How could the gap be neurobiologically real, given all that I have just said? Assume we had an account of how the brain produces mental causation, and an account of how it produces the experiences of rational agency, how do you get rational indeterminism into your account of brain function?

The only way I know to approach such a problem is to begin by reminding ourselves of what we already know. We know, or at least we think we know, two things that bear on the case. First we know that our experiences of free action contain both indeterminism and rationality and that consciousness is essential to the forms that these take. Second we know that quantum indeterminism is the only form of indeterminism that is indisputably established as a fact of nature.[6]

It is tempting, indeed irresistible, to think that the explanation of the conscious experience of free will must be a manifestation of quantum indeterminism at the level of conscious rational decision making. Previously I never could see the point of introducing quantum mechanics into discussions of consciousness. But here at least is a strict argument requiring the introduction of quantum indeterminism.

Premise 1. All indeterminism in nature is quantum indeterminism.

---

[5] On my view rationality is not a separate faculty, rather the constraints of rationality are already built into intentional phenomena such as beliefs and desires and into thought processes. So a neurobiological account of mental phenomena would already be an account of the rational constraints on such phenomena. For a more detailed presentation of this view and the reasons for it, see my *Rationality in Action* (MIT Press, 2001).

[6] Chaos theory, as I understand it, implies unpredictability but not indeterminism.

Premise 2. Consciousness is a feature of nature that manifests indeterminism.

Conclusion: Consciousness manifests quantum indeterminism.

Our aim now is to keep following relentlessly the implications of our assumptions. If Hypothesis 2 is true and if quantum indeterminism is the only real form of indeterminism in nature, then it follows that quantum mechanics must enter into the explanation of consciousness. This conclusion does not follow on Hypothesis 1. As long as the gap is epiphenomenal, then no indeterminism in the causal apparatus is essential to explain how consciousness is caused by and realized in brain processes. This is important for contemporary research. The standard lines of research, both on the building block model and the unified field model, make no appeal to quantum mechanics in explaining consciousness. If Hypothesis 2 is true these cannot succeed, at least not for volitional consciousness.[7]

But even assuming we had a quantum mechanical explanation of consciousness, how do we get from indeterminism to rationality? If quantum indeterminacy amounts to randomness then quantum indeterminacy by itself seems useless in explaining the problem of free will because free actions are not random. I think we should take the question, 'What is the relation between quantum indeterminacy and rationality?' in the same spirit in which we take the question, 'What is the relation between brain micro processes and consciousness?' or the question, 'What is the relation between visual stimuli, brain processes, and visual intentionality?' In the latter two cases we know in advance that the system features are caused by and realized in the micro processes, so we know that the causal features of the system-level phenomena are entirely explainable by the behaviour of the micro phenomena. As I have repeated to the point of tedium, the causal relations have the same *formal* structure as the causal relations between molecular movements and solidity. We also know that it is a fallacy of composition to suppose that the properties of the individual elements must be properties of the whole. Thus for example, the electrical properties of the individual atoms are not properties of the whole table, and the fact that a particular action potential is at 50 Hz does not imply that the whole brain is oscillating at 50 Hz. Now exactly analogously, the fact that individual micro phenomena are random does not imply randomness at the system level. The indeterminacy at the micro level may (if Hypothesis 2 is true) explain the indeterminacy of the system, but *the randomness at the micro level does not thereby imply randomness at the system level.*

VII. Conclusion

I said at the beginning that obdurate philosophical problems arise when we have a conflict between deeply held inconsistent theses. In the case of the mind-body

---

[7] For an explanation of the distinction between the building block model and the unified field model, see John R. Searle, 'Consciousness', *Annual Review of Neuroscience*, 2000, Vol. 23, pp. 557–78.

problem we resolved the inconsistency by a kind of compatibilism. Once we abandon the assumptions behind the traditional Cartesian categories then naive materialism is consistent with naive mentalism. We could not make such a compatibilism work for the free will problem, because the thesis that every human act is preceded by causally sufficient conditions remains incompatible with the thesis that some are not. Once we sorted out the issues we found two possibilities, Hypothesis 1 and Hypothesis 2. Neither is very appealing. If we had to bet, the odds would surely favour Hypothesis 1, because it is simpler and fits in with our overall view of biology. But it gives a result that is literally incredible. When I gave this lecture in London someone in the audience asked, 'If Hypothesis 1 were shown to be true would you accept it?' The form of the question is: 'If free rational decision making were shown not to exist, would you freely and rationally make the decision to accept that it does not exist?' Notice that he did not ask, 'If Hypothesis 1 were true would the neuronal processes in your brain produce the result that your mouth made affirmative noises about it?' That question at least is in the spirit of Hypothesis 1, though even that goes too far, because it asks me freely and rationally to make a prediction, something that is impossible on the Hypothesis. Hypothesis 2 is a mess, because it gives us three mysteries for one. We thought free will was a mystery, but consciousness and quantum mechanics were two separate and distinct mysteries. Now we have the result that in order to solve the first we have to solve the second and invoke one of the most mysterious aspects of the third to solve the first two. My aim in this article is to continue the line of attack begun in my earlier writings and to follow out the competing lines of reasoning as far as they will go. There is, I am sure, much more to be said.

Introduction to Derek Parfit's Lecture

Ted Honderich

Derek Parfit, born of medical doctors teaching in missionary hospitals in China, was educated at Eton and in Oxford, where he studied modern history. After a year at Columbia and Harvard, where he turned to philosophy, he became a fellow of All Souls College in Oxford, and is now an Emeritus Fellow. He is also a regular visiting professor at Harvard, New York University, and Rutgers. To his commitment to philosophy he adds one to photography.

If you saw somebody distinctive in the Broad in Oxford a year ago and somebody similar yesterday, what would make them the same person? What is the criterion of personal identity, of being a particular person? There once was the idea, and still is, that they would have to be one and the same *self, subject,* or maybe *soul*—an internal and unphysical entity, one that has experience rather than somehow consists in it. There is also the second idea, argued for by Bernard Williams among others, that the two would have to be one body—there would have to be *physical continuity.*

There is the third idea whose origin is assigned to Locke in the 17th century. It is that the person today is the person of a year ago if today's person remembers, as their own, actions that were performed by the person a year ago, and also the person today may be acting on an intention to visit Oxford formed by the person a year ago, and also have some identical beliefs and the like. In sum, there is *psychological continuity.* Parfit is best known for his formidable development, partly in terms of further ideas of uniqueness, cause, and brain, of what is called this Lockean idea. That was in his uniquely methodical and regulating book *Reasons and Persons.*

To these three responses to the problem of personal identity has more recently been added what has been known as the idea of *animalism,* that two persons are the same person if they are the same animal or human animal—if there is what is also called *biological continuity.* Parfit takes and speaks of this as the view that personal identity is a matter of *same human being,* and so in the title of his lecture denies that we as individual persons are individuated as human beings.

It is his main concern in his lecture to refute this view but also, so to speak, to learn from it. Proceeding by imagined cases or thought experiments like those that have been the main content of the philosophy of personal identity, he first considers objections by animalists to the Lockean idea, and then considers problems for animalism or biological continuity and also for the Lockean view and how the views do or do not solve them.

Partly prompted by animalism, he moves thereafter to the *Embodied Part View* of personal identity and then on to the principal contention of the lecture, that the truth about personal identity is the *Embodied Person View.* It is mainly a development of his original Lockeanism—a development to the effect that each person is an embodied conscious, thinking, and controlling part of a body, animal, or organism. It is no more a physicalism about personal identity than he originally had in mind. As remarked elsewhere, he continues to find physicalism implausible but rejects Cartesian dualism, and has not thought about the mind-body problem, regarding it as too difficult.

What follows in the lecture is consideration of objections to the Embodied Part and the Embodied Person View, much of this consideration by way of the proposition that the pronouns 'I' and 'you' are in a way ambiguous. Finally the possibility is considered of whether the lecturer has undermined his own original case by his development of it. He also considers a strengthening of what was an upshot of his original view—that personal identity cannot be what matters, or anyway what matters as much to us as before we come to understand it rightly.

All of the lecture is a typically indefatigable train of argument. It is a sequence of particular proofs, or particular propositions akin to proofs, that add up to something about as approximate to proof of a whole theory as the unique difficulty of philosophy allows. It is a lecture like others in this volume that are more in need of encouragement in advance for readers than summary. It is also a lecture ending in generosity to animalist opponents, including Paul Snowdon, Eric Olson, and others.

Inclined as I myself am to a developed kind of Lockean and indeed Parfitian view of personal identity, I ask but one question. In philosophy and elsewhere, there is endless concern with *subjectivity* in connection with consciousness. Is it the same fact as personal identity conceived in a way like the one defended in the lecture?

12

We Are Not Human Beings

Derek Parfit

1

We can start with some science fiction. Here on Earth, I enter the *Teletransporter*. When I press some button, a machine destroys my body, while recording the exact states of all my cells. This information is sent by radio to Mars, where another machine makes, out of organic materials, a perfect copy of my body. The person who wakes up on Mars seems to remember living my life up to the moment when I pressed the button, and is in every other way just like me.

Of those who have thought about such cases, some believe that it would be I who would wake up on Mars. They regard Teletransportation as merely the fastest way of travelling. Others believe that, if I chose to be Teletransported, I would be making a terrible mistake. On their view, the person who wakes up would be a mere Replica of me.

This disagreement is about personal identity. To describe such disagreements, we can first distinguish two kinds of sameness. Two black billiard balls may be qualitatively identical, or exactly similar. But they are not numerically identical, or one and the same ball. If I paint one of these balls red, it will cease to be qualitatively identical with itself as it was; but it will still be one and the same ball. Consider next a claim like, 'Since her accident, she is no longer the same person'. This claim involves both senses of identity, since it means that *she*, one and the same person, is *not* now the same person. That is not a contradiction, since it means that this person's character has changed. This numerically identical person is now qualitatively different.

When people discuss personal identity, they are often discussing what kind of person someone is, or wants to be. That is the question involved, for example, in an identity crisis. But I shall be discussing our numerical identity. In our concern about our own futures, that is what we have in mind. I may believe that, after my marriage, I shall be a different person. But that does not make marriage death. However much

I change, I shall still be alive if there will be someone living who will be me. And in my imagined case of Teletransportation, my Replica on Mars would be qualitatively identical to me; but, on the sceptic's view, he wouldn't *be* me. *I* shall have ceased to exist. That, we naturally assume, is what matters.

In questions about numerical identity, we use two names or descriptions, and we ask whether these refer to the same person. In most cases, we use descriptions that refer to people at different times. Thus, when using the telephone, we might ask whether the person to whom we are speaking now is the same as the person to whom we spoke yesterday. To answer such questions, we must know the *criterion* of personal identity over time, by which I mean: the relation between a person at one time, and a person at another time, which makes these one and the same person. We can also ask what kind of entity we *are*, since entities of different kinds continue to exist in different ways.

Views about what we are, and how we might continue to exist, can be placed, roughly, in three main groups. On some views, what we are, or have as an essential part, is a soul: an immaterial persisting entity, which is indivisible, and whose continued existence must be all-or-nothing. Even if we don't believe in immaterial souls, many of us have some beliefs about ourselves, and personal identity, that would be justified only if some such view were true. Though such views make sense, and might have been true, I shall not discuss them today, since we have strong evidence that no such view is true.

Of the other views, some can be called *Lockean*. Locke famously defined a person as 'a thinking intelligent being that has reason and reflection and can consider itself as itself, the same thinking thing in different times and places'.[1] Lockean criteria of identity appeal to the kind of psychological continuity that, in my imagined case, holds between me and my Replica. The Lockean view that I have earlier defended, which I called

the Narrow, Brain-Based Psychological Criterion States: If some future person would be uniquely psychologically continuous with me as I am now, and this continuity would have its normal cause, enough of the same brain, this person would be me. If some future person would neither be uniquely psychologically continuous with me as I am now, nor have enough of the same brain, this person would *not* be me. In all other cases, there would be no answer to the question whether some future person would be me. But there would be nothing that we did not know.

On this view, my Replica would not be me, since he would not have my brain. That, I claimed, would not matter, since being destroyed and Replicated would be as good as ordinary survival. I shall later return briefly to that claim. The other main kind of view appeals not to psychological but to biological continuity, and is now often called *Animalist*.

---

[1] John Locke, *Essay Concerning Human Understanding*, Book II, Chapter XXVI, Section 9.

In considering this disagreement, I shall first describe some Animalist objections to the various Lockean views that were put forward, in the nineteen sixties, seventies, and eighties, by such people as Shoemaker, Quinton, Perry, Lewis, and me. As Snowdon, Olson, and other Animalists pointed out, we Lockeans said nothing about the human beings—or to use a less ambiguous phrase, the human animals—that many of us think we are.

If persons are, in the Lockean sense, entities that can think about themselves, and whose continued existence essentially involves psychological continuity, a human embryo or fetus is not a person. But this fetus is, or becomes, a human animal. This animal's body, Lockeans claim, later becomes the body of a Lockean person. Animalists ask: What then happens to the human animal? It would be convenient for Lockeans if this animal retired from the scene, by ceasing to exist, thereby leaving its body under the sole control of the newly existing person. But that is not what happens. Most human animals continue to exist, and start to have thoughts and other experiences. So if Lockeans distinguish between persons and human animals, their view implies that whenever any person thinks some thought, a human animal also thinks this thought. Every thinking of a thought has two different thinkers. That conclusion seems absurd. As McDowell writes: 'surely there are not two lives being led here, the life of the human being... and the life of the person.'[2] We can call this the *Too Many Thinkers Problem*.

There may also be an *Epistemic Problem*. If there are two conscious beings thinking all my thoughts, the person and the animal, how could I know which one I am? If I think I am the person, Animalists object, I might be mistaken, since I may really be the animal.

There is a third problem. Snowdon pointed out that, on Locke's definition, human animals qualify as persons.[3] So if Lockeans distinguish persons from human animals, they must admit that, on their view, all of our thoughts and other experiences are had by two persons, one of whom is also an animal. This objection may seem decisive, by undermining the whole point of this Lockean distinction. We can call this the *Too Many Persons Problem*.

Several Lockeans have suggested answers to these objections. Shoemaker, for example, argues that, if we claim animals to be entities whose criterion of identity is biological, and requires the continued existence of much of their bodies, such animals could not think, or have other mental states, since the concepts that refer to mental states apply only to entities whose criterion of identity is psychological.

---

[2] John McDowell, 'Reductionism and the First Person', in *Reading Parfit*, edited by Jonathan Dancy (Blackwell, 1997), 237.

[3] P. F. Snowdon, 'Persons, Animals, and Ourselves', in *The Person and the Human Mind*, edited by Christopher Gill (Oxford University Press, 1990), page 90.

Though these human animals might seem to have thoughts and experiences, that would not really be true.[4]

Baker argues that the animal and the person are both constituted by the same body, which gives them an ontological status that is in between being one and the same entity and being two, separately existing entities. For that reason, Baker claims, though there are, strictly, two different thinkers thinking each of our thoughts, we can count these thinkers as if they were one.[5]

We can next distinguish between concepts which are *substance sortals*, in the sense that they apply to some persisting entity whenever it exists, and *phase sortals*, which apply to some entity, in the present tense, only while this entity has certain properties. Two such phase sortals are 'teenager' and 'caterpillar'. When we reach the age of 20, we cease to be teenagers, but we don't thereby cease to exist. Nor do caterpillars cease to exist when they become butterflies.

I have earlier suggested that, in response to these Animalist objections, Lockeans should claim that the concept of a person is another phase sortal.[6] On this view, we are human animals who began to exist as an embryo or fetus though we were not then persons in the Lockean sense. And if we suffered brain damage which made us irreversibly unconscious, we would continue to exist, though we would have ceased to be persons. One of Locke's aims was to describe persons in the way that makes most sense of our practical and moral beliefs. 'Person', Locke writes, 'is a forensic term', applying only to responsible rational beings. We could keep this part of the Lockean view if we claim that we have certain reasons, and certain principles apply to us, only while we are persons. For example, I might point to an ultrasound image of an embryo or fetus, saying 'There I am. That was me', but adding that, since I was not then a person, it would not have been wrong for some doctor to kill me. We might make similar claims about the concept of a human being. We might say that, just as an acorn with one green shoot sprouting is not yet an oak tree, an embryo is not yet a human being. And some other moral principles apply to us, we might claim, only after we become human beings.

Lockeans, I now believe, need not retreat to any such claim. There is another, stronger, Lockean view that can answer the Animalist objections that I have described. This view also avoids some problems that face Animalist views. So I shall next describe these other problems.

---

[4] Sydney Shoemaker, 'On What We Are', in *The Oxford Handbook of the Self*, edited by Shaun Gallagher (Oxford University Press, 2011). In what follows, I shall not be rejecting Shoemaker's view, but proposing another, simpler way of thinking about ourselves.

[5] Lynne Rudder Baker, *Persons and Bodies* (Cambridge University Press, 2000).

[6] In my 'Persons, Bodies, and Human Beings', written around 1992, published in *Contemporary Debates in Metaphysics*, edited by John Hawthorne, Dean Zimmerman, and Theodore Sider (Blackwell, 2008).

2

Most Animalists believe that we shall continue to exist if and only if our bodies continue to exist, and to be the bodies of living animals. Williams even claimed that
persons *are* bodies.[7] But suppose that, in

Transplanted Head, my body is fatally diseased, as is Williams's brain. Since we have, between
us, only one good brain and body, surgeons bring these together. My head is successfully
grafted onto the rest of Williams's headless body.

On Williams' view, he would wake up with my head, being psychologically just like
me and mistakenly believing that he was me.

Most of us would find that claim incredible. Suppose that you knew both Williams
and me, and you visit the resulting person in the post-operative recovery room. You
see my head on the pillow, and have a long conversation with someone whom you
assume to be me. If some nurse then lifted the blankets on the bed, and you saw the
rest of what you knew to be Williams' body, you wouldn't conclude that you *weren't*,
as you assumed, talking to me. You would believe that the person with my head
would be me. As many Animalists concede, this widely held belief, which some call
the *Transplant Intuition*, provides a strong objection to their view.

Olson suggests that Animalists can explain why most of us find this objection plausible.[8] In all actual cases, Olson claims, when some present person is psychologically
continuous with some past person, that is strong evidence that these people have the
same body, thereby being one and the same person. So it is not surprising that we
mistakenly believe that, if our brain and psychology were transplanted into a different body, we would wake up in that other body. We would find this Brain-Based
Psychological Criterion just as plausible, even if, as Animalists believe, this criterion
is false.

These claims do not, I believe, answer this objection to Animalism. When we
compare different proposed criteria of identity, we should consider cases in which
these criteria would conflict. If in such imagined cases Criterion A seems much more
plausible than Criterion B, we cannot defend B by saying that A seems plausible only
because, in all or most actual cases, A coincides with B. Suppose that, on the *Finger
Print Criterion*, some future person would be the same as some present person if and
only if these people have qualitatively identical finger prints. In rejecting this view, we
could point out that, if some plastic surgeon remoulded the tips of someone's fingers,
we would all believe that this person would continue to exist, with the same brain
and psychology, though with different finger prints. Finger Printists might reply that,
if this Brain-Based Psychological Criterion seems more plausible when it conflicts

---

[7] Bernard Williams, 'Are Persons Bodies?', in *Problems of the Self* (Cambridge University Press, 1973).
[8] Eric Olson, 'Animalism and the Remnant Person Problem', henceforth 'Animalism', Sections 1 and 2,
in *Metaphysics of the Self,* edited by J. Goncalves (Peter Lang, *forthcoming*).

with the Finger Print Criterion, that is only because, in nearly all actual cases, people with the same brain and psychology also have the same finger prints. That would be a weak reply. If the Finger Print Criterion seems much less plausible when these criteria conflict, that is a strong objection to this criterion. Similar remarks apply to the Transplant Intuition. If it seems very plausible that the person with my head but the rest of Williams' body would be me, that is a strong objection to the Animalist claim that this person would be Williams.

Some Animalists assume that all animals have the same criterion of identity over time. Since many animals, such as oysters, do not even have psychologies or brains, these Animalists could not accept a Brain-Based Psychological Criterion of animal identity. But other Animalists might claim that different kinds of animal continue to exist in different ways, and with different criteria of identity. At least in the case of human beings, they might say, the animal goes with the brain. These Animalists would then agree that, in *Transplanted Head,* the resulting person would be me.

This version of Animalism may now seem to coincide with this Lockean view, thereby ending this disagreement. But that is not so. We should distinguish between our cerebra, or upper brains, and our brain stems. It is our cerebrum on which all of our distinctive mental activity depends. The brain stem controls the functioning of our body in other ways. Most Animalists believe that, if our cerebrum were destroyed, but our brain stem continued to maintain the functioning of our heart, lungs, and most of our other organs, we the human animal would continue to exist, though in an unconscious vegetative state, or coma.

We can therefore add some details to our imagined case. We can suppose that, in *Transplanted Head,* my brain stem would be left behind. It is only my head and cerebrum that would be successfully grafted onto Williams' brain stem and the rest of Williams' body. With its brain stem retained, my body would then continue to be the body of a living though unconscious animal. It would be implausible to claim that this would now be a *different* animal, because the animal that used to have this body had gone with its cerebrum into a different body.

Suppose next that in another case, which we can call

Surviving Head, my head and cerebrum are not grafted onto someone else's brain stem and body, but are kept alive and functioning by an artificial support system.

As before, you visit the post-operative recovery room, see my head on the pillow, and talk with what you take to be me. If the nurse lifted the blankets on the bed, and you saw not a human body but an artificial support system, you wouldn't believe that the conscious being to whom you had been talking *wasn't* me. Some Animalists might claim that this conscious being would be the same animal as me. But there is now a different objection to this view. This conscious being would be a person, in the Lockean sense. But this person, whose physical basis is only an artificially supported head, would not seem to be an animal.

To strengthen this objection, suppose that, in

Surviving Cerebrum, what is removed from my body is not my head, but only my cerebrum, which is then kept functioning by an artificial support system. The resulting entity is conscious, as the neuro-physiological evidence shows. There is also some device which enables this conscious being to communicate with the outside world, since the brain activity involved in certain voluntary mental acts enables this being to spell out the words of messages to us, and some other device enables us to send replies. In this way you have conversations with this conscious being, who claims to be me, seems to have all my memories, and starts to dictate the rest of my unfinished book.

As before, this conscious rational being would be a Lockean person, whom many of us would believe to be me. But it would be harder for Animalists to defend the claim that this conscious being, whose physical basis is only a cerebrum, is an animal, and the same animal as me.

It is worth supposing, however, that some Animalists make this claim. These people might say that an early embryo is a human animal, though it lacks most of the properties of a living organism. The same would be true, they might claim, of my detached, artificially supported cerebrum.

If Animalists made this claim, their view would cease to be an alternative to Lockean views. On the Lockean Brain-Based Psychological Criterion, some future person would be me if this person would be uniquely psychologically continuous with me, because he would have enough of my brain. This criterion implies that, in *Surviving Cerebrum*, the conscious being would be the same person as me. When Animalists entered this debate, their main claim was that such psychological criteria of identity are seriously mistaken, because we are human animals, so that our criterion of identity must be biological. If these Animalists now claimed that, in *Surviving Cerebrum*, the conscious rational being would be a living animal, who would be me, these people would be claiming that the true criterion of identity for developed human animals is of this Lockean psychological kind.[9] Since these Animalists would now be Lockeans, I shall here consider only those other, Non-Lockean, Animalists who would believe that, in *Surviving Cerebrum*, the conscious being, though a Lockean person, would not be an animal.

This fact, these Animalists might say, is compatible with their view, which claims only that most persons are animals. There might be some conscious beings that are Lockean persons but aren't animals. But we could then ask: How would this conscious being be related to the human animal, Parfit, who used to have this cerebrum?

Animalists have two alternatives. They might claim that, when my cerebrum is detached from the rest of my body, a new conscious rational being comes into existence. But, as Johnston and Olson write, that claim would be hard to believe. It is hard

---

[9] These Animalists would be adding only that these Lockeans had failed to point out that their criterion also applies to human animals. That would be no objection to this Lockean view.

to see how we could create a new conscious being merely by disconnecting my cerebrum from the rest of my body.

Suppose next that, after this conscious being spends many days communicating with us, my cerebrum is detached from its artificial support system and successfully grafted onto some other human animal's brain stem and body. The resulting being would then be a human animal. But what would happen to the conscious being which existed for a period on its own, as a non-animal? It would be convenient for Animalists if this Lockean person, who is not an animal, would cease to exist when my cerebrum was grafted onto the rest of someone else's body. But it is hard to see how, merely by connecting this conscious being to the rest of this body, we would thereby cause this being to cease to exist. Animalists object to the way in which, when Lockeans describe how a young human animal becomes a person, Lockeans implausibly assume that the animal then retires from the scene. The same problem arises here the other way round. Animalists cannot plausibly assume that, when my cerebrum is grafted onto this animal's body, this Lockean person would retire from the scene. As Olson writes:

Animalism seems to imply that the detached brain would be a person who comes into being when the brain is removed and ceases to exist when the brain goes into a new head. And that seems absurd.[10]

Olson calls these the *Creation and Destruction Problems*.

To avoid these problems, Animalists might instead claim that this conscious being already existed when my cerebrum was in my body, and that this being would continue to exist both while it is artificially supported, and after it is grafted into another human animal's body. But if Animalists made this claim, they would face another version of the Too Many Thinkers Problem. As well as the human animal thinking my thoughts, there would be another conscious being that was not an animal, thinking all the same thoughts. This problem, moreover, isn't raised only by this imagined case. It applies to every actual fully developed human animal. On this version of the Animalist view, all of any human animal's thoughts are also thought by another, different, conscious being.

Animalists, Olson writes, therefore face this dilemma:

if your brain thinks now, there are too many thinkers; if it doesn't, things can gain or lose mental capacities in an utterly baffling way.[11]

Olson calls this the *Thinking Parts Problem*. This problem, he writes, is 'considerably more serious than animalism's unintuitive consequences in brain-transplant cases', adding that 'it has no obvious solution'.[12]

---

[10]   Olson, 'Animalism', Abstract.   [11]   Olson, 'Animalism', end of Section 5.
[12]   Eric Olson, *What Are We?* (Oxford University Press, 2007), 216.

3

This problem has, I believe, an obvious solution. According to some Lockeans, as I have said, the person and the animal are both constituted by the same body, in a way that makes them, though not numerically identical, not wholly separate either. On this view, though it is strictly true that each thought is thought by two thinkers, the person and the animal, we can count these thinkers as if they were one.

According to another, better view, we are not animals, or human beings. We are what McMahan calls the conscious, thinking, and controlling parts of human beings. We can call this the *Embodied Part View*. The Thinking Parts Problem has a thinking parts solution.

On this view, the Creation and Destruction Problems disappear. If my cerebrum were detached from the rest of my body and artificially supported, no new conscious being would mysteriously come into existence. Nor would a conscious being mysteriously disappear if my cerebrum were later successfully grafted onto another human body. The same conscious being would exist throughout, first as the thinking, controlling part of one human animal, then existing for a while on its own, then becoming the thinking, controlling part of a different human animal.

This view also avoids the Too Many Thinkers Problem. Animals digest their food by having a part, their stomach, that does the digesting. Animals sneeze by having a part, their nose, that does the sneezing. These facts do not create a Too Many Digesters or Too Many Sneezers Problem. Human animals think, we can similarly claim, by having a part that does the thinking. There are not too many thinkers here.

Some Animalists consider this Embodied Part View. Olson writes:

If we are neither animals nor material things constituted by animals, we might be parts of animals.

But Olson then rejects this view, calling it 'a desperate ploy', and doubting whether anyone 'seriously advocates' this view.[13]

Olson rejects this view because he assumes that an animal's thinking part would have to be claimed to be its brain. Though Olson calls it 'just about conceivable that the brain view might be true', he does not include this view among the 'live options' that are worth considering. Johnston similarly claims that, if we accept the view that brains can think, we shall be led to absurd conclusions.[14]

What Olson calls the brain view is, however, only one version of the Embodied Part View. This version is not, I believe, absurd. Some other Animalists claim that,

---

[13] Olson, Animalism, start of Section 7.
[14] Mark Johnston, 'Human Beings Revisited: My Body is Not an Animal', in *Oxford Studies in Metaphysics*, Volume 3, edited by Dean Zimmerman (Oxford University Press, 2007), 54–5.

rather than having bodies, we *are* bodies. On that view, it is our bodies that have our experiences, and think our thoughts. If these other Animalists came to accept the Embodied Part View, they might claim that the animal's conscious thinking part is not its body but its cerebrum or upper brain. Rather than saying, for example, that Einstein's body discovered the theory of general relativity, they would say that Einstein's brain made this discovery. Many people would find that claim more plausible. In a well-known radio quiz programme, people compete for the title *Brain of Britain*. And Hercule Poirot says, tapping his forehead, 'These little grey cells. It is "up to them"'.

If we are Embodied Part Theorists, however, we need not make such claims. The thinking part of a human animal, we could say, is related to this animal's cerebrum or upper brain in a way that is roughly similar to that in which this animal is related to its whole body. Most of us distinguish between ourselves and our bodies. If we deny that human animals *are* their bodies, we could similarly deny that the thinking part of these animals is their upper brain.

In what seems to me the best of the few published defences of the Embodied Part View, McMahan claims that we are the *minds* of human animals. McMahan calls this the *Embodied Mind View*.[15]

Some Animalists come close to accepting this view. Carter imagines a case in which President Nixon's brain is transplanted into the empty skull of Senator McGovern. Nixon's mind, Carter claims, would then become McGovern's mind. And Carter writes:

McGovern's mind may... remember being part of a person who stepped onto a certain helicopter after resigning as President.[16]

If we transferred Nixon's brain into McGovern's body, Carter adds, McGovern might bear some moral responsibility for Nixon's decision to bomb Cambodia, since the mind that used to be Nixon's but is now McGovern's would be 'the mind that once decided to do this awful thing'.

Since Carter claims that our decisions are made by our minds, we might expect him to claim that we, the decision-makers, *are* these minds. On that view, in Carter's imagined case, we would not unjustly hold McGovern responsible for Nixon's earlier decisions. But Carter rejects this view, writing:

since people have arms and legs and minds don't, people can't be identified with minds.[17]

[15] Jefferson McMahan, *Killing at the Margins of Life* (Oxford University Press, 2002), Chapter 1. The Embodied Parts Proposal was independently suggested by Ingmar Persson, in his 'Our Identity and the Separability of Persons and Organisms', *Dialogue*, 1999. But Persson rejected this view, on what seem to me overly sceptical grounds. See also his 'Self-Doubt: Why We Are Not Identical To Things of Any Kinds', *Ratio*, December 2004, and his magisterial *The Retreat of Reason* (Oxford University Press, 2005).

[16] William R. Carter, 'How to Change Your Mind', *Canadian Journal of Philosophy*, May 1989, 13.

[17] Carter, 'How to Change Your Mind', 7, note 9.

Some other people would object that, just as we shouldn't claim that *brains* think, or make decisions, we shouldn't claim that *minds* think, or make decisions. Johnston, for example, writes:

If we are saying that something is… thinking… the subject of predication should be an animal or person.[18]

Embodied Part Theorists can make similar claims. On a third version of this view, human animals think by having a conscious thinking part which is a person in the Lockean sense. We can call this the *Embodied Person View*. This, I believe, is the best version of the Embodied Part View.[19]

Though Olson claims that the Thinking Parts Problem has no obvious solution, this problem, he writes, 'is no reason to prefer any other view to Animalism'.[20] That is not so. This problem is a strong reason to prefer the Embodied Part View, since this is the only view on which the Thinking Parts Problem disappears.

Nor is this view merely a philosophical invention, since it states more clearly what many non-philosophers already believe, or would after reflection believe. Olson writes:

no one thinks that we are heads.

No one, we should agree, thinks that we are *just* heads. But we might be *embodied* heads. And most of us would believe that, for us to survive, it would be enough that our head survives, and continues to be the head of a conscious being. The body below the neck is not an essential part of us.

We can next mention the actual cases of those conjoined twins who share all or most of the same body below the neck, but have two heads, and have different thoughts and other experiences. No one doubts that these are the heads of two different people.

It may be less obvious that, for us to survive, it would be enough that our cerebrum survives. If those who love me, rather than seeing my head on a pillow, saw only an artificially supported cerebrum floating in a vat, they might doubt that I was still there. But as the dictated messages would show, the conscious being based on this cerebrum would be psychologically just like me, seem to have all my memories, etc. After reflection most of us would believe that I *was* still there. Whether I have continued to exist could not depend on whether my functioning cerebrum retained its outer covering of bone and skin, so that this conscious being still looked like me.

There are many actual cases of another relevant kind. One such case is that of Nancy Cruzan, whose cerebrum ceased to function, but whose brain stem maintained her body in a vegetative state for seven years until a US Supreme Court ruling granted her

---

[18] Mark Johnston, 'My Body is Not an Animal', in *Oxford Studies in Metaphysics*, Volume 4, edited by D. Zimmerman (Oxford University Press, 2006), 54. There is much highly relevant material, which I hope to discuss elsewhere, in Johnston's *Surviving Death* (Princeton University Press, 2010).
[19] Though we can also apply the Embodied Part View to such animals as dogs, whose conscious, thinking and controlling part may be at best a borderline case of a Lockean person.
[20] Olson, *What Are We?* note 13, 216.

parents' request to have an artificial feeding tube removed. On Cruzan's gravestone her parents had inscribed:

Departed January 11 1983... At Peace December 26 1990

When Cruzan's cerebrum was irreparably damaged, her parents came to believe, Cruzan the person departed from her body, though the human animal continued to exist with its heart beating and its lungs breathing until, after the feeding tube was removed, the heart stopped and the animal was at peace.

Nor are we merely appealing to such intuitions. We have reasons to make such claims. While defending Animalism, Olson writes:

if there are now two things thinking your thoughts, one doing it on its own and the other such that its thinking is done for it by something else, you are the one that thinks on its own.[21]

But this plausible *own-thinker principle* supports, not Animalism, but the Embodied Person View. The animal's thinking is done for it by something else, the part whose physical basis is the cerebrum. This human animal could not think on its own, since without this part it could not think at all. But the conscious thinking part *can* think on its own, as it would do in some of the imagined cases that we have been considering. If, as Olson claims, we are 'the one that thinks on its own', we are not the animal but this conscious thinking being, the Lockean embodied person.

When Johnston discusses these cases, he appeals to something like the own-thinker principle. Johnston considers the suggestion that, though the person and the animal think the same thoughts, that is not puzzling, since there are not two separate thinkers here. On this view:

(1) the person 'counts as a thinker derivatively', since the person thinks only '*because* the animal does'.

Johnston rejects this view, claiming that it 'gives the wrong result'. In his words:

if I had to pick which of two things I am identical with, the person or the animal, a good rule would be: Pick the thing which is *non-derivatively* the subject of mental acts. And on the present proposal... it is the animal, and not the person, that is non-derivatively the subject of mental acts.... But the result we wanted is that I am identical with the person.[22]

Since this proposal gets things the wrong way round, the obvious next suggestion is that:

(2) we are identical, not with the animal, but with the person, which is the non-derivative thinker, and the subject of our mental acts.

[21] Olson, 'Animalism', Section 5, quoting from Roderick Chisholm, *Person and Object* (Open Court, 1976), 104.
[22] Johnston, 'My Body is Not an Animal', 50.

Johnston comes close to accepting (2), since he discusses the view that any human animal has 'a mental organ dependent on its brain, whose operation constitutes the animal's thinking', and he also claims that, as persons, we should take ourselves to be 'the non-derivative or primary source of the thought in us'. These claims support the view that:

(3) we, who are persons, are the part of the animal that does the thinking.

Johnston, however, rejects (3). Summarizing what is shown by the Too Many Thinkers Problem, Johnston writes:

Olson has a sound argument here... one that must condition all further discussion of personal identity. *We are animals.*[23]

Johnston adds only that we, who are persons, are not essentially animals, since he believes that, in cases like *Surviving Head* or *Cerebrum*, we would continue to exist as persons, though we would have ceased to be animals. Though Johnston's other claims imply that we are the part of the animal that does the thinking, Johnston's belief that we *are* animals leads him to reject that conclusion.

4

I turn now to possible objections to the Embodied Part View, whose best form I have claimed to be the Embodied Person View.

One objection is that, as Carter claims, we can't *be* our minds, since we have arms and legs and our minds don't. Discussing the view that we are brains rather than minds, Olson similarly writes:

Is it really a serious view... that we are about four inches tall and weigh about three pounds?[24]

We can call this the *Physical Properties Objection*. On this objection, we have many physical properties which cannot be had by our conscious thinking part, whether we claim this part to be a brain, or a mind, or a Lockean person. Since we have such physical properties, we must be human animals, rather than some part of these animals.

This objection can be answered. If we are *embodied* persons, as I believe, we can explain how and why we can intelligibly claim ourselves to have the physical properties of our bodies. We already do that now if we distinguish between ourselves and our bodies, as when I say that I am 6 foot tall and weigh 160 pounds because my body has these properties.

We sometimes use 'I' and 'me' more widely, to refer to more than our bodies. I might say, for example, that I have been splashed with mud, though it was only my trousers that were splashed. And if I were a veiled Islamic woman, I might say that someone had seen

[23] Johnston, 'My Body is Not an Animal', 48.   [24] Olson, *What are We?* 76.

me, though this person saw only my clothes. If we are the conscious controlling part of an animal, we are very closely related to the rest of this animal's body, in which we can feel sensations, and with which we can see, hear, smell, and touch the world around us. As Descartes wrote, while defending his soul-involving version of the Embodied Part View, this controlling part is not lodged in our body merely in the way in which a pilot is lodged in a ship. Since we can explain how and why, on the Embodied Part View, we can claim ourselves to have the properties of our bodies, the Physical Properties Objection fails.

We can next return to the Epistemic Problem, which is held to count against all views which distinguish between a person and a human animal. On such views, Olson writes:

how could you ever know which one you are? You may think you're the person. But whatever you think, the animal thinks too. So the animal would... believe that *it* is a person... Yet it is mistaken. If you *were* the animal and not the person, you'd still think you were the person. So for all you know, you're the one making the mistake.[25]

Olson here assumes that pronouns like 'I' and 'you' are unambiguous, and must always refer to the same thing.

That is not, I believe, true. We use 'I' in different senses, or ways. It is often claimed that the word 'I' unambiguously refers to the speaker of the sentence in which 'I' is used, or to the thinker of an I-involving thought. But this claim itself illustrates the ambiguity. The speaker of any sentence may be a human animal. But when we think I-involving thoughts, we may not be intending to refer to a human animal. We can think of ourself as the direct thinker of these thoughts, whatever this thinker is. This thinker might be, not the animal, but the part of the animal that does the thinking, which I am calling the Lockean person.

If our pronouns are in this way ambiguous, the Epistemic Problem partly disappears. In describing this problem, Olson writes:

Suppose you were the animal rather than the person.

But we can't usefully *suppose* either that we are the animal, or that we are the person, since we would then be supposing falsely that the words 'I' and 'we' must always refer to the same thing. Some uses of these words may refer to an animal, and others to a person. The names of nations have a similar ambiguity, since they may refer to a nation-state, as in the claim 'France declared war', or to a part of the Earth's surface, as in the claim 'France is roughly hexagonal'. We shouldn't claim that France must be either a nation-state or a part of the Earth's surface, though we don't know which.

It will help to make our pronouns more precise. In our thoughts about ourselves, we can use the phrase 'Inner-I' to refer to the Lockean person, and 'Outer-I' to refer to the human animal. We can use similar senses of Inner- and Outer- me, you, he, she, we, and us. Suppose next that someone thinks both:

(A) Inner-I am the person, the conscious, thinking, controlling part of this animal, which is directly thinking this thought,

---

[25] Eric Olson, 'Thinking Animals and the Reference of "I"', *Philosophical Topics*, Spring, 2002.

and

(B) Outer-I am the animal that is indirectly thinking this thought, by having a part, Inner-I, that does the thinking.

On the Embodied Person View, the person and the animal both think both these thoughts. And, as thought by either thinker, both thoughts are true.

It might be objected that, when the animal believes that:

(A) Inner-I am the person,

the animal would be falsely believing that *it* is the person, since it would be using the pronoun 'Inner-I' and the verb 'am' to have a belief about itself. But that is not so. The animal would understand these new, more precise pronouns, by having a part that understands them, and the animal believes (B) as well as (A), by having a part that does the believing. If these uses of the word 'am' seem misleading, we could restate these thoughts as:

(C) Inner-I *is* the person that directly thinks these thoughts, and Outer-I *is* the animal that indirectly thinks them.

We can use 'is' rather than 'am' when thinking about ourselves, as General De Gaulle did whenever he thought 'De Gaulle is the saviour of France'. As before, whether (C) is thought directly by the person, or indirectly by the animal, (C) is true.

Return now to Olson's claim that, if there were two thinkers of all our thoughts, the person and the animal, neither thinker could know which one it was. When Olson presents this objection, he discusses the version of Teletransportation which I called *the Branch Line Case*.[26] Suppose that the new improved replicator scans my brain and body without destroying them, and then makes a Replica of me, in a room that is just like mine. Olson claims that, because I and my Replica would be exactly similar, in exactly similar surroundings, each of us would believe that he was me, and neither could know which of us was right. Similar remarks apply, Olson claims, to the Lockean view which distinguishes between the person and the animal. But this analogy is misleading. When I and my Replica both believe ourselves to be me, and then wonder who is right, these are two different conscious mental processes, or episodes of thinking. No such claim applies to the Lockean view. On this view, just as there is only a single episode of sneezing when the animal sneezes by having a part, its nose, that does the sneezing, there is only a single episode of thinking when the animal thinks by having a part that does the thinking.

Consider next Johnston's claim that we should take ourselves to be 'the *non-derivative* or primary source of the thought in us'. We can distinguish two kinds

[26] Eric Olson, 'Personal Identity', Section 6, *Stanford Encyclopaedia of Philosophy*, 2002.

of derivative thinking. Some of our thinking is derivative in the sense that we are merely thinking again what someone else thought first, and led us to think. Platonists, for example, might derivatively think what Plato thought. The Moon similarly shines at night, in a derivative way, by reflecting light that comes from the Sun, which is the Solar System's non-derivative or primary source of light. But no such claim applies to the animal and its conscious, thinking part. When a human animal thinks by having a part that thinks, there is nothing that corresponds to the derivative shining of the Moon. There are not two thinkers here, one of whom thinks in a derivative way by thinking again what the other thinks. The animal's thoughts are derivative in a second, stronger sense. When Inner-I the Lockean person thinks some thought, we can truly say that Outer-I the animal thereby thinks this thought. But the animal does not itself do any thinking. The animal cannot think in what Olson calls the *strict* or non-derivative sense.

On the objection that we are discussing, if there was both a person and an animal which think all the same thoughts, neither could know whether it was the animal or the person. This objection can now be answered. When Descartes asked what he could know, despite the arguments for scepticism, he thought:

I think, therefore I am.

Descartes concluded that he could know that he was an immaterial thinking substance. As Lichtenberg objected, Descartes should have thought only:

This is the thinking of a thought, so at least some thinking is going on.

Descartes' *Cogito* leaves it open in what sense, or way, any thought must have a thinker. This question we can also leave open here. We can assume that any conscious being that can think about itself, and its identity, is at least a person in the Lockean sense, whatever else this being may be. We are supposing that someone thinks:

(C) Inner-I is the person that is directly thinking these thoughts, and Outer-I is the animal that is indirectly thinking them, by having a part that is doing the thinking.

To explain the meaning of the pronoun 'Inner-I', we can claim that, when used in some thought, this pronoun refers to the person that is the direct thinker of this very thought. When any direct thinker uses 'Inner-I', knowing what this phrase means, this thinker knows that it thereby refers to itself. So in thinking (C), Inner-I the person would know that it is not the animal but the person.

We can next ask what the animal could know. Just as the animal thinks some thought only by having a part, the Lockean person, that does the thinking, the animal can know something only by having a part, the person, that knows this thing. Since the person knows that Outer-I is the animal that indirectly thinks these thoughts, the animal thereby knows, in its derivative way, that Outer-I is this animal. Nor could the animal be mistaken, since the animal cannot make any mistake except by having a thinking part that makes this mistake, and this part, the Lockean person, would not be mistaken.

There is, I conclude, no Epistemic Problem. And if Lockeans appeal to the Embodied Person View, they can answer the other Animalist objections to Lockean views. Since the animal thinks only by having a part that thinks, there are not too many thinkers here. And since the animal is a person only in the derivative sense of having a Lockean person as a part, there are not too many persons here.

5

The title of this lecture claims that we are not human beings, in the sense that means: human animals. Some of my remarks may seem to have undermined that claim. If our pronouns are ambiguous, as I have suggested, how can I hope to show that *we* are not human beings, or animals, but are the conscious, thinking, controlling parts of these animals?

I have not undermined that claim. If we resolved the ambiguity of our pronouns, by distinguishing the inner and outer senses, these senses would not have equal status, or equal importance in our conceptual scheme.

Return to my imagined case in which my head and cerebrum would be successfully grafted onto someone else's brain stem and the rest of that person's body. My own brain stem would maintain the functioning of the rest of my body, which would remain the body of a living but unconscious human animal.

Most of us would believe that, in this case, it would be I who would later wake up, with my head and the rest of this other person's body. If we used these more precise pronouns, we would then be believing that it would be Inner-I, the Lockean person, who would wake up, and continue my life with a new body below the neck. Outer-I the human animal would continue to exist in a vegetative state. But that would not affect Inner-Me, the person. And if we imagined ourselves about to undergo this operation, most of us would believe that we would be the person who woke up again, not the animal that lingered on in a vegetative state.

Since the inner senses of pronouns have more importance, we can now express these senses in the old familiar, briefer way. I hereby announce that, from now on, I shall use the word 'I' in the different, more precise sense that I have expressed with the phrase 'Inner-I'. I invite Inner-you, the other Lockean persons in this room, to do the same. We can then truly claim that we are not human beings in the sense that refers to human animals, but are the most important parts of these animals, the parts that do all the things that are most distinctive of these human animals, as conscious, thinking, rational beings.

Olson considers the objection that, since our pronouns are ambiguous, there is no single answer to the question of which entity we are. Though he is an Animalist, Olson then writes:

If the word 'I' in my mouth sometimes refers to a thinking thing and sometimes to an unthinking thing... [such as my body] then our concern is with the thinking thing. Never mind the referential role of personal pronouns. This is an essay in metaphysics. Our question is about the nature of the beings holding the enquiry. So we can rephrase our question.... What sorts of beings think our thoughts...?[27]

The answer, I have claimed, is: Lockean persons. Olson also writes:

Surely it couldn't turn out that there is something other than me that thinks my thoughts, whereas I myself think them only in some loose, second-rate sense?[28]

That is true, since Olson is such a Lockean person, the part of a human animal that thinks Olson's thoughts in the strict, first-rate sense.

If, as I have argued, we are not the animals that we call human beings, what difference does that make?

The most direct moral implications apply to the first part of every human being's life, and to the last part of many human beings' lives. According to the Catechism of the Catholic Church, 'Human life must be... protected absolutely from the moment of conception. From the first moment of his existence, a human being must be recognized as having the rights of a person.... The first right of the human person is his life' (1992). Many people make similar claims.

If we, who are Lockean persons, are not human beings, these claims do not apply to us. Nor do such claims apply when our cerebrum has died, so that we have ceased to exist, though our brain stem keeps the human animal alive. As McMahan claims, neither early abortion, nor removing a feeding tube from such a human being, would kill one of us. Though such acts raise moral questions, they do not violate the rights of persons.

If we are not human animals, that in one way makes little theoretical difference. In a book whose final proofs I corrected a few months ago, my first sentence is:

We are the animals that can both understand and respond to reasons.[29]

It was only while preparing this talk that I came to believe that we *aren't* animals, but are the conscious, thinking, controlling parts of these animals. But though my book's first sentence is, I now believe, misleading, I would not revise that sentence, but would only add a qualifying note. My sentence is close enough to being true. We are each part of a human animal, and we make this animal able, in a derivative way, to understand and respond to reasons. Outer-We are, in that sense, rational animals, because Inner-We are rational persons.

---

[27] Olson, *What Are We?*, note 13, 13.   [28] Olson, *What Are We?*, note 13, 79.
[29] Derek Parfit, *On What Matters* (Oxford University Press, 2011).

There are some other theoretical implications. For those who believe that we don't have souls, in the sense of persisting immaterial substances, one of the main recent philosophical disagreements has been between Lockean or psychological theories, and Animalist or biological theories. Animalism, Shoemaker writes, 'presents a powerful challenge to neo-Lockean views'. The 'crux of the current debate... [is] whether this challenge succeeds'.[30] I have tried to show that it does not. Animalists rightly claimed that Lockeans should not ignore the question whether we are animals, and Animalists put forward forceful objections to most Lockean views. But if Lockeans revise their claims, by turning to the Embodied Person View, these objections can, I have claimed, be answered. And this view also avoids some strong objections to Animalism. If Animalists also turned to this view, this disagreement would be resolved, and we together would have made philosophical progress.

I shall end with a more personal remark. In my earlier writings about these questions, my main aim was not to defend a Lockean criterion of personal identity, but to argue that, in our thoughts about our identity, or what is involved in our continuing to exist, most of us have, at some level, various false beliefs. We believe, for example, that if we are about to lose consciousness, it must either be true, or be false, that we shall wake up again. Such beliefs, I argued, are mistaken. Personal identity is not as deep, and simple, as most of us take it to be. Even if we did not know whether we would ever wake up again, we might know the full truth about what was going to happen. Since we have such false beliefs about what is involved in our continued existence, we may misunderstand the rational and moral importance of personal identity. On the true view, I claimed, though we have reasons for special concern about our future, these reasons are not given, as we assume, by the fact that this will be *our* future. Nor will our death be as significant as most of us believe. In my somewhat misleading slogan, personal identity is not what matters.

In defending these claims, I appealed in part to the imagined case in which two future people would be psychologically continuous with me as I am now, because each person would have one half of my cerebrum. But this is only one example. And I have found it hard to convince some people that, in other cases, personal identity is not what matters. I cannot persuade these people, for example, that if they were about to be destroyed and replicated, it would not matter that their future Replica would not be them, so that they would never wake up again.

If Animalism were true, it would be easier to defend these claims. Suppose again that, because your body below the neck is fatally diseased, as is someone else's cerebrum, doctors will successfully graft your head and cerebrum onto this other person's brain stem and headless body. According to Animalists, it would be this other person who would later wake up with your head, being psychologically just like you, and mistakenly believing that he or she was you. If we accepted this Animalist view, it would be easier to see that personal identity is not what matters. It would be clear

---

[30] Sydney Shoemaker, 'Persons, Animals, and Identity', *Synthese*, 2008, 315.

that, if someone would later wake up with your head, and would be psychologically just like you, it would have no practical or moral importance that this person would not be you. While defending his biological, Animalist view, Olson similarly writes:

In divorcing our identity from psychological continuity, the Biological Approach would entail that these relations of practical concern are even less reliably connected to with numerical identity than Parfit and Shoemaker have argued.[31]

If, as I have argued, Animalism is not true, I cannot defend my claims about what matters by appealing to this imagined case. That gives me a reason to *wish* that Animalism were true. But this is not a reason to *believe* that Animalism is true. So I regret that Animalism—a view that is highly plausible, widely accepted, and was strangely neglected until Snowdon, Olson, and others gave it the prominence that it deserves—seems not to be true.

---

[31] Eric Olson, *The Human Animal* (Oxford University Press, 1997), 71–2.

Introduction to Anthony Kenny's Lecture

Ted Honderich

Sir Anthony Kenny was born in Liverpool, studied and became a Catholic priest in Rome, got the D.Phil in philosophy in Oxford, questioned the Church's doctrine, married, and was excommunicated. Among the places in which he has taught philosophy is Balliol College in Oxford, of which he also became Master. His yet more relevant distinction on the present occasion is his very many books, samples being *Action, Emotion and Will* (1963), *The Five Ways: St. Thomas Aquinas' Proofs of God's Existence* (1980), *Wittgenstein* (1975), *The Metaphysics of Mind* (1990), *A Life in Oxford* (1997), and nothing less than *A New History of Western Philosophy* (2012).

The lectures in the present volume demonstrate the fact that lecturers from the same lectern may have somewhat different ideas of their audiences, and give somewhat different kinds of lecture. This is one such that the familiar words 'needs no introduction' are true of it. If no paragraph of it allows for confusion of it with popular philosophy, its attention to concepts and argument is accompanied by a determination to be understood. If it is philosophy that is indeed concentration on the logic of ordinary intelligence, and is learned and respectful of several philosophical pasts, it is also as pellucid as any in this volume.

Here and elsewhere, then, the role of an introduction can be little more than a chairman's promise of the interest of a subject that is not part of the monthly round of everyone, in this case God—and also a promise of the interest of a wider subject, that of the nature of the epistemic facts of knowledge, certainty, truth, belief, reason, scepticism, faith, and the relationships between them, not excluding that of their relative values. In particular, what is the good of faith? And what class of degree is to be awarded to the atheism of he who also informed us of the selfish gene, the distinguished ethologist and evolutionary biologist, Richard Dawkins?

Some preliminary thought of some of these matters is followed by consideration of the traditional arguments for the existence of God. The ontological proof, essentially the proposition that God exists by definition of himself, is not saved by a latter-day scholasticism of logicians about possible worlds. Nor is God's existence established by religious experience.

More attention is given to the argument from design, and in particular the matter of teleology, in its vulgar and maybe true form the idea that the occurrence of effects explains the occurrence of their causes. There is arresting reflection here on the anthropic principle, particular clarifications and developments of the idea that the nature of something requires the existence of a certain kind of cause of it. Who could deny the central idea here? And who can be untouched by the lecturer's attention to Dawkins' consideration of the principle? As much attention is given to religious belief taken as a scientific hypothesis initially on a par with other such hypotheses. Here a range of epistemic attitudes is considered, first credit for it being given to Aquinas.

I summarize no more, except to remark, first, that faith, after close examination, is deemed not a virtue but a vice, and to report, second, that the lecture may indeed achieve for you its goal, which is the conclusion that belief in God, possibly false, is as reasonable as disbelief, and third, to note the judgement that at least religious narratives are properly regarded as metaphor and to be moved into the category of poetry rather than history.

Like any good lecture, this one forms questions in your mind. Is the God in whom it is said to be reasonable to believe a lesser one than the one allowed by faith—and by the hope and promise provided by traditional religion? Should we keep in mind that the history of science, mighty science, is itself importantly a history of literal theories taken as true—and derived from or at least motivated by metaphor?

13

Knowledge, Belief, and Faith

Anthony Kenny

The nature of knowledge and its relation to certainty, belief, and doubt has been a philosophical topic ever since philosophy began. Philosophers in ancient Greece established a number of truths about knowledge. (1) Knowledge can only be of what is true. (2) A belief is only knowledge if it can appeal to some kind of warrant. (3) One who claims knowledge must have a resolute commitment to the proposition claimed to be known. If I claim to know something, then I exclude the possibility of being at some later time rightly converted to a different view.

Ancient philosophers, however, tended to demand too high a level of warrant for knowledge. Lurking behind much ancient epistemology was a fundamental logical fallacy. "Whatever is knowledge must be true" may be interpreted in two ways.

(1) Necessarily, if p is known, p is true
(2) If p is known, p is necessarily true.

(1) is uncontentiously true; but if (2) is taken as equivalent to it then only necessary truths can be known. Such a position is suggested from time to time by passages in Plato and Aristotle.

From Augustine onwards philosophers of various schools agreed that in addition to knowledge of necessary truths there was also knowledge of contingent, empirical matters. For a truth to be known it did not need to be self-evident: it could also be evident to the senses. However, a modern epistemological fallacy took the place of the ancient one. Descartes and Locke thought that the way something struck one could guarantee its truth: Descartes spoke of "clear and distinct perception", and Locke spoke of an "evident lustre" attaching to certain propositions. But there is no purely internal method of discovering which of one's beliefs deserve the name of knowledge. The best one can hope for is to acquire proficiency in attaching the right degree of commitment to each belief.

It is important for human beings to strike the right balance in belief. One can err by believing too much or believing too little. The person who believes too much suffers from the vice of credulity; the person who believes too little is guilty of excessive incredulity or scepticism. If you believe too much your mind will be cluttered with many falsehoods; if you believe too little you will be deprived of much valuable information. Let us call the virtue which stands in the middle between scepticism and credulity the virtue of rationality.

It was Aristotle who first showed us that virtues stand in a mean, that is to say that each virtue is flanked by two opposing vices. Aristotle did not himself identify any virtue which had belief as its field of operation. That is because he focussed his attention on those mental conditions, such as knowledge and understanding, that have only truth as their object. Because only what is true can be known, there was no need for Aristotle to identify a virtue which was possessing just the right amount of knowledge: one cannot—in any literal sense—know too much. But belief, as Aristotle well knew, is a state of mind that may be true or false. If p is false, then I do not know that p, however much I may think I do; but a belief of mine may be false and yet remain a perfectly genuine belief. There is room, then, for a virtue that determines the mean of belief.

Plato in the *Theaetetus* offered a definition of knowledge as a true thought with a *logos*. He found himself unable, however, to explain what was this *logos* that turned true belief into knowledge. However, his definition began a tradition of defining knowledge as justified true belief. This definition was classical over millennia, but in the last century a number of philosophers have cast doubt on this traditional definition.

Peter Geach once wrote to me "Belief is a disposition, expressed in acts of judgement, though not only that way... [It] is verbally expressed in assertion, which answers to acts of judgement... Knowledge differs from belief by being a capacity not a disposition. No added factor can turn true belief into knowledge: the Theaetetus problem is a pseudo-problem."

There is indeed knowing how as well as knowing that, so that one cannot define knowledge tout court as a kind of belief. But knowing that p does involve believing that p: that is to say, it involves a similar disposition to judge and assert that p. "I know that p but I don't believe that p" is absurd.

However, a true belief that p is not sufficient to constitute knowledge that p. I may believe that p, but be quite ready to change my mind if evidence turns up that not-p. But if I claim to know that p, I have a much stronger commitment to the truth of p. I am claiming that nothing should make me change my mind about it. No doubt I realize that I may, at some future date, change my mind; but so long as I am claiming knowledge I am claiming that I would be wrong to do so.

Of course, we often claim to know that p, and later find out that p is false. That shows that we did not ever know that p, however strongly we thought we did. I cannot then say "I knew that p, but p was false"; rather, I say, "I was certain that p, but p was false". Certainty involves the same degree of commitment as knowledge—I cannot say "I am certain that p, but p is false". However, the concept of certainty does not have the same conceptual link to truth as the concept of knowledge.

In this paper I want to address the general epistemological problem of the nature of knowledge, certainty, and belief. But I want to take as a focus for discussion one particular topic of belief, namely belief in God. I want to consider how far such belief is reasonable. As a text on which to hang the discussion I will take Richard Dawkins' book *The God Delusion* (Bantam 2006; henceforth GD). I find myself in agreement with perhaps 90% of what Dawkins says, and I shall have little to say about the areas of our agreement. But because of the 10% difference between us I end up in quite a different position with regard to the rationality of religion.

Though, like Dawkins, I am not myself a believer, I take a much more tolerant view than he does of the possibility that religious belief may be reasonable. I differ from him, that is to say, about the relationship between faith and reason. It is wrong to make too stark and simple a contrast between faith and reason. Indeed in these days of post-post-modernism it is often the proponents of faith who are loudest in their defence of the rights of reason.

Faith and reason are sometimes presented as two contrasting sources of information about religious matters. Thus a Christian theologian might maintain that there are some truths about God (e.g. that he is omnipotent) that can be discovered by unaided reason, while there are others (e.g. that there are three persons in a single God) that cannot be attained without the grace of faith. But at least since St Thomas Aquinas there has been a traditional Christian teaching that while some truths are not attainable by pure reason, no revealed doctrines are contrary to reason and faith is itself a reasonable frame of mind. Later in this paper I shall address the distinction between natural theology (the work of unaided reason) and religious faith (which is claimed to be the work of grace). For the present, like Dawkins, I will lump the two together as "belief in God".

Let me begin by saying that I am in accord with Dawkins in rejecting traditional philosophical arguments for the existence of God, whether ontological, cosmological, or experiential.

I believe that critics of the ontological argument, from Aquinas to Frege, have shown that it fails to establish the existence of God. If it were valid, then "God exists" would be an analytic proposition: "exists" would be a predicate that was tacitly contained in the subject "God". But as Kant insisted, all statements of real existence are synthetic, and "exists" is not a predicate at all. Abelard in the twelfth century and Frege in the nineteenth century urged us to rephrase statements of existence so that "exists" does not even look like a predicate. "Angels exist" should be formulated as "some things are angels". This has the advantage that it does not make it appear that when we say "angels do not exist" we are first positing angels and then rejecting them.

However, this is not a final solution of the ontological argument, because the question may be raised about what counts as something. Does our quantifier range over possible as well as actual objects? If so, then, following the lead of some recent theist philosophers, we may argue thus. A necessary being is one that exists in all possible worlds. So defined, a necessary being must exist in our world, the actual world. Our world would not exist unless it were possible; so if God exists in every possible world, he must exist in ours.

I believe that the framework of this argument, the apparatus of possible worlds, is philosophically incoherent, though I must admit that it is accepted by many atheist as well as theist philosophers. I believe that Kant was right to insist that whether there is something in reality answering to a concept of mine cannot itself be part of my concept. A concept has to be determined prior to being applied to reality, otherwise we have nothing definite to try out on the world. That there is a God cannot be part of what we mean by God. (Still less can it be *all* that we mean by God, as is contended by those who tell us that God's essence is existence.)

I also agree with Dawkins that God's existence cannot be established by appeal to experience. If there is a God with the attributes ascribed to him by Western theism then he cannot be the subject of any cognitive activity analogous to the operation of our senses. We cannot have a sixth sense that detects that God is here and not there, as we can see that something is red at one end and not at another, or which detects that God was here a moment ago and is not now, as we can hear a noise that suddenly stops. The whole context within which talk of sense-experience makes sense is lacking in the case of an alleged *sensus divinitatis*.

Aquinas' famous five ways are given a swift despatch by Dawkins. I think that he misdescribes them in some ways; but even if Aquinas is given a lot more rope, I agree that he hangs himself in the end. Nearly forty years ago I wrote a book to that effect (*The Five Ways*, Routledge 1969). However, one of Aquinas' proofs, the fifth way, deserves further treatment. It resembles the argument from design, Kant's physico-theological proof. Its case is that the ordinary teleology of non-conscious agents in the universe entails the existence of an intelligent universal orderer.

In considering this argument we must begin by recognizing that there is a difference between design and purpose. Design differs from purpose because design is purpose preceded by an idea: a thought, or blueprint, in somebody's mind. If the world is designed, then there was a precedent idea in the mind of the creator—what, in the fourth gospel, is called the *logos* or Word. In our kind of mind, the idea that precedes an artefact is not anything simple or timeless, but something that gets built up by research and experiment. The argument from design can only establish its conclusion if it is possible for there to be a quite different kind of mind: a divine, extra-cosmic, simple, and eternal mind. That, to my mind, is the greatest difficulty with the argument.

If we are to attribute intelligence to any entity—limited or unlimited, cosmic or extra cosmic—we have to take as our starting point our concept of intelligence as exhibited by human beings: we have no other concept of it. Human intelligence is displayed in the behaviour of human bodies and the thoughts of human minds. If we reflect on the actual ways in which we attribute words such as "know" "believe" "think" "design" "control" to human beings, we realize the immense difficulty there is in applying them to a putative being which is immaterial, ubiquitous, and eternal. With a degree of anthropomorphism we can apply mentalistic predicates to animals, computers, institutions; to organisms that resemble us or artefacts that are our creations; but there are limits to anthropomorphism, and an extra-cosmic intelligence appears to me to be outside those limits. It is not just that we do not, and cannot, know what goes on in God's mind; it is that we cannot really ascribe a mind to a God at all. The language that we use to describe the contents of human minds operates within a web of links with bodily behaviour and social institutions. When we try to apply this language to an entity outside the natural world, whose scope of operation is the entire universe, this web comes to pieces, and we no longer know what we are saying.

Most critics of the argument from design—particularly since Darwin—quarrel not with the conclusion but the premises of the argument. They object to the appeal to the apparent existence of teleology in the world around us.

In the course of history teleology has received drastically different treatments by different great philosophers. One of Aristotle's four causes was the final cause, the end, the purpose, the good to be achieved by some action. Aristotle, more than any other philosopher, emphasized the importance of teleology in the world; but he was no supporter of the argument from design, because he was well aware of the distinction between design and purpose. The budding of a rose and the building of a spider's web were no less teleological than human activities; but Aristotle knew better than to attribute consciousness to roses and spiders. Teleology, for him, was a basic fact about the cosmos, and no extra-cosmic designer was needed to explain it.

It was Aquinas who formulated the argument from purpose to design. Things without awareness, he argued in the fourth way, do not tend towards a goal unless directed by something with awareness and intelligence, in the way that an arrow is aimed by an archer. The ultimate designer, the arch-archer, we call God.

Descartes revolutionized philosophy by expunging teleology altogether. He eliminated, outside the human realm, purpose as well as design. Final causation, he thought, was a piece of scholastic nonsense. He rejected the explanation of gravity in terms of attraction between bodies, on the grounds that this postulated in inert entities knowledge of a goal or terminus.

With Darwinism we return to the position of Aristotle: the world contains purpose but not, outside the human realm, design. It is sometimes thought that Darwinism gave the final death-blow to teleology; but that is the opposite of the truth. Darwinian scientists have not given up the search for final causes. On the contrary, contemporary biologists are much more adept at discerning the functions of structures and behaviour than their ancient, medieval, or Cartesian predecessors. Darwin agreed with Aquinas against Aristotle that teleology was not a basic fact, but something needing explanation. His achievement was to make teleological explanation respectable by offering, in natural selection, a recipe for translating it into a naturalistic explanation that made no call on design.

Natural selection, however, cannot be offered as the sole and sufficient explanation of the history of the universe. When neo-Darwinians offer to explain the entire cosmos, I find difficulties at three main points: the origin of language, the origin of life, and the origin of the universe.

Language is conventional, that is to say it is governed by rules. Being rule-governed is different from being governed by causal laws. Rules differ from such laws in several ways. Rules may be broken; not so causal laws, short of a miracle. To be governed by a rule you must be conscious of it at least to the extent that you are aware of any breach of it. But there is no need for you to be aware of being governed by a causal law: the planets know nothing of Kepler's laws.

The problem with an evolutionary account of language is this. Explanation by natural selection of the origin of a feature in a population presupposes the occurrence of that feature in particular individuals of the population. Natural selection might favour a certain length of leg, and the long-legged individuals in the population might outbreed the others. But for that kind of explanation of features to be possible, it must be possible to conceive the occurrence of the feature in single individuals. There is no problem in describing a single individual as having legs n metres long. But there is a problem with the idea that there might be a single human language-user.

It is not easy to see how the human race may have begun to use language because language-using individuals outbred the non-language users. This is not a difficulty in seeing how spontaneous mutation could produce a language-user; it is the difficulty of seeing how anyone could be described as a language-using individual at all before there was a community of language-users.

Of course, there are animal systems of communication that have some similarity with human language, and human pets can respond to names and obey commands. But human language is separated by a gulf from the communicative abilities of other animals. The essential logical feature of human language is not that it contains nouns and verbs, but rather that it contains negation, conditionality, quantification, and modality. It is the words "not" "if" "some" and "therefore" that are the marks of rationality; and there are no animal equivalents of these.

If it is difficult to see how language could originate by natural selection, it is even more difficult to see how life could originate that way. However successful natural selection may be in explaining the origin of particular species of life, it clearly cannot explain how there came to be such things as species at all. That is to say, it cannot explain how there came to be true breeding populations, since the existence of such populations is one of the premises on which explanations in terms of natural selection rest as their starting point.

This is a point which is accepted, and indeed stressed, by Dawkins in his recent book. The origin of life, he says, is a question for chemists, and he is no chemist. The chemists haven't been able to replicate the origin of life, but maybe they will soon. In the meantime, Dawkins is happy to accept that it came about by a lucky chance: after all, if there are a billion billion planets, then the odds are a billion to one that life will have started on a billion of them, of which the earth is one. But when he turns to the ten million different species of life on our planet, each well adapted to a particular way of life, and asks "Could we get away with the 'huge number of planets' argument to explain all these separate illusions of design? No we could not, repeat not. Don't even think about it. This is important, for it goes to the heart of the most serious misunderstanding of Darwinism. It doesn't matter how many planets we have to play with, lucky chance could never be enough to explain the lush diversity of living complexity on Earth in the same way as we used it to explain the existence of life here in the first place. The evolution of life is a completely different case from the origin of life."(GD, 138.)

To explain the origin of life, Dawkins invokes a planetary version of the anthropic principle. He states it thus.

We exist here on Earth. Therefore, the Earth must be the kind of planet that is capable of generating and supporting us, however unusual, even unique, that kind of planet is. However small the minority of planets with just the right conditions of life may be, we necessarily have to be on one of that minority, because here we are thinking about it. (GD, 135)

On the face of it, the planetary conditions for our support are immensely improbable and call for explanation. No, says this anthropic principle, far from being improbable they are necessary; and necessary truths call for no explanation.

We need to look more closely at the use of "necessary" here. There are at least two senses of the word "necessary". Something is metaphysically necessary if it follows from necessary truths. But there is also epistemic necessity, which is the counterpart of epistemic possibility. P is epistemically possible when we can say "for all we know to the contrary p may be the case". If not-p is not epistemically possible, then p is epistemically necessary. Something may be epistemically necessary without being metaphysically necessary: as I write it is epistemically necessary, but not metaphysically necessary, that George W. Bush is President of the U.S. The anthropic principle argues from the epistemic necessity of conditions favourable to human life to their metaphysical necessity.

The anthropic principle is usually presented in a cosmic rather than a planetary version. Martin Rees has listed six fundamental constants that are believed to hold throughout the universe. If any one of these differed very slightly from its actual value life in the universe would be impossible. How are we to explain this fine tuning? It is here that the anthropic principle is invoked: the constants had to have that value or we would not be here to calculate them.

Dawkins is aware of the difficulty here, and borrows from John Leslie the analogy of a man sentenced to death by firing squad. It is just possible that all ten men of the firing squad will miss their victim. With hindsight the survivor who finds himself in a position to reflect upon his luck can cheerfully say "Well, obviously they all missed or I wouldn't be here thinking about it." "But he could still" Dawkins says "forgivably, wonder why they all missed." I suggest that the word "forgivably" should be replaced by "most reasonably".

Dawkins' answer to the puzzle is that (as Rees maintains, in company with Giordano Bruno) that there are many universes; the laws and constants of any one universe are by-laws. "The anthropic principle" as Dawkins puts it "kicks in to explain that we have to be in one of those universes (presumably a minority) whose by-laws happened to be propitious to our eventual evolution and hence contemplation of the problem." (GD, 145.)

Dawkins is in fact offering two different answers to the problem. The anthropic principle says there is nothing to be explained—there was not improbability in the case, but necessity. The multiverse thesis says that there is indeed something to be explained, and it is to be explained by a priori probability. This can be done if we simply call into existence billions of universes—all, ex hypothesi, inaccessible to scientific inquiry.

The first explanation is a fallacy, resting on confusion between epistemic and metaphysical necessity. The second explanation is a piece of metaphysical speculation (in Rees no less than in Bruno). Its only merit is that it provides an alternative to intelligent design.

So far we have been discussing the kind of universe we have. But why is there a universe of any kind? The most fundamental reason of postulating an extra-cosmic agency of any kind is surely the need to explain the origin of the universe itself. Most philosophical arguments for the existence of God are only sophistications of the cry of the simple believer "God must exist, else where did the world come from?"

It is wrong to say that God provides the answer to the question "Why is there something rather than nothing?" As Bede Rundle has shown in an engaging book with that title (OUP, 1999), that question is ill-conceived; the proposition "there is nothing" cannot be given a coherent sense, and therefore there is no need to ask why it is false. It is not the existence of the universe that calls for explanation, but its coming into existence.

At a time when philosophers and scientists were happy to accept that the universe had existed for ever, there was no question of looking for a cause of its origin, only of looking for an explanation of its nature. But when it is proposed that the universe began at a point of time measurably distant in the past, then it seems perverse simply to shrug one's shoulders and decline to seek any explanation. We would never, in the case of an ordinary existent, tolerate a blithe announcement that there was simply no reason for its coming into existence, and it seems irrational to abandon this principle when the existing thing in question is all pervasive, like the universe. If only an intelligent creator were conceivable, he would surely be a more persuasive solution to the problem.

My reaction to the difficulty of either proving or disproving God's existence is agnosticism: to say that we do not know either way. Often, both theist and atheist philosophers, instead of offering arguments, adopt a strategy that might be called grabbing the default position—that is, a tactic of throwing the burden of proof on the opponent. But it is agnosticism that is the true default position. A claim to knowledge needs to be substantiated, ignorance only has to be confessed. Moreover, a claim to know that God exists, or a claim to know that God does not exist, is an absolute commitment. The profession of doubt is no such thing.

Dawkins is contemptuous of agnosticism, and prefers atheism. He believes that he has an argument to disprove God's existence. A designer God, he maintains, cannot be used to explain organized complexity, because any God capable of designing anything would have to be complex enough to demand the same kind of explanation in his own right (GD, 109). He calls this argument "The Ultimate Boeing 747 argument", in tribute to Fred Hoyle who once said that the probability of life originating on earth is no greater than the chance that a hurricane, sweeping through a scrapyard, would have the luck to assemble a Boeing 747. God, according to Dawkins, is the ultimate 747.

A traditional theist would say that Dawkins' argument misrepresented the notion of God in two ways. First of all, God is as much outside the series complexity/simplicity as he is outside the series mover/moved. He is not complex as a protein is, nor for that matter is he simple as an elementary particle is. He has neither the simplicity nor the complexity of material objects. Secondly, he is not one of a series of temporal contingents, each requiring explanation in terms of a previous state of the universe: unchanging and everlasting. He is outside the temporal series. What calls for explanation is the origin of organized complexity that is to be explained. But God had no origin and is neither complex nor organized.

The principle that what is complex must be designed by what is even more complex is a metaphysical principle, because it is meant to apply outside the world of science as well as within it. As a metaphysician myself I have no objection to the use of metaphysical principles. But is this one valid? Even on earth is it true that a designer must be more complex than his creation? Is it metaphysically impossible for a human to design a computer containing more bytes than there are cells in the human brain? This, it may be objected, is an inappropriate comparison; but doesn't that show that even at this level the notion of complexity is not a simple notion, and there are various kinds of complexity?

In particular, since design is purpose preceded by an idea, we need to consider the notion of complexity as applied to thinking. A thought, or idea, does not have the same complexity as its expression in a written design or blueprint would have. A thought does not have spatial or temporal parts in the way that the sentence that expresses it has. A thought is a unified whole, and is not made up of a succession of parts in the way that a sentence is made up of successive words. Even in our mundane world, therefore, there is reason to doubt Dawkins' principle.

However, Dawkins addresses the question not only at the metaphysical level. Elsewhere he claims that the existence of God is a scientific hypothesis like any other. A universe with a supernaturally intelligent creator, he says, is a very different kind of universe from one without. He agrees that the difference is not easy to test in practice but whether God exists is a scientific question to which one day we may know the answer and in the meantime we can say something about the probabilities (GD, 48).

He sets up a spectrum of probabilities, between opposite certainties.

1   I know there is a God
2   I do not know but strongly believe
3   I am uncertain but inclined to believe
4   I think God's existence and non-existence equiprobable
5   I am uncertain but inclined to be sceptical
6   I think God's existence is very improbable
7   I know there is no God.

Dawkins places himself in category 6, as a de facto atheist. He could equally well be described as an agnostic, if an agnostic is, as its etymology suggests, someone who does not *know* whether there is a God or not.

Interestingly, Aquinas in his treatment of faith (Summa Theologiae II-IIae, 2, 1) sets up exactly the same spectrum. He calls (1) scientia (2) opinio (3) suspicio (4) dubitatio; which we may translate as (1) knowledge (2) conviction (3) guess (4) doubt.[1]

The scales given by Aquinas and Dawkins are an interesting way of classifying different degrees of commitment to a proposition, but they are inadequate to provide a total classification of epistemic states. States of mind are to be distinguished along not one but three axes: degree of commitment, conformity to the facts, type of warrant. Thus, e.g. knowledge differs from certainty not by degree of commitment, but by the fact that knowledge is only of the truth but certainty can be false. Again, in talking of certainty we must distinguish first, second, and third person. Contrast "I am certain that p but p is false" "You are certain that p but p is false" "It is certain that p but p is false".

We must take into account not only commitment and veracity, but warrant. John Locke says we should not entertain any proposition with greater assurance than the evidence it is built on will warrant. "Whoever goes beyond this measure of assent, it is plain, receives not truth in the love of it, loves not truth for truth-sake, but for some other by-end" (Essay 4, xvi). John Henry Newman contested this, and showed that knowledge need not be based on evidence. I may be justifiably certain of something

---

[1] Actuum enim ad intellectum pertinentium quidam habent firmam assensionem absque tali cogitatione [= weighing up of alternatives] sicut cum aliquis considerat ea quae scit vel intelligit: talis enim consideratio iam est formata. Quidam vero actus intellectus habent quidem cogitationem informem absque firma assensione: sive in neutram partem declinent, sicut accidit dubitanti; sive in unam partem magis declinent sed tenentur aliquo levi signo, sicut accidit suspicanti; sive uni parti adhaereant, tamen cum formidine alterius, quod accidit opinanti.

and yet there be no evidence for it because it is itself more certain than anything that could be offered in evidence.

We laugh to scorn the idea that we had no parents though we have no memory of our birth; that we shall never depart this life, though we can have no experience of the future; that we are able to live without food, though we have never tried; that a world of men did not live before our time, or that the world has no history. (*Grammar of Assent*, 117)

Wittgenstein, following Newman, identified a set of propositions of which we are certain, but where our certainty is not based on evidence and is not the result of any inquiry. He gave as examples "the earth has existed for many years past" "cats do not grow on trees" "human beings have forebears". He was not willing to say that we knew such propositions, but he said that they stood fast in our picture of the world; they had a fundamental role which was not the result of, but prior to, our methods of inquiry and evidence gathering (*On Certainty*).

In a number of works Alvin Plantinga has argued that belief in God may be regarded as basic in this way: a person may be within her epistemic rights in believing in God without having any proof or evidence of God's existence. Bertrand Russell was asked what he would say if he died and was confronted by God asking why he had not believed in him. "Not enough evidence, God, not enough evidence." If Newman, Wittgenstein, and Plantinga are right, Russell's answer does not deserve a pass.

Plantinga thinks that belief in God can be as basic an item in someone's noetic structure as the belief that other people have minds. I don't myself accept that belief in the existence of God can rightly occupy a basic role comparable to the existence of other people, but rather than explain why I think that, I want to make a distinction long overdue between simple belief in God's existence, and actual religious faith.

Faith, as I understand it, is the acceptance of the testimony of a sacred text or of a religious community. The two, in fact, go together, because if the sacred texts are taken as guides to practical life, their authority is inseparable from the authority of the religious officials whose role is to interpret them. In the Judeo-Christian tradition for instance the very notion of "the Bible" as a single entity depends on the various authorities throughout our history who have established the canon. However impressive individual books may be, to see them as elements of a single revelation containing some or all of the other books is already tacitly to accept a religious authority that defines the canon. One might gather together the works of Homer, Hesiod, Aeschylus, Sophocles, Euripides, Herodotus, and Thucydides into an epitome of Greek thought. The anthology would share a common cultural tradition and cohere as well or ill as the Bible does. But we would not treat it as a single book, to be treated differently from all other books, because there has never been a Hellenic rabbinate or episcopate to canonize such a collection.

The common characteristic of faith in almost all religious traditions is its irrevocability. A faith which is held tentatively is no true faith. It must be held with the same degree of certainty as knowledge. In some traditions the irrevocability of faith is reinforced by the imposition of the death penalty for apostasy, which is the abandonment of faith.

Aquinas, from whom I have drawn my account of religious faith, notes that it does not fit into the categorization of mental states which he, anticipating Dawkins, set out. "The state which is belief involves a firm adhesion to one side of the question. In this a believer is in the same position as someone who has knowledge or understanding; and yet his assent is not warranted by any clear vision, so that in that respect he resembles someone who doubts, guesses, or is convinced."[2]

Faith, then, resembles knowledge in being irrevocable, but differs from it in being a commitment in the absence of adequate evidence. This is well brought out by Newman. He says that the grounds on which faith is accepted—the evidence for there having been a revelation, for the divine authority of books or teachers—is a matter of conjecture, not of knowledge. "It starts from probability, yet it ends in peremptory statements... It believes an informant amid doubt, yet accepts his information without doubt."

It is religious faith, rather than theistic belief, that is the main target of Dawkins' book. "What is really pernicious is the practice of teaching children that faith itself is a virtue. Faith is an evil precisely because it requires no justification and brooks no argument... Suicide bombers do what they do because they really believe what they were taught in their religious schools: that duty to God exceeds all other priorities, and that martyrdom in his service will be rewarded in the gardens of Paradise." (GD, 308.)

It is too much to say that faith requires no justification: many religious people offer arguments not just for belief in God but for their particular creed. What is true is that the kinds of arguments they offer cannot be claimed to have anything like the degree of warrant that would justify the irrevocable commitment of faith.

It is true that faith brooks no argument, not in the sense that the faithful are unwilling to offer responses to criticisms, but that no argument will make a true believer give up his faith, and this is something he is resolved on in advance of hearing any argument.

Some years ago I expressed an opinion similar to Dawkins' complaint. "Faith" I wrote "is not, as theologians have claimed, a virtue, but a vice, unless a number of conditions can be fulfilled. One of them is that the existence of God can be rationally justified outside faith. Secondly, whatever are the historical events which are pointed to as constituting the divine revelation must be independently established as historically certain." (*What is Faith*, OUP, 1992, 57.)

It is a particular difficulty for the rationality of faith that there are so many alleged revelations that conflict with each other. One thing we know for certain is this: if any

---

[2] Sed actus iste qui est credere habet firmam adhaesionem ad unam partem, in quo convenit credens cum sciente et intelligente; et tamen eius cognitio non est perfecta per manifestam visionem, in quo convenit cum dubitante, suspicante, et opinante.

sacred text is literally true, then most are literally false. Of course, the incompatibility between conflicting revelations leaves it open as a logical possibility that just one of them is true while all the others are false. This is certainly not a possibility that can with decency be ruled out a priori by someone who believes that just by existing in this universe we are defeating odds of a billion to one. It seems to me, however, that if there is any truth in any religious revelation it is more likely that each of them is a metaphor for a single underlying truth that is incapable of being expressed in literal terms without contradiction. In this way religion would resemble poetry rather than science.

To say that religious language is not literal, and to say that different religious creeds therefore do not contradict each other, is not to say that all religions are of equal worth. The mode of utterance of Shakespeare and that of William McGonagall is poetic in each case; that does not mean that the writings of each of them display an equally valuable insight into human nature. But the fact that theological language cannot be literal provides a reason for toleration in religion. That is to say, theological propositions cannot contradict each other in the straightforward way in which empirical propositions do. Hence, there is not the head-on clash between different theologies, and different religions, which has been used to justify the persecution and killing of one religious group by others.

Dawkins' book suggests that all those who believe in God are unreasonable in so doing. I disagree. Those who claim to know that there is a God, I have agreed, are making a claim that is not justified; but so too are those who claim to know there is no God. But a belief in God, falling short of certainty, is not open to the same objection. A belief may be reasonable, though false. If two oncologists tell you that your tumour is benign, then your belief that it is benign is a reasonable belief even if, sadly, it is false. In the case of many people in many cultures, I maintain, religious belief, even if false, may well be reasonable. (So, too, may tentative, non-dogmatic atheism.) But I think belief in God reasonable only if it is based on considerations available to all humans: not if it is claimed on the basis of a special message to oneself or to the group that one belongs.

Because I think belief in God can be reasonable I think Dawkins is wrong to object to bringing up children in belief in religion. The education of children is impossible without narrative and ceremony, and growing up is a matter of knowing what to discard and what to maintain. I doubt if Dawkins objects to telling children about Santa Claus; it does not lead to an adult society of bigoted Santaclausians. Many intellectual Christians, as they mature, abandon other bits of the Christmas story: I know priests in good standing who do not believe that Jesus was born in Bethlehem. Disbelieving in religious narratives, however, does not necessarily mean discarding them: it means, as I suggested earlier, removing them from the history section of one's mind into the poetry section. I agree with Dawkins that faith, as an irrevocable commitment, is not reasonable when given to a false proposition. But I see nothing unreasonable in believers having the degree of commitment to their church, synagogue, or mosque that they might have to a political party or social community.

It is the degree of commitment involved in faith, rather than its religious object, that is what is really objectionable; and the history of nazism, fascism, and communism made this abundantly clear in the last century. Not all fanaticism is religious fanaticism, and I found unconvincing Dawkins' attempt to show that Hitler was a closet Catholic.

In answer to the question whether religious people are better or worse than non-religious people, a friend of mine gave a sage answer. "Religion" he said "makes nice people nicer and makes nasty people nastier".

When arguing, a moment ago, that religious language should be treated as metaphorical I mentioned that metaphorical propositions do not contradict each other in the way that bigots believe. But of course much religious language is in the imperative mood, and even if propositions don't contradict each other, commands certainly can. The question then arises, how should one deal with commands emanating from a religious position that one believes to be literally false? This is a practical, political question, not a merely philosophical one.

Like Dawkins I believe that the state owes no special respect to religious beliefs as such. Religious conscientious objectors should be treated on equal terms with atheist objectors who oppose a war on moral grounds: general pacifism has no priority over qualified pacifism. Religious bodies, in order to obtain tax exemption as charities, should be under an obligation to prove public benefit—that is, benefit that can be assessed as such by others than co-religionists.

On the other hand, it may be said that one of the great benefits that religion has conferred on the human race is that it has instilled into people's hearts the idea that the governments they live under are not the supreme arbiters of right and wrong: that there is an authority superior even to the most omnicompetent totalitarian government. A world in which everyone believed that there was no moral authority superior to their rulers would not necessarily be preferable to a world in which everyone saw rulers as answerable to God.

Of course, there can be a world which is worse than either: a world in which rulers believe they have a special message from God authorizing their policies in peace and war.

Introduction to Noam Chomsky's Lecture

Ted Honderich

Noam Chomsky, born in Philadelphia, has for 52 years been a unique shaper of the science of linguistics. He has for 45 years been the greatest intellectual of the Left. His work in linguistics is also a contribution to the philosophy of mind, in particular a proof of what once were called innate ideas and a refutation of functionalism as well as the behaviourism that preceded it. His lecture here is itself philosophical in its line of argument.

That argument is that there are reasons for judgement against our democracies and a compliant intellectual class, reasons that are not only truths. They are *simple and available* truths. The main one is that there are obvious inconsistencies with respect to those democracies and that class, obvious offences against universality, hence failings that in effect deprive our democracies and compliance with them of reasons, since reasons are of their nature general. If you think or say both of the propositions *p* and *not-p* your final failure is not a falsehood. It is that you think and say nothing. You have no thought.

There are other simple truths. One is that facts matter. In particular, no sense can be made or reflection carried forward productively in denial or ignorance of history, say of American support and instigation of terrorism in South America. For me, I guess there is also the truism that typical pronouncements of our democratic leaders carry no information, even in the technical sense familiar in linguistics. For me, there is a truism too about the financing of suffering, and other truisms about defence, including so-called anticipatory self-defence. Also, implicit if not explicit in the lecture, there is the proposition that there are known wrongs that can precede any general theory of right and wrong—and must shape the construction of any principle of right and wrong.

Given the inconsistencies of our democracies and their intellectuals and ourselves, you do not necessarily have to engage in further thinking, say the forming and defending of such a principle, in order to judge our democracies and those who serve them. You do not have to spend time with the total happiness principle—the Principle of Utility. Or the circularity of conservative principles of fairness in the sense of desert or retribution or what is earned or owed. Or the question-begging deriving of John Rawls' principles of justice. Or the 'principle' that everybody and all states serve their own interest, so depended on by the state of Israel that denies Chomsky admission to it. You do not necessarily need to spend time, as I have, on the Principle of Humanity: that we must take all and only rational means to the end of getting and keeping people out of bad lives, these defined plainly in terms of fundamental human desires.

The simple truths make for a response to what may be taken as hard problems, respected as such. They are in fact problems without solutions, problems owed to the abandoning of universality. One is the problem of understanding terrorism without allowing that we have long been engaged in it. Another is the problem of defensibly defining international crime or offences against human rights in accord with the intention to limit them to the actions and policies of the other side.

To defend universality and consistency and to defend the imperative of facts, I say myself, is to do what is more valuable than Descartes' 'I think, therefore I am', or Hume's declaration that each of us espies no inner self as distinct from the unity that is our ongoing conscious existence, or Lichtenberg's smaller dictum to put beside and against Descartes'—'I think, therefore there is thinking going on'.

Still, I would not agree that time spent on clarifying and defending a general principle of right and wrong is not time well spent. To demonstrate inconsistency, if wonderfully valuable, is in fact to leave open which of two things is right, at any rate to leave it only assumed or implicit. To eschew a general principle also may be to put in some doubt your own consistency, and to be more uncertain what is to be added to a list of implicit wrongs.

But you will not need telling that these words of mine on Chomsky are those of an ally, admirer of his work and independence and personal courage, and friend. Your obligation is to test his words for logic and fact. The obligation of actually thinking is another moral truism. Think your way through the lecture and look at a book or two or three of the very many of his behind it. Say *Necessary Illusions: Thought Control in Democratic Societies*, or *Power and Terror: Post-9/11 Talks and Interviews*, or *How the World Works*. Or make some other choice from the long, long list at the end of the best guide to them, the linguist Neil Smith's *Chomsky: Ideas and Ideals*, mainly on the linguistics.

14

Simple Truths, Hard Problems: Some Thoughts on Terror, Justice, and Self-Defence

Noam Chomsky

To dispel any false expectations, I really am going to keep to very simple truths, so much so that I toyed with suggesting the title 'In Praise of Platitudes,' with an advance apology for the elementary character of these remarks. The only justification for proceeding along this course is that the truisms are widely rejected, in some crucial cases almost universally so. And the human consequences are serious, in particular, with regard to the hard problems I have in mind. One reason why they are hard is that moral truisms are so commonly disdained by those with sufficient power to do so with impunity, because they set the rules.

We have just witnessed a dramatic example of how they set the rules. The last millennium ended, and the new one opened, with an extraordinary display of self-adulation on the part of Western intellectuals, who praised themselves and their leaders for introducing a 'noble phase' of foreign policy with a 'saintly glow,' as they adhered to 'principles and values' for the first time in history, acting from 'pure altruism,' following the lead of the 'idealistic new world bent on ending inhumanity,' joined by its loyal partner who alone comprehends the true nobility of the mission, which has now evolved even further into the 'Bush messianic mission to graft democracy onto the rest of the world'—all quoted from the elite press and intellectuals. I am not sure there is any counterpart in the none-too-glorious history of modern intellectual elites. The noblest achievement was a 'normative revolution' in the 1990s, which established a 'new norm in international affairs': the right of the self-designated 'enlightened states' to resort to force to protect suffering people from evil monsters.[1]

---

[1] For sources, see my *New Military Humanism* (Common Courage, 1999), *A New Generation Draws the Line* (Verso, 2000), and *Hegemony or Survival* (Metropolitan, 2003, updated 2004). I will keep here to citations not easy to locate in fairly standard work, or in recent books of mine, including these.

As anyone familiar with history knows, the normative revolution is not at all new; it was a constant refrain of European imperialism, and the rhetorical flights of Japanese fascists, Mussolini, Hitler, Stalin, and other grand figures were no less noble, and quite possibly just as sincere, so internal documents reveal.

The examples given to justify the chorus of self-acclaim collapse on the slightest examination, but I would like to raise a different question, bearing on how rules are established: why was the 'normative revolution' in the decade of the 1990s, not the 1970s, a far more reasonable candidate?

The decade of the 1970s opened with the Indian invasion of East Pakistan, saving probably millions of lives. It closed with Vietnam's invasion of Cambodia, ousting the Khmer Rouge just as their atrocities were peaking; before that, US State Department intelligence, by far the most knowledgeable source, was estimating deaths in the tens or hundreds of thousands, not from 'mass genocide' but from 'brutal rapid change,' awful enough, but not yet approaching the predictions of high US officials in 1975 that a million might die as a result of the carnage of the earlier years of bombing and atrocities. Their effects have been discussed in the scholarly literature, but perhaps the simplest account is the orders that Henry Kissinger transmitted, in the usual manner of the obedient bureaucrat, from President Nixon to the military commanders: 'A massive bombing campaign in Cambodia. Anything that flies on anything that moves.'[2] It is rare for a call for war crimes to be so stark and explicit, though it is normal for it to be considered entirely insignificant among the perpetrators, as in this case; publication elicited no reaction. By the time of the Vietnamese invasion, however, the charges of genocide that had aroused mass fury from the moment of the Khmer Rouge takeover in April 1975, with a level of fabrication that would have impressed Stalin, were finally becoming plausible. So the decade of the 1970s was indeed framed by two authentic cases of military intervention that terminated awesome crimes.

Even if we were to accept the most extreme claims of the chorus of adulation for the leaders of the 'enlightened states' in the 1990s, there was nothing that comes close to the humanitarian consequences of the resort to force that framed the decade of the 1970s. So why did that decade not bring about a 'normative revolution' with the foreign policy of the saviours basking in a 'saintly glow'?

The answer is simplicity itself, but apparently unstateable; at least, I have never seen a hint of it in the deluge of literature on this topic. The interventions of the 1970s had two fundamental flaws: (1) They were carried out by the wrong agents, *them*, not *us*; (2) Both were bitterly denounced by the leader of the enlightened states, and the perpetrators of the crime of terminating genocide were harshly punished, particularly Vietnam, subjected to a US-backed Chinese invasion to teach the criminals a lesson for bringing Pol Pot's crimes to an end, then severe sanctions,

[2] Elizabeth Becker, 'Kissinger Tapes Describe Crises, War and Stark Photos of Abuse,' *New York Times*, May 27, 2004.

and direct US-UK support for the ousted Khmer Rouge. It follows that the 1970s could not have brought about a 'normative revolution,' and no one has ever suggested that it did.

The guiding principle is elementary. Norms are established by the powerful, in their own interests, and with the acclaim of responsible intellectuals. These may be close to historical universals. I have been looking for exceptions for many years. There are a few, but not many.

Sometimes the principle is explicitly recognized. The norm for post-World War II international justice was established at Nuremberg. To bring the Nazi criminals to justice, it was necessary to devise definitions of 'war crime' and 'crime against humanity.' Telford Taylor, chief counsel for the prosecution and a distinguished international lawyer and historian, has explained candidly how this was done:

Since both sides in World War II had played the terrible game of urban destruction—the Allies far more successfully—there was no basis for criminal charges against Germans or Japanese, and in fact no such charges were brought... Aerial bombardment had been used so extensively and ruthlessly on the Allied side as well as the Axis side that neither at Nuremberg nor Tokyo was the issue made a part of the trials.[3]

The operative definition of 'crime' is: 'Crime that you carried out but we did not.' To underscore the fact, Nazi war criminals were absolved if the defence could show that their US counterparts carried out the same crimes.

Taylor concludes that 'to punish the foe—especially the vanquished foe—for conduct in which the enforcer nation has engaged, would be so grossly inequitable as to discredit the laws themselves.' That is correct, but the operative definition also discredits the laws themselves, along with all subsequent tribunals.

Taylor provides this background as part of his explanation of why US bombing in Vietnam was not a war crime. His argument is plausible, further discrediting the laws themselves. Some of the subsequent tribunals are discredited in perhaps even more extreme ways, such as the Yugoslavia vs. NATO case now being adjudicated by the International Court of Justice. The US was excused, correctly, on the basis of its argument that it is not subject to the jurisdiction of the Court in this case. The reason is that the US signed the Genocide Convention (which is at issue here) with a reservation stating that it is inapplicable to the United States.

In an outraged comment on the efforts of Justice Department lawyers to demonstrate that the president has the right to authorize torture, Yale Law School Dean Howard Koh—who, as Assistant Secretary of State, had presented Washington's denunciation of all forms of torture to the international community—said that 'The notion that the president has the constitutional power to permit torture is like

[3] Telford Taylor, *Nuremberg and Vietnam: an American Tragedy* (Times Books, 1970).

saying he has the constitutional power to commit genocide.[4] The same legal advisers should have little difficulty arguing that the president does indeed have that right.

The Nuremberg Tribunal is commonly described by distinguished figures in the field of international law and justice as 'the birth of universal jurisdiction.'[5] That is correct only if we understand 'universality' in accord with the practice of the enlightened states, which defines 'universal' as 'applicable to others only,' particularly enemies.

The proper conclusion at Nuremberg and since would have been to punish the victors as well as the vanquished foe. Neither at the postwar trials nor subsequently have the powerful been subjected to the rules, not because they have not carried out crimes—of course they have—but because they are immune under prevailing standards of morality. The victims appear to understand well enough. Wire services report from Iraq that 'If Iraqis ever see Saddam Hussein in the dock, they want his former American allies shackled beside him.'[6] That inconceivable event would be a radical revision of the fundamental principle of international justice: tribunals must be restricted to the crimes of others.

There is a marginal exception, which in fact underscores the force of the rule. Punishment is permissible when it is a mere tap on the wrist, evading the real crimes, or when blame can be restricted to minor figures, particularly when they are *not like us*. It was, for example, considered proper to punish the soldiers who carried out the My Lai massacre, half-educated half-crazed GIs in the field, not knowing who was going to shoot at them next. But it was inconceivable that punishment could reach as far as those who planned and implemented Operation Wheeler Wallowa, a mass murder operation to which My Lai was a very minor footnote.[7] The gentlemen in the air-conditioned offices are like us, therefore immune by definition. We are witnessing similar examples right now in Iraq.

We might return in this connection to Kissinger's transmission of Nixon's orders on bombing Cambodia. In comparison, the widely reported admission by Serbia of involvement in the Srebrenica massacre does not merit much attention. The prosecutors at the Milosevic Tribunal face difficulties in proving the crime of genocide because no document has been discovered in which the accused directly orders such a crime, even lesser ones. The same problem has been faced by Holocaust scholars, who of course have no doubt of Hitler's responsibility, but lack conclusive

    [4] Edward Alden, 'US INTERROGATION DEBATE: Dismay at attempt to find legal justification for torture,' *Financial Times*, June 10, 2004.
    [5] Justice Richard Goldstone, 'Kosovo: An Assessment in the Context of International Law,' Nineteenth Morgenthau Memorial Lecture, Carnegie Council on Ethics and International Affairs, 2000.
    [6] Michael Georgy, 'Iraqis want Saddam's old U.S. friends on trial,' *Reuters*, January 20, 2004.
    [7] On this and other such operations, based in part on unpublished investigations of *Newsweek* Saigon bureau chief Kevin Buckley, see Chomsky and Edward Herman, *The Political Economy of Human Rights*, vol. I (South End, 1979).

direct documentation. Suppose, however, that someone were to unearth a document in which Milosevic orders the Serbian air force to reduce Bosnia or Kosovo to rubble, with the words 'Anything that flies on anything that moves.' The prosecutors would be overjoyed, the trial would end, and Milosevic would be sent off to many successive life sentences for the crime of genocide—a death sentence, if it followed US conventions. One would, in fact, be hard put to find such an explicit order to carry out genocide—as the term is currently employed with regard to crimes of enemies—anywhere in the historical record. In this case, after casual mention in the world's leading newspaper, there was no detectable interest, even though the horrendous consequences are well known. And rightly, if we adopt, tacitly, the overriding principle that we cannot—by definition—carry out crimes or have any responsibility for them.

One moral truism that should be uncontroversial is the principle of universality: we should apply to ourselves the same standards we apply to others—in fact, more stringent ones. This should be uncontroversial for everyone, but particularly so for the world's most important citizens, the leaders of the enlightened states, who declare themselves to be devout Christians, devoted to the Gospels, hence surely familiar with its famous condemnation of the Hypocrite. Their devotion to the commandments of the Lord is not in question. George Bush reportedly proclaims that 'God told me to strike at al Qaida and I struck them, and then He instructed me to strike at Saddam, which I did,' and 'now I am determined to solve the problem of the Middle East,'[8] also at the command of the Lord of Hosts, the War God, whom we are instructed by the Holy Book to worship above all other Gods. And as I mentioned, the elite press dutifully refers to his 'messianic mission' to solve the problem of the Middle East, in fact the world, following our 'responsibility to history to rid the world of evil,' in the president's words, the core principle of the 'vision' that Bush shares with Osama bin Laden, both plagiarizing ancient epics and children's fairy tales.

I am not sufficiently familiar with the sayings of Tony Blair to know how closely he approaches this ideal—which is quite familiar in Anglo-American history. The early English colonists in North America were following the word of the Lord as they slaughtered the Amalekites in the 'New Israel' that they were liberating from the native blight. Those who followed them, also Bible-waving God-fearing Christians, did their religious duty by conquering and possessing the promised land, ridding it of millions of Canaanites, and proceeding to war against the Papists in Florida,

---

[8] Arnon Regular, *Ha'aretz*, May 24, 2003, based on minutes of a meeting between Bush and his hand-picked Palestinian Prime Minister, Mahmoud Abbas, provided by Abbas. See also *Newsweek*, 'Bush and God,' March 10, 2003, with a cover story on the beliefs and direct line to God of the man with his finger on the button. Also 'The Jesus Factory,' PBS Frontline documentary, on the 'religious ideals' that Bush has brought to the White House, 'relevant to the Bush messianic mission to graft democracy onto the rest of the world'; Sam Allis, 'A timely look at how faith informs Bush presidency,' *Boston Globe*, April 29, 2004. White House aides report concern over Bush's 'increasingly erratic behavior' as he 'declares his decisions to be "God's will"'; Doug Thompson, publisher, *Capitol Hill Blue*, June 4, 2004.

Mexico, and California. Throughout they were defending themselves from the 'merciless Indian savages'—unleashed against them by George III, as the Declaration of Independence proclaims—at other times from the 'runaway negroes' and 'lawless Indians' who were attacking innocent Americans according to John Quincy Adams in one of the most celebrated State Papers in American history, written to justify Andrew Jackson's conquest of Florida in 1818, and the opening of the murderous Seminole wars. The event was of some significance for other reasons: it was the first executive war in violation of the constitutional requirement that only Congress can declare war, by now so fully the norm that it is scarcely noted— norms being established in the conventional way.

In his later years, long after his own grisly contributions were past, Adams did deplore the fate of 'that hapless race of native Americans who we are exterminating with such merciless and perfidious cruelty.' This is 'among the heinous sins of this nation, for which I believe God will one day bring [it] to judgment,' Adams believed. The first US Secretary of War had warned many years earlier that 'a future historian may mark the causes of this destruction of the human race in sable colours.' But they were wrong. God and the historians are slow in fulfilling this task. Unlike Bush and Blair, I cannot speak for God, but historians speak to us in mortal tongues. In a typical example, two months ago one of the most distinguished American historians referred in passing to 'the elimination of hundreds of thousands of native people' in the conquest of the national territory—off by a factor of ten, apart from the interesting choice of words. The reaction was null; it would be somewhat different if we were to read a casual comment in Germany's leading newspaper that hundreds of thousands of Jews were eliminated during World War II. There is also no reaction when a highly regarded diplomatic historian explains in a standard work that after their liberation from English rule, the colonists 'concentrated on the task of felling trees and Indians and of rounding out their natural boundaries.'⁹ It is all too easy to multiply examples in scholarship, media, school texts, cinema, and elsewhere. Sports teams use victims of genocide as mascots, usually with caricatures. Weapons of destruction are casually given similar names: Apache, Blackhawk, Comanche helicopters; Tomahawk missiles; and so on. How would we react if the Luftwaffe named its lethal weapons 'Jew' and 'Gypsy'?

The British record is much the same. Britain pursued its divine mission in the evangelization of Africa, while exercising in India 'a trusteeship mysteriously placed in their hands by Providence,' easy to comprehend in a country 'where God and Mammon seemed made for each other.'¹⁰ Figures of the highest moral integrity

⁹ Gordon Wood, '"Freedom Just Around the Corner": Rogue Nation,' *New York Times Book Review*, March 28, 2004; Thomas Bailey, *A Diplomatic History of the American People* (Appleton-Century-Crofts, 1969).

¹⁰ Historians Thomas Pakenham and David Edwards, cited by Clifford Langley, 'The Religious Roots of American Imperialism,' *Global Dialogue*, Winter-Spring 2003.

and intelligence gave a secular version of the creed, strikingly John Stuart Mill in his extraordinary apologetics for British crimes, written just as they peaked in India and China, in an essay now taken to be a classic of the literature of 'humanitarian intervention.' It is only fair to note that there were different voices. Richard Cobden denounced Britain's crimes in India and expressed his hope that the 'national conscience, which has before averted from England, by timely atonement and reparation, the punishment due for imperial crimes, will be roused ere it be too late from its lethargy, and put an end to the deeds of violence and injustice which have marked every step of our progress in India'—echoing Adam Smith, who had bitterly condemned 'the savage injustice of the Europeans,' particularly the British in India. Cobden hoped in vain. It is hardly much of a relief to recognize that their continental counterparts were even worse, in deed, denial, and self-adulation.

While quoting Cobden we might recall another of his maxims, highly pertinent today, and also qualifying as a moral truism: 'no man had a right to lend money if he knows it to be applied to the cutting of throats'[11] or, a fortiori, to sell the knives. It does not take an extensive research project to draw the appropriate conclusions with regard to the regular practice of the leading enlightened states.

The common response of the intellectual culture, some memorable exceptions aside, is entirely natural if we abandon the most elementary of moral truisms, and declare ourselves to be uniquely exempt from the principle of universality. And so we do, constantly. Every day brings new illustrations. The US Senate has just lent its consent to the appointment of John Negroponte as Ambassador to Iraq, heading the world's largest diplomatic mission, with the task of handing over sovereignty to Iraqis to fulfil Bush's 'messianic vision' to bring democracy to the Middle East and the world, so we are solemnly informed. The appointment bears directly on the principle of universality, but before turning to that, we might raise some questions about other truisms, regarding evidence and conclusions.

That the goal of the Iraq invasion is to fulfil the president's messianic vision is simply presupposed in news reporting and commentary, even among critics, who warn that the 'noble' and 'generous' vision may be beyond our reach. As the London *Economist* posed the problem a few weeks ago, 'America's mission' of turning Iraq into 'an inspiring example [of democracy] to its neighbours is facing obstacles.'[12] With considerable research, I have not been able to find exceptions in the US media, and with much less research, elsewhere, apart from the usual margins.

One might inquire into the basis for the apparently near universal acceptance of this doctrine in Western intellectual commentary. Examination will quickly reveal that it is based on two principles. First, our leaders have proclaimed it, so it must be true, a principle familiar in North Korea and other stellar models. Second, we must

---

[11] Cited by Pier Francesco Asso, 'The "Home Bias" Approach in the History of Economic Thought,' in J. Lorentzen and M. de Cecco (eds.), *Markets and Authorities* (Elgar: UK, 2002).

[12] 'Another intifada in the making,' 'Bloodier and sadder,' *Economist*, April 17, 2004.

suppress the fact that by proclaiming the doctrine after other pretexts have collapsed, our leaders are also declaring that they are among the most accomplished liars in history, since in leading their countries to war they proclaimed with comparable passion that the 'sole question' was whether Saddam had disarmed. But now we must believe them. Also obligatory is the dispatch deep into the memory hole of the ample record of professed noble efforts to bring democracy, justice, and freedom to the benighted.

It is, again, the merest truism that pronouncements of virtuous intent by leaders carry no information, even in the technical sense: they are completely predictable, including the worst monsters. But this truism also fades when it confronts the overriding need to reject the principle of universality.

The doctrine presupposed by Western commentary is accepted by some Iraqis too: one percent agreed that the goal of the invasion is to bring democracy to Iraq according to US-run polls in Baghdad last October—long before the atrocities in April and the revelations of torture. Another five percent felt that the goal is to help Iraqis. Most of the rest took for granted that the goal is to gain control of Iraq's resources and use Iraq as a base for reorganizing the Middle East in US interests[13]—a thought virtually inexpressible in enlightened Western commentary, or dismissed with horror as 'anti-Americanism,' 'conspiracy theory,' 'radical and extremist,' or some other intellectual equivalent of four-letter words among the vulgar. In brief, Iraqis appear to take for granted that what is unfolding is a scenario familiar from the days of Britain's creation of modern Iraq, accompanied by the predictable and therefore uninformative professions of virtuous intent, but also by secret internal documents in which Lord Curzon and the Foreign Office developed the plans to establish an 'Arab facade' that Britain would rule behind various 'constitutional fictions.' The contemporary version is provided by a senior British official quoted in the *Daily Telegraph*: 'The Iraqi government will be fully sovereign, but in practice it will not exercise all its sovereign functions.'[14]

Let us return to Negroponte and the principle of universality. As his appointment reached Congress, the *Wall Street Journal* praised him as a 'Modern Proconsul,' who learned his trade in Honduras in the 1980s, during the Reaganite phase of the current incumbents in Washington. The veteran *Journal* correspondent Carla Anne Robbins reminds us that in Honduras he was known as 'the proconsul,' as he presided over the second largest embassy in Latin America, with the largest CIA station in the world—perhaps to transfer full sovereignty to this centrepiece of world power.[15]

Robbins observes that Negroponte has been criticized by human rights activists for 'covering up abuses by the Honduran military'—a euphemism for large-scale state

[13] Walter Pincus, 'Skepticism About U.S. Deep, Iraq Poll Shows, Motive for Invasion Is Focus of Doubts,' *Washington Post*, November 12, 2003. Richard Burkholder, 'Gallup Poll of Baghdad: Gauging U.S. Intent,' Government & Public Affairs, October 28, 2003.

[14] Anton La Guardia, Diplomatic Editor, 'Handover still on course as UN waits for new leader to emerge,' *Daily Telegraph*, May 18, 2004.

[15] Robbins, 'Negroponte Has Tricky Mission: Modern Proconsul,' *Wall Street Journal*, April 27, 2004.

terror—'to ensure the flow of US aid' to this vital country, which was 'the base for Washington's covert war against Nicaragua.' The main task of proconsul Negroponte was to supervise the bases in which the terrorist mercenary army was armed, trained, and sent to do its work, including its mission of attacking undefended civilian targets, so the US military command informed Congress. The policy of attacking such 'soft targets' while avoiding the Nicaraguan army was confirmed by the State Department and defended by leading American liberal intellectuals, notably *New Republic* editor Michael Kinsley, who was the designated spokesman for the left in television commentary. He chastised Human Rights Watch for its sentimentality in condemning US international terrorism and failing to understand that it must be evaluated by 'pragmatic criteria.' A 'sensible policy,' he urged, should 'meet the test of cost-benefit analysis,' an analysis of 'the amount of blood and misery that will be poured in, and the likelihood that democracy will emerge at the other end'—'democracy,' as US elites determine, their unquestionable right. Of course, the principle of universality does not apply: others are not authorized to carry out large-scale international terrorist operations if their goals are likely to be achieved.

In this case the experiment was a grand success, and is indeed highly praised. Nicaragua was reduced to the second-poorest country in the hemisphere, with sixty percent of children under two afflicted with anaemia from severe malnutrition and probable permanent brain damage,[16] after the country suffered casualties during the terrorist war that in per capita terms would be comparable to 2.5 million dead in the US—a death toll 'significantly higher than the number of US persons killed in the US Civil War and all the wars of the twentieth century combined,' in the words of Thomas Carothers, the leading historian of the democratization of Latin America, who writes from the standpoint of an insider as well as a scholar, having served in Reagan's State Department in the programmes of 'democracy enhancement.' Describing himself as a 'neo-Reaganite,' he regards these programmes as 'sincere,' though a 'failure,' because the US would tolerate only 'top-down forms of democracy' controlled by traditional elites with firm ties to the US. This is a familiar refrain in the history of the pursuit of visions of democracy, which Iraqis apparently comprehend, even if we choose not to. It is worth stressing the word 'choose,' because there is no shortage of evidence.

Negroponte's primary task as proconsul in Honduras was to supervise the international terrorist atrocities for which the US was condemned by the World Court in a judgment that reached well beyond Nicaragua's narrow case, shaped by its Harvard legal team to avoid factual debate, since the facts were conceded. The Court ordered Washington to terminate the crimes and pay substantial reparations—all ignored on the official grounds that other nations do not agree with us so we must 'reserve to ourselves the power to determine' how we will act and which matters fall 'essentially within the domestic jurisdiction of the United States, as determined by the

---

[16] *Envío* (UCA, Jesuit University, Managua), November 2003.

United States,' in this case the actions that the Court condemned as the 'unlawful use of force' against Nicaragua; in lay terms, international terrorism. All consigned to the ashcan of history by the educated classes in the usual manner of unwanted truths, along with the two supporting Security Council resolutions vetoed by the US, with Britain loyally abstaining. The international terrorist campaign received passing mention during Negroponte's confirmation hearings, but is considered of no particular significance, thanks to the exemption of our glorious selves from the principle of universality.

On the wall of my office at MIT, I have a painting given to me by a Jesuit priest, depicting the Angel of Death standing over the figure of Salvadoran Archbishop Romero, whose assassination in 1980 opened that grim decade of international state terrorist atrocities, and right before him the six leading Latin American intellectuals, Jesuit priests, whose brains were blown out in 1989, bringing the decade to an end. The Jesuit intellectuals, along with their housekeeper and her daughter, were murdered by an elite battalion armed and trained by the current incumbents in Washington and their mentors. It had already compiled a bloody record of massacres in the US-run international terrorist campaign that Romero's successor described as a 'war of extermination and genocide against a defenseless civilian population.' Romero had been killed by much the same hands, a few days after he pleaded with President Carter not to provide the junta with military aid, which 'will surely increase injustice here and sharpen the repression that has been unleashed against the people's organizations fighting to defend their most fundamental human rights.' The repression continued with US aid after his assassination, and the current incumbents carried it forward to a 'war of extermination and genocide.'

I keep the painting there to remind myself daily of the real world, but it has turned out to serve another instructive purpose. Many visitors pass through the office. Those from Latin America almost unfailingly recognize it. Those from north of the Rio Grande virtually never do. From Europe, recognition is perhaps ten percent. We may consider another useful thought experiment. Suppose that in Czechoslovakia in the 1980s, security forces armed and trained by the Kremlin had assassinated an Archbishop who was known as 'the voice of the voiceless,' then proceeded to massacre tens of thousands of people, consummating the decade with the brutal murder of Vaclav Havel and half a dozen other leading Czech intellectuals. Would we know about it? Perhaps not, because the Western reaction might have gone as far as nuclear war, so there would be no one left to know. The distinguishing criterion is, once again, crystal clear. The crimes of enemies take place; our own do not, by virtue of our exemption from the most elementary of moral truisms.

The murdered Jesuits were, in fact, doubly assassinated: brutally killed, and unknown in the enlightened states, a particularly cruel fate for intellectuals. In the West, only specialists or activists even know their names, let alone have any idea of what they wrote. Their fate is quite unlike that of dissident intellectuals in the domains of official enemies, who are well known, widely published and read, and highly honoured for their courageous resistance to repression—which was indeed harsh, though it did not begin to compare with what was endured by their counterparts under Western rule in the same years. Again, the differential treatment makes good sense, given our principled exemption from moral truisms.

Let us move on to some hard problems. Perhaps none is more prominent today than 'the evil scourge of terrorism,' particularly state-backed international terrorism, a 'plague spread by depraved opponents of civilization itself' in a 'return to barbarism in the modern age.' So the plague was described when the 'war on terror' was declared—not in September 2001 when it was *re-declared*, but twenty years earlier, by the same people and their mentors. Their 'war on terror' instantly turned into a murderous terrorist war, with horrifying consequences in Central America, the Middle East, southern Africa, and elsewhere, but that is only history, not the history crafted by its custodians in the enlightened states. In more useful accepted history, the 1980s are described by scholarship as the decade of 'state terrorism,' of 'persistent state involvement, or "sponsorship," of terrorism, especially by Libya and Iran.' The US merely responded with 'a "proactive" stance toward terrorism,'[17] and the same was true of its allies: Israel, South Africa, the clandestine terror network assembled by the Reaganites, and others. I will put to the side the radical Islamists organized and trained for the cause—not to defend Afghanistan, which would have been a legitimate goal, but to bloody the official enemy, probably prolonging the Afghan war and leaving the country in ruins, soon to become much worse as Western clients took over, with subsequent consequences that we need not mention. Gone from acceptable history are millions of victims of the real 'war on terror' of the 1980s, and those seeking to survive in what is left of their devastated lands. Also out of history is the residual 'culture of terror,' which 'domesticates the aspirations of the majority,' to quote the survivors of the Jesuit intellectual community in El Salvador, in a conference surveying the actual but unacceptable history.

Terrorism poses a number of hard problems. First and foremost, of course, the phenomenon itself, which really is threatening, even keeping to the subpart that passes through the doctrinal filters: *their* terrorism against *us*. It is only a matter of time before terror and weapons of mass destruction are united, perhaps with horrendous consequences, as has been discussed in the specialist literature long before the 11 September atrocities. But apart from the phenomenon, there is the problem of definition of 'terror.' That too is taken to be a hard problem, the subject of scholarly literature and international conferences. At first glance, it might seem odd that it is regarded as a hard problem. There are what seem to be satisfactory definitions—not perfect, but at least as good as others regarded as unproblematic: for example, the official definitions in the US Code and Army Manuals in the early 1980s when the

---

[17]   Martha Crenshaw, *Current History, America at War*, December 2001.

'war on terror' was launched, or the quite similar official formulation of the British government, which defines 'terrorism' as 'the use, or threat, of action which is violent, damaging or disrupting, and is intended to influence the government or intimidate the public and is for the purpose of advancing a political, religious, or ideological cause.' These are the definitions that I have been using in writing about terrorism for the past twenty years, ever since the Reagan administration declared that the war on terror would be a prime focus of its foreign policy, replacing human rights, the proclaimed 'soul of our foreign policy' before.[18]

On closer look, however, the problem becomes clear, and it is indeed hard. The official definitions are unusable, because of their immediate consequences. One difficulty is that the definition of terrorism is virtually the same as the definition of the official policy of the US, and other states, called 'counter-terrorism' or 'low-intensity warfare' or some other euphemism. That again is close to a historical universal, to my knowledge. Japanese imperialists in Manchuria and North China, for example, were not aggressors or terrorists, but were protecting the population and the legitimate governments from the terrorism of 'Chinese bandits.' To undertake this noble task, they were compelled, reluctantly, to resort to 'counter-terror,' with the goal of establishing an 'earthly paradise' in which the people of Asia could live in peace and harmony under the enlightened guidance of Japan. The same is true of just about every other case I have investigated. But now we do face a hard problem: it will not do to say that the enlightened states are officially committed to terrorism. And it takes little effort to demonstrate that the US engages in large-scale international terrorism according to its own definition of the term, quite uncontroversially in a number of crucial cases.

There are related problems. Some arose when the UN General Assembly, in response to Reaganite pressures, passed its strongest condemnation of terrorism in December 1987, with a call on all states to destroy the plague of the modern age. The resolution passed 153 to 2, with only Honduras abstaining. The two states that opposed the resolution explained their reasons in the UN debate. They objected to a passage recognizing 'the right to self-determination, freedom, and independence, as derived from the Charter of the United Nations, of people forcibly deprived of that right, particularly peoples under colonial and racist regimes and foreign occupation.' The term 'colonial and racist regimes' was understood to refer to South Africa, a US ally, resisting the attacks of Nelson Mandela's ANC, one of the world's 'more notorious terrorist groups,' as Washington determined at the same time. And 'foreign occupation' was understood to refer to Washington's Israeli client. So, not surprisingly, the US and Israel voted against the resolution, which was thereby effectively vetoed—in fact, subjected to the usual double veto: inapplicable, and vetoed from

---

[18]   See, inter alia, my *Pirates and Emperors* (1986; updated edition, South End-Pluto, 2002). For review of the first phase of the 'war on terror,' see Alexander George (ed.), *Western State Terrorism* (Polity, Blackwell, 1991).

reporting and history as well, though it was the strongest and most important UN resolution on terrorism.

There is, then, a hard problem of defining 'terrorism,' rather like the problem of defining 'war crime.' How can we define it in such a way as to violate the principle of universality, exempting ourselves but applying to selected enemies? And these have to be selected with some precision. The US has had an official list of states sponsoring terrorism ever since the Reagan years. In all these years, only one state has been removed from the list: Iraq, in order to permit the US to join the UK and others in providing badly needed aid for Saddam Hussein, continuing without concern after he carried out his most horrifying crimes. There has also been one near-example. Clinton offered to remove Syria from the list if it agreed to peace terms offered by the US and Israel. When Syria insisted on recovering the territory that Israel conquered in 1967, it remained on the list of states sponsoring terrorism, and continues to be on the list despite the acknowledgment by Washington that Syria has not been implicated in sponsoring terror for many years and has been highly cooperative in providing important intelligence to the US on al-Qaeda and other radical Islamist groups. As a reward for Syria's cooperation in the 'war on terror,' last December Congress passed legislation calling for even stricter sanctions against Syria, nearly unanimously (the Syria Accountability Act). The legislation was recently implemented by the president, thus depriving the US of a major source of information about radical Islamist terrorism in order to achieve the higher goal of establishing in Syria a regime that will accept US-Israeli demands—not an unusual pattern, though commentators continually find it surprising no matter how strong the evidence and regular the pattern, and no matter how rational the choices in terms of clear and understandable planning priorities.

The Syria Accountability Act offers another striking illustration of the rejection of the principle of universality. Its core demand refers to UN Security Council Resolution 520, calling for respect for the sovereignty and territorial integrity of Lebanon, violated by Syria because it still retains in Lebanon forces that were welcomed there by the US and Israel in 1976 when their task was to carry out massacres of Palestinians. The congressional legislation, and news reporting and commentary, overlook the fact that Resolution 520, passed in 1982, was explicitly directed against Israel, not Syria, and also the fact that while Israel violated this and other Security Council resolutions regarding Lebanon for twenty-two years, there was no call for any sanctions against Israel, or even any call for reduction in the huge unconditional military and economic aid to Israel. The silence for twenty-two years includes many of those who now signed the Act condemning Syria for its violation of the Security Council resolution ordering Israel to leave Lebanon. The principle is accurately formulated by a rare scholarly commentator, Steven Zunes: it is that 'Lebanese sovereignty must be defended only if the occupying army is from a country the United States opposes, but is dispensable if the country is a US ally.'[19] The principle, and the news reporting and

---

[19] Zunes, 'U.S. Policy Towards Syria and the Triumph of Neoconservatism,' *Middle East Policy*, Spring 2004.

commentary on all of these events, again make good sense, given the overriding need to reject elementary moral truisms, a fundamental doctrine of the intellectual and moral culture.

Returning to Iraq, when Saddam was removed from the list of states supporting terrorism, Cuba was added to replace it, perhaps in recognition of the sharp escalation in international terrorist attacks against Cuba in the late 1970s, including the bombing of a Cubana airliner killing seventy-three people and many other atrocities. These were mostly planned and implemented in the US, though by that time Washington had moved away from its former policy of direct action in bringing 'the terrors of the earth' to Cuba—the goal of the Kennedy administration, reported by historian and Kennedy adviser Arthur Schlesinger in his biography of Robert Kennedy, who was assigned responsibility for the terror campaign and regarded it as a top priority. By the late 1970s Washington was officially condemning the terrorist acts while harbouring and protecting the terrorist cells on US soil in violation of US law. The leading terrorist, Orlando Bosch, regarded as the author of the Cubana airline bombing and dozens of other terrorist acts according to the FBI, was given a presidential pardon by George Bush Number 1, over the strong objections of the Justice Department. Others like him continue to operate with impunity on US soil, including terrorists responsible for major crimes elsewhere as well for whom the US refuses requests for extradition (from Haiti, for example).

We may recall one of the leading components of the 'Bush doctrine'—now Bush Number 2: 'Those who harbour terrorists are as guilty as the terrorists themselves,' and must be treated accordingly, the president's words when announcing the bombing of Afghanistan because of its refusal to turn over suspected terrorists to the US, without evidence, or even credible pretext as later quietly conceded. Harvard International Relations specialist Graham Allison describes this as the most important component of the Bush Doctrine. It 'unilaterally revoked the sovereignty of states that provide sanctuary to terrorists,' he wrote approvingly in *Foreign Affairs*, adding that the doctrine has 'already become a de facto rule of international relations.' That is correct, in the technical sense of 'rule of international relations.'

Unreconstructed literalists might conclude that Bush and Allison are calling for the bombing of the United States, but that is because they do not comprehend that the most elementary moral truisms must be forcefully rejected: there is a crucial exemption to the principle of universality, so deeply entrenched in the reigning intellectual culture that it is not even perceived, hence not mentioned.

Again, we find illustrations daily. The Negroponte appointment is one example. To take another, a few weeks ago the Palestinian leader Abu Abbas died in a US prison in Iraq. His capture was one of the most heralded achievements of the invasion. A few years earlier he had been living in Gaza, participating in the Oslo 'peace process' with US-Israeli approval, but after the second Intifada began, he fled to Baghdad, where he was arrested by the US army and imprisoned because of his role in the hijacking of the cruise ship Achille Lauro in 1985. The year 1985 is regarded by scholarship as the peak year of terrorism in the 1980s; Mideast terrorism was the top story of the year, in a poll of editors. Scholarship identifies two major crimes in that year: the hijacking of the Achille Lauro, in which one person, a crippled American, was brutally murdered; and an airplane hijacking with one death, also an American. There were, to be sure, some other terrorist crimes in the region in 1985, but they do not pass through the filters. One was a car-bombing outside a mosque in Beirut that killed eighty people and wounded 250 others, timed to explode as people were leaving, killing mostly women and girls; but this is excluded from the record because it was traced back to the CIA and British intelligence. Another was the action that led to the Achille Lauro hijacking in retaliation, a week later: Shimon Peres' bombing of Tunis with no credible pretext, killing seventy-five people, Palestinians and Tunisians, expedited by the US and praised by Secretary of State Shultz, then unanimously condemned by the UN Security Council as an 'act of armed aggression' (US abstaining). But that too does not enter the annals of terrorism (or perhaps the more severe crime of 'armed aggression'), again because of agency. Peres and Shultz do not die in prison, but receive Nobel prizes, huge taxpayer gifts for reconstruction of what they helped destroy in occupied Iraq, and other honours. Again, it all makes sense once we comprehend that elementary moral truisms must be sent to the flames.

Sometimes denial of moral truisms is explicit. A case in point is the reaction to the second major component of the 'Bush Doctrine,' formally enunciated in the National Security Strategy of September 2002, which was at once described in the main establishment journal Foreign Affairs as a 'new imperial grand strategy' declaring Washington's right to resort to force to eliminate any potential challenge to its global dominance. The NSS was widely criticized among the foreign policy elite, including the article just cited, but on narrow grounds: not that it was wrong, or even new, but that the style and implementation were so extreme that they posed threats to US interests. Henry Kissinger described 'The new approach [as] revolutionary,' pointing out that it undermines the 17th-century Westphalian system of international order, and of course the UN Charter and international law. He approved of the doctrine but with reservations about style and tactics, and with a crucial qualification: it cannot be 'a universal principle available to every nation.' Rather, the right of aggression must be reserved to the US, perhaps delegated to chosen clients. We must forcefully reject the most elementary of moral truisms: the principle of universality. Kissinger is to be praised for his honesty in forthrightly articulating prevailing doctrine, usually concealed in professions of virtuous intent and tortured legalisms.

To add just one last example that is very timely and significant, consider 'just war theory,' now undergoing a vigorous revival in the context of the 'normative revolution' proclaimed in the 1990s. There has been debate about whether the invasion of Iraq satisfies the conditions for just war, but virtually none about the bombing of Serbia in 1999 or the invasion of Afghanistan, taken to be such clear cases that discussion is superfluous. Let us take a quick look at these, not asking whether the attacks were right or wrong, but considering the nature of the arguments.

The harshest criticism of the Serbia bombing anywhere near the mainstream is that it was 'illegal but legitimate,' the conclusion of the International Independent Commission of Inquiry headed by Justice Richard Goldstone. 'It was illegal because it did not receive approval from the UN Security Council,' the Commission determined, 'but it was legitimate because all diplomatic avenues had been exhausted and there was no other way to stop the killings and atrocities in Kosovo.'[20]

Justice Goldstone observed that the Charter may need revision in the light of the report and the judgments on which it is based. The NATO intervention, he explains, 'is too important a precedent' for it to be regarded 'an aberration.' Rather, 'state sovereignty is being redefined in the face of globalization and the resolve by the majority of the peoples of the world that human rights have become the business of the international community.' He also stressed the need for 'objective analysis of human rights abuses.'[21]

The last comment is good advice. One question that an objective analysis might address is whether the majority of the peoples of the world accept the judgment of the enlightened states. In the case of the bombing of Serbia, review of the world press and official statements reveals little support for that conclusion, to put it rather mildly. In fact, the bombing was bitterly condemned outside the NATO countries, facts consistently ignored.[22] Furthermore, it is hardly likely that the principled self-exemption of the enlightened states from the 'universalization' that traces back to Nuremberg would gain the approval of much of the world's population. The new norm, it appears, fits the standard pattern.

Another question that objective analysis might address is whether indeed 'all diplomatic avenues had been exhausted.' That conclusion is not easy to maintain in the light of the fact that there were two options on the table when NATO decided to bomb—a NATO proposal and a Serbian proposal—and that after seventy-eight days of bombing, a compromise was reached between them.[23]

A third question is whether it is true that 'there was no other way to stop the killings and atrocities in Kosovo,' clearly a crucial matter. In this case, objective analysis happens to be unusually easy. There is vast documentation available from impeccable Western sources: several compilations of the State Department released

---

[20] The Independent International Commission on Kosovo, 'The Kosovo Report,' 23 October, 2000, http://reliefweb.int/sites/reliefweb.int/files/resources/6D26FF88119644CFC1256989005CD392-thekosovoreport.pdf (Oxford University Press, 2000).

[21] Goldstone, 'Kosovo: An Assessment in the Context of International Law.'

[22] For review see New Military Humanism.

[23] For details, see my A New Generation Draws the Line (Verso, 2000), which also reviews how NATO instantly overturned the Security Council resolution it had initiated. Goldstone, in 'Kosovo: An Assessment in the Context of International Law,' recognizes that the resolution was a compromise, but does not go into the matter, which aroused no interest in the West.

in justification of the war, detailed records of the OSCE, NATO, the UN, a British Parliamentary Inquiry, and other similar sources.

There are several remarkable features of the unusually rich documentation. One is that the record is almost entirely ignored in the vast literature on the Kosovo war, including the scholarly literature.[24] The second is that the substantive contents of the documentation are not only ignored, but consistently denied. I have reviewed the record elsewhere, and will not do so here, but what we discover, characteristically, is that the clear and explicit chronology is reversed. The Serbian atrocities are portrayed as the cause of the bombing, whereas it is uncontroversial that they followed it, virtually without exception, and were furthermore its anticipated consequence, as is also well documented from the highest NATO sources.

The British government, the most hawkish element of the alliance, estimated that most of the atrocities were attributable not to the Serbian security forces, but to the KLA guerrillas attacking Serbia from Albania—with the intent, as they frankly explained, to elicit a disproportionate Serbian response that could be used to mobilize Western support for the bombing. The British government assessment was as of mid-January, but the documentary record indicates no substantial change until late March, when the bombing was announced and initiated. The Milosevic indictment, based on US and UK intelligence, reveals the same pattern of events.

The US and UK, and commentators generally, cite the Racak massacre in mid-January as the decisive turning point, but that plainly cannot be taken seriously. First, even assuming the most extreme condemnations of the Racak massacre to be accurate, it scarcely changed the balance of atrocities. Second, much worse massacres were taking place at the same time elsewhere but aroused no concern, though some of the worst could have easily been terminated merely by withdrawing support. One notable case in early 1999 is East Timor, under Indonesian military occupation. The US and UK continued to provide their military and diplomatic support for the occupiers, who had already slaughtered perhaps one-fourth of the population with unremitting and decisive US-UK support, which continued until well after the Indonesian army virtually destroyed the country in a final paroxysm of violence in August-September 1999. That is only one of many such cases, but it alone more than suffices to dismiss the professions of horror about Racak.

In Kosovo, Western estimates are that about 2000 were killed in the year prior to the invasion. If the British and other assessments are accurate, most of these were killed by the KLA guerrillas. One of the very few serious scholarly studies even to consider the matter estimates that 500 of the 2000 were killed by the Serbs. This is the careful and judicious study by Nicholas Wheeler, who supports the NATO bombing on the grounds that there would have been worse atrocities had NATO not bombed.[25]

---

[24] The only detailed reviews I know of are in my books cited in the two preceding notes, with some additions from the later British parliamentary inquiry in *Hegemony or Survival*.

[25] Nicholas Wheeler, *Saving Strangers: Humanitarian Intervention and International Society* (Oxford, 2000).

The argument is that by bombing with the anticipation that it would lead to atrocities, NATO was preventing atrocities, maybe even a second Auschwitz, many claim. That such arguments are taken seriously, as they are, gives no slight insight into Western intellectual culture, particularly when we recall that there were diplomatic options and that the agreement reached after the bombing was a compromise between them (formally at least).

Justice Goldstone appears to have reservations on this matter as well. He recognizes—as few do—that the NATO bombing was not undertaken to protect the Albanian population of Kosovo, and that its 'direct result' was a 'tremendous catastrophe' for the Kosovars—as was anticipated by the NATO command and the State Department, followed by another catastrophe particularly for Serbs and Roma under NATO-UN occupation. NATO commentators and supporters, Justice Goldstone continues, 'have had to console themselves with the belief that "Operation Horseshoe," the Serb plan of ethnic cleansing directed against the Albanians in Kosovo, had been set in motion before the bombing began, and not in consequence of the bombing.' The word 'belief' is appropriate: there is no evidence in the voluminous Western record of anything having been set in motion before the international monitors were withdrawn in preparation for the bombing, and very little in the few days before the bombing began, and 'Operation Horseshoe' has since been exposed as an apparent intelligence fabrication, though it can hardly be in doubt that Serbia had contingency plans, at present unknown, for such actions in response to a NATO attack.

It is difficult, then, to see how we can accept the conclusions of the International Commission, a serious and measured effort to deal with the issues, on the legitimacy of the bombing.

The facts are not really controversial, as anyone interested can determine. I suppose that is why the voluminous Western documentary record is so scrupulously ignored. Whatever one's judgment about the bombing, not at issue here, the standard conclusion that it was an uncontroversial example of just war and the decisive demonstration of the 'normative revolution' led by the 'enlightened states' is, to say the least, rather startling—unless, of course, we return to the same principle: moral truisms must be cast to the flames, when applied to us.

Let us turn to the second case, the war in Afghanistan, considered such a paradigm example of just war that there is scarcely even any discussion about it. The respected moral-political philosopher Jean Bethke Elshtain summarizes received opinion fairly accurately when she writes approvingly that only absolute pacifists and outright lunatics doubt that this was uncontroversially a just war. Here, once again, factual questions arise. First, recall the war aims: to punish Afghans until the Taliban agree to hand over Osama bin Laden without evidence. Contrary to much subsequent commentary, overthrowing the Taliban regime was an afterthought, added after several weeks of bombing. Second, there is quite good evidence bearing on the belief that only lunatics or absolute pacifists did not join the chorus of approval.

An international Gallup poll after the bombing was announced but before it began found very limited support for it, almost none if civilians were targeted, as they were from the first moment. And even that tepid support was based on the presupposition that the targets were known to have been responsible for the 11 September attacks. They were not. Eight months later, the head of the FBI informed the press that after the most intensive international intelligence inquiry in history, the most that could be said was that the plot was 'believed' to have been hatched in Afghanistan, while the attacks were planned and financed elsewhere. It follows that there was no detectable popular support for the bombing, contrary to confident standard claims, apart from a very few countries; and of course Western elites. Afghan opinion is harder to estimate, but we do know that after several weeks of bombing, leading anti-Taliban figures, including some of those most respected by the US and President Karzai, were denouncing the bombing, calling for it to end, and charging the US with bombing just to 'show off its muscle' while undermining their efforts to overthrow the Taliban from within.

If we also adopt the truism that facts matter, some problems arise, but there is little fear of that.

Next come the questions of just war. At once, the issue of universality arises. If the US is unquestionably authorized to bomb another country to compel its leaders to turn over someone it suspects of involvement in a terrorist act, then, a fortiori, Cuba, Nicaragua, and a host of others are entitled to bomb the US because there is no doubt of its involvement in very serious terrorist attacks against them: in the case of Cuba going back forty-five years, extensively documented in impeccable sources, and not questioned; in the case of Nicaragua, even condemned by the World Court and the Security Council (in vetoed resolutions), after which the US escalated the attack. This conclusion surely follows if we accept the principle of universality. The conclusion of course is utterly outrageous, and advocated by no one. We therefore conclude, once again, that the principle of universality has a crucial exception, and that rejection of elementary moral truisms is so deeply entrenched that even raising the question is considered an unspeakable abomination. That is yet another instructive comment on the reigning intellectual and moral culture, with its principled rejection of unacceptable platitudes.

The Iraq war has been considered more controversial, so there is an extensive professional literature debating whether it satisfies international law and just war criteria. One distinguished scholar, Michael Glennon of the Fletcher School of Law and Diplomacy, argues forthrightly that international law is simply 'hot air' and should be abandoned, because state practice does not conform to it: meaning, the US and its allies ignore it. A further defect of international law and the UN Charter, he argues, is that they limit the capacity of the US to resort to force, and such resort is right and good because the US leads the 'enlightened states' (his phrase), apparently by definition: no evidence or argument is adduced, or considered necessary. Another respected scholar argues that the US and UK were in fact acting in accord with the

UN Charter, under a 'communitarian interpretation' of its provisions: they were carrying out the will of the international community, in a mission implicitly delegated to them because they alone had the power to carry it out.[26] It is apparently irrelevant that the international community vociferously objected, at an unprecedented level— quite evidently, if people are included within the international community, but even among elites.

Others observe that law is a living instrument, its meaning determined by practice, and practice demonstrates that new norms have been established permitting 'anticipatory self-defence,' another euphemism for aggression at will. The tacit assumption is that norms are established by the powerful and that they alone have the right of anticipatory self-defence. No one, for example, would argue that Japan exercised this right when it bombed military bases in the US colonies of Hawaii and the Philippines, even though the Japanese knew very well that B-17 Flying Fortresses were coming off the Boeing production lines, and were surely familiar with the very public discussions in the US explaining how they could be used to incinerate Japan's wooden cities in a war of extermination, flying from Hawaiian and Philippine bases.[27] Nor would anyone accord that right to any state today, apart from the self-declared enlightened states, which have the power to determine norms and to apply them selectively at will, basking in praise for their nobility, generosity, and messianic visions of righteousness.

There is nothing particularly novel about any of this, apart from one aspect. The means of destruction that have been developed are by now so awesome, and the risks of deploying and using them so enormous, that a rational Martian observer would not rank the prospects for survival of this curious species very high, as long as contempt for elementary moral truisms remains so deeply entrenched among educated elites.

---

[26] Carston Stahn, 'Enforcement of the Collective Will after Iraq,' *American Journal of International Law*, Symposium, 'Future Implications of the Iraq Conflict,' 97:804–23, 2003. For more on these matters, including Glennon's influential ideas and his rejection of other moral truisms, see my article and several others in *Review of International Studies* 29.4, October 2003, and *Hegemony or Survival*.

[27] See Bruce Franklin, *War Stars* (Oxford, 1988).

Introduction to Alasdair MacIntyre's Lecture

Ted Honderich

Alasdair MacIntyre is a Scot whose higher education was in the universities of London, Manchester, and Oxford. He then taught in several English and in many American universities. His line of publications, the first in his early 20s, includes the books *Against the Self-Images of the Age* (1971), *After Virtue* (1981), *Whose Justice, Which Rationality?* (1988), *Three Rival Versions of Moral Inquiry* (1990), and *Dependent Rational Animals* (1999). The individuality of these books, their strength and their singular entry into the history of moral philosophy and morality, have given him true distinction in moral, social, and political philosophy. His line of commitments has had in it Marxism, an Aristotelian ethics of the virtues, his own thinking spoken of by others as communitarianism, objection to liberal and other capitalism, and Catholicism. He is now professor emeritus of philosophy at Notre Dame University and a research fellow at London Metropolitan University.

The lecture takes as one example a man of whom it is said that in a sense he might be anybody, but he *is* a scheduler of German passenger and freight trains. He resists a charge of moral failure having to do with whatever was carried by the trains, including Jews to extermination camps. His defence is that he did his duty, which was scheduling and the like, and he did not have anything to do with what trains carried. He fulfilled his role as instructed, did not fail in his responsibility, and so he bears no guilt. MacIntyre directs us to subjects that must arise in consideration of such a defence, gives due attention to many facets. He enriches moral philosophy by way of a kind of sociology, what might be called moral sociology, and also by way of thought on what might be called personhood in society.

His first consideration of moral agency, of being a moral agent, of being responsible, includes reflection on discriminating what is incidental in an action from what is not. This, inevitably, has to do with standards of a social and cultural order in which one exists. Being a moral agent, further, sometimes requires at least questioning accepted social structures, structures which may in fact threaten the possibility of being a moral agent.

There is much that needs to be added about understanding a moral agent. One thing is that to know that one is such an agent is to know that one has a personal identity as well as a social role. One must also be a practically rational individual, an accountable one, and respect two demands, those of integrity and constancy. One has to ask in particular what a social and cultural order needs its inhabitants not to know. For someone to become and be such a moral agent, certain milieus of dialogue and inquiry are necessary. These, of which more is said in what follows, are of prime importance. They may be missing.

Also given large importance is the fact of what is called compartmentalization. Consideration of it begins from some research having to do with the morality of decision-making in the electric power industry in America. There is the example of a man who is both a company executive and a parent, and consideration of norms within insulated spheres, of the ethics of deception including lying, and of the divided self. In the case of the railwayman, it is added that his existence is one that includes what in fact are not lacks or absences but rather active refusals and denials by that self, that co-author of its moral and social situation.

What is concluded by MacIntyre, taking all into account, is that the railwayman *is* morally guilty.

That cannot be to suppose that such persons as the scheduler are unique, let alone unique to such societies as the Nazi one. MacIntyre does not concern himself explicitly with differences and similarities between the culpable railwayman and the mentioned company executive. There is to my mind the implication that there are facts of individual moral guilt within our own societies, in our own social and cultural orders. Further, as with Germany past, there are also guilts of other kinds on the part of whole social and political orders. I myself take it that these may include, although they are not mentioned, our own governments, political classes, democracies, so-called democracies, so-called democracies that are also racist, and so on.

The lecture and the rest of MacIntyre's work raise hard questions, one being the way and extent to which a verdict as to guilt or innocence can be judged, let alone demonstrated. Another, very different, is whether it is reasonable to engage in reflective morality without some decent knowledge of its history, conceivably going back to Aristotle. The question can leave you not only envious of MacIntyre's work but uneasy about your thinking or unthinking life in a society.

15

Social Structures and their Threats to Moral Agency

Alasdair MacIntyre

1. The Case of J

Imagine first the case of J (who might be anybody, *jemand*). J used to inhabit a social order, or rather an area within a social order, where socially approved roles were unusually well defined. Responsibilities were allocated to each such role and each sphere of role-structured activity was clearly demarcated. These allocations and demarcations were embodied in and partly constituted by the expectations that others had learned to have of those who occupied each such role. For those who occupied those roles to disappoint those expectations by failing to discharge their assigned responsibilities was to invite severe disapproval and other sanctions. To refuse to find one's place within the hierarchies of approved roles, or to have been refused a place, because judged unfit for any such role, was to be classified as socially deviant and irresponsible.

The key moral concepts that education had inculcated into J were concepts of duty and responsibility. His fundamental moral beliefs were that each of us owes it to others to perform her or his assigned duties and to discharge her or his assigned responsibilities. A good human being performs those duties, discharges those responsibilities, and does not trespass into areas that are not her or his concern. A philosopher who comes across the likes of J will understand his attitudes as cultural parodies, in part of Plato (conceiving of justice as requiring 'that each do her or his own work and not meddle with many things' *Republic* 433a) and in part of Kant (doing one's duty just because it is one's duty and not for the sake of any further end), authors who had influenced J's school teachers. A sociologist will entertain the suspicion that in certain types of social order it may be only in the form of parodies that some types of concept can continue to find expression. But for the moment let us put this thought to one side and return to J.

J, like everyone else, occupied a number of roles. He was a father, the treasurer of his sports club, and in wartime had been a noncommissioned officer. Afterwards he spent his working career in the service of the railways, rising to a position in which he was responsible for scheduling passenger and freight trains, monitoring their drivers' performance, and coping with break-downs. Early in that career he had been mildly curious about what 'his' trains carried: commuters or vacationers, pig-iron or cattle. But he was instructed firmly by his superiors to take *no* interest in such questions, but to attend *only* to what belonged to his role, so as not to be irresponsibly distracted. Hence he acquired the habit of taking no cognizance of what his trains carried, a habit that endured through a later period, when the freight consisted in munitions and the passengers were Jews on their way to extermination camps. When still later J was questioned about this, he said sincerely: 'I did not know. It was not for someone in my position to know. I did my duty. I did not fail in my responsibilities. You cannot charge me with moral failure.' Was J's defence adequate?

2. Moral Agency

To many the answer will be obvious and that answer is 'No'. Their answer presupposes a widely shared conception of moral agency. On this view to be a moral agent is to be justifiably held responsible. Responsible for what? For one's actions, certainly, but for one's actions in at least three respects. First moral agents so conceived are justifiably and uncontroversially held responsible for that in their actions which is intentional. Secondly they may be justifiably held responsible for incidental aspects of those actions of which they should have been aware. And thirdly they may be justifiably held responsible for at least some of the reasonably predictable effects of their actions.

It is in spelling out the second and third of these that we encounter complexities. Consider two examples. I intentionally in my role as examiner award the prize to the competitor with highest marks, incidentally awarding the prize to the most arrogant competitor, and having reasonable grounds for predicting that the effect of the award will be to make him even more objectionable. But in this case it is my responsibility, because of my role, to ignore these latter considerations. Contrast a second example. I intentionally return a handgun to its owner, as my role in the lost property office requires, incidentally and, as it happens, knowingly returning it to someone dangerously paranoid, and having reasonable grounds for predicting that in consequence someone innocent will be harmed. In this case, because I am aware of these latter aspects of my action, I am justifiably held responsible for them, and, even if I had not known what I did, I might, at least in certain circumstances, be justifiably held responsible for not having found out what I should have found out. What the first example makes clear is that we may indeed sometimes be able to rebut charges that we were responsible for not taking cognizance of certain facts by citing a role that required us not to take account of them. And what the second example makes clear is that sometimes we are justifiably held responsible for not having made ourselves aware of certain facts about our actions, whatever the requirements of our role may have been.

How is the one type of case to be discriminated from the other? Two remarks are sufficient, not to answer this question, but to return us to the case of J. The first is that it is part of the responsibility of moral agents, on this view of moral agency, to know how at the level of practice to discriminate between such cases, and to give reasons for so discriminating, in the light of the best standards available. One reason, although only one, why children, the mentally retarded, and those suffering from some kinds of brain damage are denied the status of moral agent, or at least of fully fledged moral agent, is that they are unable to do this. And, if we hold J responsible for knowing what he was doing, whatever the requirements of his role might have been, we are ascribing to J just such a power of reasonable discrimination. Yet we are entitled to hold J responsible only if the best standards available to J would have warranted him in making those reasonable discriminations that we judge that he ought to have made. So what were the best standards available to J?

Here a second remark is to the point. J had been taught that the unquestionably best standards were in fact the standards defining and governing the role requirements of his social order. His habits of mind and action had been formed in a culture in which the truth of this claim was generally taken for granted, so that those whose expectations were that J would do what his role required, and who held him accountable, shared his view that the established standards were the unquestionably best standards. So, if we condemn J, we are treating him as justifiably responsible, not only for his actions and for his knowledge of them, and not only also for his practical reasoning, but in addition for having failed to question the hitherto unquestioned. We are taking the view that responsible deliberation requires that on occasion one puts established standards in question, whatever verdict about them one may arrive at in the end.

Moral agents, that is to say, are on this view justifiably held responsible for the standards governing the reasoning from which their actions flow and they have to understand themselves as thus responsible. When J attempted to rebut the accusations advanced against him by saying that he had discharged all his responsibilities, he laid himself open to the questions of what reason he had for taking his socially assigned responsibilities to be his only responsibilities and of what reason he had for continuing to believe that the established standards governing his deliberations were the best standards. By having failed to ask, let alone to answer these questions, J's defence of his deliberate setting of limits to his knowledge also fails, or rather it fails, provided that we are justified in ascribing to J the full powers of moral agency. But is it possible that we are not so justified?

That human beings have by their specific nature a capacity for recognizing that they have good reason to acknowledge the authority of evaluative and normative standards that are independent of those embodied in the institutions of their own particular social and cultural order, and so share equally in a capacity to be able to transcend in thought the limitations of those established standards, has been a widely held doctrine. Disagreements about what these evaluative and normative standards prescribe and what awareness of their authority consists in have not precluded widespread agreement in ascribing to normal adult human beings as such a capacity that makes them responsible as individuals for not putting their established social and cultural order to the question, if and when they have occasion to do so. So it would seem that it can be justifiably asserted of J that as a normal human being he must have had the powers of moral agency and therefore had the responsibility for doing what he failed to do.

Yet questions arise. If we were to spell out further what it is to be a moral agent, it would be crucial to note that one cannot be a moral agent without understanding oneself as a moral agent at the level of one's everyday practice and that one cannot exercise the powers of a moral agent, unless one is able to understand oneself as justifiably held responsible in virtue of one's ability to exercise those powers. But there are good reasons for believing that how human beings are able to understand themselves depends in key part upon and is always in some ways limited by the nature of the social and cultural order they inhabit. The question therefore is: are there or might there be types of social structure that would prevent those who inhabited them from understanding themselves as moral agents? Or if this seems to envisage too extreme a state of affairs, are there or might there be types of social structure that seriously threaten the possibility of understanding oneself as a moral agent and so of acting as a moral agent?

3. What is it to Understand Oneself as a Moral Agent?

What then is it to understand oneself as a moral agent at the level of everyday practice? Three characteristics of such self-understanding are relevant. First, I have to understand myself as and to present myself to others as someone with an identity other than the identities of role and office that I assume in each of the roles that I occupy. I have to understand myself as someone who brings with her or himself to each role qualities of mind and character that belong to her or him *qua* individual and not *qua* role-player. It is a mistake to think of the relationship of individuals to roles as being the same as or closely similar to that of stage actors to the dramatic parts that they play. For the lives of individuals are constituted in large part by the various roles that they play, although they are generally able to reflect upon their role-playing in ways that are not dictated by those same roles. It is characteristically, even if not only, in *how* they play out their roles that individuals exhibit their individual character. What more there is to individuals than their role-playing also includes the continuities of each individual's history, as they move from role to role, from one sphere of social activity to another. My awareness of and understanding of myself as an individual is exhibited in and partly constituted by the various acknowledgments of that individuality by others and my ability to respond to those others as individuals and not just as role-players. This mutual acknowledgment of our individuality characterizes some of our social relationships rather than others and some of our social relationships more markedly than others. And central among such acknowledgments are those judgments in which we evaluate individuals as individuals, in respect of their virtues and the goodness of their lives. But initially such judgments, we should note, just as much as our judgments about individuals as role-players, are generally governed by socially established standards. We all begin unquestioningly with the unquestioned.

Secondly, moral agents have to understand themselves not just as individuals, but as practically rational individuals. If moral agents are to be able to put in question those socially established standards, both standards defining and governing their roles and standards to which they appeal in evaluating individuals, they are going to have to understand themselves as entitled to rationally justifiable confidence in the critical judgments about those standards at which they arrive. Confidence is necessary, because these are practical judgments that are to provide them with reasons that will issue in action. Rationally justifiable confidence is necessary, because the critical response of the moral agent has to be distinguished from, and to present itself to others as distinguished from, mindless deviance and revolt. So the moral agent has to be entitled to confidence in her or his own moral judgments, when they are of the form 'Even though it is almost universally agreed in this social order that in these circumstances someone in my role should act thus, I judge that I should act otherwise.' What entitles someone to confidence in such judgments?

We are always liable to error in making particular moral judgments, sometimes intellectual errors such as going beyond the evidence or relying upon some unsubstantiated generalization, sometimes moral errors such as being over-influenced by our liking and disliking of particular individuals or projecting on to a situation some unrecognized phantasy or exhibiting either insensitivity to or sentimentality about suffering. And our intellectual errors are often rooted in moral errors. We need therefore to have tested our capacity for moral deliberation and judgment in this and that type of situation by subjecting our arguments and judgments systematically to the critical scrutiny of reliable others, of co-workers, family, friends. Such others, of course, are not always reliable and some may influence us in ways that strengthen the propensity to error. So to have confidence in our deliberations and judgments we need social relationships of a certain kind, forms of social association in and through which our deliberations and practical judgments are subjected to extended and systematic critical questioning that will teach us how to make judgments in which both we and others may have confidence. But this is not all.

Moral agents also have to understand themselves as accountable, not only in their roles, but also as rational individuals. The responsibilities that are socially assigned to roles are defined in part by the types of accountability that attach to each of them. For each role there is a range of particular others, to whom, if they fail in their responsibilities, they owe an account that either excuses or admits to the offence and accepts the consequences. Without such accountability the notion of responsibility would be largely empty. For failure in responsibility would lack those consequences, the enforcement of which is an important aspect of the social recognition of roles. But, if the notion of responsibility is deprived of significant content, when responsibility is detached from accountability, what follows about the responsibility of moral agents *qua* moral agents? To whom are they to understand themselves as accountable? To at least two sets of individuals and groups: those with whom they have engaged together in critically informed deliberation and those whose hitherto unquestioning reliance on the established standards of the social order they challenge by their deliberation and their action. To the former they owe an account of why they take it that their reasons for action have been able to withstand the strongest criticisms so far directed against them. To the latter they owe an account of why their reasons for challenging the established standards are good reasons. In giving such accounts they are inviting those who have hitherto accepted the established standards also to engage with them in critical deliberative conversation. And in understanding themselves and those others as accountable, they understand themselves and those others as moral agents.

Accountability to particular others, participation in critical practical enquiry, and acknowledgment of the individuality both of others and of oneself are all then marks of the social relationships and mode of self-understanding that characterize the moral agent. Strip away those social relationships and that mode of self-understanding and what would be left would be a seriously diminished type of agency, one unable to transcend the limitations imposed by its own social and cultural order. Moral agency thus does seem to require a particular kind of social setting.

There must therefore be a place in any social order in which the exercise of the powers of moral agency is to be a real possibility for milieus in which reflective critical questioning of standards hitherto taken for granted is an activity that is at home. These too must be milieus of everyday practice in which the established standards are, when it is appropriate, put to the question at the point at which they dictate to everyday practice and not just in an abstract and general way. The necessary presupposition of such questioning is some more or less shared conception of what it is to be a good human being that focuses upon those qualities which individuals possess or fail to possess *qua* individuals, independently of their roles, and which are exemplified in part by their capacity or their lack of capacity to stand back from and reconsider their engagement with the established role-structures. And we may remind ourselves that just this capacity to stand back was what J lacked.

Those qualities are the virtues and in different times and places the catalogue of the virtues is not always the same and particular virtues are sometimes understood differently. But there is a core notion of the virtues as qualities of human beings as such and, central to it, there is an acknowledgment of two virtues, without which the other virtues cannot be possessed. To those virtues I give their traditional names of 'integrity' and 'constancy'. To have integrity is to refuse to be, to have educated oneself so that one is no longer able to be, one kind of person in one social context, while quite another in other contexts. It is to have set inflexible limits to one's adaptability to the roles that one may be called upon to play.

Constancy, like integrity, sets limits to flexibility of character. Where integrity requires of those who possess it that they exhibit the same moral character in different social contexts, constancy requires that those who possess it pursue the same goods through extended periods of time, not allowing the requirements of changing social contexts to distract them from their commitments or to redirect them. So individuals with these two virtues will learn not only how to occupy some determinate set of roles within their social order, but also how to think of their goods and of their character independently of the requirements of those roles. They will, that is to say, be inhabitants of not just one, but of two moral systems, that of the established social order with its assignment of roles and responsibilities and that developed within those milieus in which that assignment has been put to the question. The degree to which these two systems are at odds with each other varies in different social and cultural orders. Those whose social and cultural order is such that the two systems present requirements that it is difficult to render compatible will be forced either to think their way through a series of more or less painful choices or to find some strategy for evading these choices.

The thinking that is needed is practical thinking, thinking that may occasionally be driven to extend its resources by opening up theoretical questions, but even then always for the sake of practice. The milieus in which such thinking is at home are, as I have already said, those of everyday practice, of the everyday life of certain kinds of family and household, of certain kinds of workplace, of certain kinds of school and church, and of a variety of kinds of local community. And what their flourishing will always be apt to generate is tension, tension that may develop into conflict between the requirements of the established social and moral order and the attitudes of those educated in those social settings that make the exercise of the powers of moral agency possible. So to be a moral agent is to have the potentiality for living and acting in a state of tension or, if need be, conflict between two moral points of view. And this is never simply or mainly a tension or a conflict between points of view at the level of abstract and general theory. It is always primarily a tension or a conflict between socially embodied points of view, between modes of practice.

The history of moral philosophy has usually been written—except for those historians influenced by Augustine, Marx, or Nietzsche—in such a way as to disguise this fact. Why does this matter? It is because it is from these tensions and conflicts, when and in so far as they are present, that morality gets an important part of its content. There are of course social and cultural orders in which tension, let alone conflict, between such rival moral systems has not yet been generated to any significant degree. But, whenever it has been so generated, it defines an area in which at least some moral agents find themselves with particular responsibilities to discharge. Consider how this might be so with regard to truthfulness, considered as one essential constituent of the human good. Both Aquinas and Kant hold that it is wrong to tell a lie in any circumstance whatsoever. But one could refrain from lying throughout one's life without having done what is required of one in one's own particular circumstance, if one is to achieve the good of truthfulness. For truthfulness requires of us that, when it is of peculiar importance that rational agents should understand some particular aspect of their lives, so that they are neither misled nor deceived, it is a responsibility of those who are truthful to disclose what is relevant to such understanding. But what it is relevant to disclose is in key part determined by the limitations of the contemporary role-structure and the ways in which its assigning of responsibilities may obscure from view just that about which the virtue of truthfulness requires that we and others should be undeceived. Conflicts about whose responsibility it is to know about what are therefore among those that in particular circumstances, especially the circumstances of distinctively modern societies, provide content for the requirements of morality. 'Always ask about any social and cultural order what it needs its inhabitants not to know' has become an indispensable sociological maxim. 'Always ask about your own social and cultural order what it needs you and others not to know' has become an indispensable moral maxim.

What degrees and kinds of tension and conflict are engendered by the incompatibilities of established role requirements and the demands of the virtues vary of course from social order to social order. There are societies in which the potentiality for such conflict has not yet been realized, societies in which conflict has been effectively contained, societies in which conflict has disrupted and fragmented, sometimes creatively, sometimes destructively. So that often a key moral question is that of how best to find our way through conflict. Notice also that the dimensions of moral conflict are more than moral, at least if morality is narrowly conceived: they are moral-cum-political, moral-cum-economic, moral-cum-religious, indeed sometimes moral-cum-religious-cum-political-cum-economic; and remember too that the established norms and values with which we may be invited to enter into conflict will commonly be to some large degree our own norms and values, the norms and values by which we have hitherto been guided. So that initially at least that conflict will be within each of us.

Such conflict is not only a matter of incompatibility between two sets of practically embodied norms and values. It is also a matter of a certain resistance to critical questioning that claims about the limitations and errors of the standpoint of the established order are apt to evoke. And we may in some cases be misled about the nature and degree of such resistance, if we are naïve in our identification of the norms and values of the established order. For there are types of social order, including our own, in which those norms themselves not only legitimate but encourage questioning, criticism, and protest, so that the set of approved social roles includes such roles as those of the Indignant Protester and the Angry Young Person and activities of criticism, and protest are themselves governed by prescribed routines. We need then to draw a line between conflict that is internal to and in no way a threat to an established order and conflict that is more radical, conflict that genuinely raises the question of whether established roles and routines can or cannot be justified in the light of the best account we have of the human good. It is conflict of this latter kind that social orders may need to contain or suppress, if they are to continue functioning as they have done.

Where then has the argument taken us? We began with the case of J, who asserted that he could not be justifiably held responsible for his part in making the massacre of Jews possible, because he did not know what or whom his trains were carrying and because it was not his responsibility to know this, given his social role and the standards defining the responsibilities of anyone occupying that role. To this it was replied that moral agents are responsible for critical scrutiny of the standards governing their practical reasoning about their responsibilities, including their responsibilities for knowledge of their actions. Therefore, if J, a psychologically normal human being, was capable of exercising the powers of moral agency, J was responsible for his lack of knowledge and so indirectly for his participation in massacring Jews. What then might have prevented J, even though a psychologically normal individual, from exercising the powers of moral agency?

How we answered this question depended upon an identification of three types of precondition for the exercise of the powers of moral agency. First, the powers of moral agency can only be exercised by those who understand themselves as moral agents, and, that is to say, by those who understand their moral identity as to some degree distinct from and independent of their social roles. To understand oneself thus is to understand that one's goodness as a human being, the answer that by one's whole way of life one gives to the question 'How is it best for a human being in my circumstances to live?', is not to be equated with one's goodness at being and doing what this or that role requires.

Secondly, the powers of moral agency can only be exercised by those who are able to justify rational confidence in their judgments about the goodness and badness of human beings and this ability requires participation in social relationships and in types of activity in which one's reflective judgments emerge from systematic dialogue with others and are subject to critical scrutiny by others. Without milieus within which such relationships and activities are effectively sustained, the possibility of the exercise of the powers of moral agency will be undermined. Those who participate in the relationships and activities of such milieus will always find themselves in potential conflict with, and often in actual conflict with, the requirements of established role-structures and therefore with those who uphold those requirements. And it is in part by defining their relationship to those conflicts that they give content to what the virtues require of them in this or that particular situation.

Moreover—and thirdly—it is only in and through such milieus that moral agents become able to understand themselves as accountable to others in respect of the human virtues and not just in respect of their role-performances. So all three preconditions can be satisfied only within social orders in which there exist milieus, spheres of activity, which sustain the relevant kind of understanding of the self, the relevant kind of critical discourse and reflection, and the relevant kind of accountability. The question therefore is: are there types of social structure that preclude the existence of such milieus, so that the very possibility of the exercise of the powers of moral agency might be threatened? The type of structure that I shall use as an example is very different in some respects from that inhabited by J. But it is worth beginning with a more extreme case.

4. The Structures of Compartmentalization

In the nineteen seventies I was a minor participant in a study of the moral dimensions of decision-making in the American electric power industry (for the principal findings see *Values in the Electric Power Industry*, ed. Kenneth Sayre, University of Notre Dame Press, 1977). One incidental discovery in the course of that study was that power company executives tended to a significant degree to answer what were substantially the same questions somewhat differently, depending on whether they took themselves to be responding *qua* power company executive or *qua* parent and head of household or *qua* concerned citizen. That is to say, their attitudes varied with their social roles and they seemed quite unaware of this. I take this to be a mild example of a peculiarly modern phenomenon that I will call compartmentalization.

Compartmentalization goes beyond that differentiation of roles and institutional structures that characterizes every social order and it does so by the extent to which each distinct sphere of social activity comes to have its own role-structure governed by its own specific norms in relative independence of other such spheres. Within each sphere those norms dictate which kinds of consideration are to be treated as relevant to decision-making and which are to be excluded. So in the power company case executives were unable even to entertain, as a serious policy alternative, reduction in the overall levels of power consumption, so long as they thought and spoke from within their sphere of activity as power company executives, but they did not suffer from the same inability when thinking and speaking as consumers or concerned citizens.

This relative autonomy of each demarcated sphere of activity is reinforced by the degree to which in contemporary advanced societies individuals encountered in each particular sphere are often not the same as those whom one meets elsewhere. When one encounters each individual only within some particular sphere, in some role that is a counterpart to one's own role in that particular sphere, then one's responses are increasingly only to the-individual-in-this-or-that-role rather than to the individual who happens to be occupying this role at this time. So individuals as they move between spheres of activity, exchanging one role for another and one set of standards for their practical reasoning for another, become to some important extent dissolved into their various roles, playing one part in the life of the family, quite another in the workplace, yet a third as a member of a sports club and a fourth as a military reservist. Within each sphere such individuals conform to the requirements imposed on their role within that sphere and there is no milieu available to them in which they are able, together with others, to step back from those roles and those requirements and to scrutinize themselves and the structure of their society from some external standpoint with any practical effect.

Consider the different forms that the ethics of deception may take in different spheres, the different answers given to such questions as 'Who is justified in deceiving whom and about what?' and 'Who has the authority to object to deception?' A first example is that of a business corporation whose chief executive officer decides to exaggerate the progress made by the corporation's scientists on a research project, with the aims both of not losing customers to rivals and of bolstering share prices. Here the scientists have no right to lie to or otherwise deceive the CEO—not to do so is a condition of their continuing employment—and they likewise have no right to speak out. The only grounds on which objection to such deception can be based, if it is to be heard, is that in the longer run deception will fail to maximize corporate profits. (A former Chairman of the Securities Exchange Commission explained his decision to endow a Chair in Business Ethics at Harvard by claiming that in the long run ethics pays.)

Contrast with this the situation of those same scientists when publishing their data in professional journals. In this context no end external to scientific enquiry is allowed to justify deception. The falsification of data warrants their exposure by other scientists and their consequent expulsion from the scientific community. So the individual who recurrently moves between the spheres of corporate activity and of independent scientific enquiry exchanges each time that he or she does so one ethics of deception for another, often without any consciousness of so doing.

That same individual will of course also move into yet other contexts with their own ethics of deception, for example the kind of social occasion in which relative strangers meet, drink in hand, anxious to make a favourable impression on prestigious people and equally anxious to avoid garrulous and insistent bores. Here deception, including lying, is generally a sanctioned aspect of the work of self-presentation—without it I might not be able to make myself sufficiently interesting—and I may defend myself from aggressive conversational intrusions by further lies. Each of these three ethics of deception does of course need further elaboration, but that elaboration would only strengthen the grounds for concluding that the norms of deception are specific to social context and that to move from one role in one sphere of activity to another in another is to move from one context-based moral standpoint to another.

We encounter a similar range of differences in contemporary attitudes to death. Contrast the attitudes to death exhibited within the sphere of family life by those mourning the death of a child in an automobile accident, with that of the executives of the corporation that manufactured the automobile, and with that of the lawyers who urge the family to sue the driver of the automobile. For family members the death is a unique loss for which nothing can compensate, for the corporate executives it contributes to an annual death rate that is an acceptable trade-off for the benefits of automobile sales to their industry and to society, and for the lawyers it has a precise financial value calculable on the basis of recent jury awards. And it is possible to adopt the attitudes dictated by any of these three perspectives only by temporarily excluding those of the other two. So those who move from extending their condolences at the grave-side to a meeting of automobile company executives reevaluating their production goals to the offices of a law firm will find the same death evaluated in ways that are not only different, but to some degree incompatible (I have treated this a little more fully in 'Some Enlightenment projects reconsidered' in *Questioning Ethics: Contemporary Debates in Philosophy*, R. Kearney and M. Dooley (eds), London: Routledge, 1998, pp. 255–6) and this often enough without any awareness of the incompatibility. Here again each sphere of activity has its own norms and values. But compartmentalization involves more than this in two respects: the degree to which each sphere of activity is insulated from others, so that considerations that would carry weight in some other sphere are deprived of it in this; and the absence of any accessible sphere of activity in which practically effective reasoning might be used to evaluate the norms and values of each particular sphere from some external point of view.

Insulation is provided by the prescribed standard responses to the introduction into the conversations within some particular sphere of considerations that are by its norms at best irrelevant, at worst distracting. So, if in a policy meeting of the Midwestern power executives one of them had proposed attempting to bring about an overall reduction in power consumption, or if at a social gathering someone were to insist that the standards of truthfulness required in scientific reports should also apply to party gossip, their remarks might be treated as a joke or ignored, but, if such a speaker persisted, they would find themselves deprived at least temporarily of their status in that sphere of activity, treated, that is, as a source of background noise rather than a participant. And the effects of insulation are reinforced by the absence from everyday life of milieus in the home, the workplace, and elsewhere in which such agents might engage in extended critical reflection with others about, for example, what conflicts the virtue of truthfulness requires us to engage in in that time and place and just how its requirements are at odds with the established ethics of deception in each sphere of activity or about what the significance of death is. Such milieus would provide agents with what they otherwise lack, an understanding of themselves as having a substantive identity independent of their roles and as having responsibilities that do not derive from those roles, so overcoming divisions within the self imposed by compartmentalization and so setting the scene for types of conflict that compartmentalization effectively suppresses.

This divided self has to be characterized negatively, by what it lacks. It is not only without any standpoint from which it can pass critical judgment on the standards governing its various roles, but it must also lack those virtues of integrity and constancy that are prerequisites for exercising the powers of moral agency. It cannot have integrity, just because its allegiance to this or that set of standards is always temporary and context-bound. And it cannot have the constancy that is expressed in an unwavering directedness, since it recurrently changes direction, as it moves from sphere to sphere. Indeed its conception of a virtue will generally be one of excellence in role performance rather than of excellence as a human being and hence what is judged excellent in one role-governed context may be very different from and even sometimes incompatible with what is judged excellent in others. (This context-bound use of the concept of a virtue parodies older conceptions and older uses and in so doing may remind us of J whose uses of moral concepts were also parodies. But for the moment let us put this resemblance to J to one side.) Lacking these, and lacking also an awareness that it lacks these, there is nothing about the self thus divided that is liable to generate conflict with what are taken to be the requirements of morality with the established order. So in so far as that self recognizes and aspires to conform to what it takes to be moral requirements, within each particular sphere of activity, it will be a morality from which the elements of potential and actual conflict are missing, a diminished morality that matches its diminished powers of agency.

It must therefore seem that so far as individuals approach the condition of this divided self, they can no longer be justifiably held responsible for their actions in anything like the ways in which moral agents are held responsible. Here, it seems, there is indeed a type of social structure that warrants for those who inhabit it a plea of gravely diminished responsibility. And we may be tempted therefore to turn immediately to the question of whether the earlier twentieth-century society that J inhabited sufficiently resembled later forms of compartmentalized social and cultural order for us to enter a similar plea on J's behalf. But this would be a mistake. For we need first to consider some further dimensions of this divided self.

It is, I shall argue, a self that is to a significant degree responsible for its own divisions. It is indeed to be characterized negatively in terms of lacks or absences, but these lacks or absences are, so I will suggest, the expression of refusals, active refusals by that self. A number of aspects of its activity are relevant. First, it can never be dissolved nor dissolve itself *entirely* into the distinctive roles that it plays in each compartmentalized sphere of activity. It exhibits for one thing a quality that both it and some others understand as a virtue of the individual as such and not just of the individual-in-this-or-that-role, a virtue that is a newcomer to the catalogue of the virtues: adaptability, flexibility, knowing chameleon-like how to take on the colour of this or that social background. And it exhibits this virtue in managing its transitions from one role to another, so that it appears, so far as possible, to be dissolved into its roles. But this appearance is, when well managed, a dramatic feat, an expression of the actor as well as of the roles enacted.

Secondly, the individual *qua* individual appears not only in managing the transitions from one role to another, but also, as I suggested earlier, in the role-playing itself. There are some roles that may seem purely mechanical, since the individual who plays the role can always be replaced by a machine: where there was once a ticket-seller, there is now a ticket-machine. But the ticket-seller always faced choices that machines never confront: *how* to play her or his role, cheerfully or sullenly, carelessly or conscientiously, efficiently or inefficiently. And for all roles, the way in which the role is enacted presupposes not only an answer to a question posed to and by the role-player: 'How is it best for me to play this role?', but also to such further questions as: 'By what standards am I to judge what is best?' and 'Should I continue to play this role in this way?' It is the inescapability on occasion of such questions that suggests that practical reasoning that is adequate for doing what a particular role requires will itself generate reasons for acting beyond those requirements and even sometimes against those requirements. To resist asking such questions, to insist upon terminating one's practical reasoning whenever it directs one beyond one's role requires a peculiar kind of self-discipline. To be able to restrict one's practical reasoning to what will enable one to discharge the responsibilities of one's socially approved roles is to have imposed on one's thinking a set of artificial restrictions. It is to have arbitrarily closed one's mind to certain possibilities of action. And, although others may provide one with motives for effecting such a closure, it is only with one's own active cooperation that the habits of mind can be developed which make such closure possible.

What is true of practical reasoning generally holds with special force of those periods during which, but for avoidance strategies, one might find that one had committed oneself to incompatible judgments. The divided self of a compartmentalized social order, in order not to have to confront incompatible attitudes to, say, truthfulness or death, has to have developed habits of mind that enable it not to attend to what it would have to recognize as its own incoherences, if it were to understand itself apart from its involvements in each of its particular roles in each distinct sphere. And to learn how to focus one's attention in this way once again requires one's active cooperation.

I conclude that what I earlier characterized as lacks or absences of the divided selves of a compartmentalized social order are better described as active refusals and denials. The divided self is complicit with others in bringing about its own divided states and so can be justly regarded as their co-author. It and those others can justifiably be called to account for what they have jointly made of themselves. They may indeed inhabit a type of social and cultural order whose structures to some large degree inhibit the exercise of the powers of moral agency. But they share in responsibility for having made themselves into the kind of diminished agent that they are. Their responsibility is that of co-conspirators, engaged together in a conspiracy that functions so that they can lead blamelessly compliant lives, able plausibly to plead lack of knowledge of as well as lack of control over outcomes for which they might otherwise be held jointly responsible. Their lack of knowledge and their lack of control are often enough real, an inescapable outcome of the structuring of roles and responsibilities in a compartmentalized social order. But they are, so I have argued, responsible and accountable for making it the case that they do not know and that they lack certain powers. They are not passive victims. To have understood this enables us to return to the case of J.

5. Once More the Case of J

I take the social structures of compartmentalization, although peculiar to the late twentieth century, to be more generally instructive, just because they provide us with a case at the extremes, a case in which, after compartmentalization has progressed beyond a certain point, many agents exhibit no awareness of responsibilities beyond those assigned to them by their roles in each particular sphere of activity, while in their practical reasoning they admit as premises only those considerations sanctioned in each context by the norms defining and governing those roles. Their lives express the social and cultural order that they inhabit in such a way that they have become unable to recognize, let alone to transcend its limitations. They do not have the resources that would enable them to move to an independent standpoint.

Both their resemblances to and their differences from J and those like him are worth remarking. Both J and those who inhabit a compartmentalized society accept unquestioningly structures that give definition to their lives by prescribing a range of roles that they are to occupy and a range of responsibilities attached to each. And it is not only what they are to do in each type of social context that is prescribed. What kind of practical reasoning it is for each of them to undertake, *qua* enactor of this or that role, what it is the responsibility of each to know, and what is not a matter for their concern or knowledge are also prescribed. And in so far as both are deprived of participation in milieus in which in the company of others they might have elaborated a standpoint external to their role-structured activities, they have become unable to pass judgment on the limitations of their judgments. These are the resemblances, but there are also striking differences.

For J and those like him exhibited an awareness of their situation that is absent from those who inhabit a compartmentalized society. J judged that this way of life was the best way of life for him and for others. It is true that he did not and perhaps could not open up this judgment to any extended reflective scrutiny. But he made it and was capable of making it proudly and defiantly. Judgments about compartmentalization and its effects upon the lives of those subject to it are necessarily third-person judgments delivered from some standpoint that has escaped those effects. J was able to deliver judgment on the organization of his social life in the first person. What kind of difference does this signify?

At least this: that, if those who inhabit a compartmentalized social order can be held responsible as co-authors of their social and moral situation, then the case for imputing such responsibility to J and those like him must be even stronger. For J actively chose not to move beyond the boundaries imposed by established role-definitions. He had made himself into what the roles said that he was. By so doing he had assented to doing, reasoning, and knowing only as the standards governing his roles prescribed. And in so assenting he had excluded the possibility of moral conflict. He did not allow himself to pass judgment on the judgments that he made in accordance with those established standards and so rendered himself unable to raise the question of what it was about which he was required to know and required to be truthful. For truthfulness as a virtue was itself defined for J by the context-bound standards governing his role-performances, so that much that truthfulness requires had become invisible.

I argued earlier that 'Always ask about your social and cultural order what it needs you and others not to know' has become in the modern world an indispensable moral maxim. J, like those subject to the limitations of a compartmentalized social order, had cooperated in making it impossible to acknowledge the authority of this maxim. But J's refusal of such knowledge made him too responsible, in cooperation with others, for not knowing what he did not know. So J's later defence of his earlier actions failed.

It has been my assumption that when J defended himself by denying that he had had the relevant knowledge, he was sincere. Some commentators have insisted that J and those like him must have had that knowledge and that therefore they were guilty, thus implying that if they had not had that knowledge, then they would have been innocent. I have contended by contrast that, even if J and those like him did not have that knowledge, they remained guilty and that their guilt was not merely individual guilt, but, in a sense that I hope has been made clear, the guilt of a whole social and cultural order.

Introduction to Jürgen Habermas' Lecture

Ted Honderich

What is called continental philosophy, which is not all of the philosophy in continental Europe, is often distinguished from philosophy in the English language, often with at least the implication that one is at least superior. Maybe, despite diversity, it is safe to say that against what is called our analytic philosophy, continental philosophy is more concerned with human experience in the sense of lived lives, often more akin to reflective literature, perhaps more informed by both the history of philosophy and several other disciplines, and less affected by physical and other sciences.

The attention paid to it in American and English universities is one fact that is relevant to the inclusion of Jürgen Habermas in the Royal Institute of Philosophy Annual Lectures. A larger justification is his achievement, the philosophy written. In terms of his long university life, he is best known for his leading role in an institute at Frankfurt University, an institute in a way Marxist in the past, one that continues to bring together philosophy with sociology, with what is probably better named social theory. In terms of his public life, Habermas is known for his liberal interventions in many German social and political controversies. He has been Germany's most eminent public intellectual.

The lecture is in part an explanation of how claims to cultural rights have come about, this being their emergence from the history of religious tolerance. But it is in the main an assertion of and argument for these cultural rights, an argument depending on an analysis of their nature. These aims of the lecture are achieved in four stages, discursively and with reprises.

(1) A distinction having been made between toleration and tolerance, behaviour and legality, consideration is given to Goethe's superiority to toleration on the ground that it involves a line drawn, not only an acceptance of behaviour on one side of the line but also a rejection of behaviour on the other side. A practice of tolerance includes intolerance. One part of Habermas' response is that

what tolerance puts on the prohibited side must be defensible in that it is owed to reciprocity in the drawing of the line, not authoritarianism or worse but rather democracy and liberal co-existence.

(2) Another part of the response to Goethe is the insistence that democracy must defend itself by drawing a line, perhaps including the outlawing of certain political parties. It must also defend against terrorism, now both politically ideological and fundamentalist in religion. But democracy must also pass a litmus test in accepting civil disobedience, and it must remember that 'enemies of the state' may be radical defenders of democracy.

(3) In reflection on kinds of reasons in this whole area, there is consideration for example of the need not merely not to tolerate racism but to condemn it. There is the necessity of demanding of racists that they give up their racism, give up their commitment to what is called an ethos and their denial of the liberal ethos.

(4) Examples are given in a footnote of many claims presumably of cultural rights, claims made and disputed, one concerning Muslim calls to prayer by loudspeaker where churches are allowed to ring their bells. There is further reflection on the necessary neutrality of the state. This and what has gone before issue and culminate in an analysis or theory of the cultural rights we have been considering. They have to do at bottom with the maintaining and protecting of personal identity, and also collective identity. They are to be distinguished from the subject of distributive justice as it can be conceived. This value of identity itself is fundamental to the defence of cultural rights. It is to me a new thought, of great interest.

Evidently philosophy can come together with other things. The resulting coalitions, no doubt, may make for gains, if gains at a price. Continental philosophy implicitly makes the case for particular wider concentration. The widening in the case of Habermas does indeed include a kind of social and political theory, to very good effect.

16

Religious Tolerance—The Pacemaker for Cultural Rights

Jürgen Habermas

(1) It was not until the 16th century that the German language borrowed the word 'Toleranz'—or tolerance—from the Latin and French, which is why in the context of the Reformation the concept immediately assumed the narrow meaning of toleration of other religious confessions.[1] In the course of the 16th and 17th centuries, religious toleration becomes a legal concept. Governments issued toleration edicts that compelled state officials and the population to be tolerant in their behaviour toward religious minorities, such as Lutherans, Huguenots, and Papists.[2] Legal acts of toleration by state authorities led to the expectation that people (as a rule the majority of the population[3]) behave tolerantly toward members of religious communities that had until then been oppressed or persecuted.

With greater precision than in German, in English the word 'tolerance' as a form of behaviour is distinguished from 'toleration', the legal act with which a government grants more or less unrestricted permission to practise one's own particular religion. In German, the predicate 'tolerant' refers to both, to a legal order that guarantees toleration and to the political virtue of tolerant behaviour. Montesquieu emphasizes the constitutive link between toleration and tolerance:

As soon as the laws of a land have come to terms with permitting several religions, they must oblige these to show tolerance also to one another.[4]

[1] See the *Allgemeine Handwörterbuch der philosophischen Wissenschaften nebst ihrer Literatur und Geschichte*, ed. Wilhelm Traugott Krug, 2nd edition (1832): 'Toleranz (von tolerare, dulden, ertragen) ist Duldsamkeit... Doch wird jenes Wort meist im engeren Sinne von religiöser Duldsamkeit gebraucht, wie das entgegengesetzte Intoleranz von der religiösen Unduldsamkeit.'

[2] In 1598, Henri IV of France issued the *Edict of Nantes*, see also the *Act Concerning Religion* passed by the Government of Maryland in 1649, the *Toleration Act* issued by the King of England in 1689 or—as one of the last instances in this chain of sovereign 'authorizations'—the 'Patent of Toleration' proclaimed by Joseph II in 1781.

[3] The case was different in Maryland, where a Catholic minority ruled over a Protestant majority.

[4] Quoted from C. Herdtle and Th. Leeb (eds), *Toleranz, Texte zur Theorie und politischen Praxis*, (Stuttgart, 1987), 49.

Through to the French Revolution the concept not only retains its link to religious addressees, but also the authoritarian connotation of *mere* toleration. That said, ever since the days of Spinoza and Locke the philosophical justifications given for religious tolerance point the absolutist state in a direction away from *unilaterally* declared religious toleration, the limits of which are defined by the authorities, and towards a conception of tolerance based on the *mutual* recognition of everybody's religious freedom. Rainer Forst contrasts the 'concept of permission' issued by the authorities who grant religious freedoms to the 'concept of respect' that concurs with our understanding of religious freedom as a civil right.[5]

Pierre Bayle already dreamed up various examples in order to force his intolerant opponents to adopt also the perspective of the other persons and to apply their own principles to their opponents, too: 'If it should thus suddenly cross the Mufti's mind to send some missionaries to the Christians, just as the Pope sends such to India, and someone were to surprise these Turkish missionaries in the process of forcing their way into our houses to fulfill their duties converting us, then I do not believe we would have the authority to punish them. For if they were to give the same answers as the Christian missionaries in Japan, namely that they had arrived to zealously famil-iarize those with the true religion who were not yet acquainted with it, and to care for the salvation of their fellow men—now if we were to string up these Turks, would it not then actually be ridiculous to find it bad if the Japanese did the same thing?'[6] Bayle, who in this respect was the forerunner of Kant, practises mutual perspective-taking. He insists on the *universalization of* those 'ideas' in the light of which we judge 'the nature of human action'.[7]

On this basis of a *reciprocal* recognition of the rules of tolerant behaviour we can find a solution to the paradox which prompted Goethe to reject toleration as insult-ing and patronizing benevolence. The ostensible paradox is that each act of toleration must circumscribe the range of behaviour everybody must accept, thereby drawing a line for what can*not* be tolerated. There can be no inclusion without exclusion. And as long as this line is drawn in an authoritarian manner, i.e. unilaterally, the stigma of arbitrary exclusion remains inscribed in toleration. Only with a *universally convinc-ing* delineation of the borderline, and this requires that all those involved *recipro-cally* take the perspectives of the others, can toleration blunt the thorn of intolerance. Everyone who could be affected by the future practice must first voluntarily agree on those conditions under which they wish to exercise mutual toleration.

The usual conditions for liberal co-existence between different religious commu-nities stand this test of reciprocity. They refer in the first place to prohibiting the use of political power for missionary purposes, and to the freedom of association that also prevents religious authorities being able to influence their members' conscience compulsorily. Only if they find intersubjective recognition across confessional

---

[5] See footnote 7.   [6] P. Bayle, quoted from Herdtle & Leeb (1987), 42.
[7] P. Bayle, quoted from Herdtle & Leeb (1987), 38.

boundaries can such specifying norms provide justifications that *out-trump* those personally maintained reasons for rejecting alien religious convictions and practices. Even if there is no historical substantiation for Jellinek's suggestion that all human rights are rooted in religious freedom, there is certainly a conceptual link between the universalistic justification for religious tolerance, on the one hand, and democracy as the basis for legitimation for a secular state, on the other.

The purported paradox dissolves if we conceive of religious freedom—covering both the right to free expression of one's own religion and the corresponding negative freedom to remain undisturbed by the others' practising their respective religions— as part of a democratic constitution. Religious tolerance can be practised in a tolerant manner precisely under those conditions which the citizens of a democratic community mutually accord one another. From the viewpoint of the democratic lawmaker who makes the addressees of such a law likewise the authors thereof, the legal act of mutual toleration melds with the virtuous self-obligation to behave tolerantly.

(2) However, the paradox does not seem to be fully resolved by the reciprocal generalization of religious freedom, since it appears to reemerge, in secular terms, at the very core of the constitutional state. A democratic order that guarantees tolerance also in terms of political freedoms, such as free speech, must take preventive protection against the enemies of that very core of the constitution. At latest since the 'legal' transition from the Weimar Republic to the Nazi régime we in Germany have become aware of the necessity of self-assertion—but equally of that strange dialectic of the self-assertion of a 'militant' democracy that is 'prepared to defend itself'.[8] Courts can on a case-by-case basis pass judgment on the limits of religious freedom, basing their conclusions on the law. However, if the constitution faces the opposition of enemies who make use of their political freedom in order to abolish the constitution that grants it, then the question arises as to the limits of political freedom in a self-referential form. How tolerantly may a democracy treat the enemies of democracy?

If the democratic state does not wish to give itself up, then it must resort to intolerance toward the enemy of the constitution, either bringing to bear the means afforded by political criminal law or by decreeing the prohibition of particular political parties (Article 21.2 of the German Constitution) and the forfeiture of basic rights (Article 18 and Article 9.2 of the same). The 'enemy of the state', a concept originally with religious connotations, resurfaces in the guise of the enemy of the constitution: be it in the secularized figure of the political ideologist who combats the liberal state, or in the religious shape of the fundamentalist who violently attacks the modern way of life *per se*. Today's terrorists seem to embody a combination of both. Yet it is precisely the agencies of the constitutional state itself who define what or who shall be classified as an enemy of the constitution. A constitutional state must perform a twofold act

---

[8] K. Loewenstein, 'Militant Democracy and Fundamental Rights', *American Political Science Review* (31), 1937; see also his *Verfassungslehre*, 3rd edition (1975), 348ff.

here: it must repel the animosity of existential enemies while avoiding any betrayal of its own principles—in other words, it is exposed in this situation to the constantly lurking danger of itself being guilty of retrogressively resorting to an authoritarian practice of *unilaterally* deciding the limits of tolerance. Those who are suspicious of being 'enemies of the state' might well turn out to be radical defenders of democracy. This is the problem: whereas the task of a seemingly paradoxical self-limitation of religious tolerance can be ceded to democracy, the latter must process the conundrum of constitutional tolerance through the medium of its own laws.

A self-defensive democracy can sidestep the danger of paternalism only by allowing the self-referentiality of the self-establishing democratic process to be brought to bear on controversial interpretations of constitutional principles. In this regard, it is something like a litmus test, how a constitutional state treats the issue of civil disobedience. Needless to say, the constitution itself decides what the procedure should be in the case of conflicts over the correct interpretation of the constitution. With a legal recognition of 'civil disobedience' (which does not mean it does not punish such acts), the tolerant spirit of a liberal constitution extends even beyond the ensemble of those existing institutions and practices in which its normative contents have become actually embodied so far. A democratic constitution that is understood as the project of realizing equal civil rights tolerates the resistance shown by dissidents who, even after all the legal channels have been exhausted, still insist on combating decisions that came about legitimately. Under the proviso, of course, that the 'disobedient' citizens plausibly justify their resistance by citing constitutional principles and express it by nonviolent, i.e. symbolic, means.[9] These two conditions again specify the limits of political tolerance in a constitutional democracy that defends itself against its enemies by non-paternalist means—and they are limits that are acceptable for its democratically minded opponents, too.

By recognizing civil disobedience, the democratic state copes with the paradox of tolerance that reoccurs at the level of constitutional law in a tolerant manner. It draws a line between a tolerant and a self-destructive handling of ambivalent dissidents in such a way as to ensure that these persons (who could in the final analysis transpire to be enemies of the constitution) nevertheless have the opportunity contrary to their image to prove themselves to actually be the true patriotic champions of a constitution that is dynamically understood as an ongoing *project*—the project to exhaust and implement basic rights in changing historical contexts.

(3) Now, pluralism and the struggle for religious tolerance were not only driving forces behind the emergence of the democratic state, but continue to stimulate its further evolution up to now. Before addressing religious tolerance as the pacemaker for multiculturalism, in the correct sense of the term, allow me to analyse the concept of tolerance

---

[9] On the problematic issue of civil disobedience see my two essays in: J. Habermas, *Die Neue Unübersichtlichkeit* (Frankfurt/Main, 1985), 79–117.

a bit further (a) and to explain the specific burden imposed on citizens by the expectation to behave tolerantly (b). For the purpose of conceptual analysis it is useful to distinguish the two kinds of reasons that are involved: reasons to reject the convictions of others and reasons to accept nevertheless common membership of essentially disagreeing people within the same political community. From the latter reasons—political reasons for civic inclusion—the third kind of reasons, I have already mentioned, can be derived—reasons for the limits of tolerance and the repression of intolerant behaviour. These legal reasons then open the door to the justification of cultural rights.

(a) The religious context of discovering tolerance brings first to mind the key component of a 'rejection based on existentially relevant conviction'. That rejection is a condition necessary for all kinds of tolerant behaviour. We can only exercise tolerance towards other people's beliefs if we reject them for subjectively *good* reasons. We do not need to be tolerant if we are indifferent to other opinions and attitudes anyway or even appreciate the value of such 'otherness'. The expectation of tolerance assumes that we can endure a form of ongoing non-concurrence at the level of social interaction, while we accept the persistence of mutually exclusive validity claims at the cognitive level of existentially relevant beliefs. We are expected to neutralize the practical impact of a cognitive dissonance that nevertheless calls for further attempts to resolve it within its own domain. In other words, we must be able to socially accept mutual cognitive dissonances that will remain unresolved for the time being. Yet such a cognitive difference must prove to be 'reasonable' if tolerance is to be a meaningful response here. Tolerance can only come to bear if there are legitimate justifications for the rejection of competing validity claims: 'If someone rejects people whose skin is black we should not call on him to be "tolerant toward people who look different"... For then we would accept his prejudice as an ethical judgment similar to the rejection of a different religion. A racist should not be tolerant, he should quite simply overcome his racism.'[10] In this and similar cases, we consider a critique of the *prejudices* and the struggle against *discrimination* to be the appropriate response—and not 'more tolerance'.

The issue of tolerance only arises after those prejudices have been eliminated that led to discrimination in the first place. But what gives us the right to call those descriptions 'prejudices' that a religious fundamentalist, a racist, the sexual chauvinist, the radical nationalist, or the xenophobic ethnocentric have of their respective 'other'? This points to the second kind of reasons. We allow ourselves those stigmatizing expressions in light of the egalitarian and universalistic standards of democratic citizenship, something that calls for the equal treatment of the 'other' and mutual recognition of all as 'full' members of the political community. The norm of complete inclusion of all citizens as members with equal rights must be accepted before all of us, members of a democratic community, can mutually expect one another to be

---

[10] R. Forst, 'Der schmale Grat zwischen Ablehnung und Akzeptanz', *Frankfurter Rundschau* (December 28, 2001).

tolerant. It is the standard of non-discrimination that first provides this expectation with moral and legal reasons that can *out-trump* the epistemic reasons for the persisting rejection of those convictions and attitudes we merely tolerate. On the base of that normative agreement, the potential for conflict in the cognitive dimension of ongoing contradictions between competing worldviews can be defused in the social dimension of shared citizenship. Thus, tolerance only begins where discrimination ends.

(b) Keeping in mind both kinds of reasons, reasons for rejection at the cognitive level, and for acceptance on the social level, we can better answer the question of which sort of burden the tolerant person is expected to carry. What exactly must this person 'endure'? As we have seen, it is not the contradiction between premises and perspectives of different worldviews that has to be 'accepted' as such: there is no contradiction in one's own head. An unresolved contradiction remains only in the interpersonal dimension of the encounter of different persons who are aware that they hold contradictory beliefs. The crux is rather the neutralization or containment of specific practical consequences of unresolved contradictions. To tolerate that pragmatic contradiction means a twofold burden: she who is tolerant may only realize the ethos inscribed in her own worldview within the limits of what everyone is accorded. The way of life prescribed by a particular religion or worldview may be realized only under conditions of equal rights for everybody. And, within these limits she must also respect the ethos of the others.

This burden is of a cognitive kind to the extent that those beliefs in which each person's ethos is rooted must be brought into harmony with the liberal norms of state and society. What this requires can be seen from the accommodation of religion in modern Europe. Every religion is originally a '*worldview*' or, as John Rawls would say, a 'comprehensive doctrine'—also in the sense that it lays claim to the authority to structure a form of life in its entirety. A religion has to relinquish this claim to an encompassing definition of life as soon as the life of the religious community is differentiated from the life of the larger society. A hitherto prevailing religion forfeits its political impact on society at large if the political regime can no longer obey just one universal ethos. Emancipated minority religions face a similar challenge. By having to deal with the fact of pluralism, religious doctrines are forced to reflect on their own relations to the environments of the liberal state and a secularized society. This results, among other things, in the renunciation of violence and the acceptance of the voluntary character of religious association. Violence may not be used to advance religious beliefs, both inside and outside the community.[11] However, the major religions must appropriate the normative foundations of the liberal state under conditions of *their own premises* even if (as in the European case of the Judaeo-Christian legacy) both evolved from the same historical context.

John Rawls has chosen the image of a module in order to describe the 'embedding' of the political morality of equal respect for everybody in different religious worldviews. The normative frame of the liberal state is a module that, because it

---

[11] J. Rawls, *Political Liberalism* (New York: Columbia U.P., 1993), 58ff.

is constructed by means of neutral or secular reasons, fits into different orthodox chains of justifications.[12] Compared with the idea of a rational religion that absorbs the moral substance shared by all religious doctrines, that image of a module has the advantage of not denying that those mutually exclusive belief-systems raise absolute claims to truth. It therefore does not need to downplay the radical thrust of a cognitively challenging tolerance. Depending on the context of the doctrine, a respectively different dogmatic solution will be found to the problem of finding justifications for human rights from within. In functional terms, religious tolerance should absorb the social destructiveness of irreconcilably persistent dissent. The latter may not tear the social bond that ties believers to those who believe in other faiths or are unbelievers. However, the functional solution requires the solving of a cognitive problem.

If conflicts of loyalty are not to simmer, the necessary role differentiation between members of one's own religious community and co-citizens of the larger society needs to be justified convincingly from one's internal viewpoint. Religious membership is in tune with its secular counterpart only if (from the internal point of view of each) the corresponding norms and values are not only different *from each other*, but if the one set of norms can consistently be derived *from the other*. If differentiation of both memberships is to go beyond a mere *modus vivendi*, then the modernization of religious consciousness must not be limited to some cognitively undiscerning attempt to ensure that the religious ethos conforms to externally *imposed* laws of the secular society. It calls instead for developing the normative principles of the secular order from within the view of a respective religious tradition and community. In many cases this makes it necessary to revise attitudes and prescriptions that (as with the dogmatic prejudice against homosexuality for example) claim support from a long-standing tradition of interpretations of holy scriptures.

(4) Thus, the cognitive demand we make of someone in expectation of tolerance is the following: he shall develop from his own worldview reasons that tell him why he may realize the ethos inscribed in that view only within the limits of what everyone is allowed to do and to pursue. Of course, these limits themselves are often up for discussion, at which point the courts decide who must accept whose ethos—the majority, that of a minority, or vice versa.[13] This brings me, following the reasons for rejection and acceptance, on to the third kind of reasons. The legal *reasons for excluding intolerant behaviour* provide the yardstick for measuring whether the state adheres to the imperative of remaining neutral and whether legislature and jurisdiction have institutionalized tolerance in the right way. Let me first discuss some familiar examples and then introduce the notion of a cultural right.

---

[12] J. Rawls, *Political Liberalism*, 11ff.

[13] See the list offered by D. Grimm in the *Frankfurter Allgemeine Zeitung* of June 21, 2002, 49: 'Can a Sikh riding a motorcycle be excused from obeying the general law to wear a helmet on grounds of his religious duty to wear a turban? Must a Jewish prisoner be offered kosher food? Does a Muslim employee have the right to briefly interrupt his work time in order to pray? Can an employee be fired because he did

Sikhs in Great Britain and the United States gained exceptions from generally bind-
ing safety regulations and are permitted to wear turbans (rather than crash helmets)
and daggers (kirpans). In Germany Jehovah's Witnesses successfully fought to be
recognized as a public-law entity ('Anstalt öffentlichen Rechts') and thereby gained
the same legal privileges our large churches enjoy. In these cases when minorities
call for equal standing, for exceptions from established laws, or for special subsidies
(e.g. for curricula transmitting the language and tradition of a minority culture), in
many cases the courts must decide who has to accept whose ethos or form of life:
must the Christian inhabitants of the village accept the call of the muezzin? Must
the local majority for strict animal protection accept the ritual slaughter of poultry
and cattle by Jewish butchers? Must the non-confessional pupils, or those of different
confessions, accept the Islamic teacher's head scarf? Must the owner of the grocery
shop accept the decision of his employee to wear what to the customers appear conspicuously strange symbols or clothes? Must the Turkish father accept coeducational
sports for his daughters at public schools?

In all these cases religious freedom tests the neutrality of the state. Frequently
neutrality is threatened by the predominance of a majority culture, which abuses
its historically acquired influence and definitional power to decide according to its
own standards what shall be considered the norms and values of the political culture which is expected to be equally shared by all.[14] This implicit fusion of the common political culture with a divisive majority culture leads to the infiltration of the
manifest legal form by inconspicuous cultural substance, thus distorting the very
procedural nature of a democratic order. After all, the moral *substance* of democratic
principles is spelled out in terms of legal *procedures* that can only build up legitimacy
because they enjoy a reputation for granting impartiality by focusing consideration
on all interests equally. Legal procedures thus stand to lose the force to found legitimacy if notions of a substantial ethical life slowly creep into the interpretation and
practice of formal requirements. In this regard, political neutrality can be violated
just as easily by the secular or laical side as by the religious camp.

For the one side, the paramount example is the *affaire foulard*, for the other,
the response of the Bavarian State government to the German Supreme Court's

---

not appear for work on the high holy days? Does an employee dismissed for this reason forfeit his entitle-
ment to unemployment benefits? Must Jewish entrepreneurs be permitted to open their businesses on
Sundays simply because for religious reasons they had to keep them shut on Saturday? Does a Muslim
pupil have the right to be exempted from PE classes because she is not allowed to show herself to other
pupils wearing sports clothes? May Muslim pupils wear headscarves in class? What is the case if the
woman concerned is a teacher at a government-owned school? Should the law be different for nuns than
it is for a Muslim teacher?... Must muezzins be allowed to broadcast their call to prayer by loudspeaker
in German cities just as churches are allowed to ring their bells? Must foreigners be allowed to ritually
slaughter animals although it contravenes the local animal protection regulations?... Must Mormons be
permitted to practise polygamy here because it is allowed them in their country of origin?'

[14] On the unity of political culture in the diversity of sub-cultures see. J. Habermas, *The Inclusion of the
Other* (Cambridge, Mass: MIT Press, 1998), 117ff.

judgment on whether crucifixes should be mandatory for classrooms in elementary schools. In the former case, the headmaster of a French school prohibited Muslim girls from wearing their traditional head scarves; in the other, the German Supreme Court agreed with the complaint brought by anthroposophical parents that there should be no crucifix in the classroom in which their daughter had to sit for lessons. In the French case, positive religious freedom is called into question; in the German case, it is the negative version which is cast into doubt. The Catholic opponents of the crucifix verdict of Germany's Supreme Court defend the religious symbol of the crucified Christ as an expression of 'Occidental values' and thus as part of a political culture which all citizens may be expected to share. This is the classical case of a political over-generalization of a regionally dominant religious practice, as it was reflected in the Bavarian Public Primary School Order of 1983. By contrast, in France the Muslim pupils were forbidden from wearing head scarves—the laical argument given was that religion is a private matter that has to be kept out of the public domain. This is the case of a secularist interpretation of the constitution that must face the challenge whether the republican interpretation of constitutional principles that prevails in France is not too 'strong' and is thus not able to avoid violating due neutrality of the state vis-à-vis legitimate claims of a religious minority to enjoy the right of self-expression and to receive public recognition.

These legal conflicts show why the spread of religious tolerance—and we have seen that it was already a driving force for the emergence of democracies—has now become also a stimulus for developing further cultural rights. The inclusion of religious minorities in the political community kindles and fosters sensitivity to the claims of other discriminated groups. The recognition of religious pluralism can fulfil the role of a pacemaker in legal development, as it makes us aware in an exemplary fashion of the *claims of minorities to civic inclusion*. One might object that the debate on multiculturalism hinges less on neglecting religious minorities than on other issues such as defining national holidays, specifying official language(s), promoting instruction for ethnic and national minorities, set quotas for women, coloured people, indigenous populations at the working place, in schools or politics. From the viewpoint of equal inclusion of all citizens, however, religious discrimination takes its place in the long list of forms of cultural and linguistic, ethnic and racial, sexual and physical discrimination, and thus functions as a pacemaker of 'cultural rights'. Let me explain what I mean by this term.

Inclusion refers to one of two aspects of the equal standing of citizens, or civic equality. Although discrimination against minorities is usually associated with social under-privileging, it is well worth keeping these two categories of unequal treatment separate. One is measured against the yardstick of *distributive justice*, the other against that of *full membership*.[15] From the viewpoint of distributive justice,

---

[15] On this distinction N. Fraser, 'From Redistribution to Recognition?' in C. Willett (ed.), *Theorizing Multiculturalism* (Oxford: Wiley-Blackwell, 1998), 19–49.

the principle of equal treatment of everybody requires that all citizens have the same opportunities to make actual use of equally distributed rights and liberties in order to realize their own particular life plans. Political struggles and social movements opposing status deprivation and fighting for redistribution are fuelled by the experiences of injustice at the level of distributive justice. By contrast, the struggles that relate to the *recognition of a specific collective identity* are based on a different kind of experience of injustice—not status deprivation but disregard, marginalization, or exclusion depending on membership in a group, considered as 'inferior' according to prevailing standards.[16] From this aspect of incomplete inclusion, overcoming religious discrimination is the pacemaker for a new kind of cultural rights.

Cultural rights serve, as does the freedom to practise one's religion, the purpose of guaranteeing all citizens equal access to those associations, communication patterns, traditions, and practices that they respectively deem important in order to develop and maintain their personal identities. Cultural rights need not in each case refer to the ascribed group of origin; the personal identity in need of protection can just as well be based on a chosen and achieved environment. Religious convictions and practices have a decisive influence on the ethical conception of believers in all cultures. Linguistic and cultural traditions are similarly relevant for the formation and maintenance of one's own personal identity. In light of this insight we need to revise the traditional conception of the 'legal person'. The individuation of natural persons occurs through socialization. Individuals socialized in this manner can form and stabilize their identity only within a network of relationships of reciprocal recognition. This should have consequences for the protection of the integrity of the legal person—and for an intersubjectivist expansion of a person concept that has to date been tailored to the narrow lens of the tradition of possessive individualism.

All rights protecting the integrity of an individual define the legal status of that person. These rights must now extend to the access to that community's matrix of experience, communication, and recognition within which people can articulate their self-understanding and maintain their identity. From this angle, cultural rights are introduced as individual rights in the first place. In line with the model of religious freedom, they are what German lawyers call 'subjective rights', designed for the purpose of granting full inclusion.[17] The point of cultural rights is to guarantee all citizens equal access to cultural environments, interpersonal relations and traditions as far as these are essential for them to form and secure their personal identity.

Yet cultural rights do not just mean 'more difference' and 'more independence' for cultural groups and their leaders. Members of discriminated groups do not enjoy

---

[16] A. Honneth, *Das Andere der Gerechtigkeit* (Frankfurt/Main: Suhrkamp, 2000), focuses specifically on these pathologies of refused recognition.

[17] Charles Taylor, *Multiculturalism and 'The Politics of Recognition' With Commentary* by Amy Gutmann (ed.), Steven C. Rockefeller, Michael Walzer, and Susan Wolf (Princeton University Press, 1992). See in the German edition my critique of the communitarian conception of cultural rights as collective rights (117–46).

equal cultural rights 'free of charge'. They cannot benefit from a morality of equal inclusion without themselves making this morality their own. The cognitive demand the liberal state makes of religious communities is all the same for 'strong' secular communities (such as national or ethnic minorities, immigrant or indigenous populations, descendants of slave cultures, etc).[18] The traditions they continue open up 'world perspectives' that, *like* religious worldviews, can come into conflict with one another.[19] Therefore, cultural groups are equally expected to adapt their internal ethos to the egalitarian standards of the community at large. Some of them may find this even tougher than do those communities who are able to resort to the highly developed conceptual resources of one or the other of the great world religions.

Anyway, the leap in reflexivity that has come to characterize the modernization of religious consciousness within liberal societies provides a model for the mind-set of secular groups in multicultural societies as well. A multiculturalism that does not misunderstand itself does not constitute a *one-way street* to cultural self-assertion by groups with their own collective identities. The coexistence of different life forms as equals must not be allowed to prompt segmentation. Instead, it requires the integration of all citizens—and their mutual recognition across cultural divisions as citizens—within the framework of a shared political culture. Citizens are equally empowered to develop what is for them their cultural identity and might appear to others as cultural idiosyncrasies, but only under the condition that all of them (across boundaries) understand themselves to be citizens of one and the same political community. From this point of view, the very same normative base of the constitution that justifies cultural rights and entitlements likewise limits a kind of aggressive self-assertion that leads to fragmenting the larger community.

[18] On the concept of such 'encompassing groups' see A. Margalit J. Raz, 'National Self-Determination' in: W. Kymlicka (ed.), *The Rights of Minority Cultures* (Oxford: Oxford University Press, 1995), 79–92, esp. 81ff.

[19] The more comprehensive the cultural life form, the stronger its cognitive content, the more it resembles a way of life structured by religious worldviews: 'The inescapable problem is that cultures have propositional content. It is an inevitable aspect of any culture that it will include ideas to the effect that some beliefs are true and some are false, and that some things are right and others wrong.' T. B. Barry, *Culture and Equality* (Cambridge, UK: Polity Press, 2001), 270.

Introduction to Bernard Williams' Lecture

Ted Honderich

Mainstream philosophy, as you have heard before now, can be taken to be a greater concentration than science's on the logic of ordinary intelligence: (i) clarity and in particular analysis, (ii) consistency and validity, (iii) completeness, and (iv) generality or summation—usually with respect to large subjects, of which the largest are some-times labelled reality, knowledge, and value. This philosophy, maybe you can also say, is *thinking about facts* as against science's *getting of facts*. But should this philosophy approximate more to science? If so, does it immediately become what falls under a pejo-rative term, *scientism*, an excessive or exclusive deference to science and its method?

The philosophical life of Sir Bernard Williams, which might have been still more fulfilled by being longer, began with Greats in Oxford, the undergraduate degree that begins with Homer and the ancient history of the Greeks and now may end with Williams among others. It was a brilliant start in life. Then followed thinking and teaching at All Souls College, University College London, Bedford College London, Cambridge, where he was provost of King's College, the University of California at Berkeley, and Oxford again. This was also a life much of which was at least in touch, by way of his marriage, with a political class of some conscience.

As a Royal Institute of Philosophy annual lecturer, he finds and advocates more in mainstream philosophy than you have heard. He allows necessarily that there is some philosophical work that is what he calls an extension of science, no doubt including not only the philosophy of science but also, say, kinds of philosophy of mind and lan-guage. But it is his principal line of thought that mainstream philosophy has been and must continue to be, or to be more of, a humanistic discipline. Its being *humanistic* is defined or spoken of as its being the attempt to *make the best sense of our life*, includ-ing our thinking. Its being a *discipline* is, as you have heard above in my other explicit words, its expressing things clearly and offering arguments, or, as he says, getting things right.

This philosophy does not and must not embrace scientism. It must not try to assimilate philosophy to the aims or the manners of the sciences—the aim of philosophy but not science is indeed to make the best sense of our life. This first proposition is to be understood and defended, perhaps mainly, in terms of a second one: that science aspires to an absolute, objective, or universal view of all that it concerns itself with. But—a third proposition—it is a mistake to think that an absolute conception of the world, in so far as that is possible, is all that matters, the only worthwhile endeavour. An absolute conception is not intrinsically superior to a conception from what is called a perspective, some point of view, a kind of locality.

As a result, a fourth and the main proposition of the lecture is that philosophy and more than philosophy must attend to history and to its own history. We cannot separate ourselves off from our history and the history of philosophy. That we must attend to our past is a necessity, at least in large part, because historiography is also a part of making sense of our existence. That we must attend to the history of philosophy is in good part the fact that without doing so we cannot in our progress understand the fullness of what we may be denying. We do not understand what we believe except by understanding what it is that we are disbelieving.

These main reflections of the lecture, together with instructive reprises and elaborations, one about what is called the vindicatory, another about what is *unhintergehbar*, basic in the sense of being beyond justification, come together with still other lines of reflection with which Williams was more engaged in his life, and reflections on morality and moral philosophy. Although he does not himself attend to the matter in his lecture, there is at least a consonance between his conception of philosophy as humanistic, his passionate recommendation with respect to it, and his conception of morality and of moral philosophy. For him it cannot be that morality is a matter of theories, of generalizations, of principles, or a principle of what is right. It is instead a matter of such considerations as personal integrity.

Look back over the lectures in this book. Can the conception of philosophy or maybe best philosophy as necessarily in a way historical be made consistent with the worth of these lectures? Is it true and enlightening that the difference of philosophy from science is that philosophy cannot aspire to objectivity? Can it be safe to eschew a general rule of what is right? Does it show misunderstanding to ask, if integrity is being true to oneself, having principles, being whole and undivided, whether Hitler could have had integrity?

Certainly neither Bernard, as I remember from his teaching of me, nor I, would hurry you into deferential agreement with any of that or with his lecture. You can look further into the questions by way of the wide range of his lovely books, reasonable in their confidence. *Morality: An Introduction to Ethics* (1972), *Problems of the Self* (1973), *Moral Luck* (1981), *Ethics and the Limits of Philosophy* (1985), and *Truth and Truthfulness* (2002). The present lecture is also reprinted in a posthumous collection of connected and supporting writings, under the title *Philosophy as a Humanistic Discipline* (2008).

17

Philosophy as a Humanistic Discipline

Bernard Williams

1. In the formula 'humanistic discipline' both the elements are meant to carry weight. This is not a lecture about academic organization: in speaking of philosophy as a 'humanistic' enterprise, I am not making the point that philosophy belongs with the humanities or arts subjects. The question is: what models or ideals or analogies should we look to in thinking about the ways in which philosophy should be done? It is an application to our present circumstances of a more general and traditional question, which is notoriously itself a philosophical question: how should philosophy understand itself?

Similarly with the other term in the phrase. It is not just a question of *a* discipline, as a field or area of enquiry. 'Discipline' is supposed to imply discipline. In philosophy, there had better be something that counts as getting it right, or doing it right, and I believe that this must still be associated with the aims of philosophy of offering arguments and expressing oneself clearly, aims that have been particularly emphasized by analytic philosophy, though sometimes in a perverse and one-sided manner. But offering arguments and expressing oneself clearly are not monopolies of philosophy. Other humanities subjects offer arguments and can express themselves clearly; or if they cannot, that is their problem. History, for instance, certainly has its disciplines, and they involve, among other things, both argument and clarity. I take history to be a central case of a humanistic study, and it makes no difference to this that history, or some aspects of history, are sometimes classified as a social science—that will only tell us something about how to understand the idea of a social science. History is central to my argument not just because history is central among humanistic disciplines, but because, I am going to argue, philosophy has some very special relations to it.

A certain limited relation between history and philosophy has been traditionally acknowledged to the extent that people who were going to learn some philosophy were expected to learn some history of philosophy. This traditional idea is not accepted everywhere now, and I shall come back to that point. It must be said, too, that this traditional concession to history was often rather nominal: many of the exercises conducted in the name of the history of philosophy have borne a tenuous relation to anything that might independently be called history. The activity was identified as the 'history of philosophy' more by the names that occurred in it than by the ways in which it was conducted. Paul Grice used to say that we 'should treat great and dead philosophers as we treat great and living philosophers, as having something to say to *us*'. That is fine, so long as it is not assumed that what the dead have to say to us is much the same as what the living have to say to us. Unfortunately, this is probably what was being assumed by those who, in the heyday of confidence in what has been called the 'analytic history of philosophy', encouraged us to read something written by Plato 'as though it had come out in *Mind* last month'—an idea which, if it means anything at all, means something that destroys the main philosophical point of reading Plato at all.[1]

The point is not confined to the 'analytic' style. There is an enjoyable passage by Collingwood in which he describes how 'the old gang of Oxford realists', as he called them, notably Prichard and Joseph, would insist on translating some ancient Greek expression as 'moral obligation' and then point out that Aristotle, or whoever it was, had an inadequate theory of moral obligation.[2] It was like a nightmare, Collingwood said, in which one met a man who insisted on translating the Greek word for a trireme as 'steamship' and then complained that the Greeks had a defective conception of a steamship. But, in any case, the points I want to make about philosophy's engagement with history go a long way beyond its concern with its own history, though that is certainly part of it.

I have already started to talk about philosophy being this or that, and such and such being central to philosophy, and this may already have aroused suspicions of essentialism, as though philosophy had some entirely distinct and timeless nature from which various consequences could be drawn. So let me say at once that I do not want to fall back on any such idea. Indeed, I shall claim later that some of the deepest insights of modern philosophy, notably in the work of Wittgenstein, remain undeveloped—indeed, at the limit, they are rendered unintelligible—precisely because of an assumption that philosophy is something quite peculiar, which should not be confused with any other kind of study, and which needs no other kind of study in order to understand itself. Wittgenstein in his later work influentially rejected essentialism, and spoke of family resemblances and so on, but at the same time he was obsessed—I do not think that is too strong a word—by the identity of philosophy as an enterprise which was utterly peculiar compared with other enterprises; this is so on Wittgenstein's view, whether one reads him as thinking that the compulsion to

---

[1] The point, in particular, of making the familiar look strange, and conversely. I have said some more about this in 'Descartes and the Historiography of Philosophy', in John Cottingham (ed.), *Reason, Will and Sensation* (Oxford: Clarendon Press, 1994).

[2] R. G. Collingwood, *An Autobiography* (Oxford: Clarendon Press, 1939), p. 63.

engage in it is pathological, or is part of the human condition.[3] It does not seem to me as peculiar as all that, and, in addition, we should recall the point which Wittgenstein invites us to recall about other things, that it is very various. What I have to say applies, I hope, to most of what is standardly regarded as philosophy, and I shall try to explain why that is so, but I shall not try to deduce it from the nature of philosophy as compared with other disciplines, or indeed deduce it from anything else. What I have to say, since it is itself a piece of philosophy, is an example of what I take philosophy to be, part of a more general attempt to make the best sense of our life, and so of our intellectual activities, in the situation in which we find ourselves.

2. One definite contrast to a humanistic conception of philosophy is *scientism*. I do not mean by this simply an interest or involvement in science. Philosophy should certainly be interested in the sciences and some philosophers may well be involved in them, and nothing I say is meant to deny it. Scientism is, rather, a misunderstanding of the relations between philosophy and the natural sciences which tends to assimilate philosophy to the aims, or at least the manners, of the sciences. In line with the point I have just made about the variety of philosophy, there certainly is some work in philosophy which quite properly conducts itself as an extension of the natural or mathematical sciences, because that is what it is: work in the philosophy of quantum mechanics, for instance, or in the more technical aspects of logic. But in many other areas, the assimilation is a mistake.

I do not want to say very much about what might be called 'stylistic scientism', the pretence, for instance, that the philosophy of mind is the more theoretical and less experimentally encumbered end of neurophysiology. It may be suggested that this kind of assimilation, even if it is to some extent misguided, at least encourages a certain kind of rigour, which will help to fulfil philosophy's promise of embodying a discipline. But I doubt whether this is so. On the contrary: since the scientistic philosophy of mind cannot embody the rigour which is in the first instance appropriate to neurophysiology, that of experimental procedures, the contributions of philosophers in this style are actually more likely to resemble another well-known phenomenon of the scientific culture, the discourse of scientists when they are off duty, the slap-dash programmatic remarks that scientists sometimes present in informal talks. Those remarks are often very interesting, but that is because they are the remarks of scientists, standing back from what they ordinarily do. There is not much reason to expect as much interest in the remarks of philosophers who are not taking a holiday from anything, but whose business is identified simply as making such remarks.

A question that intrigues me and to which I do not know the answer is the relation between a scientistic view of philosophy, on the one hand, and, on the other, the well-known and highly typical style of many texts in analytic philosophy which seeks

---

[3] The former view was expressed, in a vulgarized form, in the literature of 'therapeutic positivism'. The latter is richly developed in the work of Stanley Cavell.

precision by total mind control, through issuing continuous and rigid interpretative directions. In a way that will be familiar to any reader of analytic philosophy, and is only too familiar to all of us who perpetrate it, this style tries to remove in advance every conceivable misunderstanding or misinterpretation or objection, including those that would occur only to the malicious or the clinically literal-minded. This activity itself is often rather mournfully equated with the boasted clarity and rigour of analytic philosophy. Now, it is perfectly reasonable that the author should consider the objections and possible misunderstandings, or at least quite a lot of them; the odd thing is that he or she should put them into the text. One might hope that the objections and possible misunderstandings could be considered and no doubt influence the text, and then, except for the most significant, they could be removed, like the scaffolding that shapes a building but does not require you after the building is finished to climb through it in order to gain access.

There is no doubt more than one force that tends to encourage this style. One is the teaching of philosophy by eristic argument, which tends to implant in philosophers an intimidatingly nit-picking superego, a blend of their most impressive teachers and their most competitive colleagues, which guides their writing by means of constant anticipations of guilt and shame. Another is the requirements of the PhD as an academic exercise, which involves the production of a quite peculiar text, one that can be too easily mistaken for a book. There are demands of academic promotion, which can encourage one to make as many published pages as possible out of whatever modest idea one may have. Now none of these influences is necessarily connected with a scientistic view of philosophy, and many people who go in for this style would certainly and correctly reject any suggestion that they had that view. Indeed, an obvious example of this is a philosopher who perhaps did more than anyone else to encourage this style, G. E. Moore. However, for all that, I do not think that we should reject too quickly the thought that, when scientism is around, this style can be co-opted in the scientistic spirit. It can serve as a mimicry of scrupulous scientific procedures. People can perhaps persuade themselves that if they fuss around enough with qualifications and counter-examples, they are conducting the philosophical equivalent of a biochemical protocol.

3. But, as I said, stylistic scientism is not really the present question. There is a much more substantive issue here. Consider the following passage by Hilary Putnam from his book of Gifford Lectures, *Renewing Philosophy*:[4]

Analytic philosophy has become increasingly dominated by the idea that science, and only science, describes the world as it is in itself, independent of perspective. To be sure, there are within analytic philosophy important figures who combat this scientism... Nevertheless, the idea that science leaves no room for an independent philosophical enterprise has reached the point at which leading practitioners sometimes suggest that all that is left for philosophy is

---

[4] Hilary Putnam, *Renewing Philosophy* (Cambridge, MA: Harvard University Press, 1992), Preface, p. x.

to try to anticipate what the presumed scientific solutions to all metaphysical problems will eventually look like.

It is not hard to see that there is a large *non sequitur* in this. Why should the idea that science and only science describes the world as it is in itself, independent of perspective, mean that there is no independent philosophical enterprise? That would follow only on the assumption that if there is an independent philosophical enterprise, its aim is to describe the world as it is in itself, independent of perspective. And why should we accept that? I admit to being rather sensitive to this *non sequitur*, because, in the course of Putnam's book (which contains a chapter called 'Bernard Williams and the Absolute Conception of the World'), I myself am identified as someone who 'views physics as giving us the ultimate metaphysical truth...'[5] Now I have never held any such view, and I agree entirely with Putnam in rejecting it. However, I have entertained the idea that science might describe the world 'as it is in itself'; that is to say, give a representation of it which is to the largest possible extent independent of the local perspectives or idiosyncrasies of enquirers, a representation of the world, as I put it, 'as it is anyway'.[6] Such a presentation I called in my jargon 'the absolute conception of the world'. Whether it is attainable or not, whether the aspiration to it is even coherent, are of course highly disputable questions.

A sign that something must have gone wrong with Putnam's argument, or with mine, if not with both, is that he supposes that the idea of an absolute conception of the world must ultimately be motivated by the contradictory and incoherent aim of describing the world without describing it: as he puts it,[7] we cannot divide language into two parts, 'a part that describes the world "as it is anyway" and a part that describes our conceptual contribution'. (The ever tricky word 'our' is important, and we shall come back to it.) But my aim in introducing the notion of the absolute conception was precisely to get round the point that one cannot describe the world without describing it, and to accommodate the fundamentally Kantian insight that there simply is no conception of the world which is not conceptualized in some way or another. My idea was not that you could conceptualize the world without concepts. The idea was that when we reflect on our conceptualization of the world, we might be able to recognize from inside it that some of our concepts and ways of representing the world are more dependent than others on our own perspective, our peculiar and local ways of apprehending things. In contrast, we might be able to identify some concepts and styles of representation which are minimally dependent on our own or any other creature's peculiar ways of apprehending the world: these would form a kind of representation that might be reached by any competent investigators of the world, even though they differed from us—that is to say, from human beings—in their sensory apparatus and, certainly, their cultural background. The objective of distinguishing

---

[5] *Renewing Philosophy*, p. 108.
[6] Bernard Williams, *Descartes: The Project of Pure Enquiry* (Harmondsworth: Penguin, 1978), p. 64.
[7] *Renewing Philosophy*, p. 123.

such a representation of the world may possibly be incoherent, but it is certainly not motivated by the aim of transcending all description and conceptualization.

I do not want to go further here into the question whether the idea of an absolute conception is coherent.[8] I mention the matter because I think that Putnam's stick, although he has got the wrong end of it, may help us in locating a scientism in philosophy which he and I actually agree in rejecting. Putnam's basic argument against the idea of the absolute conception is that semantic relations are normative, and hence could not figure in any purely scientific conception. But describing the world involves deploying terms that have semantic relations to it: hence, it seems, Putnam's conclusion that the absolute conception is supposed to describe the world without describing it. Let us pass over the point that the argument seems to run together two different things: on the one hand, *using* terms that have semantic relations to the world, and, on the other, *giving an account* of those semantic relations: I shall concentrate on the latter.[9] Let us also grant for the sake of the argument the principle, which is certainly disputable, that if semantic relations are normative, it follows that an account of them cannot itself figure in the absolute conception. It does not follow that the absolute conception is impossible. All that follows is that an account of semantic relations, in particular one given by the philosophy of language, would not be part of the absolute conception. But—going back for a moment to the purely *ad hominem* aspect of the argument—I never claimed that it would be; and in a related point, I said that, even if the absolute conception were attainable and it constituted knowledge of how the world was 'anyway', it was extremely doubtful that we could know that this was so.[10]

So why does Putnam assume, as he obviously does, that if there were to be an absolute conception of the world, philosophy would have to be part of it? I doubt that he was simply thrown by the Hegelian associations of the word 'absolute', with their implication that if there is absolute knowledge, then philosophy possesses it. What perhaps he does think is the conjunction of two things: first, that philosophy is as good as it gets, and is in no way inferior to science, and, second, that if there were an absolute conception of the world, a representation of it which was maximally independent of perspective, that would be better than more perspectival or locally conditioned representations of the world. Now the first of these assumptions is, as it were, half true: although philosophy is worse than natural science at some things, such as discovering the nature of the galaxies (or, if I was right about the absolute conception, representing the world as it is in itself), it is better than natural science at other things, for instance making sense of what we are trying to do in our intellectual activities. But the second assumption I have ascribed to Putnam, that if there were an absolute

[8] An outstanding discussion is A. W. Moore, *Points of View* (Oxford: Clarendon Press, 1997).

[9] This is the point that should be relevant to the question whether philosophy would form part of the content of the absolute conception. Moreover, if Putnam wanted to say that any statement which merely contained terms governed by normative semantic relations was itself normative, he would have to say that every statement was normative.

[10] *Descartes*, pp. 300–303.

conception, it would somehow be better than more perspectival representations—that is simply false. Even if it were possible to give an account of the world that was minimally perspectival, it would not be particularly serviceable to us for many of our purposes, such as making sense of our intellectual or other activities, or indeed getting on with most of those activities. For those purposes—in particular, in seeking to understand ourselves—we need concepts and explanations which are rooted in our more local practices, our culture, and our history, and these cannot be replaced by concepts which we might share with very different investigators of the world. The slippery word 'we' here means not the inclusive 'we' which brings together as a purely abstract gathering any beings with whom human beings might conceivably communicate about the nature of the world. It means a contrastive 'we'; that is to say, humans as contrasted with other possible beings; and, in the case of many human practices, it may of course mean groupings smaller than humanity as a whole.

To summarize this part of the argument, there are two mistakes to hand here. One is to suppose that just because there is an uncontentious sense in which all our conceptions are ours, it simply follows from this that they are all equally local or perspectival, and that no contrast in this respect could conceivably be drawn from inside our thought between, for instance, the concepts of physics and the concepts of politics or ethics. The other mistake is to suppose that if there is such a contrast, and one set of these concepts, those of physical science, are potentially universal in their uptake and usefulness, then it follows from this that they are somehow intrinsically superior to more local conceptions which are humanly and perhaps historically grounded. The latter is a scientistic error, and it will remain one even if it is denied that the contrast can conceivably be drawn. People who deny the contrast but hold on to the error—who believe, that is to say, that there can be no absolute conception, but that if there were, it would be better than any other representation of the world—these people are counterfactually scientistic: rather as an atheist is really religious if he thinks that since God does not exist everything is permitted.

Because Putnam assumes that if there were such a thing as an absolute conception of the world, the account of semantic relations would itself have to be part of it, he also regards as scientistic the philosophical programme, which has taken various forms, of trying to give an account of semantic relations such as reference in non-normative, scientific, terms. It might be thought there was a question whether such a programme would necessarily be scientistic, independently of Putnam's particular reasons for thinking that it would; but in fact this question seems to me to be badly posed. The issue is not whether the programme is scientistic, but whether the motivations for it are, and this itself is a less than clear question. I take it as obvious that any attempt to *reduce* semantic relations to concepts of physics is doomed. If, in reaction to that, the question simply becomes whether our account of semantic relations is to be consistent with physics, the answer had better be 'yes'. So any interesting question in this area seems to be something like this: to what extent could the behaviour of a creature be identified as linguistic behaviour, for instance that of referring to something, without that creature's belonging to a group which had something like a culture, a general set of rules which governed itself and other creatures with which it lived? Related questions are: is language a specifically human activity, so far as terrestrial species are concerned, in the sense that it is necessarily tied up with the full human range of self-conscious cultural activities? Again, at what stage of hominid evolution might we conceive of genuine linguistic behaviour emerging? These questions seem to me perfectly interesting questions and neither they, nor their motivation, is scientistic. What would be scientistic would be an *a priori* assumption that they had to have a certain kind of answer, namely one that identified linguistic behaviour as independent of human cultural activities in general, or, alternatively, took the differently reductive line, that cultural activities are all or mostly to be explained in terms of natural selection. I shall not try to say any more about this aspect of the subject here, except to repeat yet again the platitude that it is not, in general, human cultural practices that are explained by natural selection, but rather the universal human characteristic of having cultural practices, and human beings' capacity to do so. It is precisely the fact that variations and developments in cultural practices are *not* determined at an evolutionary level that makes the human characteristic of living under culture such an extraordinary evolutionary success.

4. What are the temptations to scientism? They are various, and many of them can be left to the sociology of academic life, but I take it that the most basic motivations to it are tied up with a question of the intellectual authority of philosophy. Science seems to possess intellectual authority, and philosophy, conscious that as it is usually done it does not have scientific authority, may decide to try to share in it. Now it is a real question whether the intellectual authority of science is not tied up with its hopes of offering an absolute conception of the world as it is independently of any local or peculiar perspective on it. Many scientists think so. Some people think that this is the only intellectual authority there is. They include, counterfactually speaking, those defenders of the humanities, misguided in my view, who think that they have to show that nobody has any hope of offering such a conception, including scientists: that natural science constitutes just another part of the human conversation, so that, leaving aside the small difference that the sciences deliver refrigerators, weapons, medicines, and so on, they are in the same boat as the humanities are.[11]

This way of defending the humanities seems to me doubly misguided. It is politically misguided, for if the authority of the sciences is divorced from any pretensions to offer an absolute conception, their authority will merely shift to the manifest fact of their predictive and technological successes, unmediated by any issue of where those successes come from, and the humanities will once again, in that measure, be disadvantaged. The style of defence is also intellectually misguided, for the same kind of

[11] A rather similar line was taken by some defenders of religion at the beginning of the scientific revolution.

reason that we have already met, that it assumes that offering an absolute conception is the real thing, what really matters in the direction of intellectual authority. But there is simply no reason to accept that—once again, we are left with the issue of how to make the best sense of ourselves and our activities, and that issue includes the question, indeed it focuses on the question, of how the humanities can help us in doing so.

One particular question, of course, is how to make best sense of the activity of science itself. Here the issue of history begins to come to the fore. The pursuit of science does not give any great part to its own history, and that is a significant feature of its practice. (It is no surprise that scientistic philosophers want philosophy to follow it in this: that they think, as one philosopher I know has put it, that the history of philosophy is no more part of philosophy than the history of science is part of science.) Of course, scientific concepts have a history: but on the standard view, though the history of physics may be interesting, it has no effect on the understanding of physics itself. It is merely part of the history of discovery.

There is of course a real question of what it is for a history to be a history of discovery. One condition of its being so lies in a familiar idea, which I would put like this: the later theory, or (more generally) outlook, makes sense of itself, and of the earlier outlook, and of the transition from the earlier to the later, in such terms that both parties (the holders of the earlier outlook, and the holders of the later) have reason to recognize the transition as an improvement. I shall call an explanation which satisfies this condition *vindicatory*. In the particular case of the natural sciences, the later theory typically explains in its own terms the appearances which supported the earlier theory, and, furthermore, the earlier theory can be understood as a special or limited case of the later. But—and this is an important point—the idea that the explanation of a transition from one outlook to another is 'vindicatory' is not defined in such a way that it applies only to scientific enquiries.

Those who are sceptical about the claims of science to be moving towards an absolute conception of the world often base their doubts on the history of science. They deny that the history is really vindicatory, or, to the extent that it is, they deny that this is as significant as the standard view supposes. I shall not try to take these arguments further, though it is perhaps worth noting that those who sympathize with this scepticism need to be careful about how they express their historical conclusions. Whatever view you take of the scientific enterprise, you should resist saying, as one historian of science has incautiously said, 'the reality of quarks was the upshot of particle physicists' practice' (the 1970s is rather late for the beginning of the universe).[12]

5. Philosophy, at any rate, is thoroughly familiar with ideas which indeed, like all other ideas, have a history, but have a history which is not notably vindicatory. I shall concentrate for this part of the discussion on ethical and political concepts, though

---

[12] Andrew Pickering, *Constructing Quarks* (Edinburgh University Press, 1984). It should be said that Pickering's history does raise important questions about interpreting the 'discovery' of quarks.

many of the considerations go wider. If we ask why we use some concepts of this kind rather than others—rather than, say, those current in an earlier time—we may deploy arguments which claim to justify our ideas against those others: ideas of equality and equal rights, for instance, against ideas of hierarchy. Alternatively, we may reflect on an historical story, of how these concepts rather than the others came to be ours: a story (simply to give it a label) of how the modern world and its special expectations came to replace the *ancien régime*. But then we reflect on the relation of this story to the arguments that we deploy against the earlier conceptions, and we realize that the story is the history of those forms of argument themselves: the forms of argument, call them liberal forms of argument, are a central part of the outlook that we accept.

If we consider how these forms of argument came to prevail, we can indeed see them as having won, but not necessarily as having won an argument. For liberal ideas to have won an argument, the representatives of the *ancien régime* would have had to have shared with the nascent liberals a conception of something that the argument was about, and not just in the obvious sense that it was about the way to live or the way to order society. They would have had to agree that there was some aim, of reason or freedom or whatever, which liberal ideas served better or of which they were a better expression, and there is not much reason, with a change as radical as this, to think that they did agree about this, at least until late in the process. The relevant ideas of freedom, reason, and so on were themselves involved in the change. If in this sense the liberals did not win an argument, then the explanations of how liberalism came to prevail— that is to say, among other things, how these came to be our ideas—are not vindicatory.

The point can also be put like this. In the case of scientific change, it may occur through there being a crisis. If there is a crisis, it is agreed by all parties to be a crisis of explanation, and while they may indeed disagree over what will count as an explanation, to a considerable extent there has come to be agreement, at least within the limits of science since the eighteenth century, and this makes an important contribution to the history being vindicatory. But in the geographically extended and long-lasting and various process by which the old political and ethical order has changed into modernity, while it was propelled by many crises, they were not in the first instance crises of explanation. They were crises of confidence or of legitimacy, and the story of how one conception rather than another came to provide the basis of a new legitimacy is not on the face of it vindicatory.

There are indeed, or have been, stories that try to vindicate historically one or another modern conception, in terms of the unfolding of reason, or a growth in enlightenment, or a fuller realization of freedom and autonomy which is a constant human objective; and there are others. Such stories are unpopular at the moment, particularly in the wide-screen versions offered by Hegel and Marx. With philosophers in our local tradition the stories are unpopular not so much in the sense that they deny them, as that they do not mention them. They do not mention them, no doubt, in part because they do not believe them, but also because it is not part of a philosophical undertaking, as locally understood, to attend to any such history. But—and this is the point I want to stress—we *must* attend to it, if we are to know what reflective attitude to take to our own conceptions. For one thing, the answer to the question whether there is a history of our conceptions that is vindicatory (if only modestly so) makes a difference to what we are doing in saying, if we do say, that the earlier conceptions were wrong. In the absence of vindicatory explanations, while you can of course say that they were wrong— who is to stop you?—the content of this is likely to be pretty thin: it conveys only the message that the earlier outlook fails by arguments the point of which is that such outlooks should fail by them. It is a good question whether a tune as thin as this is worth whistling at all.

However, this issue (the issue roughly of relativism) is not the main point. The real question concerns our philosophical attitude towards *our own* views. Even apart from questions of vindication and the consequences that this may have for comparisons of our outlook with others, philosophers cannot altogether ignore history if they are going to understand our ethical concepts at all. One reason for this is that in many cases the content of our concepts is a contingent historical phenomenon. This is for more than one reason. To take a case on which I am presently working, the virtues associated with truthfulness, I think it is clear that while there is a universal human need for qualities such as accuracy (the dispositions to acquire true beliefs) and sincerity (the disposition to say, if anything, what one believes to be true), the forms of these dispositions and of the motivations that they embody are culturally and historically various. If one is to understand our own view of such things, and to do so in terms that are on anyone's view philosophical—for instance, in order to relieve puzzlement about the basis of these values and their implications—one must try to understand why they take certain forms here rather than others, and one can only do that with the help of history. Moreover, there are some such virtues, such as authenticity or integrity of a certain kind, which are as a whole a manifestly contingent cultural development; they would not have evolved at all if Western history had not taken a certain course. For both these reasons, the reflective understanding of our ideas and motivations, which I take to be by general agreement a philosophical aim, is going to involve historical understanding. Here history helps philosophical understanding, or is part of it. Philosophy has to learn the lesson that conceptual description (or, more specifically, analysis) is not self-sufficient; and that such projects as deriving our concepts *a priori* from universal conditions of human life, though they indeed have a place (a greater place in some areas of philosophy than others), are likely to leave unexplained many features that provoke philosophical enquiry.

6. There are other respects, however, in which historical understanding can seem not to help the philosophical enterprise, but to get in the way of it. If we thought that our outlook had a history which was vindicatory, we might to that extent ignore it, precisely as scientists ignore the history of science. (One can glimpse here the enormous and implausible assumptions made by those who think that philosophy can ignore its own history.) But if we do not believe that the history of our outlook is vindicatory,

then understanding the history of our outlook may seem to interfere with our commitment to it, and in particular with a philosophical attempt to work within it and develop its arguments. If it is a contingent development that happens to obtain here and now, can we fully identify with it? Is it really *ours* except in the sense that we and it happen to be in the same place at the same time?

To some extent, this is one version of a problem that has recurred in European thought since historical self-consciousness struck deep roots in the early nineteenth century: a problem of reflection *versus* commitment, or of an external view of one's beliefs as opposed to an internal involvement with them—a problem, as it might be called, of historicist weariness and alienation. It may be a testimony to the power of this problem that so many liberal philosophers want to avoid any question of the history of their own views. It may also be significant in this connection that so much robust and influential political philosophy comes from the United States, which has no history of emerging from the *ancien régime*, since (very roughly speaking) it emerged from it by the mere act of coming into existence.

One philosopher, and indeed an American philosopher, who has raised the question within the local tradition is Richard Rorty, and he has suggested that the answer to it lies in irony:[13] that *qua* political actors we are involved in the outlook, but *qua* reflective people (for instance, as philosophers) we stand back and in a detached and rather quizzical spirit see ourselves as happening to have that attachment. The fact that 'qua' should come so naturally into formulating this outlook shows, as almost always in philosophy, that someone is trying to separate the inseparable: in this case, the ethically inseparable, and probably the psychologically inseparable as well, unless the ironist joins the others (the outlook that Rorty calls 'common sense') and forgets about historical self-understanding altogether, in which case he can forget his irony as well, and indeed does not need it.

In fact, as it seems to me, once one goes *far enough* in recognizing contingency, the problem to which irony is supposed to provide the answer does not arise at all. What we have here is very like something that we have already met in this discussion, the phenomenon of counterfactual scientism. The supposed problem comes from the idea that a vindicatory history of our outlook is what we would really like to have, and the discovery that liberalism, in particular (but the same is true of any outlook), has the kind of contingent history that it does have is a disappointment, which leaves us with at best a second best. But, once again, why should we think that? Precisely because we are not unencumbered intelligences selecting in principle among all possible outlooks, we can accept that this outlook is ours just because of the history that has made it ours; or, more precisely, has both made us and made the outlook as something that is ours. We are no less contingently formed than the outlook is, and the formation is significantly the same. We and our outlook are not simply in the same

[13] Richard Rorty, *Contingency, Irony and Solidarity* (Cambridge University Press, 1989), especially Chapters 3 and 4.

place at the same time. If we really understand this, deeply understand it, we can be free of what is indeed another scientistic illusion, that it is our job as rational agents to search for, or at least move as best we can towards, a system of political and ethical ideas which would be the best from an absolute point of view, a point of view that was free of contingent historical perspective.

If we can get rid of that illusion, we shall see that there is no inherent conflict among three activities: first, the first-order activities of acting and arguing within the framework of our ideas; second, the philosophical activity of reflecting on those ideas at a more general level and trying to make better sense of them; and third, the historical activity of understanding where they came from. The activities are in various ways continuous with one another. This helps to define both intelligence in political action (because of the connection of the first with the second and the third), and also realism in political philosophy (because of the connection of the second with the first and the third). If there is a difficulty in combining the third of these activities with the first two, it is the difficulty of thinking about two things at once, not a problem in consistently taking both of them seriously.

7. In fact, we are very unlikely to be able to make complete sense of our outlook. It will be in various ways incoherent. The history may help us to understand why this should be so: for instance, the difficulties that liberalism has at the present time with ideas of autonomy can be traced in part to Enlightenment conceptions of the individual which do not fully make sense to us now. In these circumstances, we may indeed be alienated from parts of our own outlook. If the incoherence is severe enough, it will present itself to us, who hold this outlook, as a crisis of explanation: we need to have reasons for rearranging and developing our ideas in one way rather than another. At the same time, we may perhaps see the situation as a crisis of legitimation—that there is a real question whether these ideas will survive and continue to serve us. Others who do not share the outlook can see the crisis of legitimation, too, but they cannot see it as a crisis of explanation for themselves, since they did not think that our outlook made sense of things in the first place. We, however, need reasons internal to our outlook not just to solve explanatory problems, but in relation to the crisis of legitimation as well. We need them, for one thing, to explain ourselves to people who are divided between our present outlook and some contemporary active rival. If things are bad enough, those people may include ourselves.

There may be no crisis. Or if there is, there will be some elements in our outlook which are fixed points within it. We believe, for instance, that in some sense every citizen, indeed every human being—some people, more extravagantly, would say every sentient being—deserves equal consideration. Perhaps this is less a propositional belief than the schema of various arguments. But in either case it can seem, at least in its most central and unspecific form, *unhintergehbar*: there is nothing more basic in terms of which to justify it. We know that most people in the past have not shared it; we know that there are others in the world who do not share it now. But for us, it is simply there. This does not mean that we have the thought: 'for us, it is simply there.' It means that we have the thought: 'it is simply there.' (That is what it is for it to be, for us, simply there.)

With regard to these elements of our outlook, at least, a philosopher may say: the contingent history has no effect in the space of reasons (to use a fashionable phrase), so why bother about it?[14] Let us just get on with our business of making best sense of our outlook from inside it. There are several answers to this, some implicit in what I have already said. One is that philosophers reflecting on these beliefs or modes of argument may turn back to those old devices of cognitive reassurance such as 'intuition'. But if the epistemic claims implicit in such terms are to be taken seriously, then there are implications for history—they imply a *different* history. Again, what we think about these things affects our view of people who have different outlooks in the present, outlooks that present themselves as rivals to ours. To say simply that these people are wrong in our terms is to revert to the thin tune that we have already heard in the case of disapproval over the centuries. It matters why these people believe what they do; for instance, whether we can reasonably regard their outlook as simply archaic, an expression of an order which happens to have survived into an international environment in which it cannot last, socially or intellectually. This matters both for the persuasion of uncommitted parties, as I have already said, but also for making sense of the others in relation to ourselves—and hence of ourselves in relation to them. Even with regard to those elements of our outlook for which there are no further justifications, there can still be explanations which help to locate them in relation to their rivals.

Above all, historical understanding—perhaps I may now say, more broadly, social understanding—can help with the business, which is quite certainly a philosophical business, of distinguishing between different ways in which various of our ideas and procedures can seem to be such that we cannot get beyond them, that there is no conceivable alternative. This brings us back to Wittgenstein. Wittgenstein influentially and correctly insisted that there was an end to justifications, that at various points we run into the fact that 'this is the way we go on'. But, if I may say again something that I have said rather often before,[15] it makes a great difference who 'we' are supposed to be, and it may mean different groups in different philosophical connections. It may mean maximally, as I mentioned earlier, any creature that you and I could conceive of understanding. Or it may mean any human beings, and here universal conditions of human life, including very general psychological capacities, may be relevant. Or it may mean just those with whom you and I share much more, such as outlooks typical

[14] This is (in effect) a central claim of Thomas Nagel's book *The Last Word* (Oxford University Press, 1997). His arguments bear closely on the present discussion. I have commented on them in a review of the book, *New York Review of Books* XLV, 18 (November 19, 1998).

[15] See e.g. 'Wittgenstein and Idealism', reprinted in *Moral Luck* (Cambridge University Press, 1981). The question of idealism is not relevant in the present context.

of modernity. Wittgenstein himself inherited from Kant a concern with the limits of understanding, from Frege and Russell an interest in the conditions of linguistic meaning, and from himself a sense of philosophy as a quite peculiar and possibly pathological enterprise. These influences guided him towards the most general questions of philosophy, and, with that, to a wide understanding of 'we', but they also conspired to make him think that philosophy had nothing to do with explanations—not merely scientific explanations (he was certainly the least scientistic of philosophers), but any explanations at all, except philosophical explanations: and they were not like other explanations, but rather like elucidations or reminders. In this sense, his ways of doing philosophy, and indeed his doubts about it, still focused on a conception of philosophy's subject matter as being exclusively *a priori*. That is a conception which we have good reason to question, and so, indeed, did he.

Once we give up that assumption, we can take a legitimate philosophical interest in what is agreed to be a more local 'us'. But it may be said that when it is specifically this more restricted group that is in question, it cannot be that there are no conceivable alternatives. Surely the history I have been going on about is a history of alternatives? But that is a misunderstanding of what, in this context, is being said to be inconceivable. History presents alternatives only in terms of a wider 'us': it presents alternative ways, that is to say various ways, in which human beings have lived and hence can live. Indeed, in those terms we may be able to conceive, if only schematically and with difficulty, other ways in which human beings might live in the future. But that is not the point. What in this connection seem to be simply there, to carry no alternative with them, are elements of our ethical and political outlook, and in those terms there are no alternatives for us. Those elements are indeed *unhintergehbar*, in a sense that indeed involves time, but in a way special to this kind of case. We can explore them on this side, in relation to their past, and explain them, and (if, as I have already said, we abandon scientistic illusions) we can identify with the process that led to our outlook because we can identify with its outcome. But we cannot in our thought go beyond our outlook into the future and remain identified with the result: that is to say, we cannot overcome our outlook. If a possible future that figures in those shadowy speculations does not embody some interpretation of these central elements of our outlook, then it may make empirical sense to us—we can see how someone could get there—but it makes no ethical sense to us, except as a scene of retrogression, or desolation, or loss.

It is connected with this that modern ethical and political conceptions typically do not allow for a future beyond themselves. Marxism predicted a future which was supposed to make ethical sense, but it notoriously came to an end in a static Utopia. Many liberals in their own way follow the same pattern; they go on, in this respect as with respect to the past, as though liberalism were timeless.[16] It is not a reproach to

---

[16] This needs qualification with regard to the more recent work of Rawls, which displays a stronger sense of historical contingency than was present in *A Theory of Justice*.

these liberals that they cannot see beyond the outer limits of what they find accept-able: no-one can do that. But it is more of a reproach that they are not interested enough in why this is so, in why their most basic convictions should seem to be, as I put it, simply there. It is part and parcel of a philosophical attitude that makes them equally uninterested in how those convictions got there.

8. I have argued that philosophy should get rid of scientistic illusions, that it should not try to behave like an extension of the natural sciences (except in the special cases where that is what it is), that it should think of itself as part of a wider humanistic enterprise of making sense of ourselves and of our activities, and that in order to answer many of its questions it needs to attend to other parts of that enterprise, in particular to history.

But someone, perhaps a young philosopher, may say: that is all very well, but even if I accept it all, doesn't it mean that there is too much that we need to know, that one can only do philosophy by being an amateur of altogether too much? Can't we just get on with it?

To him or her I can only say: I entirely see your, that is to say our, problem. I accept that analytic philosophy owes many of its successes to the principle that small and good is better than broad and bad. I accept that this involves a division of labour. I accept that you want to get on with it. I also admit something else, that it is typically senior philosophers who, like senior scientists, tend to muse in these expansive ways about the nature of their subject. As Nietzsche says in a marvellous passage about the philosopher and age:[17]

It quite often happens that the old man is subject to the delusion of a great moral renewal and rebirth, and from this experience he passes judgments on the work and course of his life, as if he had only now become clear-sighted; and yet the inspiration behind this feeling of well-being and these confident judgments is not wisdom, but *weariness*.

However, there are things to be said about how one might accept the view of philoso-phy that I am offering, and yet get on with it. Let me end by mentioning very briefly one or two of them. One thing we need to do is not to abandon the division of labour but to reconsider it. It tends to be modelled too easily on that of the sciences, as divid-ing one field or area of theorizing from another, but we can divide the subject up in other ways—by thinking of one given ethical idea, for instance, and the various con-siderations that might help one to understand it. Again, while it is certainly true that we all need to know more than we can hope to know—and that is true of philosophers who work near the sciences, or indeed in them, as well—it makes a difference what it is that you know you do not know. One may not see very far outside one's own house, but it can be very important which direction one is looking in.

---

[17] Friedrich Niezsche, *Daybreak*, sec. 542.

Moreover, it is not only a matter of research or philosophical writing. There is the question of what impression one gives of the subject in teaching it. Most students have no interest in becoming professional philosophers. They often take away an image of philosophy as a self-contained technical subject, and this can admittedly have its own charm as something complicated which can be well or badly done, and that is not to be despised. It also in some ways makes the subject easier to teach, since it less involves trying to find out how much or how little the students know about anything else. But if we believe that philosophy might play an important part in making people think about what they are doing, then philosophy should acknowledge its connections with other ways of understanding ourselves, and if it insists on not doing so, it may seem to the student in every sense quite peculiar.

We run the risk, in fact, that the whole humanistic enterprise of trying to understand ourselves is coming to seem peculiar. For various reasons, education is being driven towards an increasing concentration on the technical and the commercial, to a point at which any more reflective enquiry may come to seem unnecessary and archaic, something that at best is preserved as part of the heritage industry. If that is how it is preserved, it will not be the passionate and intelligent activity that it needs to be. We all have an interest in the life of that activity—not just a shared interest, but an interest in a shared activity.

Introduction to David J. Chalmers' Lecture

Ted Honderich

David Chalmers came from Australia to Oxford as a Rhodes Scholar, furthered his work in neuroscience and philosophy in several American universities, and is now professor of philosophy at New York University and also director of the Centre for Consciousness at the Australian National University. He has also been the moving spirit of the principal international conference on consciousness at the University of Arizona. He has the distinction of insisting, to science in particular, on 'the hard problem' with respect to consciousness, which term he put into the contemporary philosophical vernacular. His response to the problem, principally in his book *The Conscious Mind* (1996), recognizes the relevant science while espousing not only what he calls a naturalistic dualism of brain and mind rather than a philosophically ordinary physicalism, but also a version of panpsychism, the idea that everything whatever has an inner conscious aspect.

His lecture below is one of the two or three in this volume that are least in need of introduction—anyway least in need of a helping hand for readers on account of assumptions made and language used. It is as clear as a bell. The headings of its seven parts tell all.

(1) The central thesis of the lecture is that there has not been an extent of consensus in philosophy, of convergence on truth rather than any other kind of consensus, with respect to about ten big problems, including mind and body, consciousness in particular, knowledge of the external world, right and wrong, god, and free will. There has not been as much consensus or convergence as in in hard science about its big problems.

(2) The argument for the central thesis rests mainly on an empirical premise and what is called a bridging premise. The empirical premise is a matter of a poll carried out of philosophers in leading departments and their extents of disagreement on thirty important questions. These included the big problems but

also questions about political commitments, aesthetic value, truth, laws of nature, time, personal identity, proper names, and so on. The argument for the central thesis also includes responses to objections to it.

(3) Admittedly, there *are* varieties of progress in philosophy, kinds of agreement— as much as is consistent with the central thesis of comparison with science.

(4) That philosophy is a matter of *argument* as distinct from proof in mathematics or scientific method in the hard sciences is an initial explanation of the disagreement in philosophy. As a result, philosophy typically issues not in agreements but in sophisticated disagreements.

(5) New philosophical methods such as those in empirical philosophy and feminist philosophy have indeed been added to those of the past. But the new methods have not changed the general situation, in particular the possibility of the denial of other people's premises in philosophy.

(6) The possible further and deeper explanation of the apparent relative lack of philosophical progress includes problems dealt with but moved from philosophy into science. The further explanation also includes some big problems in philosophy not being about truth, the existence of verbal disputes, greater distance from the data, and what are called sociological and psychological effects.

(7) The prospects for more progress in philosophy at least bring up the question of whether such problems as that of consciousness are mysteries beyond our human minds. But since that has not been shown, we don't have to give up, we can keep at philosophy.

That this lecture of exemplary good order leaves your introducer to it with less to do also leaves him more free to think about questions. One is that of how close what you have heard is to the proposition that philosophy is *harder* than science—maybe the question of whether science's being less hard is to be regarded as a shortcoming of philosophy. I don't think so. And does disagreement in science need more recognition than is given to it? That is brought to mind by something mentioned in passing, what without deference to science is called by me the mess that is the applying of fundamental physics to the world, the interpretation of the mathematics of quantum mechanics.

And would it be fair to suppose that the lecture itself, being an instance of metaphilosophy, philosophy about philosophy, applies to itself? Is *it* not quite up to snuff? And can there be conceivably be any inferiority in philosophy's asking questions which include right and wrong, democracy, and the general fact of being conscious? Could they, so to speak, be avoidable, a matter of choice? And what is to be said of the bearing of this lecture on Bernard Williams' lecture? And vice versa?

18

Why Isn't There More Progress in Philosophy?

David J. Chalmers

Is there progress in philosophy?[1] I have two reactions to this question. First, the answer is obviously yes. Second, it is the wrong question. The right question is not "Is there progress?" but "Why isn't there more?"

We can distinguish three questions about philosophical progress. The Existence Question: is there progress in philosophy? The Comparison Question: is there as much progress in philosophy as in science? The Explanation Question (which tends to presuppose a negative answer to at least one of these two questions): why isn't there more progress in philosophy?

What we might call a glass-half-full view of philosophical progress is that there is some progress in philosophy. The glass-half-empty view is that there is not as much as we would like. In effect, the glass-half-full view consists in a positive answer to the Existence Question, while the glass-half-empty view (or at least one salient version of it) consists in a negative answer to the Comparison Question. These views fall between the extremes of a glass-empty view which answers no to the Existence Question, saying there is no progress in philosophy, and a glass-full thesis which answers yes to the Comparison Question, saying there is as much progress in philosophy as in science (or as much as we would like).

Of course the glass-half-full thesis and the glass-half-empty thesis are consistent with one another. I think for almost anyone deeply involved with the practice of philosophy, both theses will ring true. In discussions of progress in philosophy, my experience is that most people focus on the Existence Question: pessimists about

  [1] I first gave a brief version of this paper at the Harvard-Australia conference on Progress in Philosophy at Harvard University in 2011. Thanks to audiences there, on subsequent occasions in Arizona, Cambridge, Fordham, Liverpool, Oslo, Rio, Santiago, and at the Royal Institute for Philosophy lecture in London. Thanks also to participants in a number of useful Internet discussions. For comments on the written version, thanks to Russell Blackford, Melissa Ebbers, Alan Hájek, Robin Hanson, John Keller, Mark Lance, Seth Lazar, Christian List, Luke Muehlhauser, Rick Repetti, and Joshua Weisberg.

philosophical progress (e.g. Dietrich 2010; Nielsen 1987; McGinn 1993) argue for the glass-empty thesis, and optimists (e.g. Stoljar forthcoming) respond by defending the glass-half-full thesis. I will focus instead on the Comparison and Explanation Questions. I will articulate a version of the glass-half-empty thesis, argue for it, and then address the crucial question of what explains it.

I should say this paper is as much an exercise in the sociology of philosophy as in philosophy. For the most part I have abstracted away from my own philosophical and metaphilosophical views in order to take an "outside view" of philosophical progress from a sociological perspective. For much of the paper I am largely saying the obvious, but sometimes the obvious is worth saying so that less obvious things can be said from there. Only toward the end will I bring in my own views, which lean a little more toward the optimistic, and see how the question of philosophical progress stands in light of them.

1 The Central Thesis

The form of a glass-half-empty thesis is: there is less progress in philosophy than some benchmark. To articulate such a thesis more precisely, one needs to articulate a measure of progress and a benchmark. The measure of progress I will use is collective convergence to the truth. The benchmark I will use is comparison to the hard sciences.

Here I take inspiration from Peter van Inwagen (2004, p. 332), who writes:

Disagreement in philosophy is pervasive and irresoluble. There is almost no thesis in philosophy about which philosophers agree. If there is any philosophical thesis that all or most philosophers affirm, it is a negative thesis: that formalism is not the right philosophy of mathematics, for example, or that knowledge is not (simply) justified true belief.

That is not how things are in the physical sciences. I concede that the "cutting edge" of elementary-particle physics looks a lot like philosophy in point of pervasive and fundamental disagreement among its respected practitioners. But there is in physics a large body of settled, usable, uncontroversial theory and of measurements known to be accurate within limits that have been specified. The cutting edge of philosophy, however, is pretty much the whole of it.

Van Inwagen's thesis is not explicitly about progress, and the general tenor of his discussion suggests something closer to a glass-empty thesis than a glass-half-empty thesis. I think that at least once the issue is made a little more precise, however, a glass-half-empty thesis is more defensible.

Here is my central thesis: There has not been large collective convergence to the truth on the big questions of philosophy.

Here the big questions of philosophy are questions like: What is the relationship between mind and body? How do we know about the external world? What are the fundamental principles of morality? Is there a god? Do we have free will? I will not try to provide a more precise list than this, but any philosopher can come up with a list of 10 or so big questions fairly easily, and I suspect that there would be a lot of overlap between these lists. We could even use these lists to operationally define the big questions: the big questions of a field at time *t* are those that members of that field would count as the big questions of the field at time *t*. For purposes of comparison, we may want to impose some regimentation on the form of the big questions, for example formulating them all as choices between a small number of mutually exhaustive options.

We can define collective convergence on an answer over a period as the increase in degree of agreement on that answer from the start of the period to the end of the period. Degree of agreement can be defined using one of various mathematical measures of agreement across a group of people on a set of issues.[2] Collective convergence (simpliciter) over a period is defined as the collective convergence on the dominant answer at the end of that period over the period. The degree of agreement at a time on answers to the big questions at the same time will usually be low, as disagreement on the answer to a question is highly relevant to making it a big question. Convergence over a period provides a more discriminating measure, which can reasonably be expected to be high in some cases and low in others. For our purposes we could choose an arbitrary period (say, from 200 years ago to today), or perhaps better, choose many different periods and take the average convergence over those periods.[3]

We can say that *large* collective convergence over a period requires as much convergence as there has been over big questions in the hard sciences in the same period. Here I will take the hard sciences to include at least mathematics and the natural sciences: paradigmatically physics, chemistry, and biology. I set aside the cognitive and social sciences, which have arguably seen less convergence on the answers to their big questions. For current purposes I do not need to take a stand on how philosophy fares relative to these.

Large collective convergence to the truth in a period requires large collective convergence to true answers to the big questions over that period. That is, we must have as much increased agreement on *true* answers to the big questions as in the hard sciences. Because of the reference to truth, large collective convergence requires a

---

[2] I leave open the question of just what measure of agreement is best for present purposes. One useful measure is Krippendorff's alpha (Krippendorff 2013, pp. 221–50), equal to $1 - (D_o/D_e)$, where D_o is the observed incidence of disagreement between respondents (summed over all pairs of respondents and all questions) and D_e is the expected incidence through chance alone. This measure can be applied to communities of different sizes (not all of whose members need have a view on a given issue) and to questions whose answers have many different sorts of structure. Disagreement is weighted by a measure of "distance" between any two answers, which makes alpha particularly helpful in comparing questions with different numbers of answers. With such a metric in hand, one can use a version of alpha to measure communal degree of agreement with a specific answer. For the purposes above, what is needed is a variant on Krippendorff's alpha that measures communal degree of agreement with a specific answer. Some rescaling may be useful (e.g. imposing a lower bound of zero and then squaring).

[3] Here I am not invoking the standard mathematical notion of convergence, which applies to infinite series or infinite times rather than discrete periods and which would require that the community eventually come arbitrarily close to universal consensus on an issue. But an element of its flavour will be present if our measure of agreement has some bias toward universal agreement (as the rescaled version of Krippendorff's alpha does), so that for example a shift from 79% to 99% of the community agreeing on an answer to a binary question counts as greater convergence than a shift from 40% to 60%.

degree of realism about the domains in question. But something like convergence to the truth is required in order that the convergence constitutes progress and not regress.

2 Argument for the Central Thesis

Here is an argument for the central thesis. It has two premises: an empirical premise and a bridging premise.

(1) Empirical premise: There has not been large collective convergence on the big questions of philosophy.

(2) Bridging premise: If there has not been large collective convergence on the big questions of philosophy, there has not been large collective convergence to the truth on the big questions of philosophy.

(3) Conclusion: There has not been large collective convergence to the truth on the big questions of philosophy.

The argument is valid. The bridging premise may look like a logical truth, but it is not. The antecedent of this conditional premise says that there is less convergence on dominant answers to the big questions in philosophy than in the hard sciences, while the consequent says that there is less convergence on true answers to those questions. These may come apart in a way that renders the conditional false if there has been strong convergence to the false (or strong convergence un-correlated with truth) in the sciences along with weak convergence to the truth in philosophy. Still, given that convergence in science is largely convergence to the truth, or merely that convergence in science is at least as likely to be convergence to the truth as convergence in philosophy, then the premise is plausible.[4]

One may worry that because most scientific theories eventually turn out to be false, most convergence in science will be convergence to the false. This worry is less pressing if we formulate questions in terms of a small number of mutually exhaustive choices, as suggested earlier. This way, convergence to the truth will require only convergence on a correct coarse-grained class of theories, rendering it much more plausible that much convergence in science has been convergence to the truth. Alternatively, if questions allow an open-ended range of answers, then invoking a metric for distance between answers (also suggested earlier) will allow that agreement on strictly speaking false theory that is relatively close to the truth constitutes a sort of convergence to the truth.

The main work in the argument is done by the empirical premise. I take it that it will be plausible to those with passing familiarity with philosophical and scientific

---

[4] Thanks to Hedda Hassel Morch and Rory Madden for pointing out ways in which the bridging premise could turn out to be false.

practice. Still, it makes a sociological claim and cannot be decisively settled from the armchair. We do not have all the empirical data required for a systematic investigation of the premise, but we have some of it.

The 2009 PhilPapers Survey (Bourget and Chalmers 2014) surveyed professional philosophers on answers to 30 important questions in philosophy. The survey was sent to the members of 99 leading departments of philosophy (largely specializing in analytic/Anglocentric philosophy) in North America, Europe, and Australasia. About 47% of the 2000 or so recipients of the survey filled out and returned the survey. Questions were posed as a choice between two, three, or four options. Respondents could indicate that they "accept" or "lean toward" one option, or give a variety of "other" answers (e.g., unfamiliar with the issue, the question is too ambiguous to answer, there is no fact of the matter, accept another option, and so on). The results (collapsing "accept" and "lean toward" answers, and collapsing "other" answers) were as follows.

(1) A priori knowledge: yes 71%, no 18%, other 11%.

(2) Abstract objects: Platonism 39%, nominalism 38%, other 23%.

(3) Aesthetic value: objective 41%, subjective 35%, other 24%.

(4) Analytic/synthetic distinction: yes 65%, no 27%, other 8%.

(5) Epistemic justification: externalism 43%, internalism 26%, other 31%.

(6) External world: non-skeptical realism 82%, skepticism 5%, idealism 4%, other 9%.

(7) Free will: compatibilism 59%, libertarianism 14%, no free will 12%, other 15%.

(8) God: atheism 73%, theism 15%, other 13%.

(9) Knowledge claims: contextualism 40%, invariantism 31%, relativism 3%, other 26%.

(10) Knowledge: empiricism 35%, rationalism 28%, other 37%.

(11) Laws of nature: non-Humean 57%, Humean 25%, other 18%.

(12) Logic: classical 52%, non-classical 15%, other 33%.

(13) Mental content: externalism 51%, internalism 20%, other 29%.

(14) Meta-ethics: moral realism 56%, moral anti-realism 28%, other 16%.

(15) Metaphilosophy: naturalism 50%, non-naturalism 26%, other 24%.

(16) Mind: physicalism 57%, non-physicalism 27%, other 16%.

(17) Moral judgment: cognitivism 66%, non-cognitivism 17%, other 17%.

(18) Moral motivation: internalism 35%, externalism 30%, other 35%.

(19) Newcomb's problem: two boxes 31%, one box 21%, other 47%.

(20) Normative ethics: deontology 26%, consequentialism 24%, virtue ethics 18%, other 32%.

(21) Perceptual experience: representationalism 32%, qualia theory 12%, disjunctivism 11%, sense-datum theory 3%, other 42%.

(22) Personal identity: psychological view 34%, biological view 17%, further-fact view 12%, other 37%.

(23)   Politics: egalitarianism 35%, communitarianism 14%, libertarianism 10%, other 41%.

(24)   Proper names: Millian 34%, Fregean 29%, other 37%.

(25)   Science: scientific realism 75%, scientific anti-realism 12%, other 13%.

(26)   Teletransporter: survival 36%, death 31%, other 33%.

(27)   Time: B-theory 26%, A-theory 16%, other 58%.

(28)   Trolley problem: switch 68%, don't switch 8%, other 24%.

(29)   Truth: correspondence 51%, deflationary 25%, epistemic 7%, other 17%.

(30)   Zombies: conceivable but not metaphysically possible 36%, metaphysically possible 23%, inconceivable 16%, other 25%.

The degree of disagreement here is striking, if unsurprising. Only one view (non-skeptical realism about the external world) attracts over 80% support. Three views (a priori knowledge, atheism, scientific realism) attract over 70% support, with significant dissent, and three more views attract over 60% support. On the other 23 questions, the leading view has less than 60% support.

Admittedly, not all of the questions are among the "big questions" of the past, but certainly some are: the questions about the external world, free will, god, knowledge, meta-ethics, metaphilosophy, mind, and normative ethics, for example. Only two of these (external world, god) have views with over 60% support (and in the case of the external world question, the consensus is somewhat misleading, since arguably the biggest question is *how* we know about the external world).

For fuller data to adjudicate the central thesis, we would need the results of the PhilPapers Survey not just in 2009, but at regular intervals in the past: 1909, 1809, and so on. At each point we would need to ask members of the philosophical community first, what they take to be the big questions of philosophy, and second, what they take to be the answers to those questions as well as to big questions from past surveys. We would also need to have analogous longitudinal surveys in other fields: the MathPapers Survey, the PhysPapers survey, the ChemPapers Survey, the BioPapers Survey, and so on. And we would need a reasonable measure of agreement at a time. I predict that if we had such surveys and measures, we would find much less convergence on answers to the big questions suggested by past surveys of philosophers than we would find for corresponding answers in other fields.

Some partial data is given by the 23 problems that David Hilbert posed for mathematics in 1900 (Hilbert 1902; Yandell 2002). Around 10 of these 23 problems have been clearly solved, leading to universal consensus, and seven have been partially solved, leading to partial consensus. A similar pattern could reasonably be expected in physics, chemistry, and biology. We can compare these results to the problems in Bertrand Russell's 1912 *The Problems of Philosophy*.[5] None of these have led to universal convergence and almost none have led to anything close.

---

[5]   Thanks to Jeremy Goodman for suggesting the Hilbert/Russell comparison.

Of course one can object to the thesis in various ways. One could argue that there has been more convergence on the big philosophical questions of the past than these case studies suggest. Alternatively, one could argue that there has been less convergence on the big scientific questions of the past than they suggest.

A version of the first objection springs from the observation that disciplines such as physics were once considered part of philosophy. If we go back to a time before the split, then insofar as the big questions of physics are among the big questions of philosophy at that point, high convergence on the former will lead to significant convergence on the latter. Still, insofar as physics was just a proper part of philosophy, and one more susceptible to convergence than the other parts, one would still expect convergence on the former to produce less convergence on the latter. It is also not entirely clear that philosophy *as we understand it* should get the credit for the convergence in physics: what was called philosophy in the past was arguably a different and broader field.

In any case, one can bypass this objection by focusing on a point after the split between physics and philosophy: 1809 or 1909, say. The objector might respond that now there will be less convergence in philosophy only because we have split off the parts of it that have made most progress. But this is to concede the central thesis and argue for a certain explanation of it, one that I consider later in the paper. Another response is that there were further splits after this point: psychology, logic, linguistics, and economics, for example. Still, I think that the questions resolved by these areas constitute a small enough fraction of the big questions of philosophy in 1809 or 1909 that even if philosophy gets credit for them, this will not bring the level of convergence in philosophy close to the corresponding level in the hard sciences.

Another version of the first objection suggests that some big philosophical questions of the past have reached consensus and so have dropped off the list of big questions even without their own disciplines branching off. Perhaps something like this is plausible for some moral and political questions, for example, such as the question of whether all people are equal, where convergence within philosophy reflects convergence in society more generally. And there may have been questions that were regarded as truly important in a period (about the viability of certain versions of idealism, say) on which there is now a consensus view. The existence of questions like this helps to make a case against a glass-empty thesis. But where a glass-half-empty thesis is concerned, it suffices to note that the proportion of questions like these is lower in philosophy than in the hard sciences.

As for the second objection, one could argue that many of the big questions of the hard sciences are themselves philosophical questions and have seen low convergence: questions about the interpretation of quantum mechanics, for example, or about the locus of natural selection. But as long as some of the big questions of the hard sciences are not philosophical questions, as is surely plausible, and as long as these are more susceptible to convergence, then we would still expect the central thesis to be true. Furthermore, insofar as this objection relies on a contrast between philosophical and nonphilosophical questions, it tends to reinforce the underlying contrast in convergence.

It could also be suggested that numerous big nonphilosophical questions in the hard sciences have met with low convergence: questions about the origins of life, for example. This is surely right, but it remains plausible that enough have seen major convergence that there is still a significant difference between the nonphilosophical and the philosophical. The case of the Hilbert problems for mathematics brings this out. The problems are mostly nonphilosophical, and although some of them are unsolved, the overall convergence on them has been quite dramatic. Something similar plausibly applies in physics, chemistry, and biology.

A final objection is that even though there is more agreement now in the hard sciences than in philosophy, these sciences may also start from a position of more agreement, resulting in a smaller *increase* in agreement in the sciences than in philosophy. This hypothesis is mathematically consistent, but I do not think it is especially plausible. Especially given a measure of agreement that is biased toward universal agreement, as discussed earlier, and given that there is considerable disagreement over the big questions of a time at that time, then the various cases in which the hard sciences (unlike philosophy) approach universal consensus will tend to yield greater overall convergence as well.

3 The Varieties of Progress

Despite this lack of convergence, it is hard to deny that the insights of Plato and Aristotle, Hume and Kant, Frege and Russell, Kripke and Lewis have involved significant philosophical progress. Correspondingly, my glass-half-empty thesis is compatible with many different glass-half-full theses, asserting the existence of various forms of progress in philosophy. We can systematize various such theses by dropping the central requirements of my central thesis one at a time.

Drop "large": There has been (non-large) collective convergence to the truth on big questions of philosophy. It is plausible that there has been major convergence on answers to a small number of the big questions of philosophy: in questions about god there appears to have been major convergence toward atheism, for example. It is also plausible that there has been minor convergence on answers to many other questions, such as toward physicalism about the mind. Of course whether one counts this convergence as convergence to the truth will depend on one's own philosophical views. Theists and dualists will hold that the convergence constitutes regress rather than progress. But if we assume optimistically that the convergence is indeed convergence to the truth, it may be that 10–20% more philosophers have true beliefs about the answers to the big questions of 1809 in 2009 than in 1809. If so, that is a sort of progress. Still, it remains plausible that convergence is greater in other areas.

Drop "collective": There has been large (non-collective) convergence to the truth on the big questions of philosophy. The central thesis is consistent with the claim that various individuals or subcommunities have themselves had large convergence to true answers on the big questions. For example, on my more optimistic days I can convince myself that over time I have converged on the truth on many of these questions. But if so, sadly, it has not led to collective convergence on the truth. Likewise, perhaps groups such as the logical empiricists or the Oxford realists have converged on the truth. But again, community-wide convergence has not ensued. Perhaps there has even been a large amount of community-wide convergence at certain local temporal periods, but if so, this convergence has not persisted over time.

Drop "big": There has been large collective convergence to the truth on (non-big) questions of philosophy. There has been large convergence on various smaller theses: the thesis that knowledge is not justified true belief, for example, and the thesis that conditional probabilities are not probabilities of conditionals. As van Inwagen suggests in the passage above, we are especially good at converging on negative theses that rule out certain specific views. There is also often convergence on conditional theses, asserting conditional connections between views. But I take it that these are not really answers to the big questions of philosophy.

Drop "convergence to the truth": There have been large collective advances (not involving convergence to the truth) on the big questions of philosophy. Certainly there are many forms of philosophical progress that do not involve convergence to the truth. It is plausible that we have a greatly increased understanding of the issues underlying the big questions. We have come to explore new views and new areas of philosophical space that we had not even conceived of earlier. We have developed new methods and better arguments. In some cases we have applied philosophy to the world. These are all certainly forms of progress. I simply note that they have not been accompanied by large collective convergence to the truth.

I want to stress that I am not simply equating progress with convergence to the truth. I am a pluralist about progress: there are many values that can be realized through philosophy, and there are many ways of advancing and realizing those values. Attaining the truth is certainly not the only such value. Still, it is certainly one such value. It follows that progress toward the truth is one form of philosophical progress.

More strongly, I think a case can be made that attaining the truth is the primary aim at least of many parts of philosophy, such as analytic philosophy. After all, most philosophy, or at least most analytic philosophy, consists in putting forward theses as true and arguing for their truth. I suspect that for the majority of philosophers, the primary motivation in doing philosophy is to figure out the truth about the relevant subject areas: What is the relation between mind and body? What is the nature of reality and how can we know about it? Certainly this is the primary motivation in my own case. So I am sympathetic to the claim that progress toward the truth has a certain primacy among the forms of philosophical progress. But even if one denies this, it is hard to deny that it is among those forms.

It is sometimes said that an obsession with truth reflects an overly scientific conception of philosophy. We should not think of philosophy as a quest for the answers. Instead it is a quest for something else: understanding, clarity, enlightenment. I agree that these are goals worth pursuing, and that philosophy can help us pursue them. And I can see why, in the absence of answers to philosophical puzzles, it might seem especially appealing to focus on these goals instead. Still, I think we should acknowledge that this reaction involves something of a lowering of our sights for philosophy. At least pretheoretically, many of us get into philosophy looking for truth and looking for answers. One can argue that this hope is naive: truth and knowledge are not to be had in philosophy, and one should settle for something different. But even if so, both the hope and its naivety are worth marking.

Why is *convergence* to the truth important, and why should we be concerned about its absence? One obvious answer is that we value knowledge, agreement is required for knowledge, and convergence goes along with increases in knowledge. A strong version of this view, suggested by van Inwagen's discussion, is that where there is sufficient disagreement among experts, no individuals can be said to know the truth. Even if some individuals have hit on good arguments for true conclusions, how can they have justified confidence that these are good arguments, when so many of their peers disagree? I am not so sure: I think that at least in some cases, a good argument can ground an individual's knowledge of a conclusion even when peers reject it. For example, I think that the presence of any number of peers who deny the existence of consciousness would not undermine my knowledge that I am conscious. Likewise, it would not undermine arguments that take this claim as a premise.

But even if agreement is not required for individual knowledge, some degree of agreement is plausibly required for *collective* knowledge. If the community of experts on a question has serious disagreement over the answer to that question, then that community cannot be said to collectively know the answer to that question, and nor can the broader community of which they are a part. Even when some individuals know the answer to a question, this individual knowledge will not usually suffice for collective knowledge, except perhaps in special circumstances such as when the community defers to these individuals.

Furthermore, we value collective knowledge. One reason that progress of the hard sciences has been so impressive is that it has plausibly enabled us—the community of inquirers—to collectively know the answers to those questions. But in the absence of sufficient agreement on the answers to philosophical questions, we cannot be said to have collective knowledge of those answers.

Of course one can argue over just what degree and pattern of agreement is required for collective knowledge. But it is highly plausible that the kind of disagreement that we observe over the answers to the big questions of philosophy suffices to undermine any claims of collective knowledge of the answers to most of those questions. Perhaps one could argue that in the survey above, a few views (non-skeptical realism about the external world, atheism, a priori knowledge) display the sort of consensus that allows collective knowledge. But even that claim would be bold, and the extension to claims with less consensus (physicalism and compatibilism, say) seems so bold as to be implausible. So I take it that the difference in agreement on the big questions in science and philosophy reflects a significant difference in the collective knowledge that we have attained. Likewise, the difference in convergence on the big questions reflects a significant difference in the increase of collective knowledge over time.

This is not to deny that we have attained a great deal of collective knowledge in philosophy. As Timothy Williamson (2006) has said, we knew much more in 2004 than in 1964, much more in 1964 than in 1924, and so on. But this collective knowledge typically does not involve answers to the big questions. It is mainly knowledge of the answers to smaller questions, of negative and conditional theses, of frameworks available to answer questions, of connections between ideas, of the way that arguments bear for and against conclusions, and so on. In the absence of convergence on the big questions, collective knowledge of the answers to those questions eludes us.

4 Philosophical Argument

I now turn to the central question: why isn't there more progress in philosophy? And in particular: why is there less convergence in philosophy than in the hard sciences?

An initial explanation, though perhaps this is merely an articulation of the phenomenon, lies in the relative power of the methods used in these domains. The hard sciences have methods—proof in the case of mathematics, and the observational/experimental method in physics, chemistry, and biology—that have the power to compel agreement on the answers to the big question. Philosophy has a method—the method of argument—that does not.

What is the difference between these methods? One difference is that the methods of experiment and proof start from widely agreed premises—observations in science, axioms in mathematics—and proceed from there to strong and surprising conclusions. We aspire to do this in philosophy too: witness Russell's remark that the point of philosophy is to start with something so simple as not to seem worth stating, and to end with something so paradoxical that no one will believe it (Russell 1918). But in practice, widely agreed premises rarely suffice to ground strong and surprising conclusions in philosophy.

There are certainly many arguments for strong conclusions in philosophy. But in the great majority of cases, they have premises that opponents can deny without too much cost, or inferences that opponents can reject without too much cost. (I focus mainly on premises, but everything I say also applies to inferences, for example by turning nondeductive inferences into tacit premises of deductive arguments.) Sometimes the denied premise is antecedently plausible, and the denial somewhat surprising. But even then the denial rarely has the implausibility of denying a mathematical axiom, or of denying a well-replicated experimental observation. So these denials are usually tenable, at least in a broadly sociological sense of tenability.

Let us say that *consensus* premises (and inferences) are those that are regarded by the community as undeniable, or at least as incurring enormous cost for anyone who denies them. A consensus premise might be denied by a few outliers, but it cannot be subject to widespread disagreement within the community. Let us say that an argument that uses only consensus premises and inferences is a decisive argument. (Note that consensus premises and decisive arguments are both defined in sociological terms.) Then the claim is that while there are decisive arguments for strong conclusions in the sciences, there are relatively few such arguments in philosophy.

There are certainly some consensus premises in philosophical arguments. After all, these premises can include mathematical axioms and empirical observations themselves, as well as the theorems and theories that are grounded in them. But mathematical premises and empirical observations alone almost never suffice to draw strong philosophical conclusions. Further premises or inferences are required to bridge from science and mathematics to philosophy, and these premises and inferences are typically deniable.

In addition to mathematical axioms and empirical observations, there are some philosophical intuitions that are extremely difficult to deny. But these intuitions are not so common (many antecedently plausible intuitions turn out to be deniable), and where they exist, it is typically difficult to draw strong philosophical conclusions from them. There are some cases where these intuitions, perhaps in conjunction with mathematical and empirical claims, allow us to draw strong and surprising conclusions. This works particularly well for negative theses, where intuitions and formal models can generate counterexamples to positive theses or other reasons to reject them. Gettier's argument from an intuition about a case to the conclusion that knowledge is not justified true belief is one example. Lewis' formal argument that conditional probabilities are not probabilities of conditionals is perhaps another. But it is notable that these negative conclusions fall far short of answers to the big questions of philosophy. Almost any argument for a positive answer to these questions involves deniable premises.[6]

---

[6] To gather data here, I ran an informal Internet survey of philosophers, asking for arguments that are near-universally regarded by philosophers as establishing their conclusions. Further candidates included the forcible-organ donation argument against simple versions of utilitarianism, Kripke's argument that necessity comes apart from apriority, Gödel's argument against versions of mathematical formalism, the argument from evil against theism, the model-theoretic argument against global descriptivism, the perfect actor argument against logical behaviourism, the multiple-realizability argument against the identity theory, Goodman's argument against purely formal inductive logic, arguments from relativity against presentism, Frankfurt's argument that moral responsibility does not require the ability to do otherwise, Hart's argument against Austin's command theory of laws, Russell's refutation of Frege's Basic Law V, Moore's open question argument against analytic naturalism, Putnam's argument for externalism about meaning, Descartes' cogito, and many others.

It is striking that the great majority of these arguments are naturally regarded as arguments for negative conclusions, in that they are arguments against fairly specific views. Of course the negative/positive distinction is not entirely clear, but we have a reasonably intuitive grasp on it. A few conclusions have a positive flavour: one's existence (the cogito), externalism (Putnam), and perhaps the necessary a posteriori (Kripke) and atheism (the argument from evil). But the first three are at best marginal candidates for answers to big questions, and the survey data suggests that the second and fourth are at best marginal cases of near-universal agreement. All this reinforces the point that decisive arguments in philosophy are rare, that decisive arguments for positive views are even rarer, and decisive arguments for positive answers to the big questions are so rare as to be almost nonexistent.

For most practitioners of philosophy, the phenomenon of premise deniability is familiar from both sides. When we give arguments for our views, we are frustrated to find opponents biting the bullet by rejecting what we took to be a plausible premise, without this serving as any sign of defeat. When we address arguments against our views, we sometimes work backwards from our rejection of the conclusion to see which premises we have to deny, and we deny them. In the best cases, we learn something from this, and we take on commitments that we might have antecedently found surprising. But these commitments are rarely untenable to maintain.

As a result, philosophical arguments typically lead not to agreement but to sophisticated disagreement. Advocates of a view learn what extra commitments they need to take on to avoid the arguments. Bad versions of a view are rejected and sophisticated versions are developed in their place. This leads to a sort of negative progress where areas of philosophical space are eliminated, but only in small fragments at a time. It is rare for a major general view (materialism or dualism, compatibilism or incompatibilism, utilitarianism or deontology) to be eliminated in this way. Instead, there are large surviving fragments involving the views needed to avoid the arguments (type-B materialism with the phenomenal concept strategy, source incompatibilism, two-level utilitarianism, theism without unrestricted benevolence or omnipotence). The same sort of elimination, fragmentation, and refinement often recurs at these lower levels. The views that survive yield a sort of fractal structure to philosophical space, akin to the Mandelbrot set with its intricate complexities at all levels, but in which large regions of space are rarely eliminated entirely.

This phenomenon might strike one as a philosophical analogue of the Duhem-Quine thesis, in a version saying that any scientific theory can be made compatible with any evidence by appropriate adjustment to the background assumptions that bridge between theory and evidence. But in practice, scientific theories are often decisively rejected in light of evidence, with revised consistent versions of the theories being rejected as untenable. In effect, some (nondeductive) inferences from evidence to scientific theory have consensus status. Theories are ruled out not by consensus evidence alone, but by consensus evidence plus consensus inferences. In the philosophical case, however, consensus evidence plus consensus inferences are much less powerful. When someone argues against a philosophical theory, there is usually at least a revision of the theory that is not just consistent but tenable in light of the consensus evidence. Those who argue against a philosophical view sometimes accuse their resourceful opponents of holding onto a degenerating research programme, but it is typically much harder to make this charge stick in philosophy than in science. This could be because philosophers apply laxer standards to their theories, so that inferences that have consensus status among scientists do not have it among philosophers, but more plausibly it is because the same sort of inferences do not suffice to settle philosophical questions.

It might also be objected that, in science, positive theories are not usually established by single experiments, but by many experiments collectively. By parity, we might hope that even if positive philosophical theories are not established by single arguments, they might be established by a number of arguments collectively. There are perhaps a few cases of negative theses being established this way: the rejection of sense-datum theories of perception may be an example. But even these cases are rare, and positive cases are even rarer. In practice, if an opponent can reject individual arguments for a thesis without too much cost, they can usually reject collections of arguments without much cost too.

Does this mean that all philosophical arguments for positive theses are unsuccessful, as van Inwagen (2006) has suggested? (Van Inwagen talks about substantive theses, but his discussion suggests that these are required to be positive theses.) This depends on what one means by success. If one defines success in sociological terms, so that success requires convincing almost everyone in a community, then we have seen that at best very few philosophical arguments for positive theses have been successful in our community. Van Inwagen defines success in idealized epistemological terms: a successful argument for a proposition p is one that would convince an audience of ideal reasoners who are initially agnostic concerning p, in the presence of an ideal opponent of p. I do not think that the sociological observations above (or the sociological observations that van Inwagen appeals to) come close to establishing that no philosophical arguments are successful in that sense. (See McGrath and Kelly, forthcoming, for more on this theme.) Human beings are simply too far from ideal for that conclusion to follow.

It also does not follow from anything I have said that all philosophical arguments are question-begging, or that they are dialectically powerless. Even when arguments have deniable premises, they often have dialectical power, in that their premises have antecedent support that does not rest on considerations too close to the conclusion. In such a case the argument does not beg the question. Even though a sophisticated and committed opponent will deny the premise, the argument might well move an agnostic observer to accept the conclusion. In practice, we often use this sort of dialectical power as a criterion for a good argument that many philosophers can agree on, even if they disagree on the argument's ultimate persuasiveness.

I am also not saying that these arguments cannot produce knowledge. Deniable premises may nevertheless be known by many people to be true. As before, while too much disagreement over a claim may undermine collective knowledge of that claim, it need not undermine individual knowledge of that claim. Likewise, an argument can ground individual knowledge even when peers reject it. This applies all the more where non-peers are concerned. For all I have said, some arguments may have premises and inferences that can only be denied unreasonably, or by nonideal reasoners.

If so, these arguments may well produce knowledge in beings more reasonable than the deniers.

So it is not straightforward to draw conclusions about lack of normative force from premises about lack of sociological success. There is perhaps an intermediate normative notion, defining a successful argument as one with the power to persuade all *competent* agnostics, where competence is some reasonably high but nonideal standard of rationality that many human philosophers meet. There is good reason to think that few philosophical arguments for positive conclusions persuade all competent philosophers, or even all competent agnostics. On the face of it, disagreement on big questions among the most able philosophers (by any reasonably neutral measure) is about as rife as disagreement among philosophers more generally. This suggests that most philosophical arguments are not successful in the normative sense tied to competence, even if they are successful in the other normative senses.

Burton Dreben once memorably said to me (on the only occasion that I met him, in St. Louis around 1994): "Great philosophers don't argue." He went on to elaborate that none of Frege, Russell, Wittgenstein, Carnap, or Quine really give arguments for their views. Of course this is not strictly true, but I think his point was that in these philosophers, the real work is not done by arguments for a thesis, but by the thesis itself, or the framework it is embedded in. A refined version of his claim (suggested to me by Gene Callahan) might say: great philosophers may argue, but their arguments are not what makes them great. A part of Dreben's thought, as I understood it, was that since arguments are so easily rebutted, giving arguments is a sign of weakness. It's better to simply assert and develop a thesis. Then one's readers have to engage with the thesis itself, without the cheap distraction of rebutting arguments for the thesis.

(Rawls (2001) elaborates on Dreben's views in a somewhat different direction: "Burt would not, of course, deny the plain fact that philosophers make many complicated arguments. But he thinks that at bottom there are no arguments one philosopher can use to convince another of a metaphysical point. At the basic level, philosophers simply rely on and appeal to different 'data.' It is a standoff with no resolution by argument. Burt has said that Quine is a metaphysician, a metaphysician of science. By that he means that Quine doesn't argue for physicalism, or scientific realism. He assumes it and works out his view from there.")

I have found it impossible to follow Dreben's advice myself. In my work I am a compulsive arguer, which no doubt leaves me subject to a modus tollens from Dreben's thesis. But certainly it is rare that these arguments bring a large sector of the population around. This is especially so when many of the people already have firm commitments, as on issues such as the mind–body problem and the theory of meaning: here it is hard to do more than bring around a few people here and there. On issues where people are initially agnostic or their commitments are weak, there can be more movement.[7] Even here the fact that such movement is limited reinforces the basic point.

The upshot is that consensus in philosophy is as hard to obtain as it ever was, and decisive arguments are as rare as they ever were. To me, this is the largest disappointment in the practice of philosophy. Once one has been doing philosophy for a while, one no longer expects arguments to produce agreement, and one deems an argument good when it merely has some dialectical power. But this is an adjustment of expectations in response to a disappointing reality. Antecedently to doing philosophy, one might have hoped that something more was possible.

5 New Philosophical Methods

Faced with the failure of traditional philosophical methods, we might look to new methods. Occasionally, new methods developed by thinkers who considered themselves philosophers have helped to resolve questions once considered philosophical: witness the development of logic, physics, psychology, and so on. It is natural to hope that new methods might produce further progress.

In the last century or so, many new philosophical methods have been developed and many old methods have been refined, in order to help reach philosophical conclusions. Empirical philosophy draws on empirical science. Formal philosophy draws on formal reasoning. Linguistic philosophy draws on the analysis of language. Phenomenology draws on phenomenological reflection. Feminist philosophy draws on consideration and analysis of gender. Crosscultural philosophy draws on multiple cultural traditions in philosophy. Experimental philosophy draws on the empirical study of philosophical judgments.[8]

All of these methods have led to new insights and to philosophical progress. All have led to new arguments for interesting conclusions. But manifestly, none of these methods have led to recent convergence on answers to the big questions of philosophy. In the wake of each of these methods, philosophical disagreement is as rife as it ever was. Even within a tradition, there are few cases where the big questions are regarded as settled. Instead, these methods have led us again to more sophisticated versions of old disagreements.

---

[7] To indulge in autobiography: I have the sense that my arguments with Andy Clark for the extended mind thesis (an area where prior commitments were relatively weak) may have brought more people around than my arguments against physicalism or for two-dimensional semantics (areas where prior commitments are strong). Even there I suspect that the thesis and the framework have brought around as many people as the arguments. Perhaps most effective of all has been the argument in "The Matrix as Metaphysics", which brings many people around to the view that if we are in a matrix scenario or that if we are brains in vats, most of our beliefs are true. (At least it does this in lecture presentations and informal discussions; there has been relatively little discussion of the argument in print.) Although people find this view initially counterintuitive, it turns out that their antecedent commitment was weak.

[8] Then there are many other methods that I am not competent to discuss. For example, Nielsen (1987) suggests that the one hope for progress in philosophy is critical theory.

In many cases, the basic problem is that of premise deniability. In the case of empirical and formal philosophy, we have already seen that empirical and formal results must be combined with further bridging premises to settle a philosophical question. In most cases, it turns out that these bridging premises can be denied. Often they are about as controversial as the conclusions they aim to establish. In some cases, empirical and formal results help to settle relatively small questions, as well as introducing and addressing new important questions. But when they are brought to bear on the big questions, it is rare that they do much to produce consensus.

There are some partial exceptions: perhaps the bearing of evolution on theism, the bearing of relativity on presentism, and the bearing of Gödel's theorem on mathematical formalism. But these exceptions are not especially common, and even in these cases, there are modified versions of the relevant views that have retained numerous serious adherents. What exceptions there are seem mainly to fall into two classes. First, there are cases where empirical methods bear strongly on areas of philosophy that focus on concrete reality, such as subfields of metaphysics and the philosophy of science. Second, there are cases where formal methods bear strongly on areas that deal with formal questions, such as the philosophy of mathematics and logic. Of course both sorts of method are often brought to bear on other areas—normative areas such as ethics and epistemology, for example—but cases in which they produce consensus are much rarer.

One might think that the philosophy of mind would be an exception, given the obvious connections to neuroscience and psychology. But even here, these sciences seem to have left the big questions—the problems of consciousness and intentionality, of mental causation and free will—wide open. Certainly there have been arguments from neuroscience and psychology to views about these problems, but in most cases the bridging premises required have been as controversial as most other philosophical claims. What has resulted is a greatly increased sophistication with scientifically informed versions of the relevant views, but not much more in the way of consensus. Perhaps the greatest bearing on these big questions about the mind has come not from these fields but from physics, where the evidence for causal closure at the microphysical level has put serious pressure on views such as interactionist dualism. But even here many have resisted the pressure, and in any case the denial of interactionism does not really amount to a positive view.

Other new methods do not even offer premises with the relative security of empirical and formal premises. In phenomenology, for example, the key phenomenological premises are typically as deniable as any other philosophical premises. Something similar may apply to feminist and crosscultural philosophy, while other methods may exhibit a mix of the two patterns above.[9] Some methods, such as feminist

---

[9] For my take on the power and limits of experimental and linguistic philosophy, see http://consc.net/papers/xphi.pdf and http://consc.net/papers/langphil.pdf respectively.

philosophy and experimental philosophy, have played a critical role, but the upshot has been largely to lessen our confidence about the answers to the big questions rather than to strengthen it.

Of course, new methods are always being developed. It still happens that issues gradually migrate from philosophy to science as methods become more rigorous and decisive: two recent examples include the development of formal semantics and the ongoing development of a science of consciousness. Still, even in these cases it would be hard to say that the new methods have led to consensus on the biggest philosophical questions that preceded their development. So while we can hope for further methods that produce convergence on the big questions, these methods will have to go well beyond what we have seen over the last century or so.

6 Explanations

So far I have given a very partial explanation of the relative lack of convergence in philosophy. There is less convergence in philosophy because the philosophical method has less power to compel agreement, and it has less power because of the phenomenon of premise deniability: arguments for strong conclusions in philosophy (unlike science and mathematics) almost always have premises or inferences that can be rejected without too much cost.

Still, this explanation stays fairly close to the surface of the phenomenon. It is natural to ask for a deeper explanation. Why are arguments from consensus premises relatively powerless to settle the big questions of philosophy? And more generally, why is there so little convergence in philosophy?

(1) *Disciplinary speciation.* The most popular answer to this question, at least among philosophers, is that the field is subject to a sort of disciplinary speciation. As I have discussed already, many new disciplines have sprung forth from philosophy over the years: physics, psychology, logic, linguistics, economics, and so on. In each case, these fields have sprung forth as tools have been developed to address questions more precisely and more decisively. The key thesis is that when we develop methods for conclusively answering philosophical questions, those methods come to constitute a new field and the questions are no longer deemed philosophical. So it is only to be expected that the questions that remain are subject to less agreement than those in other disciplines.

There is certainly something to this explanation. The key thesis is plausible and the central thesis seems to follow from it. Still, I think there are some limits on this explanation.

I have already noted one limit: the fields that have split off have not always answered the big philosophical questions that preceded them. Psychology has not done much to settle the mind–body problem, for example, and linguistics has not really settled the deepest philosophical questions about meaning. Logic and physics have come closer, but even here it is arguable that they have not settled some of the biggest antecedent philosophical questions. Now, it might be said that the smaller philosophical questions that these fields settle nevertheless correspond to the big questions in the new fields, thereby explaining the central thesis about relative convergence. Still, one wants an explanation of why the *antecedent* big questions in philosophy have been so hard to answer. Insofar as these big questions have not been resolved by disciplinary speciation, then speciation cannot answer that question.

A more general objection is that although the speciation thesis may explain, de dicto, why there is less convergence on big questions in philosophy than on big questions elsewhere, we also want a de re explanation, concerning those big questions, of why *they* in particular receive so little convergence. One hypothesis is that this is simply a matter of luck: all questions are equally apt for convergence, and through random luck some have received convergence (and thereby speciated) sooner than others. But setting aside this implausible hypothesis, the relative lack of convergence on these questions is presumably explained by something distinctive about those questions and their relation to us. We can then ask just what distinctive feature or features of these questions explain the lack of convergence. Speciation does not have the power to answer this question, so a further answer is required.

(2) *Anti-realism.* One answer is that there is no convergence to the truth because there are no objective truths to be had in the relevant domains. Where there is objective truth, it serves as a sort of magnet for convergence, but in its absence there is simply an unruly body of opinion which we should not expect to converge. Many philosophers will have sympathy for this line in some areas. I have sympathies with anti-realism about ethics and some questions in ontology. Still, this leaves plenty to be realist about. And even accepting moral anti-realism, say, leaves open why there is so little convergence on the question of moral realism itself. Of course there remains the possibility of global philosophical anti-realism, but this is not an especially plausible or attractive view.

(3) *Verbal disputes.* Another answer is that there is little convergence because participants are talking past each other. Each side is using key terms in different ways and each is correct where their own use of the term is concerned. In "Verbal Disputes" I argued that verbal disputes are common in philosophy. For example, I think many debates in the philosophy of free will and the philosophy of language have a significant verbal element. And I think that resolving verbal disputes can lead to philosophical progress. Still, often when we clarify the key terms in a partly verbal dispute, we find that a substantive dispute remains. And there is a core of fundamental questions (including many normative questions, as well as the mind–body problem and other issues involving "bedrock" philosophical concepts, in the terms of "Verbal Disputes") for which the diagnosis of a verbal dispute seems quite implausible.

(4) *Greater distance from data.* An answer naturally suggested by the discussion of decisive arguments is that there is less convergence in philosophy than in science because philosophy tends to concern domains that are remote from clear data. To put this in a Quinean mode, philosophical theses are a long way from the periphery in the network of belief. Still, on the face of it, the same goes for many highly theoretical claims in science, for example concerning the distant past and the very small. And plausibly the same goes for mathematics. In that case one might point to mathematical axioms and intuitions as data, but this then raises the question of why we don't have analogous philosophical data to settle philosophical questions. So this option tends to relabel the problem rather than solve it.[10]

(5) *Sociological explanations.* It is natural to suppose that sociological factors play a role in preventing convergence. When our arguments are not universally accepted, we often chalk this up partly to our opponents' professional background, or to false assumptions that are widespread in the profession, or to professional or emotional attachment to alternative views.

I think there is no denying that sociological factors play a major role in determining which philosophical views are widely accepted at a time. The unpopularity of the analytic-synthetic distinction in the decades after "Two Dogmas of Empiricism" was certainly not uncorrelated with Quine's position of power in the profession and his impact on graduate students. Still, many of the relevant sociological factors are also at play in the sciences. So to explain a difference with the sciences, one has to either point to relevant sociological differences, or combine the sociological explanation with other distinctive features of philosophical questions.

Some potential sociological differences include the hypothesis that philosophers are rewarded for disagreement more than in the sciences, that they are more tolerant of dissent, or that they have been trained to have higher standards for acceptance of views. One could also point to differences in funding, training, and research structures. Still, it is hard to believe that the difference in convergence between, say, the human genome project and the mind–body problem merely comes down to these sociological factors. So sociological explanations work best when they are combined with further theses about the distinctiveness of philosophical questions. For example, one could suggest that the greater distance between data and philosophical theses makes it easier for sociologically grounded resistance to a thesis to get a grip.

(6) *Psychological explanations.* Closely related are psychological explanations, holding that there is something distinctive about human minds or about philosophers'

---

[10] It is also worth noting (as Larry Solum suggested to me) that the social sciences have much less convergence than the hard sciences despite being less remote from data than philosophy. An interesting general question is whether the lack of convergence in social sciences and in philosophy should receive different explanations or a uniform explanation. My suspicion is the former: for example, the complexity and messiness of social systems seems especially relevant in the social sciences but less relevant in philosophy.

minds that prevents convergence on philosophical questions. Perhaps there is some psychological flaw that prevents us from recognizing philosophical truth, for example. At some level some explanation like this must be part of the story: at least if ideal reasoners could converge on the truth, then our failure can be marked down to the nonideality of our reasoning. But now the crucial questions will be: what are the respects in which our reasoning is nonideal, and what are the respects in which philosophical questions are distinctive, such that this nonideality of our reasoning prevents us from converging to the truth on philosophical questions?

To sum up, it appears that what is needed is an account of how philosophical questions are distinctive, and an account of why questions of that sort produce little convergence. The most obvious version of the second account would be an account of relevant aspects of our psychology or sociology. That would yield a sort of two-component "lock-and-key" explanation, suggesting an imperfect match between our key (human psychology or sociology) and an intellectual lock (philosophical questions). Alternatively, one could perhaps give a version of the second account on which philosophical questions turn out to be "objectively" hard and not just hard for humans. That would be a sort of lock-and-key account on which the key is characterized in terms of species-neutral epistemology rather than human psychology. It is not clear just what this objective hardness would come to, and it is not clear why we should expect that philosophical questions are objectively hard in this sense, so perhaps the human-centred version is more plausible. Either way, the lock-and-key strategy seems to be a promising one. We just need to give the right accounts of the lock and the key.

(7) *Evolutionary explanations.* It is sometimes suggested (e.g. by McGinn 1993) that there is a Darwinian explanation for the lack of progress in philosophy. The rough idea is that we did not evolve to be good at philosophy, since on the evolutionary environment there were no selection pressures that favoured philosophical ability or anything that strongly correlates with it. Perhaps there is something to this, though it would take some work to explain why the same does not apply to the ability to do abstract mathematics or highly theoretical science. In any case this sort of explanation will work best in conjunction with a psychological explanation, and raises the same crucial questions discussed under that topic.

I think all seven of these explanations may be partially correct. I do not think that they collectively provide a full explanation of the phenomenon as they stand, though. To do that, many of the details would need to be fleshed out. In particular, we still need a good account of just what is distinctive about philosophical questions such that they lead to lack of convergence. Only (2) and (4) really address this, but (global anti-realism aside) (2) only applies in some cases, while (4) is too close to a restatement of the phenomenon. It ought to be possible to provide an account of this distinctiveness that meshes with psychological, evolutionary, and perhaps sociological explanations to provide a full account of the lack of convergence. But for now I think this remains an open question.

7 The Prospects for Further Progress

Finally: what are the prospects for further philosophical progress? Is it possible that we may eventually converge to the truth on the big questions of philosophy?

To get a grip on this, we need to address the question of whether the answers to these questions are even knowable in principle, by sufficiently ideal reasoners. Here I will just flag my own positive view on this question. In *Constructing the World*, I argued for a scrutability thesis (called Fundamental Scrutability in the book) holding that all truths are a priori entailed by fundamental empirical truths concerning fundamental natural properties and laws. It follows (roughly) that if someone could know all the fundamental empirical truths and reason ideally, they could know all the truths, including all the philosophical truths.

Of course the scrutability thesis can be denied. If it is false, then even ideal reasoning from fundamental empirical truths may not enable us to know the philosophical truth. One could preserve a modified version of the thesis by expanding the fundamental truths in the base to include certain philosophical truths: fundamental normative and ontological principles, say. But then the fundamental truths themselves may lie beyond an ideal epistemological grasp. Either way, if philosophical truths are not scrutable from an appropriate basis, we should not expect convergence to the truth even in a community of ideal reasoners. This would be an extreme version of the view discussed above on which philosophical questions are objectively hard.

If the scrutability thesis is true, on the other hand, a more optimistic view ensues. The thesis does not entail that we can know all the philosophical truths, but it provides a useful way to classify the cases where we fall short, and more generally to classify cases where we fail to converge. First, there are cases of anti-realism about a domain, where there is no philosophical truth to know. Second, there are cases where multiple parties all know philosophical truths, but where verbal disputes get in the way of their recognizing their agreements. Third, there are cases where we are ignorant of relevant fundamental empirical truths. Fourth, there are cases where our reasoning is nonideal.

I think that many of the hardest cases in philosophy fall into the last category: questions whose answers are knowable by ideal reasoners, but not (yet) known by us. This then raises the key question: are the answers knowable or unknowable by humans?

McGinn (1993) and van Inwagen (2009) have advocated unknowability: humans are just not smart enough to answer the big questions. The idea is that there is some level of intelligence or aptitude that would suffice to answer these questions, but that humans fall below that level.

Van Inwagen argues for this conclusion as follows. He suggests that it is implausible that we are much above that level, given the lack of progress to date, and that it is antecedently improbable that we should be just barely at that level. So it is much more likely that the level lies above us. I am not so sure about this argument. I think we already know that for a vast range of questions, humans are just barely at the level for doing them well: scientific and mathematical questions, for example. Because of this, it is arguable that we lie at a special intelligence threshold at which an extraordinarily wide range of questions come to be within our grasp over time. It is not obvious whether or not philosophical questions fall within that range, but it is not obviously more likely that they do not than that they do.

If McGinn and van Inwagen are right, it remains open that we could answer philosophical questions by first improving our intelligence level, perhaps by cognitive enhancement or extension. Alternatively, we could construct artificial beings more intelligent than us, who will then be able to construct artificial beings more intelligent than them, and so on. The resulting intelligence explosion might lead to creatures who could finally answer the big philosophical questions.

If McGinn and van Inwagen are wrong, on the other hand, then we may eventually answer philosophical questions without radical cognitive enhancement. We may need to develop new methods, increased discipline, new sorts of insights, and perhaps there will need to be a conceptual revolution or two, but none of this will lie outside human capacity. It may turn out that there is a curve of increasing philosophical sophistication such that past a certain point on the curve major progress is possible. We are not there yet, but we are working our way toward it.

It is not obvious whether McGinn and van Inwagen are right or wrong. The question of whether the big philosophical questions are humanly solvable is itself a big metaphilosophical question. Like other big questions in philosophy, it is one we do not currently know the answer to. Both answers to this metaphilosophical question seem to be open, and we do not currently have strong reasons to favour either one.

If we don't know which of these two options obtains, then I think to do philosophy we can make the working assumption that it is the second: the questions are answerable by us but as yet unsolved. Then we can simply do philosophy as well as we can, doing our best to come up with those new insights, methods, and concepts that might finally lead to us answering the questions. After all, we are still learning to do philosophy well. To see how far it can take us, we have to keep doing philosophy.

References

Bourget, D. and Chalmers, D. J. 2014. What do philosophers believe? *Philosophical Studies* 170:465–500.

Chalmers, D. J. 2011. Verbal disputes. *Philosophical Review* 120:515–66.

Chalmers, D. J. 2012. *Constructing the World*. Oxford University Press.

Dietrich, E. 2010. There is no progress in philosophy. *Essays in Philosophy* 12: 329–44.

Hilbert, D. 1902. Mathematical problems. *Bulletin of the American Mathematical Society* 8:437–79.

Kelly, T. & McGrath, S. forthcoming. Are there any successful philosophical arguments? In (J. Keller, ed.) *Being, Freedom, and Method: Themes from van Inwagen*. Oxford University Press.

Krippendorff, K. 2013. *Content Analysis: An Introduction to its Methodology*, 3rd edition. Sage Publishing.

McGinn, C. 1993. *Problems in Philosophy*. Oxford University Press.

Nielsen, K. 1987. Can there be progress in philosophy? *Metaphilosophy* 18:1–30.

Rawls, J. 2001. Afterword. In (J. Floyd & S. Shieh, eds) *Future Pasts: The Analytic Tradition in Twentieth-Century Philosophy*. Oxford University Press.

Russell, B. 1912. *The Problems of Philosophy*. Williams and Norgate.

Russell, B. 1918. "The Philosophy of Logical Atomism". The Monist 28:295–527. Reprinted as *The Philosophy of Logical Atomism*. Taylor and Francis. 2009.

Stoljar, D. forthcoming. *Philosophical Progress: In Defense of a Reasonable Optimism*.

Van Inwagen, P. 2004. Freedom to break the laws. *Midwest Studies in Philosophy* 28:334–50.

Van Inwagen, P. 2006. *The Problem of Evil: The Gifford Lectures*. Oxford University Press.

Van Inwagen, P. 2009. *Metaphysics* (third edition). Westview Press.

Williamson, T. 2006. Must do better. In (P. Greenough & M. Lynch, eds) *Truth and Realism*. Oxford University Press.

Yandell, B. H. 2002. *The Honors Class: Hilbert's Problems and their Solvers*. A. K. Peters.

Subject Index